Firm Valuation and Asymmetric Foreign Exchange Exposure

Measuring and Managing Foreign Exchange Exposures in a Strategic Real Option Framework

von

Thierry Leutwiler

Tectum Verlag
Marburg 2006

Leutwiler, Thierry:
Firm Valuation and Asymmetric Foreign Exchange Exposure.
Measuring and Managing Foreign Exchange Exposures
in a Strategic Real Option Framework.
/ von Thierry Leutwiler
- Marburg : Tectum Verlag, 2006
Zugl.: Oestrich-Winkel, Univ. Diss. 2005
ISBN 978-3-8288-8992-7

Tectum Verlag
Marburg 2006

Acknowledgments

This book has been published from my doctoral dissertation. I would like to thank the members of my Doctoral Thesis Supervisory Committee at the European Business School in Oestrich-Winkel, in particular Professor Ulrich Hommel and Professor Onno Lint, for their assistance in formulating the subject, understanding the critical issues, and for helping me to develop and complete the work.

I am indebted to scores of people for having pursuaded me to undertake this endeavour and infused it with their enthusiasm. Special thanks go to my current and former colleagues, professors and fellow students at HEC Lausanne, New York University, EBS Oestrich-Winkel, KPMG Consulting, and LogicaCMG Consulting.

I dedicate this book to the memory of my parents, and to my dear wife Min-Joo for her support and cheerfulness.

Thierry Leutwiler   Oestrich-Winkel, 9th of September 2005

Contents

1. Introduction

1.1 Background

An important issue for corporate managers and investors is how exchange rate fluctuations affect a firm's market value. This relation is a firm's economic foreign exchange exposure. Managing this exposure has become increasingly important since the breakdown of the Bretton-Woods system of fixed exchange rates in 1973. The international financial environment of firms has become riskier in part because exchange rates volatility has increased dramatically and significant and prolonged deviations of exchange rates from their purchasing power parity values have been observed. An other reason is that firms are operating more internationally as a result of the globalization of goods markets.

A. Evolution of Foreign Exchange Risk Management

Well-known cases of companies having lost considerable market shares or been put into financial distress as a result of large scale exchange rate changes[1] have ignited a growing awareness of the importance of managing foreign exchange exposure[2]. The emerging importance of the risk management function has been supported by the rapid growth of the market for financial derivative instruments, advances in risk management systems technology, and more sophisticated risk and exposure measurement methods.

The perspective on the risk management function has become more strategic. Efficient risk management is increasingly seen as being a potential source of competitive advantage over competitors. According to this view, the objective of risk management is to reduce exposure to adverse exchange rate changes by hedging downside exposure, while enabling the firm to exploit opportunities arising from exposures to beneficial exchange rate changes. An implication of pursuing a value-maximizing rather than a variance-minimizing approach to the management of exposures is that risk management activities are becoming more coordinated with capital budgeting and

---

[1] Examples often mentioned are the US firms Caterpillar and Kodak, or the German car producers Volkswagen and Porsche on the US market. See Bodnar and Gebhardt (1998), Levich (1998), p. 572.
[2] See, e.g., Miyamoto (2003) for a survey showing that firms are increasingly trying to manage their economic exposures.

corporate strategy. Rather than being a problem to be dealt exclusively by the treasury office, foreign exchange exposure management is now often viewed as a general management issue. However, although the benefit of a risk management approach integrating various corporate functions and different types of risks is increasingly recognized, the effects of an integrated approach on exposure measurement has been the subject of little analysis. This study shows that a strategic real options framework offers a promising way to describe and value foreign exchange exposures within an integrated risk management approach.

B. Foreign Exchange Exposures of Flexible Firms

A firm's economic foreign exchange exposure measures the exposure of its contractual cash flows, which are nominally fixed in foreign currency, and of its non-contractual cash flows, which are risky in terms of foreign currency. As such, converted domestic currency cash flows may not only be affected by shifts in exchange rates, but also by changes in foreign cash flows. The impact that exchange rate changes have on input and output prices and quantities depends in part on the firm's decisions on where to locate production, whether to alter its prices after an exchange rate change, and so forth. The ability to make adjustments in costs and revenues structure depends on the firm's operating flexibility. Operating flexibility can be interpreted as providing real options that can be used to control the distribution of cash flows over time. Operating flexibility does not presume any value implication but is potentially valuable.

Exposures are frequently measured and hedged within a linear framework, although insights based on structural exposure models predict, except under restrictive assumptions, non-linear exposures[3]. Exposure linearity implicitly assumes that the current operating and financial structure is static and unaffected by exchange rate changes. This is plausible over very short horizons. Over longer horizons, a firm is likely to exercise options. For example, an exporter's exposure may be low if it has the flexibility to shift sales rapidly and at low costs between various foreign markets as a function of the prevailing exchange rate. A firm's endogenous flexibility makes its cash flows distribution and exposure dependent on the exchange rate level. A non-

---

[3] For example in case of a firm under perfect competition with production inflexibility. See, e.g., Ware and Winter (1988).

linear exposure profile implies that endogenous changes in competitive positions and firms' strategic responses should be incorporated into exposure measurement.

C. Foreign Exchange Exposure Asymmetries

Because exchange rate changes of different nature present firms with different strategic opportunities, the exercise rule of real options is likely to be function of the exchange rate. A firm will respond differently to appreciations relative to depreciations, and to small relative to large exchange rate changes. Correspondingly, exposure asymmetries will reflect the possibility for firms to be affected in a significant different way to exchange rate appreciation relative to depreciation, and/or to small relative to large exchange rate changes. In this study we examine the economic rationales for endogenous corporate behavior[4] and the possibility that exposure could take very different values for some exchange rate ranges. Factors of exposure asymmetries include operating flexibility but also financial flexibility. The value effect associated with exposure asymmetries is function of the real options and financial flexibility options payoffs, which in turn depend on industry structure, flexibility bounds, and so forth.

D. Analyzing Foreign Exchange Exposure in a Strategic Real Option Framework

Traditionally, foreign exchange exposure has been analyzed in industrial organization models of cash flow determination. The early models examine the role of industry structure in partial equilibrium (perfect competition or monopoly), and ignore indirect effects through consumers, suppliers and competitors. Exposure takes a more complex and ambiguous form in general equilibrium models, which allow for strategic interactions between oligopolists[5].

These theoretical studies are closely related to an other branch of the economic literature that examines the effects of exchange rate changes on corporate pricing. This includes the work on pricing-to-market (PTM) and exchange rate pass-through (ERPT), which emphasize the relations between industry structure and corporate

---

[4] The effect on exposures of expected ex-post operating adjustments in response to exchange rate changes will be examined here, and not how the firm can hedge a given exposure with real means.
[5] See, e.g., Luehrman (1990), Marston (2001).

pricing strategies based on exchange rate considerations. In spite of the importance of pricing on foreign exchange exposure, there is little research investigating this relation[6]. Microeconomic models of PTM and hysterisis predict exposure asymmetries. Based on strategic objectives or capacity constraints, PTM models predict asymmetric ERPT behavior between exchange rate appreciations and depreciations and asymmetric exchange rate sensitivity of profit margins. Hysterisis models, for example, predict exposure asymmetries from the endogenous decisions to enter and leave foreign markets.

Microeconomic models clarify the channels of influence of exchange rate fluctuations on firm value. However, they are characterized by several shortcomings that make them not directly relevant in terms of corporate risk management. To have a complete discussion on exposure asymmetries, one needs a fundamentally different conceptual framework that comprises at least the following aspects:

- *Model of valuation*: microeconomic models examine the exposure of single-period cash flows rather than of firm value. What ultimately matters in terms of risk management is the effect of exchange rate changes on firm value.

- *Models of adjustments of variables over the estimation period*: models of exposure are static and the dynamic adjustment mechanisms of prices, exchange rates, and other variables are not modeled. Furthermore, what is examined in these models is the effect of actual ex-post adjustments. But what matters in terms of exposure is the *expected* effect of these endogenous adjustments. For example, there is an enormous amount of literature on exchange rate pass-through and pricing-to-market, but much less has been written on the effect on exposure of pricing flexibility under exchange rate uncertainty[7]. As such, one needs a probabilistic rather than a deterministic framework to assess the distribution of the effect of ex-post adjustments.

- *Model of firm's behavior based on corporate finance principles*: in microeconomic models, corporate behavior is analyzed at a general level that does not allow direct inferences for risk management policies.

---

[6] A contribution is Bodnar et al. (2002).
[7] An example is Chang and Lapan (2001).

- *Model with multiple sources of uncertainty:* other factors than exchange rates can affect a firm's exposure, through their impact on foreign currency cash flows.

The real option analytical approach is based on a dynamic multi-period framework that can be used for describing and valuing exposures in a way that is consistent with risk management objectives. It is better suited to describe the corporate behaviors leading to exposure asymmetries and interpret their effects in terms of value. However, most real option models assume a firm in monopoly. In imperfectly competitive markets, real options can have more complex payoffs because of strategic competition. Whereas in perfect competition, market constraints dictate that the firm's only decisions are whether and how much to produce, in imperfect competition, firms must assess the likely response of competitors, consumers, and foreign governments to their range of possible actions. The implication is that a firm can be indirectly exposed through its strategic interactions with other market participants. For an oligopolist, exposure asymmetries reflect the payoffs of "strategic real options"[8]. More recent real options contributions have modeled the effect of strategic interactions using the traditional microeconomic approach used in industrial organization and dynamic game theory.

E. Comments on Empirical Studies of Asymmetric Exposures

Empirical studies are generally based on econometric models that do not constitute direct tests of structural models, and that do not use direct measures of cash flows in their estimation of exposures; they test the plausibility of theoretical predictions inferred from these structural models. This branch of the literature uses a kind of "short-cut" and measures in reduced-form models how exchange-rate movements affect stock returns at the firm and industry level. A reason why theoretical models are not directly applicable for multi-firm empirical studies or large-scale cross-firm comparisons of exchange rate exposures is that they examine specific situations and would require extensive and often unreliable accounting data to be tested.

This market value approach has generally produced puzzling empirical estimates of exposure. Although several studies show that foreign exchange exposures appear to be

---

[8] Strategic options are defined as the "future opportunities that are created by today's investments", whereas real options are defined as "the subset of strategic options in which the exercise decision is largely triggered by market-priced risk, a risk that is captured in the value of traded security". See Amram and Kulatilaka (2000), p. 10.

related to the types of activities in which firms engage, one common issue is why most companies do not display significant exchange rate exposures[9]. Some studies find significant exposure measures, but the estimated exposure coefficients are unstable over time and with signs contradicting conventional theoretical predictions. The low occurrence of significant equity exposures seems particularly puzzling given the frequency with which exchange rates are mentioned by finance managers and investors as a factor of corporate performance[10]. The difficulty in identifying statistically significant and economically meaningful estimates of exposure has cast doubts on the usefulness of these market-based reduced-form estimations of exchange rate exposure. The issue essentially boils down to determine whether the lack of supporting empirical evidence for the theory exists because exchange rates in fact do not significantly impact firm value, for example if firms are able to insulate themselves through hedging, or because the complexity of the relation is not well captured by theoretical models, or because the relation has not been adequately examined in econometric tests. These three aspects are investigated throughout the study.

Several shortcomings characterize the hypothesis of exposure asymmetries that have been tested in empirical studies:

(i)   *Based on pricing-to-market models:* implications of asymmetric pricing-to-market behavior in terms of exposure cannot be drawn without qualifiers. First, exposure asymmetries are viewed as being the result of asymmetric profit margins sensitivities caused by asymmetric pricing behavior. This is likely to be incorrect over a valuation period, when adjustments in quantities are important. Second, these pricing models assess the actual effects of ex-post adjustments on profitability. What matters for exposure, however, is the expected distribution of the pricing effects. Pricing flexibility rather than exchange-rate pass-through (ERPT) decisions make exposure asymmetric.

---

[9] Typically, empirical studies based on regression estimation of foreign exchange exposures at the industry level have found that substantially less than half of the industries in a country display significant exposures at even a 10 percent significant level in either direction. See, e.g., Jorion (1990).

[10] For example, in January 2004, during the long slide of the US-dollar against the euro, Merrill Lynch cut its rating on Volkswagen's stock to sell, citing the German automaker's foreign exchange exposure and, more particularly, the weak US-dollar. See McLannahan and P.F. Larsen, 2004, Out for the Count: the reaction of Europe's auto manufactures to the sinking dollar provides an object lesson for other sectors, CFO Magazine, Feb. 17.

(ii) *Assume that the value of real options is proprietary:* the effects on exposure of real options are examined in partial equilibrium and strategic interactions with other market participants are ignored. For most international corporations the value of real options cannot be assumed to be fully proprietary.

(iii) *Based on structural models that emphasize single-period cash flows:* what ultimately matters is the exposure of firm value. The focus on short term cash flows implies that strategic and capital structure issues are not dealt with. Typically, these models do not consider the influence on economic exposure of contractual exposures, the effect trough the cost of capital and taxes.

(iv) *Ignore the interaction between real options:* typically, these studies examine the effects of real options on firms specialized in a specific sector of activity. The interpretation of asymmetries for multinational corporates (MNCs), which hold portfolios of options, is more complex.

Finally, the empirical methodological shortcomings that could explain their findings are generally not given sufficient attention.

1.2 Objective, Scope, and Contribution of the Thesis

Much of what has been written about corporate risk management focuses primarily on justifying and explaining the use of derivative instruments in hedging exposures to interest rates, foreign exchange rates, and commodity prices. Much less has been written about the identification of these risks and exposures, and on how to devise optimal hedging strategies based on exposure characteristics. The general objectives of the study are threefold:

I.   Analysis of the sources of foreign exchange exposure asymmetries under various industry structures. Emphasis is placed on the exposure asymmetries of firms operating in oligopolistic industries, where strategic interactions between market participants play an important role to a firm's exposure.

II. Empirical test on the stock markets valuation of exposure asymmetries.

III. Evaluation of the implications of exposure asymmetries in terms of hedging strategies.

The contributions and methodology of the analysis can be outlined as below.

Analysis of the Effects of Operating and Financial Flexibilities on Exposures

Exposure asymmetries reflect a firm's real options and financial flexibility options expected payoffs. We show that in presence of strategic real options and financial flexibility options, exposure can take complex forms and cannot be generalized analytically. It is eventually a firm-specific and empirical matter. The analytical objectives are as follows. The *first objective* is to show the relevance of the real option framework to describe and value foreign exchange exposures. We examine the insights of the microeconomic literature on exposure within a real option valuation framework. This shows the limitations of analyzing exposure in static, single-period cash flow models and the relevance of adopting a dynamic multi-period real option valuation framework.

The *second objective* is to show that exposure predictions from standard real option models may be invalid (i) for firms operating in oligopolistic industry structure, (ii) for firms with bounds on flexibility. Oligopolistic models of exposure and models of corporate pricing show that the payoffs of real options can be negative under these two conditions. The *third objective* is to show the necessity of an integrated approach of exposure measurement. Specifically, we show the importance of (i) incorporating financial flexibility options into the analysis: the interaction between real options and financial flexibility options complexify the nature of exposure asymmetries, (ii) incorporating all factors of foreign currency cash flow volatility into the analysis: foreign cash flows fluctuate in nominal terms as a result of market conditions, possibly because of exchange rates, but also because of business, political, and macroeconomic factors[11], (iii) incorporating portfolio/netting effects over a firm's cash flows: typically, international firms are engaged in various activities and product lines.

This analysis of exposure asymmetries gives insights on some "puzzling" results found in the empirical literature. The sign of exposure does not necessarily depend on whether a firm is long or short in foreign currency. We identify several explanations

---

[11] Strictly speaking, we should refer to the uncertainty of local cash flows rather than foreign cash flows, since even firms with no international trading activities can be affected by exchange rate changes. The reference to foreign cash flows is made to emphasize the distinction between exposure from a conversion effect and from a competitive effect. These concepts are clarified in chapter 2.

for negative exposures: (i) negative real option payoffs as a result of strategic competition: in oligopolistic industries, a firm does not have full control over the value of its options. Strategic competition with other firms can destroy the value of its options, (ii) negative real option payoffs as a result of bounds on flexibility, (iii) effects of other factors on foreign currency cash flows. The shifts back and forth of exposure signs observed in virtually all empirical studies can be explained by switching options or changes in industry competitive structure. For example, it could be that a firm produces in one country if the exchange rate has some value and in an other country if it has a different value.

Evidence on Stock Market's Valuation of Exposure Asymmetries

An important question is whether stock markets value exposure asymmetries. An econometric test of exposure asymmetry is performed for a sample of German corporations. Since Germany is a very open economy, we expect to find relatively large and significant estimates of exposure. The hypothesis of exposure asymmetries justifies the use of GARCH models. Exposure asymmetries create departures from cash flow distribution normality and introduce conditional heteroskedasticity.

The results of various empirical specifications are compared to test the robustness of our results. Detailed explanations are proposed for our findings, grouped into those based on theories and those based on empirical methodological shortcomings. Throughout, the empirical analysis gives an overview of the vast empirical literature, by reviewing stylized facts, discussing methodological issues and the importance of model specification.

Risk Management Implications of Exposure Asymmetries

The results of this study have implications for elaborating hedging strategies. The discussion evolves around four aspects:

(a) The implication of exposure asymmetries for risk management objectives: hedging the net present value of the firm is not appropriate for flexible firm.

(b) The suitability of linear/non-linear derivatives: exposure asymmetries provide an economic rationale for hedging with currency options, either as variance-minimizing or value-maximizing hedges. Currency options are adequate to increase firm value by tailoring inter-temporal and intra-temporal hedges consistent with corporate investments and financing decisions.

(c) The efficiency of currency derivatives: because foreign currency cash flows' uncertainty may be function of other factors than exchange rates, currency derivatives are not always efficient to hedge foreign exchange exposures. The relation between real price risk and quantity risk indicates the sources of exposure uncertainty and the effectiveness of currency hedges.

(d) The suitability of a strategic real options framework to identify and manage foreign exchange exposures: the possibility of exposure asymmetries is conducive towards a more integrated and strategic approach of the risk management function that take into consideration the influence of three sets of determinants: firms' strategic options, industry competitive factors, the interrelation between financial hedging and strategic options.

1.3 Thesis Outline

This book is broadly divided into seven chapters and two parts as follows. The fundamental properties of foreign exchange exposure are defined sufficiently for the scope of this dissertation in the first part of this book. Part one *"valuation of asymmetric foreign exchange exposures"* presents the conceptual framework that will be used to analyze corporate foreign exchange exposure asymmetries. Interpretation of our exposure estimates will be based on part one. Chapter 2 assesses the theoretical literature on foreign exchange exposure. It specifies the mechanisms by which exchange rate changes affect firms' value, and identifies firm- and industry-specific determinants of foreign exchange exposure. This chapter shows that for non-financial corporations, for which cash flows are uncertain and difficult to measure, economic exposure essentially depends on the industry competitive environment in which the firm operates. Chapter 3 assesses the asymmetric effects of real options on exposure whereby firms can alter their marketing strategy or production strategy in response to exchange rate movements, and of financial flexibility options. Chapter 4 examines the theoretical arguments suggesting that exposure is asymmetric for oligopolistic firms.

Part two *"empirical evidence and risk management implications"* assesses the main findings and methodological issues of the empirical literature, statistically investigates the exposure of German corporations, and discusses the implications of exposure asymmetries in terms of real and financial hedging. Chapter 5 tests empirically the hypothesis of exposure asymmetry for a sample of German corporations, and reviews the significant findings and contributions of the empirical literature. This chapter concludes with a discussion on the implications of exposure asymmetries in terms of estimation methods. In chapter 6, we evaluate the implications of asymmetric exposures in terms of risk management strategies. We conclude with a discussion of our main findings and some suggestions for further research in chapter 7.

PART ONE: VALUATION OF ASYMMETRIC FOREIGN EXCHANGE EXPOSURES

2. Foreign Exchange Exposure and Corporate Competitiveness

Real exchange rate shifts affect firms' competitiveness by modifying their relative input and output prices. This in turn has an impact on their current and future cash flows, and thereby their values. The expected exchange rate sensitivity of firm value to a unit of unexpected exchange rate change is measured by the concept of foreign exchange exposure[1]. In this chapter, we examine first the relevance of exchange rate fluctuations in terms of economic corporate performance. Second, we emphasize that foreign exchange exposure is to a large extent a competitive exposure that is determined mainly by the industry structure in which a firm operates. Section 2.1 examines the various definitions of exposure in terms of their economic relevance. Section 2.2 reviews the concepts of exchange rate risk and exposure. Section 2.3 discusses the effects of real exchange rate changes on corporate competitiveness. Section 2.4 examines the channels of influence of exchange rate fluctuations on firm value and the role of industry structure.

2.1 Economic Relevance of Exchange Rates for Corporate Performance

What should matter to shareholders and managers is corporate performance in terms of current and future real cash flows. Accordingly, an economically relevant measure of foreign exchange exposure should determine to what extent the real value of a firm would be affected by exchange rates fluctuations. This implies that an economic measure of exposure should be *(i) cash flow based, (ii) forward-looking*, and *(iii) in real terms*. The exposure metrics used in practice, however, frequently do not display these characteristics and are unsuited for risk management purposes. Three types of exposure measurement, *translation exposure, contractual exposure*, and *competitive exposure* are commonly used. As a background to understanding the properties of each

---

[1] See Adler and Dumas (1984).

type of exposure measurement, it is helpful to be aware of the context in which they were developed. Improved methods of foreign exchange exposure measurement were devised as a response to the shortcomings of the existing methods, and evolved against a background of progressive globalization and a progressively greater need to measure foreign exchange exposure[2].

A. Translation Exposure

Translation exposure arises when a multinational corporation has foreign subsidiaries and that its consolidated balance sheet is affected by changes in exchange rates[3]. Translation exposure has two shortcomings that make it inappropriate for risk management. First, it is a *retrospective measure*: it focuses on the effect of exchange rate changes on the book value of assets and liabilities as measured in the firm's balance sheet. Book values represent historical values that do not reflect the effects of exchange rate changes on current and future cash flows[4]. Second, it is an *incomplete measure*: even if these historical book values were adjusted to reflect prospective economic values, translation exposure would still be an incomplete measure of economic exposure. All items on a balance sheet indeed represent future cash flows, but not all future cash flows of a firm appear on a balance sheet[5].

For these reasons, translation exposure often bears little relationship to a firm's economic exposure, and it has long been advocated that firms should not actively manage their translation exposures[6]. However, despite these shortcomings, it is necessary from an accounting standpoint in the preparation of a multinational company's financial statements. Furthermore, accounting data are often the only data that are readily available. It is thus important that if treasurers use these data to make hedging decisions, they be aware of these limitations and make appropriate adjustments.

---

[2] See Heckman (1989) for an account of these theoretical developments.
[3] Consolidation refers to the translation of the financial statements of the firm's foreign subsidiaries into the currency in which the parent firm reports its accounts. For details, see, e.g., Shapiro (1999).
[4] The only cash flow implication of translation exposure is through its effect on taxes, and this impact is generally small. See Sercu and Uppal (1995), p. 516.
[5] For example, cash flows from contracts for future sales or purchases are not included in translation exposure. See Shapiro (1999), pp. 276-277.
[6] See, e.g., Dufey (1972).

B. Accounting and Economic Contractual Exposure

Contractual exposure measures the "change in value of outstanding nominal financial obligations incurred prior to a change in the exchange rate but not due to be settled until after the exchange rate change"[7]. It arises when a firm acquires contractual nominal positions denominated in foreign currency[8]. These contractual undertakings ultimately get reflected in future cash flows because the asset or liability is still outstanding. Since contractual exposure is forward-looking and cash flow oriented, it is economically relevant.

From an accounting perspective, translation exposure is the exposure of a firm's balance sheet, whereas contractual exposure is the exposure of the income statement[9]. As such, contractual exposure focuses on the exposure of foreign currency denominated transactions that are planned or forecast to occur within the next reporting period[10]. But a distinction needs to be drawn between the accounting and economic definitions of contractual exposure (see Appendix A):

(i)   *time at which exposure arises*: in accounting, the time at which exposure arises corresponds to the *transaction date*, whereas the economically relevant date is the *commitment date*[11].

(ii) *exchange rates for calculation*: the exchange rates for accounting calculation are actual exchange rates, whereas expected exchange rates should be used from an economic point of view[12].

(iii) *estimation period*: contractual cash flows can be exposed over a longer period than the next accounting period. Long term contractual exposures are for example common in the construction industry[13].

---

[7] See Bodnar (1999), p. 1. Contractual cash flows include expenses and revenues "when a firm purchases or sells goods or services on credit with foreign currency prices", borrowing and lending funds when repayment is to be made in a foreign currency, dividend, interest, lease payments, royalty and licensing receipts, et cetera. See Bodnar (1999), p. 1.

[8] Transactions that are "highly probable" based on the firm's historical business line and market shares, but that have no legal basis yet, are called "anticipated transaction exposures". See Eiteman et al. (2000). Hagelin and Pramborg (2001) distinguish the "exposure of committed transactions", and the "exposure of identifiable anticipated transactions".

[9] For example Levich (1998), pp. 572-575, subdivides accounting exposure into translation exposure (exposure of the balance sheet) and transaction exposure (exposure of the income statement).

[10] See Levich (1998), p. 575.

[11] See Stulz (2000), ch. 8, p. 3, Bodnar (1999), pp. 1-2.

[12] See Bodnar (1999), pp. 1-2.

[13] See Demacopoulos (1989).

Because what ultimately matters is the exposure of firm value, it is essential to recognize the long term competition effects on *local* currency cost and revenue streams resulting from exchange rate changes. Because contractual exposure ignores the exposure of ongoing operating cash flows, it is an incomplete measure of economic exposure for non-financial firms, which possess essentially real assets that generate non-contractual cash flows. However, contractual exposure could be an adequate measure of economic exposure in two cases. First, it is a relatively comprehensive measure of economic exposure for *financial institutions*, which have mostly financial assets that generate contractually fixed returns. Second, it can estimate a non-financial firm's *short term economic exposure*, since, over a short time period, the majority of a firm's cash flows may be contractual. Although economic exposure is the exposure of firm value, a manager might be interested in a short term measure of exposure for risk management purposes. The objective of risk management is to increase firm value, but most of its rationales are cash flow based.

Figure 2. 1 Comparison of Timing of Different Exposure Measures[14]

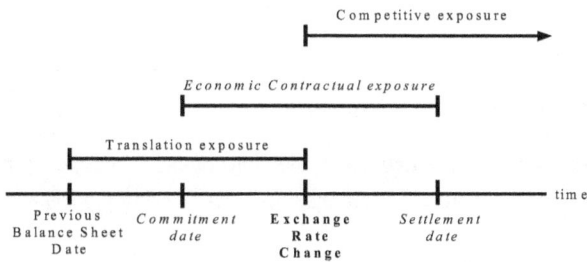

---

[14] Adapted from Bodnar (2004), p. 2, Shapiro (1999), p. 266.

C. Competitive Exposure of Unlevered Cash Flows

Competitive exposure measures the exchange rate sensitivity of non-contractual cash flows[15]. The cash flows considered are those from operations and not those implied by changes in value of existing assets or liabilities[16]. A distinction needs to be made between the definition of operating cash flows used in accounting and in finance textbooks. Operating cash flow, in the accounting sense, does not properly measure cash flows that stem directly from the firm's operations (see Appendix J)[17]. First, it includes cash flows arising from the financing of the firm, including interest and dividends. Second, it does not account for the required capital expenditures that a firm or project may require to keep it operating (these appear in the investing cash flow portion of the cash flow statement).

For these reasons, the term *unlevered cash flows*[18] or *free cash flows*[19] rather than *operating cash flow* is more appropriate in reference to competitive exposure. The economic impact of exchange rate fluctuations on firm value is captured by combining contractual and competitive exposures, the two cash flow related measures[20]. Figure 2.1 above shows the timing of the impact of exchange rate changes for each definition of exposure.

2.2 Foreign Exchange Risk and Exposure

The term "risk" is sometimes defined as the "uncertainty of environmental variables that reduce corporate performance predictability"[21]. Accordingly, *foreign exchange risk*

---

[15] Competitive exposure is sometimes called operating exposure or economic exposure. See, e.g., Flood and Lessard (1986) or Levich (1998), p. 578. The term competitive exposure is more appropriate than operating exposure because it explicitly includes the strategic implications of exchange rate changes on firms' behavior. This is advocated for example by Stulz (1999), ch. 8, p. 17. Operating exposure typically refers to exposure measures that evaluate the effect of exchange rate changes on the profitability of the firm's current operations while holding other economic variables constant. See Stulz and Williamson (1996), p. 9. It is not correct to define competitive exposure as equivalent to economic exposure because contractual exposure is also cash flow related and economically relevant.
[16] See Sercu and Uppal (1994), p. 488.
[17] See Grinblatt and Titman (2002), p. 304.
[18] See Grinblatt and Titman (2002), p. 304.
[19] See Copeland et al. (1994).
[20] See Shapiro (1999), p. 317. The term "cash flow exposure" is used as a synonym for economic exposure. See Shapiro (1999), p. 785.
[21] See Miller (1992), p. 312.

is the uncertainty about the future spot rate, or the exchange rate volatility as measured statistically by the standard deviation[22]. Since the value of a firm may not depend on exchange rates, even though exchange rates might be extremely volatile and unanticipated, it is more appropriate to define foreign exchange risk as the uncertainty or lack of predictability in corporate outcome variables such as profits, cash flows, or firm value, due to exchange rate fluctuations[23]. Accordingly, the standard deviation of exchange rates should be referred to as "exchange rate uncertainty" rather than risk.

A firm is said to be exposed to exchange rate uncertainty if it is expected to be affected by unexpected exchange rate changes. The concept of foreign exchange exposure indicates "how relevant" an unexpected exchange rate change would be in terms of firm value. As such, exposure can be interpreted as a "sensitivity" measure indicating how foreign exchange risk is related to exchange rate uncertainty:

a) *Exposure to Unexpected Changes in Exchange Rates Volatility*

If a firm's exposure is nonzero, an increase in the volatility of exchange rates could result in an increase in the volatility of the firm's cash flows and value. In expression [2.1], the exposure measures the relationship between foreign exchange risk and exchange rate volatility:

[2.1] $\sigma^2(_tX_{t+n}S_t) =_t X_{t+n} \times S_t \times \sigma^2(S_t)$

where $\sigma^2(\ )$ is the standard deviation's operator, $_tX_{t+n}$ is a measure of foreign exchange exposure assessed over an estimation period t to $t+n$, and $\sigma^2(S_t)$ is the exchange rate volatility evaluated at t^{24}. Foreign exchange risk over the future period t to $t+n$, $\sigma^2(_tX_{t+n}S_t)$, is the product of the measure of exchange rate uncertainty, $\sigma^2(S_t)$, by the measure of exposure, $_tX_{t+n}$, converted into domestic currency. Since exchange rate risk refers to the volatility of firm value in domestic currency, exposure is a measure in foreign currency, and S_t is the price of the foreign currency in units of domestic currency. Whereas the measure of risk is a positive number, exposure can

---

[22] See, e.g., Adler and Dumas (1984).
[23] See, e.g., Levi (1996) or Miller (1992).
[24] See Coval (1998), March 30, p. 2, Booth (1996), Stulz (2000), ch. 8, p. 28, Levi (1996), p. 303, Levich (1998), p. 566.

take a positive or negative sign depending on whether the firm is adversely or positively affected by currency fluctuations.

Unexpected changes in exchange rate volatility can have long term effects on a firm's competitive position. For instance, exchange rate volatility can make the financial information released by firms noisy, with the consequence of making it more difficult for investors to monitor firms' performance and for firms to attract capital for investment.

b) *Exposure to Unexpected Changes in Exchange Rate Level*

If a firm's exposure is nonzero, an adverse change in the exchange rate can reduce its value. Expression [2.1] can be interpreted in terms of changes in variable levels rather than in terms of volatility. In that case, the expected impact of an unexpected exchange rate change, measured over the estimation period t to $t+n$, is obtained by multiplying exposure by an exchange rate change at t[25]. In expression [2.2], competitive exposure can be assimilated to *a real* amount in foreign currency, which indicates what the magnitude of unexpected *real* losses or gains, in home currency, that corresponds to a given unexpected *nominal* change in exchange rate is expected to be[26]:

[2. 2] $[Gain / Loss]_t^{t+n} = {}_t X_{t+n} (\Delta S_t)$

where ΔS_t is an unexpected exchange rate change at t. Whereas firms have no control on the uncertainty of exchange rates, they can adjust their exposure, for instance through derivatives.

What matters for risk management are unexpected gains or losses that increase the volatility of cash flows. Anticipated exchange rate variations should be reflected into the firm's current market valuation and have no effect at the time the exchange rate changes actually occur. However, in the case of competitive exposure, even if the exchange rate is predictable, its effect on corporate performance may not necessarily be predictable. This results from the fact that competitive *risk* is function of two

---

[25] See, e.g., Sercu and Uppal (1995).
[26] See Coval (1998), March 30, p. 3., Stulz (2000), p. 15.

sources of uncertainty: the uncertainty of the exchange rate and the uncertainty of the foreign currency cash flows.

2.3 Exchange Rates Misalignment and Corporate Competitiveness

The purchasing power parity (PPP) relationship indicates whether changes in nominal exchange rates have an impact on the real value of a firm. The exchange rate is the relative price of domestic to foreign goods, so departures from PPP affect a firm's international competitiveness by changing the costs of its inputs relative to those of its competitors and the relative price of its output purchased by its consumers[27].

The change in competitiveness then affects a firm's current and future cash flows and value. The exchange rate index to be used for exposure measurement differs whether cash flows are contractually fixed or not:

- *Contractual exposure* measures the exposure of cash flows that are fixed in nominal currency. Since prices have been contractually fixed and cannot be adjusted to nominal exchange rate changes, the relevant exchange rate for exposure calculation is the expected nominal exchange rate at the time of payment (settlement date)[28].

- *Competitive exposure* concerns non-committed nominal cash flows; prices have not been set and adjustment can take place in response to a nominal exchange rate change. In that case, the real exchange rate is relevant for exposure measurement.

If *absolute PPP* holds, the real exchange rate equals unity, as a result of foreign prices translated into the home currency being equal to domestic prices[29]. Under absolute PPP, the change in the nominal exchange rate is determined by its movements back towards the assumed equilibrium, which is the nominal exchange rate that corresponds to a real exchange rate equal to one. *All other things remaining equal*, when the nominal exchange rate returns to its PPP value, the initial competitive position of the firm prior to the exchange rate shock would be restored. If *relative PPP* holds, the expected change in real exchange rate is zero. The real exchange rate is expected to be

---

[27] PPP theory predicts that relative prices are correlated with exchange rates but does not presuppose a causal link between relative prices and exchange rates. See Levich (1998), pp. 103-104.

[28] See Stulz (2000), ch. 8, p. 17 and p. 22, Bodnar (1999), pp. 1-2.

[29] If foreign prices translated into the home currency are higher than domestic prices, then the real exchange rate is greater than unity.

constant, but not necessarily equal to unity. This implies that nominal exchange rate changes that are not compensated with differences in inflation rates affect firms' international competitiveness[30].

If PPP holds, firms should have little exposure. But the practical relevance of PPP measures is subject to several difficulties:

(a) *Changes in the equilibrium real exchange rate:* the exchange rate might actually not revert to its initial equilibrium value. Real exchange rates could change permanently if a real shock affects one country but not its trading partners[31], e.g., real shocks in real income or real interest rates.

(b) *Corporate planning horizons shorter than period for exchange rate mean reversion:* in contrast to the view prevailing in the 1980s, there now appears to be a consensus in the academic literature that long run PPP holds. However, deviations from PPP have been reported to be substantial in the short and medium term, and the mean reversion process of exchange rates towards their PPP value is usually long lasting[32]. Treasurers, who typically have to consider planning horizons that are much shorter, must deal with PPP deviations and their impact on short-term cash flow and long-term competitiveness[33].

(c) *Difficulty to calculate a relevant PPP measure:* a calculated PPP exchange rate is a proxy for the "true" real exchange rate and can be prone to *measurement error*[34]. Furthermore, it can be difficult to calculate a comprehensive PPP measure in terms

---

[30] If absolute PPP holds, then so will relative PPP. But the reverse is not necessarily true; relative PPP may hold even if there are persistent deviations in the average absolute price levels across countries. See Giddy (1994), p.129, for a discussion on why absolute PPP is an implausible theory.

[31] Levich (1998), p. 117: "assuming that the long-run real exchange rate is constant is of course a convenience, one that might plausibly be based on the assumption that while real shocks occur, they may affect all countries more or less equally, leaving the long-run real exchange rate unchanged".

[32] Frankel and Rose (1996) use a panel of 150 countries and 45 annual post World War II observations and show strong evidence of mean-reversion. PPP deviations are eroded at a rate of approximately 15% annually which put the half-life of deviations from PPP at about 4 years. Abuaf and Jorion (1990) use annual data for the period 1900 to 1972 and monthly data for the period 1973 to 1987 for 10 industrial countries, and find support for the long-run PPP in both periods, but with substantial short-term deviations, that appear to take about 3 years to be reduced in half.

[33] For companies in certain structured settings, this mean reversion property can be exploited in the hedging strategies. See Froot (1993). This property can also be exploited for forecasting exchange rates at long horizon. See, e.g., Mark (1994) or Chinn and Meese (1995).

[34] Measurement error is defined as the "fraction of the variance of the PPP real exchange rate that has no counterpart in the true real exchange rate". See Sjaastad (1998).

of input and output prices that are relevant for the cash flows of a firm[35]. Aggregate PPP measures based on economy-wide price indices, such as wholesale prices or consumer prices are not directly informative. To have some relevance, one needs to know how closely these price indices represent the price behavior of a firm's inputs and outputs.

(d) *PPP is not a sufficient condition for the absence of exposure*: first, nominal exchange rate changes can affect real cash flows if there is *nominal taxation of gains in foreign currency*: regardless of whether PPP holds, government tax policies could be a source of exposure, if they imply the taxation of nominal rather than real income. Suppose that a company's foreign affiliate has debt in its base currency (foreign currency). The base currency depreciates relative to the parent company's currency, in line with inflation. There is no real exchange rate change and PPP holds. The tax on the nominal interest paid in home currency by the parent company is reduced, although the real value and cost of the foreign currency debt has not changed[36]. Second, although they capture a large proportion of an exchange rate impact, changes in relative prices do not tell the entire story in terms of corporate competitiveness, especially in the short run[37]. *Changes in productivity* can also play a role. A strong currency can put a firm to greater efficiency and give it a competitive edge that outweighs any disadvantage from the exchange rate[38].

2.4 Foreign Exchange Exposure and Industry Structure

2.4.1 Foreign Exchange Exposure with Real Price Risk and Quantity Risk

A. Channels of Influence of Exchange Rates Fluctuations on Firm Value

In order to understand economic exposure, it is necessary to consider how a firm generates its current and future cash flows. In expression [2.3] the value of a German firm consists of discounted contractual and non-contractual cash flows from various currencies:

---

[35] See Dufey and Srinivasulu (1983), Pringle and Connolly (1993). See Demacopoulos (1989) for real exchange rate calculation for the U.S. construction sector.
[36] See Demacopoulos (1989), pp. 46-47, Sercu and Uppal (1995), pp. 516-527.
[37] See Flood and Lessard (1986), p. 27, The Economist, August 18th 2001, p. 50, for a discussion on empirical evidence.
[38] Changes in productivity could, for example, be induced by exchange-rate related changes in wages.

[2. 3] $$V_t = \sum_{t=0}^{T} \frac{CF_{Euro,t}}{(1+i_{Euro,t})^t} + \sum_{t=0}^{T} \frac{CF_{\$,t} s_{Euro/\$}}{(1+i_{\$,t})^t} + \sum_{t=0}^{T} \frac{CF_{Yen,t} s_{Euro/Yen}}{(1+i_{Yen,t})^t} + \ldots\ldots$$

where the value of a firm at time t (V_t) is defined as the summation of the firm's cash flows (CF_t) over time discounted back to their present value by an appropriate discount factor (i_t), i.e. $V_t = \sum_{t=0}^{T} CF_t / (1+i_t)^t$, with $t = 0$ to T. Cash flows in each currency are discounted at their own appropriate interest rate and multiplied by a nominal spot exchange rate. The German firm generates foreign currency cash flows whose real value in home currency may be affected by nominal changes in exchange rates[39]. Foreign currency cash flows in US-dollar, for example, can be expressed as[40]:

[2. 4] $$CF_{\$,t} = \mathrm{Re}\,venue_{\$,t} - Costs_{\$,t} - Taxes_{\$,t} - Investments_{\$,t}$$

$$= (p_{\$,t} \times q_{\$,t}^S) - (FC_{\$,t} + VC_{\$,t} \times q_{\$,t}^P) - T_{\$,t} - I_{\$,t}$$

where cash flows, which are equal to after-tax profits plus net investment, are expressed as revenues defined as the quantity of goods sold $(q_{\$,t}^S)$ times the price unit $(p_{\$,t})$, minus costs defined as the sum of a fixed component $(FC_{\$,t})$ plus a variable component $(VC_{\$,t})$ times the number of goods produced $(q_{\$,t}^P)$, minus corporate taxes (T) and investments (I). Accordingly, the cash flow impact of an exchange rate change is equal to its impact on sales minus its impact on costs of good sold, minus its impact on taxes, and minus its impact on investment[41]. This decomposition of firm value is the starting point to think through in greater detail how exchange rate changes could affect firm value, by thinking how prices, profit margins and quantities could change in response to an exchange rate change.

B. Determinants of Foreign Exchange Exposure

Although economic exposure is conceptually clear, its determination is complex. The "determinants" of foreign exchange exposure refer to the factors that determine *how* exchange rates affect a firm value. They determine to what extent a firm's competitive

---

[39] For example if purchasing power parity does not hold.
[40] See Stulz (2000), ch. 8, p. 26.
[41] For an empirical study estimating the foreign exchange exposure of investments, see Campa and Goldberg (1995).

position is affected by exchange rate changes. An accurate picture of competitive exposure depends on a detailed list of assumptions regarding how a firm, its competitors, suppliers, and customers may respond to an exchange rate change, and it is impossible to generalize how all these factors interact to determine a firm's exposure. However, it is reasonable to assume that exposure can be functionally described by a parsimonious set of determinants and that it is not purely random. These determinants can be categorized as follows:

- *Firm's activities, as reflected by its current operating and financial structure*: the type and extent of a firm's activities is defined by the proportion of exports and imports, the involvement in foreign operations and foreign investments, the proportion of imported / locally produced inputs, and so forth.

- *Market structure*: the key determinant of economic exposure is the competitive structure of the industry in which the firm operates, because industry structure characterizes the exchange rates elasticity of a firm's local currency cash flows.

- *Strategic options,* whereby firms can alter their marketing strategy or production strategy in response to exchange rate changes. Exposure measures should not estimate the effect of exchange rate changes on the profitability of a firm's current (ex-ante) operations, but on the profitability adjusted for ex-post operating adjustments that are expected to be implemented in response to exchange rate changes.

- *Hedging activities*: the extent to which a firm and its competitors offset their exposures through operational and financial hedging.

- *Government policies*: this includes both domestic and foreign fiscal and monetary policies[42].

- *Risk factors affecting foreign currency cash flows*: foreign currency cash flows fluctuate in nominal terms according to local market conditions, e.g., exchange rates but also business and political factors.

C. Specification of Exchange Rate Effects on Cash Flows and Firm Value

---

[42] See Oxelheim and Wihlborg (1987), p. 115.

Quantity Risk and Real Exchange Rate/Price Risk

Unexpected exchange rate fluctuations can lead to variations in domestic cash flows as a result of two sources of risk[43]:

- *Real exchange rate risk/domestic real price risk*: real domestic price risk results from nominal exchange rate uncertainty and foreign currency prices uncertainty.

- *Quantity risk*: uncertainty regarding quantities, e.g., sales projections can be uncertain.

For an international trading firm, "quantity risk" is the uncertainty of *real* foreign cash flows, and "real price risk" the uncertainty of the real exchange rate. Competitive exposure is uncertain because cash flows fluctuate in *nominal* foreign currency terms, primarily as function of market conditions. They can be affected by multiple factors including market risks such as exchange rate risk, but also political, country and business risks[44].

Contractual exposure is associated with *nominal* domestic price risk only and is therefore constant. Because there is no uncertainty regarding the amount of nominal foreign currency cash flows to be hedged, contractual exposures are generally simple to analyze and to hedge. Typically, the assumption of measuring the effect of exchange rate changes on firm value, "while holding other economic variables constant" implicitly assumes contractual exposure.

Conversion Effect and Competitive Effect

Competitive exposure comprises two effects: a *competitive effect* and a *conversion effect*[45]. The conversion effect results from the necessity to convert foreign currency cash flows into home currency[46]. The competitive effect is the "sensitivity of the local

---

[43] See e.g., Stulz (2000), ch. 8, p. 8, Gay et al. (2001), Taft and Brown (2001). Quantity risk is sometimes associated with business risk, whereas price risk is associated with financial risk. See, e.g., CorporateMetrics (1999).

[44] For example, the power of local labor and business interests, the macroeconomic environment and policies and country sources of economic risk. See Demacopoulos (1989).

[45] See, e.g., Flood and Lessard (1986), p. 26, Glaum (1990), p 68. The "competitive effect" and the "competitive exposure" are sometimes viewed as equivalent, but they are conceptually different.

[46] The existence of a conversion effect depends on the *currency of invoice*, i.e. currency of settlement, whereas the *currency of denomination* is the currency in which prices are set and sales generated.

currency cash flows to changes in the exchange rate", whereas the conversion effect is "the one-for-one mapping of the resulting local currency cash flows" into the firm's home currency[47]. For an international trading firm, this corresponds to the sensitivity of its foreign currency cash flows to exchange rates. For a firm with purely domestic activities, this is the sensitivity of its home currency cash flows to exchange rates.

The competitive effect refers to the influence of exchange rate changes on quantity risk and depends on the structure of the markets in which the firm sells its products and sources its inputs. It can be described by breaking it down into a *profit margin effect* and a *volume effect*[48]. The combination of the effects on profit margins with the quantity impacts fully describes the effect of exchange rate changes on revenues, costs and profits. This competitive effect makes it difficult to estimate economic exposure and eliminate it through hedging[49].

Market Structure and Currency of Determination

A firm's competitive exposure is largely determined by (a) the *structure of the markets in which it sells its products*: the industry structure in the output market is characterized by the location and currency denomination of key competitors[50], consumers' characteristics, and so forth, (b) the *structure of the markets in which a firm (and its competitors) purchase their inputs*[51]: for example, the competitive structure of inputs markets determines the degree of substitutability between local and imported factors of production. Markets' structure will, in turn, determine (i) the *quantity impacts* (unit sales or purchases) and (ii) the *currency of determination* of the price of goods. The exchange rate impact on revenues, costs, and profits is fully described by combining the first factor, which describes quantity impacts with the second factor, the price movements[52].

---

[47] See Flood and Lessard (1986), p. 26. The definition of "competitive effect" does not imply that the firm competes with other firms, but that its competitive position, such as the degree of attractiveness to consumers, has been altered.

[48] See Lessard and Lightstone (1986), p. 108. The volume effect is sometimes called "market share effect". See, e.g., Bodnar et al. (2002), p. 209.

[49] Competitive exposure is referred to as "residual exposure" for that reason. See Levi (1996).

[50] Exporters, for instance, can have little exposure if they compete in the foreign market with domestic firms; it they compete with foreign firms, however, their exposure can be substantial.

[51] See Flood and Lessard (1986).

[52] See Flood and Lessard (1986), pp. 29-34.

The conversion effect is by definition associated with the currency in which foreign cash flows are denominated (*currency of denomination*). The competitive effect is determined primarily by market characteristics, not by the currency in which prices are denominated. It is function of the real exchange rate that matters for the firm's international competitiveness (*currency of determination* or *currency habitat of price*[53]). While domestic currency cash flows are by definition not subject to a conversion effect, they may be subject to a competitive effect. The identification of a firm's currency of determination necessitates an industry competitive analysis[54]. This essentially consists in identifying a firm's input or output price's most stable currency or basket of currencies. This will generally be the currency in which much of the production or sales of the product take place. A reason is that in highly competitive markets, firms have little flexibility to protect their profit margins by adjusting their foreign prices and are therefore more exposed.

The notion of currency of determination implies that a purely domestic firm (non-traded goods sector[55]) with no apparent linkage with the international economy could be exposed, through its interaction with other market participants that are exposed. The example of regional electric utilities illustrates this point[56]. They have no foreign currency accounts on their books, and consequently no accounting contractual or translation exposures. But they will be exposed if they have customers whose demands for electricity are affected by exchange rate changes.

At a macroeconomic level, a purely local firm's exposure can depend on the capital-labor ratio in its industry. An appreciation deteriorates the price competitiveness of domestic products and reduces the range of domestic products that are exportable. Trade theory predicts that the relative price change at a country level, resulting from a domestic currency appreciation, will induce a shift of resources from traded to non-traded activities[57]. The reallocation of resources causes the market value of capital in

---

[53] In most cases a price's currency habitat consists of a basket of currencies. For example, "the price of wine will likely have the lowest variability in a basket which includes the Dollar, Franc, and Lira". See Coval (1998), March 16, p. 49.

[54] For example, Weyerhauser, an U.S company, found that its US$ cash flows were exposed to the Swedish Krona, the home currency of Weherhauser's main competitors. See Adler (1995), p. 167.

[55] See Levich (1998), p. 567, Levi (1996), p. 334. The distinction between traded (exported/imported) and non-traded (exclusively produced and consumed locally) goods, e.g., the housing and construction sectors, is determined by transaction costs and tariffs that segment markets.

[56] See Adler and Dumas (1984), p. 41. See also DeRosa (1996).

[57] This happens "as long as capital is more sector-specific than other inputs to production", which means that for medical services, car repair for example, we should not observe this phenomenon. See Bodnar (1998), p. 314.

non-traded goods activities to rise, in the short run, relative to the market value of capital in traded goods activities. This implies that companies producing non-traded goods should see an increase in their market value in response to an appreciation of the domestic currency[58].

2.4.2 Impact on Operating and Financial Structure: Real and Nominal Effects

A. Relation Between Real and Nominal Effects

Equation [2.5] clarifies the effects characterizing a firm's foreign revenue exposure:

[2. 5]
$$(q \cdot p^h) \cdot \frac{1}{p^h} = q \cdot p^f \cdot s \cdot \frac{1}{p^h}$$

q	quantity sold which is function of currencies of determination, s^d, and market conditions represented by x: $q = f(s^d, x)$.
p^h	domestic currency price.
p^f	foreign currency price as a function of s^d and x: $p^f = f(s^d, x)$.
s	*nominal* exchange rate used for conversion.
$(q \cdot p^f)$	*nominal* foreign currency cash flow.
$[(q \cdot p^f)/p^h]$	*real* foreign currency cash flow.
$[(q \cdot p^h)/p^h]$	*real* domestic currency cash flow.

Exposure is *a real* amount of foreign currency cash flows which relates changes in *nominal* exchange rate to changes in a *real* amount of domestic currency cash flows. If absolute PPP holds, the purchasing power in terms of q in the two countries is identical. Exposure changes if the *real* amount of foreign currency cash flows changes:

$$d\left[\frac{(q \cdot p^f)}{p^h}\right] = \left[\frac{\partial[(q \cdot p^f)/p^h]}{\partial s^d} \cdot \partial s^d\right] + \left[\frac{\partial[(q \cdot p^f)/p^h]}{\partial x} \cdot \partial x\right]$$

The exposure will be different depending on how changes in s^d or x affect the firm's ability to generate real foreign cash flows by modifying its competitive position and inducing changes in its operating and financial structure.

---

[58] See Bodnar (1998), p. 314, Burda and Wyplosz (1997), Levich (1998), pp. 567-568.

- **Quantity risk** refers to the uncertainty of q associated with s^d and x, whereas **real price risk** refers to the uncertainty of the real exchange rate.

- **Competitive effects** refer to the effects of *nominal* exchange rate changes on *real* foreign currency cash flow, $\partial[(q \cdot p^f)/p^h]/\partial s$, whereas the **conversion effect** refers to the impact of nominal exchange rate changes on nominal domestic currency cash flow, $\partial(q \cdot p^h)/\partial s$. The relation between real foreign currency cash flows and nominal exchange rate can equivalently be assessed through the relation between real exchange rate/price risk and quantity risk.

- Foreign currency cash flows $(q \cdot p^f)$ fluctuate in nominal terms according to market conditions, i.e., q and p^f fluctuate as a function of s^d and x, and have real effects on firm value.

- Foreign exchange risk results from quantity risk and **real domestic price risk**/real exchange rate risk: this means that the real effect on cash flows of a nominal exchange rate change can be influenced through operating measures, either through adjustments in quantities q, or changes in real foreign costs, or changes in real foreign prices (p^f/p^h). Adjustments in the nominal foreign currency price, by affecting the domestic real price/real exchange rate, will influence the real effect of exchange rate changes on cash flows. This justifies exchange rate pass-through policies to manage real foreign exchange exposures.

As a result of uncertainties in s^d and x, the exposure can be non-linear but also linear and stochastic. Exposure non-linearities arise when *nominal* exchange rate changes affect the firm's *real* foreign currency cash flows, e.g., negative correlation for an exporter implies that the firm will experience increasing (declining) sales volume at the same time as the domestic currency is strengthening (weakening). In that case, exposure is function of exchange rate variations and level. On the other hand, if foreign cash flows are affected by factors other than the exchange rate, exposure is linear and stochastic.

B. Real Effects of Changes in Competitiveness

The exposure of a non-contractual foreign cash flow will be relatively *greater than* the exposure of a fixed foreign cash flow[59]. Figure 2.2 shows the concave/convex exposure profile BOB^* of a firm with a long foreign currency position, e.g. an exporter. S_T is the nominal exchange rate and CF_T^d are real domestic cash flows:

- a *real* exchange rate/*real* price depreciation improves the firm's competitiveness and leads to a more than proportional increase in exporting profits.

- a *real* exchange rate/*real* price appreciation deteriorates the firm's competitiveness and leads to a more than proportional decrease in exporting profits.

Figure 2. 2 Real Impact of Competitive Effects[60]

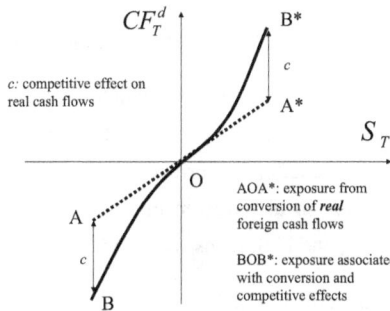

The sufficient condition for exposure non-linearity is changes in competitiveness reflecting changes in foreign currency profit margins. Operating flexibility, i.e., flexibility to make ex-post adjustments in quantities or *nominal* foreign prices is not a necessary condition for non-linearity. Suppose an exporter with domestic costs. A depreciation will make the firm more competitive in the foreign market *through more competitive costs*. Profit margins and profits in domestic currency increase even if nominal foreign currency revenues are unchanged. Even if the firm has no operating flexibility, the nominal depreciation has a real effect on domestic profits. The linear component of exposure reflects the nominal effect associated with the conversion of a real foreign cash flow with a nominal exchange rate.

---

[59] See Bodnar et al. (2002), p. 212.
[60] Contractual exposure cannot be represented in the same graph, since adjustments for inflation are made after conversion of foreign cash flows.

2.4.3 Industry Structure, Operating Flexibility, and Competitiveness Effects

Structural models examine exposure by modeling the impact of exchange rate changes on firms' cash flows and emphasize the importance of the competitive structure of the industry in which firms operate[61]. Supply/demand conditions determine the sensitivity of a firm's foreign currency price and quantities to exchange rate changes. Microeconomic theory is helpful to distinguish the effects of exchange rate changes on a firm's prices, revenues, costs, operating margin, and overall profits. To illustrate, we consider the exposure of a firm under perfect competition and monopoly[62].

A. Competitive and Conversion Effects Under Perfect Competition

A German firm exports in the U.S. market, which is perfectly competitive. The marginal revenue of selling in the U.S. is fixed and does not depend on the actions of the German firm. Inputs to production are priced domestically, i.e., they are available from domestic markets that are insulated from international conditions. German firms produce with costs in euro (€) and U.S. firms with US$ costs.

Figure 2.2(a) illustrates the effect of a real € appreciation. A real € appreciation deteriorates the firm's competitiveness through its costs. There is a change in € costs expressed in US$. In perfect competition, price equals marginal costs. The change in profit margins *expressed in US$* then induces adjustments in production/sales.

The initial € price is p_0^{ϵ} and is given by point *a* on the demand curve corresponding to the quantity that equalizes marginal revenue (*MR*) and marginal cost (*MC*). A € appreciation deteriorates the firm's competitive position in the U.S. market by altering its inputs relative prices. The firm has to charge a lower € price and leave the US$ price unchanged. The *MC* curve in € is unaffected since the firm's costs are in €, but

---

[61] See the neo-classical models of Shapiro (1974), Hodder (1982), Hekman (1985), Choi (1986), Flood and Lessard (1986), Luehrman (1990), von Ungern-Sternberg and von Weizsacker (1990), Bessembinder (1992), Levi (1994), Levi (1996), Fridberg (1998), Marston (2001), Bodnar et al. (2002).
[62] Textbook analysis in terms of demand and supply curves can be found in Flood and Lessard (1986), Lessard and Lightstone (1986), Levi (1996), pp. 330-362, Stulz and Williamson (1996), Stulz (2000).

total € costs are exposed through changes in quantity sold[63]. The demand curve in €
shifts down to D_1, by the extent of the US$ depreciation if there is no inflation. The
firm produces at **b**, with a lower € price and level of sales. Revenues decrease by,
$q_1 q_0 a p_0^\epsilon p_1^\epsilon b$, total costs by $q_0 q_1 ab$, and profits by $p_0^\epsilon ab p_1^\epsilon$. There is a decrease in € cash
inflows[64]. Figure 2.2(b) shows the curves in US$. The US$ price is $p_0^\$$. If MC, the
input costs incurred in € in Germany, but expressed in US$, shifts to MC', quantity
diminishes to q_1. The revenue in terms of US$ decreases by $q_0 q_1 ba$. If the US$ MC
curve shifts upward to MC'', and the demand curve shifts to D_2 (MR curve shifts to
MR'' in figure 2.2a), sales in the U.S. are no longer profitable[65].

Figure 2. 2 German Exporter and Euro Appreciation in Perfect Competition[66]

(a)Input priced domestically (curves in terms of €)	(b)Input priced domestically (curve in terms of US$)	(c)Input priced internationally (curves in terms of €)

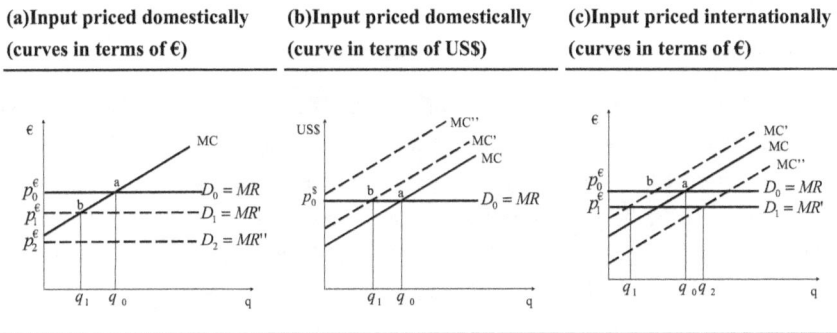

The general prediction is that a decline in the real value of a country's currency makes
its exports and import-competing goods more competitive. Conversely, an appreciating
home currency should hurt the country's exporters and those producers competing with
imports. This analysis highlights the following aspects:

---

[63] Production costs in domestic currency are sensitive to exchange rate fluctuations if either some
inputs are priced in foreign currency units or cost varies with the quantity produced which in turn
varies with exchange rates. See Knetter (1992), p. 2.
[64] Underlying this prediction is the assumption that the costs of the firm are largely denominated in the
home currency, while revenues are contingent on the relative purchasing power of foreign currencies.
[65] The firm's exposure may still be low for example if it has the "operational flexibility to shift sales
rapidly and at low cost away from the US". See Stulz (2000), ch. 8.
[66] See, e.g., Levi (1996), Stulz (2002), ch. 8.

a) *Interaction between competitive and conversion effects*: an exporter located in a country with an appreciating currency has a cost disadvantage relative to firms in countries with stable or declining real currency value, and this decline in competitiveness will reduce future export profits. In perfect competition, competitive effects and conversion effects are of the same sign: when the € appreciates, the German firm loses US$ profits relative to an unchanged € (competitive effect), but the US$ is worth less so those losses are not as costly (conversion effect). When the € depreciates, the German firm increases its US$ profits at a time when the US$ has increased in value.

b) *Tradeoff between natural hedging and strategic flexibility effects*: we consider three cases:

- *Case 1 - natural hedge:* the € appreciates. The firm incurs production costs in the U.S., in US$. In that case, the US$ *MC* curve remains unchanged. This creates a natural hedge by offsetting revenue exposure trough cost exposure.

- *Case 2 – production flexibility*: the € *depreciates*. The firm incurs production costs in Germany, in €. The firm has production flexibility and increases its sales because of its improved competitiveness. Expected profits increase as a result of this flexibility. If the firm had a natural hedge in place (costs in US$), profits would increase, but less than with flexibility. By setting the natural hedge, the firm gives up some profits associated with production flexibility.

- *Case 3 – switching flexibility:* the firm can switch between production costs in the U.S. in US$ and in Germany in €. When the € appreciates, the firm produces in the U.S. and its profits are similar to case 1. When the € depreciates, the firm produces in Germany in € costs (case 2). The profits *over time* are potentially higher than under both previous cases. There is a potential value advantage from this switching flexibility against having inflexible production either in Germany or U.S. Since it is costly to switch between production modes, the value of the flexible strategy and the inflexible strategy will depend on the comparison between the cost savings and the costs of switching between the two operating modes. Natural hedging and flexibility are discussed in chapter 6/6.3.4.

c) *Changes in competitiveness make exposure non-linear*: the reduced competitiveness because of the lower profit margin *expressed in* US$ induces changes in quantities. But suppose that the firm has no flexibility to adjust quantities. US$ revenues remain unchanged, US$ marginal and total costs are higher, and the profit margin in € is lower. The implication is that even if the ex-ante operating structure is unchanged ex-post (no production/sales flexibility), the exposure is non-linear. Only contractual exposures are linear.

d) *Effect of purchasing power parity law*: in the long run, the € price will tend to decrease by the combined rate of depreciation and US inflation, according to the PPP law. In a situation without German inflation and where all inputs are non-tradable, *MC* in € will remain, at least in the short run, as it was before the appreciation. However, if inputs are priced internationally, or if there is inflation, the *MC* curve will shift upwards or downwards, both in terms of € and US$, depending on the predominant effect between inflation in US and tradable inputs' prices (figure 2.2c). A € appreciation reduces the € price of inputs, while inflation has the opposite effect[67].

B. Competitive and Conversion Effects Under Monopoly

In monopoly, the firm's exposure is lower due to the ability to adjust the local price. Unlike perfect competition where price equals marginal costs, in monopolistic competition price is greater than marginal cost. The more competitive the environment, the more the markup will be defined by the competition. As a consequence, foreign prices are more sensitive in monopolistic than in competitive environment, resulting in higher variations of foreign cash flows[68].

In less competitive environments, a firm can have more control over pricing. The German exporter faces a downward-sloping demand curve, implying that a key exposure determinant is the price-elasticity of demand[69]. A € appreciation makes the exporting goods more expensive in terms of the US$ and this results in a U.S. demand decline. Figure 2.3(a) illustrates curves in € and figure 2.3(b) in US$ with input

---

[67] If production costs decrease, it can be shown that if profits are being made, an exporter's total revenues will decrease more than total costs, and so profits will diminish. Local costs often rise with some time lag following a depreciation. See Eiteman et al. (2000).

[68] See Demacopoulos (1989).

[69] The demand function of the monopolist could be interpreted more generally in an oligopolitic framework if we consider the elasticities to be associated with a residual demand curve that takes into account the firm's perceptions of competitors responses to changes in the firm's price. See Levi (1994).

domestically priced. The € price of goods sold in the U.S. is p_0^ϵ before the US$ depreciation. As the US$ depreciates, for each quantity sold, the demand and the MR curves in € falls by the extent of the US$ depreciation. The € price falls to p_1^ϵ and the quantity exported to q_1. Since costs are incurred in €, the MC curve in € is unaffected. With a downward sloping curve, the domestic currency price reduction from p_0^ϵ to p_1^ϵ is smaller than the vertical shift in the demand curve (ac>ab), i.e., less than the US$ depreciation, and sales decrease by a smaller fraction than in perfect competition.

Figure 2.3 German Exporter and Appreciation of the home currency (€) in an Imperfectly Competitive Market[70]

(a) Curves in terms of home currency (€)   (b) Curves in terms of foreign currency (US$)

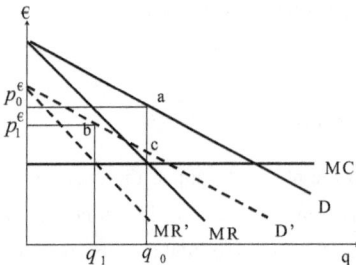

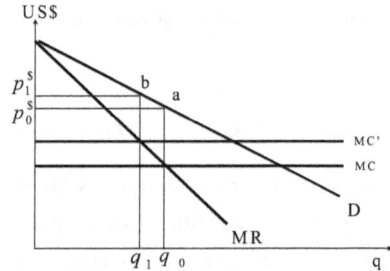

Variations in costs are correlated with the relative output prices in US$. The exporter's competitive position in the U.S. market is affected not only through changes in relative input costs like under perfect competition, but also through changes in relative foreign output prices in US$[71]. The US$ price is related to the € costs, through the effect of quantity changes on marginal costs. By increasing the US$ price, the exporter pass-through some of the costs increase. This mitigates the adverse effect that an increased € cost (expressed in US$) has on competitiveness by adjusting the US$ mark-up.

---

[70] For simplicity, the marginal costs are assumed to be independent of the quantity produced.
[71] For a firm operating in a monopolistic market, a change in q will always produce a change in p and as costs are assumed constant, the mark-up will vary. A change in the firm's markup will modify the sensitivity of cash flows for all level of cash flows.

In figure 2.3(b), before the US\$ depreciation, the US\$ price is $p_0^\$$. As the US\$ depreciates, there is no effect on the demand curve in US\$, but the MC curve shifts to MC'. The costs incurred in Germany but expressed in terms of US\$ increase in proportion to the US\$ depreciation. The net effect is to reduce the quantity exported to q_1 and increase the US\$ price to $p_1^\$$. This reduces profit margin and profit. However, the firm can increase its US\$ price without losing its entire market share and protect partially its profit margins. The profit margin and level of profits are higher than in the case of perfect competition, but the exchange rate sensitivity of its profits is lower.

Pricing flexibility and the extent of exchange-rate-pass-through (ERPT) depend on supply/demand conditions in the foreign market[72]:

- *Demand-side effect - convexity of the demand curve in the export market*: this determines how the elasticity of demand and mark-ups varies with price (along the demand curve). The higher the convexity of the demand curve, the lower the ERPT, i.e., if demand becomes more (less) elastic as local currency prices rise, the optimal foreign currency markup charged by the exporter will fall (rise) as the foreign currency depreciates. The firm will pass-through relatively less adverse foreign currency depreciation.

- *Supply-side effect - change in marginal cost:* production costs in domestic currency are sensitive to exchange rate fluctuations if either (i) some inputs are priced in foreign currency or (ii) marginal costs vary with the quantity produced which in turn varies with exchange rates[73].

Since firms in the *import sector* face a lower € price for foreign goods, the quantity demanded and the price-cost margins increase. Whereas the value of the firm in the import sector increases, the value of the firm in the *import-competing sector* is reduced, since the demand and price-cost margins of an import-competing firm is lower[74]. The overall exposure of a *multinational corporation* is more complex, and offsetting effects can come into play. The profitability of a foreign subsidiary could be enhanced by the same rate movement that reduces the return on exports from the home plant.

---

[72] See, e.g., Dornbush (1987), Marston (1990), Clark and Faruquee (1997).
[73] See Knetter (1992), p. 2.
[74] See, e.g., Levi (1996).

2.4.4 Industry Structure, Corporate Pricing, and Natural Hedging Effects

A. Exposure in Partial Equilibrium

A multi-market monopoly model of foreign exchange exposure assumes a monopolist which practices price discrimination between markets[75] (calculations in Appendix B). It produces its inputs for production domestically and exports in k separate destination markets, indexed by i. The firm sets prices and takes quantities, and solves a static profit maximization problem, where the exchange rate is the only source of uncertainty. An expression for the firm value can be written as[76]:

$$[2.6] \qquad V = \pi \left[\frac{(1-\tau)}{\rho} \right] = \left(\sum_{i=0}^{k} s_i p_i q_i - c \sum_{i=0}^{k} q_i \right) \left[\frac{(1-\tau)}{\rho} \right]$$

where V is the market value of the firm, $\sum_{i=0}^{k} s_i p_i q_i$ the total revenue, $c \sum_{i=0}^{k} q_i$ the total cost, ρ the risk-adjusted shareholder opportunity cost of capital, τ the tax rate, s_i the exchange rate in units of home currency per unit of currency i, p_i the product price in country i, q_i the quantity sold in country i, c the marginal cost of production at home, which is assumed to be constant. Expressed in terms of elasticity, the exposure of the firm can be written as:

$$[2.7] \qquad \frac{\partial V}{\partial s_j} \cdot \frac{s_j}{V} = \eta_j \cdot \frac{\left[s_j q_j \left(p_j - \dfrac{c}{s_j} \right) (1-\tau) \right] \cdot \dfrac{1}{\rho}}{V}$$

This shows that a firm operating in a relatively more competitive environment should be more exposed and that an exchange rate appreciation could hurt exporters. The exposure to currency j depends on the price-elasticity of the firm's product in the foreign market j, η_j; on the profit from exports to country j which is the per unit mark-up of the firm in the foreign market j[77], $(p_j - c/s_j)$, times the volume of firm sales in the foreign market, q_j; on the corporate tax rate and opportunity cost of capital. If the

---

[75] This part is based on the models of Levi (1994), pp. 38-43, and Marston (2001), pp. 151-153.
[76] In Levi (1994), a term representing net monetary asset/liability position in currency i is added. This does not affect the main conclusions of this model. Since the value of assets and liabilities located in foreign countries ultimately gets reflected in cash flows, cash flow is all that matters to firm value. See Pringle and Connolly (1993), p.70.
[77] Mark-up is defined as "per-unit profit measured in currency j".

ratio term on the left side in equation [2.7] is positive, exports to market j are profitable, and exposure will be greater, the higher the elasticity of the demand. Several determinants of exposure could change over time, supporting the intuition that exposure is time varying[78]. One important source of time-variation is likely to be due to changes over time in real operations (i.e., imports and exports). The exposure of the firm can be expressed as:

[2. 8]
$$\frac{\partial V}{\partial s_j} = (p_j q_j) \frac{(1-\tau)}{\rho}$$

This model assumes input cost incurred in domestic currency. If we suppose a two country case where inputs are produced in the country where the product is exported, the exposure of profits is equal to the initial level of net revenue denominated in foreign currency, and exposure is proportional to the initial level of foreign currency based net revenue[79].

[2. 9]
$$\frac{\partial V}{\partial s_j} = (p_j q_j - c q_j) \frac{(1-\tau)}{\rho} \qquad j = 1,2$$

The exposure is not directly dependent on the price elasticity of demand or on marginal cost *"once the level of net revenues based in foreign currency is taken into account"*, although net revenues themselves are still dependent on these two factors. Two insights are of direct interest for this study:

- *Indirect exposure effects arise through competitive interactions*: in [2.8] and [2.9], exposure would disappear if the firm ceased any international trading activities. In [2.8] exposure is the initial level of foreign currency revenue, whereas in [2.9] it is equal to the initial level of foreign currency profits. Yet we know from our discussion on the currency of determination that firms can be exposed even if they have purely "local" activities only, through their interactions with other market participants which are exposed. To account for that possibility, the interactions among firms and with consumers need to be analyzed (see chapter 4).

---

[78] Allayannnis (1997) empirically shows that exchange rate exposure is time-varying.
[79] See Marston (2001), pp. 151-153 and pp. 160-162. The introduction of imported inputs in addition to domestic inputs would make profit-maximizing output dependent on more than one exchange rate and thereby greatly complicate the analysis. See Levi (1994).

- *In monopoly/partial equilibrium, the exposure is linear[80]:* exposure forecast does not necessitate the evaluation of demand elasticities and marginal costs. All that matters for exposure measurement is the level of foreign currency based net revenue or the level of home based costs, depending on how profits are measured[81]. The exposure in [2.9] can be hedged with linear variance-minimizing hedges, e.g. natural hedges by matching foreign currency costs and revenues, geographical diversification, or linear derivatives.

B. Pricing-to-Market

In the model above, profit-maximizing price setting is based on expression [2.10]:

[2. 10]
$$p_j^h = \frac{c}{s_j\left(1-\dfrac{1}{\eta_j}\right)} \qquad p_j^f = \frac{c}{\left(1-\dfrac{1}{\eta_j}\right)} \; \forall j \qquad \eta_j = -\frac{p_j dq_j}{q_j dp_j}$$

This equalizes the marginal revenue from sales in each market to the common marginal cost. The firm is said to price discriminate or *price-to-market*[82]. This tells how to set prices in foreign currency p_j^f and domestic currency p_j^h, according to the common marginal cost c, the exchange rate, and the elasticities of demand η_j [83]. A low price will be set for the price-sensitive market and a high price for the market that is relatively price insensitive. In this way it maximizes its overall profits. When an exchange rate change occurs, the exporter will adjust the prices charged to the foreign markets, depending on how the exchange rate change has affected (i) marginal cost (through changes in quantity or input prices), or (ii) the elasticity of export demand. The former effect will spillover to the other destination markets, while the latter is destination-specific.

---

[80] Marston (2001), pp. 160-162, shows that this result holds for a firm following a Stackelberg strategy in a duopoly. Because exposure is easily forecast in that case, firms could manage it through simple financial instruments such as forward contracts.

[81] See Marston (2001), p. 152.

[82] See, e.g., Varian (1992) pp. 248-49, or Varian (1999), p. 422 and p. 434ss, and pp. 440-444 on third-degree price discrimination.

[83] The elasticity of demand is greater than 1 for a profit maximizer. See Varian (1999), p. 416, Levi (1996), p. 358.

Pricing-to-Market (PTM) theories describe price discrimination strategies that firms use to cope with exchange rate fluctuations. They explain a firm's pricing behavior from the fact that a firm with some market power to segment between markets will maximize its profits through price discrimination. Typically, PTM implies that "prices charged by exporters in their home currency for the exact same good, differ across destination markets, depending on different price elasticity of demand, even when the cost of serving different customers is the same, and that these differences can be explained by exchange rate differences alone"[84].

---

[84] See Goldberg and Knetter (1996).

3. Foreign Exchange Exposure with Real Options and Financial Flexibility Options

The analysis so far suggests that foreign exchange exposure depends to a large extent on the impact that exchange rates are expected to have on prices and quantities of inputs and outputs. Operating flexibility gives a firm the possibility to adjust operationally to exchange rate changes. It enables adjustments in costs and revenues structure and can be interpreted and valued as real options. Exposure asymmetries reflect a firm's expected real options payoffs associated with nominal exchange rate fluctuations. Flexibility is typically expected to convexify the exposure profile and increase expected firm value by mitigating the exposure to adverse exchange rate changes while increasing the exposure to beneficial exchange rate changes. The plan of this chapter is as follows. Section 3.1 highlights the shortcomings of analyzing foreign exchange exposure in a static framework. Section 3.2 and 3.3 examine the stochastic properties of asymmetric exposures and define exposure asymmetries. Section 3.4 shows how to value real options under real exchange rate/price risk and quantity risk. Section 3.5 examines the possibility of negative flexibility value because of bounds on flexibility. Sections 3.6 and 3.7 respectively analyze the effects of operating and financial flexibility on exposure.

3.1 Foreign Exchange Exposure with Multi-Period Flexibility

A. Dynamic Perspective on Foreign Exchange Exposure

A firm's foreign exchange exposure can be assimilated to a regression coefficient from a *cross-sectional* regression across possible future exchange rates values. It is represented graphically by the slope of a function having the conditional expectation (at a time t) of the firm's real value at a future time period T, $E_t(V_T|S_T)$, as the dependent variable, against each possible values of real exchange rate at time T, S_T, as the independent variable[1]. This function (figure 3.1 below) is called the *"foreign*

---

[1] See, e.g., Sercu and Uppal (1995), p. 504. The horizon at which exposure is estimated is thus $(T-t)$.

exchange exposure profile" of the firm's value. V_T corresponds to the level of firm value resulting from an unexpected exchange rate change.

Figure 3. 1 Foreign Exchange Exposure Profile of a Firm's Value at Time T[2]

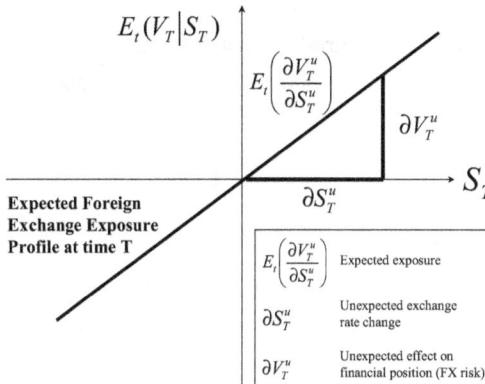

A linear exposure profile is static in the sense that the distribution of foreign cash flows over the valuation period is assumed to remain unchanged (ex-post) after an exchange rate change. The definition of exposure in the finance literature generally implicitly assumes a linear exposure. Exposure is assimilated to a partial derivative measuring the change in firm value in response to an infinitesimal exchange rate change, over a time period, "*while holding other economic variables constant*"[3]. This definition suggests a focus on the very short run. Over the longer run, other variables vary, with the implication that exposure measures should evaluate, not the expected effect of exchange rate changes on the firm's current (ex-ante) profitability, but on the firms' expected profitability adjusted for ex-post structural changes that are anticipated to take place in response to exchange rate shocks:

- First, a firm could *exercise real options* implying changes in suppliers, pricing policy, product design, and so forth[4]. For example, after an exchange rate change, a firm's exposure may still be low, if it has the operational flexibility to shift sales rapidly and at low cost to an other market.

---

[2] See, e.g., Smith (1995), p.23, Smithson et al. (1995), Sercu and Uppal (1995), p. 470.
[3] See Levich (1998), pp. 568-569. In other words, competitive effects are ignored.
[4] See Levich (1999), pp. 571-572, Stulz (2000), ch. 8, on the time dimension of exposure.

- Second, *other economic events or developments* could be expected to occur after exchange rate changes. Government trade or exchange rate policies could be implemented, new competitors could enter the market, or the exchange rate might revert to its purchasing power parity value.

These expected adjustments in a firm's economic environment and operating/financial structure generate exposure non-linearities, that is, the exposure is function of the exchange rate level.

B. Risk Management Relevance of Structural Models of Exposure

Traditionally, foreign exchange exposure has been analyzed in static industrial organization models of cash flow determination. However, since the objective of risk management is ultimately to maximize shareholder wealth, one needs a *valuation model of exposure.* Structural models of exposure typically examine the exposure of a single-period cash flow and do not directly address valuation issues. An analysis in terms of cash flows can be misleading if the exchange rate effects through the cost of capital are important. Changes in net cash flows do not necessarily translate into changes in firm value when the level of capitalization varies over time. If a firm raises new capital, e.g. through debt/equity financing or through retention of earnings, and invest this capital in projects generating returns equal to the cost of capital, there will be no increase in shareholder value even though net cash flows have increased from the investments[5]. A valuation model of exposure should integrate four related features:

- *Probabilistic models of variables adjustments over the estimation period* [6]: the firm's operating and financial adjustments, the industry structure and the exchange rate, should be viewed within dynamic processes over the valuation period.

---

[5] See Miller (1994), p. 14, based on Rappaport (1986).
[6] Hekman (1985), p. 84, argues that in order to examine the effect of exchange rate risk on value would require "*at least* an implicit model of valuation which might specify the effects of exchange risk on the discount rate or, through agency costs, on the expected values of cash flows". Flood and Lessard (1986), p. 26, argue that "in order to have a complete discussion on the implications of exchange rate changes on firm value, it is necessary to have a firm valuation model and models that examine intertemporal price and exchange rate adjustment mechanism".

- *Model of corporate behavior:* models of exposure do not describe the corporate motivations and financial implications that lead to a firm's strategic responses. Typically, the costs of making these adjustments are examined at a general level.

- *Model with multiple sources of uncertainty:* the assumption that exchange rates are the only source of uncertainty can be justified if we are concerned with the volatility of profit within about a year. At such frequencies, nominal exchange rates are generally highly volatile and weakly related to fundamentals. But if one is concerned with exchange rate exposure over longer horizons, the assumption of independent exchange rate uncertainty is not justified[7].

- *Model of capital structure:* contractual exposure arises from the acquisition of contractual nominal positions in foreign currency. The firms' financial structure can affect economic exposure and either mitigate or exacerbate the exposure of operating cash flows. Structural models of exposure typically ignore the role of capital structure and financial flexibility and the related issues on tax shields, dividend policy, and so forth.

These shortcomings highlight the potential of real options models to describe and value the exposure profile of risky cash flows.

C. Time Path of Foreign Exchange Exposure over the Valuation Period

It is critical to conduct the analysis of economic exposure in a dynamic framework, and in terms of a projected stream of cash flows over a multi-period planning horizon[8]. There are two reasons for this: (i) real assets need to be valued based on discounted cash flows[9], (ii) this is necessary for economic interpretation and to understand the problematic from the perspective of a corporate manager. Insights from economic models need to be interpreted in a discrete-time framework that values flows at each

---

[7] See Friberg and Vredin (1996), p. 12.
[8] Stock variables, such as firm value, represent net present values at time zero, whereas flow variables represent cash flow from operations.
[9] Real assets are tangible assets and intangible assets, e.g., in the form of managerial flexibility, used to carry on the firm's activities. A tangible asset is a physical asset, such as plant, machinery, and offices. An intangible asset is a nonmaterial asset, such as technical expertise, a trademark, or a patent. See Brealey and Myers (2000), p. 1067-72.

period[10]. This necessitates thinking of unexpected exchange rate changes in a probabilistic sense. "Exposure to unexpected exchange rate changes" is to be thought of as exposure to exchange rate uncertainty defined by a probability distribution. A high exchange rate standard deviation implies that the probability of departures from the mean is higher. As such, departures from PPP are not fully unexpected but more or less likely. A valuation framework is useful to highlight the irrelevance of statements such as "risk management might be unnecessary because the exchange rate reverts after a shock to its PPP value in the long run". What matters to firms is the effect on cash flows and value during the exchange rate mean reversion. Even if long term PPP holds, the short run exposure is critical and risk management justified since the firm must survive an exchange rate shock *to get to the long run[11]*.

The stochastic processes underlying domestic cash flow volatility are the real exchange rate/price risk and quantity risk. The time path of cash flow exposure over the valuation period is dependent on the time path of exchange rates and of foreign currency cash flows. The domestic cash flow exposure in any given time period will depend on the[12]:

(a) *time path of the currencies of denomination* used for converting foreign cash flows.

(b) *time path of foreign currency cash flows*: with real options, cash flows can follow different paths, depending on the operating adjustments made in each period in response to exchange rate changes. This implies assessing the time path of quantities, foreign currency prices, costs. This in turn requires estimating the dynamic of currencies of determination and other factors of foreign currency cash flow volatility, and evaluating the hysteretic effects that are sources of cash flow and exposure path dependencies between periods.

Expected exposures vary with time. Over the valuation period, changes will take place in the expectations about future exchange rates, and the expectations about future cash flows, based on business/project performance as well as macroeconomic prices data[13].

---

[10] Sick (1995), p. 648, discusses this aspect. The exchange rate is also often specified in discrete time for easier economic interpretation. See, e.g., Kogut and Kulatilaka (1994), p. 127.
[11] This is discussed in Levich (1998), p. 572.
[12] See Demacopoulos (1989), p. 104.
[13] See Demacopoulos (1989), p. 103. Exposure forecasts may depend on the horizon at which it is estimated, since the exchange rate forecasting ability may be better at longer horizons. See Froot (1993), Mark (1995).

Real option valuation (ROV) analysis permits the valuation of cash flows that can take different paths over the valuation period because of endogenous multi-period flexibility. With managerial flexibility, the ROV method is more appropriate than traditional valuation methods.

D. Exposure Estimation Period and Duration

Although the exposure of firm value is what ultimately matters for risk management, a manager might have to estimate exposure over shorter time periods depending on the "intermediate" risk management targets pursued. For instance, if the exposure needs to be assessed to avoid default and bankruptcy, the deadlines for making specific payments and meeting covenants will define the period over which exposure is computed. If the reason is to minimize the present value of tax payment, the manager will be concerned about the tax year. If it is to enable the implementation of a strategic plan, the manager will assess the exposure of funds over the planning period[14]. At long horizons, purchasing power parity (PPP) may hold, but the relevant planning period for exposure measurement is usually much shorter.

Exposure measures depend on the length of their estimation periods. Over a short estimation period, economic exposure is mostly a contractual exposure, which could be insignificant, since contractual cash flows can be easily hedged. At longer horizons, most cash flows are non-contractual. The *duration* of exposure depends on the effect of exchange rate changes on a firm's particular forms of competitive advantage. This depends mostly on (1) the firm's ability to preserve its sources of competitive advantages, as measured by the expected time required for the restructuring of operations in response to exchange rate changes[15], and (2) the expected exchange rate behavior over the estimation period.

3.2 Stochastic Properties of Asymmetric Foreign Exchange Exposures

Operating and financial flexibility make the exposure asymmetric and induce departures from normality of the cash flow and firm value distributions. In the

---

[14] Examples from Stulz and Williamson (1996).
[15] See, e.g, Srinivasulu (1981).

literature, exposure asymmetries are defined in general terms[16]. Exposure asymmetries are referred to as the *asymmetry of the exposure profile* associated with the non-differentiability/structural breaks of the exposure profile at some exchange rates, or/and the *asymmetric effects* between exchange rate appreciation/depreciation[17] or between large/small exchange rate changes[18]. However, focusing on the shape of the exposure profile or asymmetry of exchange rate effects is confusing. With these definitions, an asymmetric exposure is non-linear or piecewise linear, but a non-linear exposure is not necessarily asymmetric. For example, if the exposure profile is curvilinear and symmetric (convex/concave), the exchange rate effects would be asymmetric between large/small exchange rate changes but at the same time the exposure profile would have a symmetric shape. As such, we associate exposure asymmetries with departures from normality of the cash flow and firm value distributions. Our analysis of exposure asymmetries will essentially evolve around the discussion of four related aspects:

(a) Payoffs of real options, financial flexibility options, strategic real options.

(b) Effect of options' payoffs on the distribution of cash flows and firm value.

(c) Effect of options' payoffs on the relation between real exchange rate/price risk and quantity risk.

(d) Effect of options' payoffs on the foreign exchange exposure profile.

---

[16] Asymmetric economic effects have been examined in other research areas. There is a literature on the asymmetric effect of exchange rate fluctuations on real output and price at the macroeconomic level, e.g., Kandil (2000); on asymmetric exchange-rate pass-though, e.g, Froot and Kemplerer (1989), Knetter (1994), Coughlin and Pollard (2000); on the asymmetric effect of monetary policy on economic activity, e.g., Garcia and Schaller (1995), Arden et al. (1998); on the asymmetric wealth effects of stock prices on consumer expenditures, e.g., Shirvani and Wilbratte (2000); on the asymmetric relation between aggregate stock returns and inflation, e.g., Domian and Gilster (1996), on the asymmetric relation between the yield spread and aggregate output, e.g., Galbraith and Tkacz (2000).

[17] See, e.g., Miller and Reuer (1995), Bradley and Moles (2001), pp. 55-59, Koutmos and Martin (2003).

[18] See Andren (2001), pp. 16-17, Di Ioro and Faff (2002).

3.2.1 Operating Flexibility and Departures from Cash Flow Distribution Normality

Several aspects need to be examined as background to our discussion on exposure asymmetries.

A. Exposure Uncertainty and Quantity Risk

Foreign exchange risk and exposure are function of two sources of uncertainties, quantity risk and real exchange rate/price risk. A firm faces quantity risk for two reasons:

(i)   *difficulty to forecast real foreign cash flows*: exposures will be imprecisely estimated if for example the volume of future transactions depends on the exchange rate. The exposure would be linear and fixed if the foreign cash flows were fully predictable. This foreign cash flow uncertainty makes exposure uncertain.

(ii) *quantity risk is unhedgeable*: because of the existence of moral hazard, there are no contracts designed to hedge against quantity risk[19].

B. Asymmetric Profit/Firm Value Distribution

Operating flexibility causes departures from cash flow distribution normality and makes exchange rate risk and exposure dependent on the exchange rate level. The cash flow distribution cannot be described with the first two moments[20]. Departures from normality are described by the skewness and by the kurtosis of the distribution:

▪ *Skewness* (third-central moment) is a measure of the asymmetry of a distribution. The skewness is positive if the "long tail" is in the positive direction. The odd moments represent measures of asymmetry.

---

[19] Moral hazard is the tendency to incur risks that one is protected against. Market insurance for quantity risk is not feasible because of moral hazard; sales can be manipulated by firms. See Chowdhry and Howe (1999).

[20] The skewness and kurtosis of a normal distribution is 0 and 3 respectively. See Jorion (1997), p. 80.

- *Kurtosis* (fourth-central moment) is a measure of the thickness of the tails of the distribution[21]. All the even moments represent the likelihood of extreme values.

3.2.2 Relation between Real Price Risk/Quantity Risk and Exposure Asymmetries

Figure 3.2 below illustrates curvilinear exposure profiles[22]. S_T and V_T are respectively the exchange rate defined as the price of foreign currency in terms of domestic currency, and firm value are time T. These exposure profiles are positively sloped. A depreciation leads to an increase in firm value, whereas an appreciation leads to a reduction of firm value.

BOB* - concave/convex and symmetric function[23]: small exchange rate changes have relatively little effect on firm value. Large exchange rate changes have relatively large effect on firm value.

COC* - concave/convex and symmetric function: small exchange rate changes have relatively large effect on firm value. Large exchange rate changes have relatively little effect on firm value.

Figure 3. 2 Curvilinear Exposure Profiles

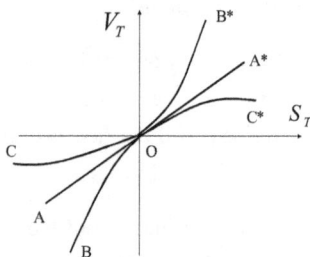

Three observations can be made on figure 3.2:

---

[21] See Greene (2000), p. 64, Verbeek (2000), p. 188. The first moment/expected value represents the reward. The second and higher central moments characterize the uncertainty of the reward. Larger values for these moments indicate greater uncertainty. See Bodie et al. (1993), pp. 161-162.
[22] See Dowling (1990), p. 37, Bartram (1999), pp. 181-182, Brown and Toft (2001), pp. 45-46. Miller and Reuer (1998) test for curvilinear foreign exchange exposures.
[23] See Archinard and Guerrien (1988), p. 186.

Asymmetry of Exchange Rate Effects and of Exposure Profile

For both BOB^* and COC^*, a large exchange rate change is not just a linear multiple of a small exchange rate change. In that sense, exposure can be viewed as being asymmetric to small/large exchange rate changes. But these exposure profiles are symmetric. For example, BOB^* represents a symmetric exposure to exchange rate appreciation/depreciation, since the slope of the curve varies at a symmetric rate on the left and right side of point O. On the other hand, an asymmetric exposure profile (curves COB*, BOC*) implies that the slope of the exposure becomes asymmetric at the exchange rate at which the firm's profit and value function become asymmetric.

Exposure Non-Linearity and Relation between Real Price Risk and Quantity Risk

If a firm exercises real options over the valuation period, its periodical real cash flows become a function of the exchange rate. Exposure non-linearities arise if quantity risk and real exchange rate/price risk are related, in other terms, if real foreign currency cash flows and the nominal exchange rate are related[24]. As such, the relation between real price risk and quantity risk defines the slope of the exposure profile. In figure 3.2 above, BOB^*, COC^*, and AOA^*, correspond respectively to a positive, negative, zero correlation. A positive correlation indicates that real exchange rate/price risk and quantity risk move in the same direction, while a negative correlation implies that they move in opposite direction[25].

Cash Flow Distribution, Exposure Profile, Relation between Real Price Risk - Quantity Risk

The relation between real price risk and quantity risk is mirrored in the firm's cash flow and firm value distribution and in the exposure profile. Suppose an exporter that has the flexibility to increase foreign sales when the exchange rate depreciates while reducing them when it appreciates. This would:

---

[24] An exception is if the exchange rate elasticity of foreign currency price is offset by the price-elasticity of demand, e.g., foreign revenue can be linearly exposed if both the exchange rate elasticity of foreign currency price and price-elasticity of demand are equal to 1 and offset each other. See CorporateMetrics Technical Document (1999), p. 43.

[25] See Pindyck and Rubinfeld (1991), pp. 22-23.

- *convexify the exposure profile* (curve COB*), by increasing its exposure to (beneficial) depreciations and reducing its exposure to (adverse) appreciations.

- *skew the cash flow/firm value distribution*: the positive correlation between real price risk and quantity risk when the exchange rate depreciates exacerbates the beneficial effects of depreciations. The negative correlation between real price risk and quantity risk when the exchange rate appreciates mitigates the adverse effects of appreciations.

The correlation between real price risk and quantity risk is often used to structure hedging strategies[26]. This can be problematic for asymmetric exposures, since the correlation is function of the exchange rate level. Covariance and correlation measure linear dependence. They measure the *linear* association between two variables. This implies that variables may be related non-linearly and yet have a zero covariance[27].

3.2.3 Exposure Profile with Threshold Exchange Rate Effects

Some factors explain why exposure could be different for certain ranges of exchange rate values. Asymmetries may stem, for example, from competitive threats or price pressures that are expected to become active for a certain range of exchange rates only[28]. As a result, the slope of the exposure profile will experience discrete shifts at some distinct exchange rate values, where the nature of the exposure changes dramatically. Because exposure will be different for some exchange rate ranges, the exposure profile will be piecewise linear/non-linear rather than curvilinear. This justifies the use of piecewise linear regressions in our empirical analysis.

---

[26] See, e.g., Brown and Toft (2001).
[27] See Pindyck and Rubinfeld (1991), pp. 22-23.
[28] There is evidence that price adjustments tend to be infrequent and often involves large discrete changes. See Kumakura (2001), p. 3.

Figure 3. 3 Piecewise Linear Exposure Profile

(a) Piecewise Constant Foreign Cash Flow[29]   (b) Piecewise-Linear Exposure Profile

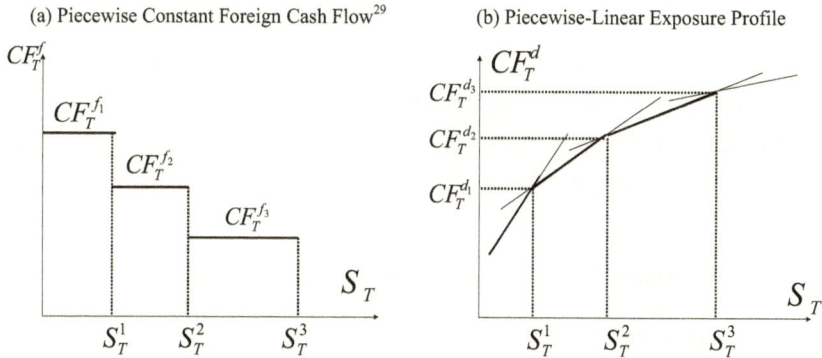

Notation: $CF_T^{f_1}$, $CF_T^{f_2}$, $CF_T^{f_3}$ are foreign currency cash flows corresponding respectively to the exchange rates S_T^1, S_T^2, S_T^3. $CF_T^{d_1}$, $CF_T^{d_2}$, $CF_T^{d_3}$ are domestic currency cash flows corresponding respectively to the exchange rates S_T^1, S_T^2, S_T^3.

The function $CF_T^d(S_T)$ in figure 3.3 (b) represents a piecewise-linear concave exposure. In the econometrics literature, the threshold or trigger exchange rate values are called *knots*[30]. At each knot, the exposure changes dramatically and displays an asymmetric behavior. $CF_T^f(S_T)$ in figure 3.3 (a) represents the function that relates foreign cash flows to the exchange rate, corresponding to the values of the slope of the exposure profile, dCF_T^d/dS_T, evaluated at each exchange rate S_T [31]. This is the underlying (before hedge) exposure.

The function $CF_T^f(S_T)$ is said to be "piecewise constant on the segments of linearity of the function $CF_T^d(S_T)$ "[32]:

[3. 1] $$\frac{CF_T^{d_2} - CF_T^{d_1}}{(S_T^2 - S_T^1)} = CF_T^{f_2} = CF_T^{f_1} + \frac{CF_T^{f_2} - CF_T^{f_1}}{(S_T^2 - S_T^1)} \cdot S_T^1 \qquad \text{if } S_T^1 < S_T < S_T^2$$

---

[29] If the number of chart bars increases to infinity, the resulting negatively sloped straight line will lead to a concave exposure (curve COC* in figure 3.2).

[30] See Greene (2000), p. 324. Piecewise linear models are special cases of a larger set of models called *spline functions*, which are functions with distinct pieces.

[31] "From duality arguments, taking the derivative dCF_T^d/dS_T yields a function representing the "currency requirements" corresponding to CF_T^d at any exchange rate S_T". See Ware and Winter (1988), p. 296.

[32] See Ware and Winter (1988), p. 296.

[3. 2] $$\frac{CF_T^{d_3} - CF_T^{d_2}}{(S_T^3 - S_T^2)} = CF_T^{f_3} = CF_T^{f_2} + \frac{CF_T^{f_3} - CF_T^{f_2}}{(S_T^3 - S_T^2)} \cdot S_T^2 \qquad \text{if } S_T^2 < S_T < S_T^3$$

Mathematically, the exposure profile is continuous but non-differentiable at the knots S_T^1, S_T^2, S_T^3. At these knots, the exposure is not defined in a unique way[33]. The characteristics of the function differ between the knots, but over the whole exchange rate range, the function is continuous[34].

3.3 Foreign Exchange Exposure Profile with Real Options

3.3.1 Linear Exposure and Normal Cash Flow Distribution

Figure 3.4 below illustrates the relationship between exchange rate distribution, foreign exchange exposure profile, and distribution of domestic currency cash flows. The domestic cash flow is linear in the exchange rate. The volatility of domestic cash flow measures exchange rate risk. S_T and CF_T^d are respectively the exchange rate and domestic currency cash flows at time T. S_T is assumed to follow a normal distribution and is the price of foreign currency in terms of domestic currency.

Figure 3. 4 Symmetric Exposure[35] - Normal Distribution of Foreign Currency Cash Flows

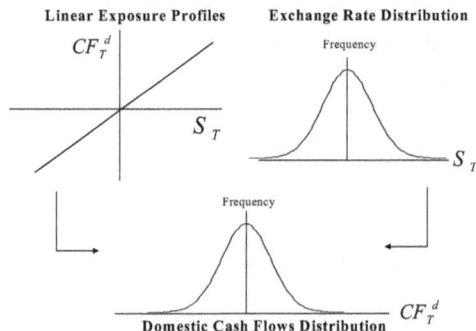

----

[33] Geometrically, this means that the tangency to the exposure profile at the knots is not uniquely defined. See Deschamps (1988), p. 99.
[34] If the exposure profile has discontinuities, the function can be made continuous by setting constraints to join the segments at the trigger points, and piecewise regression methods (restricted regressions known as *spline functions*) can still be used. See Greene (2000), pp. 324-325.
[35] Adapted from Jorion (1997), p. 189.

The assumption of normal cash flow distribution implies/reflects the following characteristics:

(a) *Linear exposure profile*: the *invariance property of normal variables* stipulates that portfolios of normal variables are themselves normally distributed[36]. This property implies that when the exposure is linear, the joint distribution (i.e. distribution of domestic cash flow) between the distribution of foreign cash flow and the exchange rate distribution is normal. Exposure linearity reflects the joint and individual normality of the variables involved. It is important to note that, in contrast to contractual exposure which is linear and fixed, the slope of the exposure profile is linear and stochastic. Foreign cash flows and exposure can vary as a result of factors unrelated to the exchange rate.

(b) *Abstraction of competitive effects*: for non-contractual cash flows, a linear exposure component results from having to convert real foreign cash flow with a nominal exchange rate. Competitive effects, which occur even if no ex-post operating adjustments are made (see section 2.4.2/chapter 2), would generate non-linearities.

(c) *Symmetric risk/return tradeoff*: since the statistical expectation/mean operator is a linear operator, exchange rate volatility has no effect on the *conditional* expected value of domestic cash flow/firm value. The effects of appreciations and depreciations offset each other.

(d) *Passive management and static operating and financial structure*: managers are assumed to be passive. An example of implausible implication is that a manager would be assumed to watch passively the firm going bankrupt as a result of a large adverse exchange rate change.

(e) *Independence of foreign exchange risk and exposure from the exchange rate*: the *conditional* variance of domestic cash flow does not depend on the exchange rate level and the volatility of the exchange rate has no effect on the exposure values.

Finance models generally ignore endogenous changes in the firm's competitive position and the firm's strategic responses. They implicitly assume a static operating structure and normal cash flow distribution, and take into account only the linear component of exposure associated with the conversion of foreign cash flows. For

---

[36] See Jorion (1997), p. 188, Spanos (1995), p. 462.

example, *portfolio theory* is built on mean-variance analysis and ignores higher moments[37]. This relies on the property that a normal distribution can be fully described by its first two moments.

3.3.2 Exposure and Cash Flow Distribution Skewness: Long/Short Real Put and Call

A. Distribution Positive Skewness and Leptokurtosis: Long Real Put and Call

Real options theory generally views exchange rate uncertainty as providing firms with an opportunity to achieve higher mean profits[38]. Investments in operating flexibility convexify the exposure profile by enabling the firm to increase its exposure to favorable exchange rate changes, while reducing its exposure to adverse exchange rate changes.

Flexibility skews and makes asymmetric the distribution of foreign and domestic cash flows. The asymmetric foreign cash flows distribution is reflected in an asymmetric exposure profile. As a consequence, there is a differential impact on firm value between exchange rate appreciation/depreciation. Figure 3.5 below shows that, assuming a "convex" exposure and a normal exchange rate distribution, the distribution of domestic cash flows is skewed and shifted to the right relative to a normal distribution. The *conditional* variance of domestic cash flows (foreign exchange risk) is relatively higher for exchange rate depreciations. Since the distribution of possible outcomes is skewed, the expected cash flow is not the same as the most likely (or modal) cash flow value[39].

---

[37] See Bodie et al. (1993), pp. 161-162.
[38] This is consistent with microeconomic theory that states that the mean profits of a price-taker are higher the more the market price fluctuates. See Oi (1961).
[39] See Brealey and Myers (2000), p. 260.

Figure 3. 5 Asymmetric Exposure - Asymmetric Distribution of Foreign Currency Cash Flows

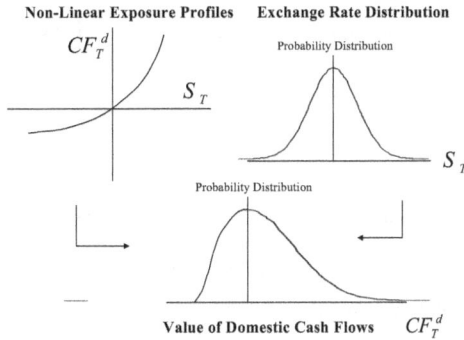

Non-Linear Exposure Profiles   Exchange Rate Distribution

Value of Domestic Cash Flows CF_T^d

Departures from normality of cash flows distribution imply:

(a) *Non-linear foreign exchange exposure profile*: the nature of the non-linearity is function of the effect on the cash flows distribution of (i) expected changes in competitiveness, (ii) the firm's expected strategic responses. Flexibility is not a necessary condition for exposure non-linearity.

(b) *Asymmetric risk/return trade-off*: the conditional variance of domestic cash flow is function of the exchange rate. If the exposure is *convex*, the exchange rate volatility affects positively expected mean profits and firm value (the distribution shifts positively since the expectation is a linear operator). In other terms, if profits/firm value increase at a increasing rate as the exchange rate becomes more favorable, exchange rate fluctuations lead to an increase in mean profits/firm value. The convexity reflects a foreign cash flow distribution that is skewed to the right. Active management of exchange rate uncertainty with real options is generally believed to lead to such convexity. Conversely, if the exposure is *concave*, exchange rate volatility has a negative effect on expected cash flow and firm value.

(c) *Conditional heteroskedasticity of cash flow/firm value variance*: there are two implications for exposure estimation: (i) expected cash flows over the valuation period varies, (ii) conditional variance of domestic cash flows/firm value over the valuation period varies since it depends on the exchange rate level. Conditional heteroskedasticity will justify the use of a GARCH model in the empirical analysis.

(d) *Dependency of foreign exchange risk and exposure on the exchange rate distribution*: we assumed a normal exchange rate distribution. Empirically, however, exchange rate changes are generally found to have distributions that are fat-tailed. The probability of extreme events is higher than the normal and lognormal models predict[40].

B. Long Real Options Put and Call Payoffs and Exposure Asymmetries

Figure 3.6 (a) below shows the real options payoffs associated with a positively skewed and shifted conditional (lognormal) cash flow distribution. Options are exercised if they are in-the-money[41]. The higher the real exchange rate/price risk or quantity risk, the higher the likelihood for the option to be in-the-money:

- *Long call on real foreign currency*: at expiration, a real call option is exercised and pays off when the expected domestic cash flow from undertaking the foreign project S is higher than the capital cost of developing the project X_C (fixed investment and adjustment costs in domestic currency). Otherwise it has no value. The call option value at expiration is $MAX [S - X_C, 0]$. S is the payoff for one unit of real foreign cash flow. X_C is the level of expected domestic cash flows at which the call is exercised. The value of the long call corresponds to the *upper tail* of the distribution. This payoff would correspond, for an exporter, to additional expected cash flows from the flexibility to increase exports when the foreign currency appreciates. To value the cash flow, we value the entire distribution, but to value the call, we value the upper tail of the distribution.

- *Long put on real foreign currency*: long put payoffs are in the *lower tail* of the distribution, which is shorter than for a normal distribution. This payoff would correspond, for an exporter, to reduced cash flows from the flexibility to decrease exports when the foreign currency depreciates. The payoffs for the put are positive when the capital cost of developing the project X_P is higher than the expected domestic cash flow from undertaking the foreign project S. The put option value at expiration is $MAX [X_P - S, 0]$.

---

[40] See Sercu and Uppal (1995), p. 256.
[41] See Copeland and Antikarov (2001), p. 10.

Figure 3. 6 (a) Probability Distribution of Domestic Cash Flows: Long Put-Call Payoffs, (b) Exposure Asymmetries with Threshold Effects[42]

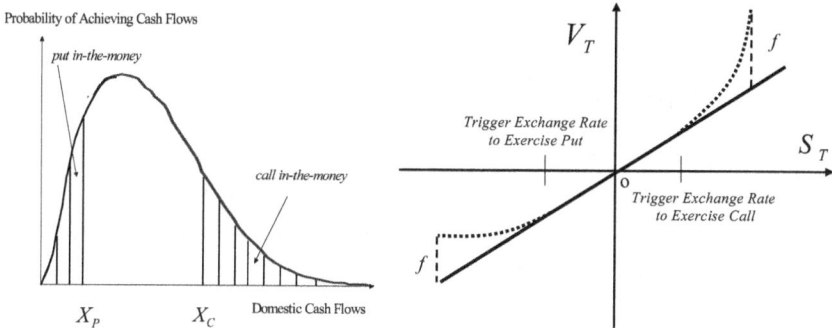

The probability distribution of firm value may (but not necessarily) also be positively skewed. Figure 3.6 (b) above shows the corresponding exposure profile of firm value V_T with threshold effects at the exchange rate levels at which options are exercised. It indicates the effect f of operating flexibility on V_T, and the trigger exchange rate values at which options are exercised. At these exchange rates, it becomes worthwhile to pay a predetermined sunk cost and exercise the options.

Options are exercised only if exchange rate changes are of a magnitude above a certain threshold. Small exchange rate changes are not large enough to trigger the exercise of real options and the exposure is linear between the trigger exchange rate levels. In the short term, the exposure might be linear at all exchange rates, because real adjustments take time to be implemented.

D. Negatively Skewed Cash Flow Distribution: Short Real Put and Call

A firm with a short put and call position would have a cash flow distribution that is negatively skewed. The exposure profile would correspond to curve BOC* in figure 3.2. This would reflect a negative (positive) relation between quantity risk and real price risk for exchange rate depreciation (appreciation). We shall discuss later the

---

[42] Adapted from Oxelheim and Wihlborg (2002), p. 20.

economic rationales that can explain negative real options payoffs and "concave" exposure profiles.

E. Symmetric Leptokurtotic Cash Flow Distribution

A cash flow CF_T^d distribution that is symmetric but leptokurtic in both tails would correspond to the exposure curve BOB^* (figure 3.7 below). This reflects a positive correlation between quantity risk and real price risk for both appreciations and depreciations. A positive correlation will *exacerbate* fluctuations in cash flows. The likelihood of extreme values is higher for both appreciations and depreciations and results in an increased volatility of domestic cash flow/firm value. Although we assume a normal exchange rate distribution, BOB^* could also correspond to an exchange rate distribution with fatter tails. Also, we saw in chapter 2 that BOB^* could correspond to the competitive exposure of an inflexible firm with a long position in foreign currency.

Figure 3. 7 Exposure Profile of *Cash Flows* at T

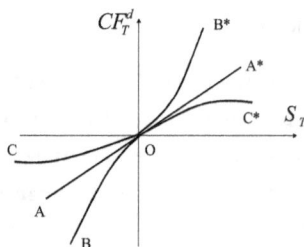

On the other hand, if the cash flow distribution is symmetric with tails shorter than for a normal distribution, the exposure profile is COC^*. This reflects a negative correlation between quantity risk and real price risk for both appreciations and depreciations. The lower likelihood of extreme values results in a decreased volatility of domestic cash flow/firm value. A negative correlation will *dampen* fluctuations in cash flows. We shall see that this could result from a firm pursuing market share expansion when the exchange rate depreciates and minimizing reduction in profit margins when it appreciates. However, the exposure *of firm value* could be convex as a result.

3.3.3 Relation between Cash Flow Exposure and Firm Value Exposure

For risk management, one needs to measure the exposure of periodic cash flows and of firm value. Exposure asymmetries imply that future cash flows are function of the exchange rate level because the firm's operating mode is endogenous to the exchange rate. A firm's cash flows exposure therefore varies over the valuation period and can have a different profile than the exposure of firm value. Economic theory is useful to understand the relation between periodic cash flow exposures and firm value exposure.

Similarly, the effect of real options on periodic cash flows can be different from the effect on firm value. A firm's flexibility could skew negatively the cash flow distribution at a given period while skewing positively the distribution of firm value. The relation depends in part on assumptions about the industry structure and the firm's operating structure (elasticity of demand, marginal costs, strategic decisions, and so forth).

Figure 3. 8 Real Option Effects on Firm Value under Exchange Rate Uncertainty

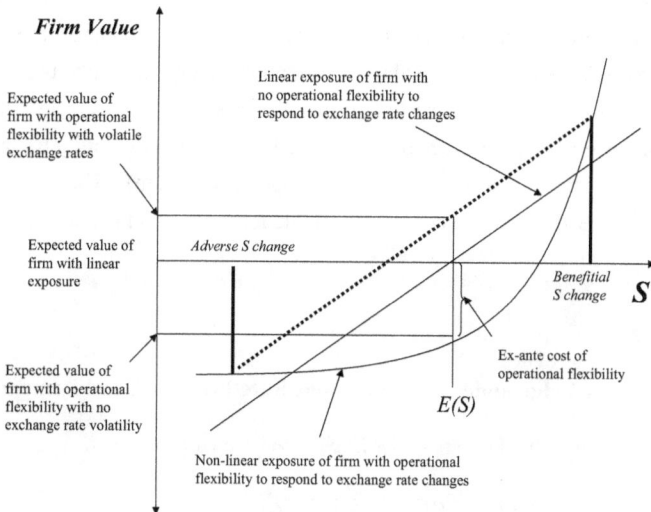

Source: adapted from Bodnar (2004), p. 9.

Figure 3.8 above shows the effect on *firm value* exposure of real options for a firm with a long position in foreign currency. The exchange rate S is the price of the foreign currency in terms of domestic currency. $E(S)$ is the expected mean value of the exchange rate. This exposure profile reflects a positively skewed firm value distribution as a result of flexibility under exchange rate uncertainty:

- *Relation between real price and quantity risks*: positive (negative) relation between quantity risk and real price risk for depreciation (appreciation) over the valuation period. For example, an exporter could sell more when the exchange rate depreciates, and sell less when it appreciates because it is less competitive. The negative correlation for appreciations implies that the quantity risk (naturally) hedges some of the price risk for adverse exchange rate changes.

- *Shape of exposure profile*: the firm's flexibility increases the exposure to beneficial exchange rate changes while decreasing the exposure to adverse exchange rate changes, making the exposure profile convex. The risk of firm value is unlimited upwards and limited downwards.

- *Effect of an increase in cash flow volatility on firm value*: the convexity of the exposure profile indicates that an increase in nominal exchange rate volatility increases expected real firm value. Real option theory generally predicts that a higher real exchange rate/price risk or quantity risk increases expected firm value. Without uncertainty, the expected firm value is lower with flexibility because of the ex-ante investment costs in flexibility (option premium). The exchange rate uncertainty needs to be of a certain magnitude for the option to be in-the-money.

3.4 Real Option Value under Real Exchange Rate/Price Risk and Demand Risk

3.4.1 Real Option Value Drivers under Exchange Rate Uncertainty

A. Real Exchange Rate/Price Risk and Quantity Risk

Exchange rate (high-frequency) volatility gives indications on the uncertainty about the long-term exchange rate levels (drift):

(i)   *Probability of real exchange rate changes and of the real option to be in-the-money:* exchange rate volatility determines the probability of departures from its mean (PPP) value, and the associated probability for a real option to be in-the-money. With higher exchange rates volatility, the probability for large exchange rates deviations from their PPP equilibrium value becomes greater[43]. A higher exchange rate volatility increases the value of having invested in flexibility by increasing the probability of exceeding the exercise price. The likelihood that cash flows be higher than X_C in figure 3.6 (a) above is higher.

(ii)   *Risk of exchange rate mean reversion[44] and option value-of-waiting:* exchange rate volatility determines the risk of exchange rate reversion to its PPP value[45], and the associated option value-of-waiting for the realization of the exchange rate. Flexibility is valuable if exchange rate volatility leads to departures from PPP that are persistent. Since sunk costs are paid to exercise options, they will be exercised only if departures from PPP are sufficiently large and expected to be persistent.

High exchange rate volatility makes it more difficult to assess the persistence of PPP departures, and increase the option value-of-waiting for the realization of the exchange rate uncertainty. The risk is that the firm exercises a real option but that the exchange rate departure from PPP quickly dissipates. A higher probability of reversion to PPP would incite the firm not to act (hysteretic behavior).

The risk of mean reversion itself could be non-linear and depend on the exchange rate level. First, there is evidence suggesting that the speed of mean reversion towards exchange rate equilibrium depends on the size of the overvaluation or undervaluation, which implies that the adjustment process may itself be non-linear[46]. This would make exposures asymmetric to small/large exchange rate changes. Second, the risk of mean

---

[43] See Kogut and Kulatilaka (1994), p. 127.

[44] See Oi (1962), p. 542, Dixit (1989), p. 634.

[45] Because the exchange rate might overshoot after a shock and the real exchange rate might revert to its mean in the long run, it is possible for the nominal and real exchange rates to reverse course after an initial shock. See Dornbusch (1976).

[46] See Taylor and Peel (2000), Holmes and Maghrebi (2002), p. 6. They examine nonlinear exposures in a Markov regime switching model.

reversion can also differ between appreciations and depreciations. In support of this hypothesis, a study shows that for Germany, exchange rates have markedly different adjustment patterns for positive gaps from PPP than negative gaps[47]. This would make exposures asymmetric to appreciations/depreciations.

When assessing the likely permanence of an exchange rate change, a move back toward equilibrium is generally considered more permanent than an exchange rate movement away from equilibrium, that is, one that is moving out of step with inflation. In practice, many of "disequilibrium" exchange rate moves can be attributed to government interference in the foreign exchange markets, whereas the adjustments back toward equilibrium are usually associated with free-market forces[48].

Real options value is also driven by *quantity risk*. A higher quantity risk has similar effects on the probability of the option to be in-the-money and on the option value-of-waiting for the realization of the uncertainty.

B. Option Value of Waiting and Foreign Exchange Exposure

The literature on "investment under uncertainty"[49] interprets operating flexibility as an option to defer an investment decision[50]. The value of waiting comes from the improved knowledge about the nature of the uncertainty as it realizes. A higher real price risk or quantity risk increases the option value for two reasons. A real option is exercised if (i) the magnitude of an unexpected change in real price or quantity is large enough for the option to be in-the-money, (ii) the unexpected change is expected to be persistent.

Accordingly, the value of the flexibility to defer an investment increases with uncertainty because: (a) it increases the probability of the option to be exercised, (b) it increases the flexibility value to wait and assess the nature of an exchange rate change. The value in real options comes from the firm's ability to wait until conditions are optimal before moving forward with a project. Real exchange rate uncertainty creates

---

[47] See Enders and Dibooglu (2001).
[48] See Bishop and Dixon (1992), p. 346.
[49] See, e.g., Pindyck (1991).
[50] See, e.g., Sercu and Uppal (1995), p. 675.

an uncertain environment decisions and incites firms to delay their investment decisions to obtain more information about the nature of an exchange rate change[51].

The real option approach can be interpreted in terms of projects or firm value (value additivity principle)[52]. The investment expenditures paid to exercise a real option have three important characteristics[53]:

(i)   *Investment is irreversible*: the exercise of an option involves an initial investment expenditure that is to some extent irreversible (sunk costs). For example, the cost paid for the right to switch to an other production facility is sunk. If the investment was fully reversible, there would be no point waiting for the realization of the exchange rate uncertainty. The effect of uncertainty is intensified as the irreversibility of investment increases.

(ii) *Investment can be delayed*: flexibility in timing introduces an option value-of-waiting which increases with uncertainty. The investments can be delayed to wait for new information about exchange rates. Ex-post adjustments can be delayed if the uncertainty about both the level and persistence of the exchange rate change is high. For example, the sunk cost to be paid to enter a new market can be delayed until realization of the exchange rate.

(iii) *Contingent on the exchange rate*[54]: when investments are irreversible and can be delayed, exchange rate uncertainty increases the value of the implicit option to wait until exchange rate uncertainty is resolved[55], meaning that the exercise of the option is less likely. The assumption is that the exchange rate uncertainty resolves gradually over time and provides additional information on whether it is worth exercising the option. In other terms, the passage of time narrows down the range of scenarios for a particular future exchange rate. As both uncertainty and irreversibility increase, the value of the option to wait and the incentive to delay the exercise of the option increase.

---

[51] See Pindyck (1991).
[52] See Brealey and Myers (2000). "If we view a firm as a collection of assets, this approach can be extended to value a firm, using cash flows to the firm over its life and a discount rate that reflects the collective risk of the firm's assets". See Damodaran (2004-a), pp. 4-8.
[53] See Pindyck (1991).
[54] See Sercu and Uppal (1995), p. 677.
[55] See Dixit and Pindyck (1994).

An illustrative case clarifies the relation between option value-of-waiting and exposure[56]. A risk-neutral investor in the U.S. must decide whether or not to buy a plant that produces one unit of output *per annum*, which is then exported to the U.K., where its sale price is fixed at £1. One period is needed to produce the single unit of output. The US$ value of revenues are constant from year to year after $t=1$[57] and are subject to exchange rate uncertainty. The assumption is that the exchange rate is uncertain at $t=0$ and that uncertainty is reduced as time goes by. The exchange rate uncertainty makes the option to postpone the decision to invest valuable because the investor can take advantage of the additional knowledge at $t=1$ to decide whether or not to undertake the project.

The exchange rate S_0 at $t=0$ is US$/£ 2. At $t=1$ it may either increase by the factor $u=1.1$ to US$/£ 2.2, or decrease by the factor $d=0.9$ to US$/£ 1.8, with equal probability $p=0.5$[58]. The exchange rate stays the same after $t=1$, which implies that an exchange rate change at t=1 is permanent. r and r^* are the current risk-free interest rates in the U.S. and U.K. respectively and are equal to 5% *p.a.* The initial investment required for this project is US$ 38.

Figure 3. 9 Event and Scenario Tree

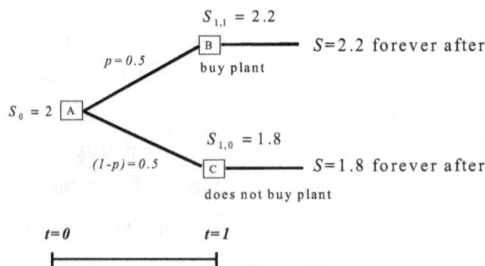

Source: Sercu and Uppal (1995), p. 678.

---

[56] This example is based on Sercu and Uppal (1995), pp. 677-679, which is similar to a numerical example in Pindyck (1991).
[57] The after-tax profit stream is a perpetuity. See Brealy and Myers (2000), p. 41.
[58] Formula that relates the up and down changes to the standard deviation of the returns on the asset: (i) $1 + \text{upside change} = u = e^{\sigma/\sqrt{h}}$, (ii) $1 + \text{downside change} = d = 1/u$. Where e = base for natural logarithms = 2.718, σ = standard deviation of (continuously compounded) returns on asset, in percent per year, h = interval as fraction of a year. See Brealey and Myers (2000), pp. 631-632.

The investor has the right to undertake the project by paying the initial investment, and the payoff to the project depends on the future evolution of the exchange rate. The option value to postpone the investment decision for one period is solved recursively[59]. At $t=1$, the present value is:

$t=1$	NPV of undertaking project	Payoffs of option value to postpone
$S_{1,1} = 2.2$	$PV_1[S_1 = 2.2] = -38 + (2.2/0.05) = \$6$	$V_1[S_1 = 2.2] = Max\{PV_1[S_1 = 2.2], 0\} = \$6$
$S_{1,0} = 1.8$	$PV_1[S_1 = 1.8] = -38 + (1.80/0.05) = -\$2$	$V_1[S_1 = 1.8] = Max\{PV_1[S_1 = 1.8], 0\} = \$0$

A static NPV uses only information available at $t=0$. It would be optimal to invest at $t=0$ if the net present value (NPV) would exceed the option value of waiting. Here, there is a valuable option-of-waiting: if we wait until $t=1$ to invest, the value of the project at $t=0$ is: $V_0[S_0 = 2] = [(0.5 \times 6) + (0.5 \times 0)]/1.05 = US\$2.86$. This exceeds the value of US\$ 2.0 if we invest at $t=0$ [60]. The value of the option to delay is the difference between the static and dynamic NPVs: 2.86-2.00=US\$ 0.86.

Several aspects are relevant in terms of exposure:

- the distribution of cash flows forecasted at $t=0$ for $t=1$ is skewed positively. This has the effect of skewing the distribution of the project value at $t=0$, and increase the expected value at $t=0$.

- the *conditional* variance of cash flows is changing based on the payouts at various parts of the tree. In a framework with more than two periods, this would imply that the discount rate varies within the decision tree and that there is conditional heteroskedasticity.

- the exposure forecasted at $t=0$ for $t=1$ is asymmetric: the asymmetry of the exposure of the project value forecasted at $t=0$ depends on the value of the option to delay the project until $t=1$.

---

[59] The stochastic dynamic programming procedure used in this type of calculations is the same as the procedure used to determine the value of an American option. See Cox et al. (1979).
[60] $NPV_0^{static}[S_0 = 2] = -38 + 2/0.05 = US\$2.0$

Because of changing discount rates within the tree, option pricing theory is necessary for discounting cash flows and a static NPV valuation approach is inappropriate. The NPV approach implies (i) forecasting expected cash flows and (ii) discounting at the opportunity cost of capital. The first step is difficult, the second is not feasible in presence of real options[61]. It is impossible to find the opportunity cost of capital because the risk of cash flow changes with the exchange rate. The NPV methodology fails to capture the value of flexibility because it assumes distribution normality. It is therefore based on expected value and dispersion of future cash flows. Whereas NPV is forced to treat future courses of action in response to exchange rate changes as mutually exclusive, ROV can combine them into a single value with a decision rule for choosing among them.

C. Comparison of Financial and Real Options

Operating flexibility is a kind of intangible real asset that has some value[62]. The value of this intangible real asset is the real option value. A real option is in turn contingent on the uncertain value of a tangible real asset. A real option gives the right, but not the obligation, to buy or sell a real asset at a predetermined cost. For competitive foreign exchange exposure, the uncertainty of the real option's underlying is driven by the volatility of the real exchange rate/price risk and quantity risk. In other terms, the domestic payoff to the real option depends on the future evolution of the nominal exchange rate and real foreign cash flows.

Table 3. 1 Comparison of Financial and Real Options

Financial Option	Real Option
Strike price	Fixed investment and switching costs (capital cost of developing the project)
Spot price	Expected cash flow from undertaking the project (underlying asset)
Time to expiration	Planning horizon
Volatility of underlying asset	Volatility of the underlying stochastic processes, e.g., real exchange rate/price risk - quantity risk.
Interest rate	Interest rate

Sources: adapted from Cohen and Huchzermeier (1998), section 21.2, Sick (1995), p. 631.

---

[61] See Brealey and Myers (2000), p. 601.
[62] See Muralidhar (1992), essay 2.

Despite the similarities between financial and real options, valuation methods of financial options cannot be directly applied to the valuation of real options. Table 3.1 above highlights the similarities between financial and real options. Making the investment is like exercising the option, and the cost of the investment is like the strike price of the option[63].

- *Real underlying asset*: whereas for a financial option the underlying asset is a nominal asset, real tangible assets underlie the value of real options. By real, it is meant an "investment in operating activities rather than the purchase of financial instruments"[64]. The underlying real tangible asset, e.g., business unit or a foreign production plant, generates risky foreign cash flows.

- *Investment in flexibility*: to acquire a real option, the firm has to make an investment in flexibility which can be viewed as an investment in lower adjustment costs. The investment expenditure made for having this flexibility is like an *option premium*. This implicit *option price* or *option premium* is paid for the right to pay a predetermined adjustment costs (*strike price*) and exercise the option.

Real options value the operating flexibility to control the value of the underlying real asset by controlling the distribution of cash flow over time. They are generally more valuable than financial options since they are generally not traded in financial markets. The financial flexibility given by currency options does not increase firm value if they are fairly priced, since they are efficiently traded in financial markets[65].

D. Real Options Value Drivers

Real options theory suggests that uncertainty has value because of the ability of firms to manage the uncertainty of cash flows. The right to defer a real investment, which is given up by exercising, is more valuable with higher volatility. Real option valuation

---

[63] See Dixit (1989), p. 621.
[64] See Kogut and Kulatilaka (1994), p. 125.
[65] See Adler (1994), p. 165. "Real assets are, in contrast to financial assets, to a little extent marked-to-market, since they are mostly intangible assets whose prices are not listed on a stock exchange". See Hayt and Song (1995). Intangible assets are mostly information intensive assets which cannot be frictionlessly traded in capital markets. See Froot and Stein (1997). "Since these options are exercisable only by the MNC and cannot be traded and purchased by individual investors in any meaningful sense, the value of the firm is enhanced by the incremental value of these options". See Kogut (1983), p. 47.

(ROV) is particularly useful for assessing foreign exchange exposures when a situation involves great real exchange rate/price risk and quantity risk, and managers have flexibility to respond. Real options have the greatest value when there is:

(1) *High uncertainty*: the value of flexibility depends critically on the volatility of cash flows. For a given degree of operating flexibility, the higher the uncertainty, the more valuable it is to have invested in flexibility. If there is no uncertainty, an investment in flexibility has no value.

(2) *High flexibility to respond to the uncertainty*: the flexibility value comes from the ability to respond to information about the real price or quantity that may be received in the future. For a given level of uncertainty, a higher flexibility implies a better ability to make value enhancing adjustments (figure 3.10 below).

Figure 3. 10 Positive Relation between Value of Flexibility and Uncertainty

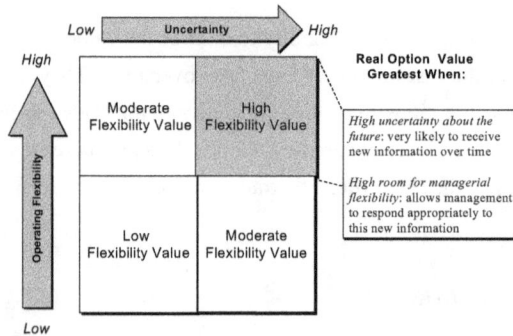

Adapted from Copeland and Antikarov (2001), p. 14, based on Copeland et al. (2000).

Table 3.2 below shows that the value of real options predominantly depends on seven variables, with the arrows indicating the effect on option value[66]. Option value increases with (1) greater uncertainty, (2) the irreversibility of investment, and (3) the

---

[66] Based on Copeland and Antikarov (2001), pp. 5-7, Cottrell and Sick (2001).

duration of the investment opportunity, and are reduced by a high 'dividend yield' or opportunity cost given by the cash flows that are foregone by not investing.

Table 3. 2 Variables that Drive the Real Options Value under Uncertainty

↑	**1. Expected Present Value of Cash Flows from Investment** An increase in the present value of the project increases the NPV (without flexibility) and as a result the ROV. ROV values both the linear and non-linear components of exposure.
↓	**2. Exercise Price / Investment Cost** A higher sunk cost to exercise the option lowers the ROV. The price that one has to pay for flexibility often exceeds the value of flexibility, which can itself be negative. A high investments costs in flexibility (option premium) reduces the ROV, e.g., cost of establishing a foreign currency production facility.
↑	**3. Time to Expire** In contrast to financial options, real options can be delayed. A longer time to expiration allows to learn more about the uncertainty and increases the ROV.
↑	**4. Uncertainty (Volatility) about the Present Value** With flexibility, an increase in uncertainty generally increases the ROV, but not always. For example, an increase in quantity risk with bounds on flexibility can decrease the ROV (see section 3.5.2)
↑	**5. Risk-free Interest Rate Over the Life of the Option** Investing has an opportunity cost. An increase in the risk-free rate increases the ROV since it increases the time value of money.
↓	**6. Cash Flows (Dividends) Lost Due to Competitors Who Have Fully Committed** Standard option theory assumes that the firm optimizes its competitive response to a predetermined competitor's action. In imperfect competition, changes in the firm's expected economic rent can occur because of the flexibility of other market participants. Higher cash flows lost to competitors decreases the ROV. The dividends that may be paid out by the underlying asset also reduces the ROV (see chapter 4).
↓	**7. Convenience Value of Possessing an Operating Project** Real option models recognize the option value-of-waiting until the uncertainty is resolved. But waiting has an opportunity cost. There is a tradeoff between the benefits of early operating adjustments and the benefits of waiting to assess the nature of the uncertainty. The value to delay can be offset by the *"convenience value of possessing an operating project"*[67].

Source: taxonomy from Copeland and Antikarov (2001), p. 7, based on Copeland et al. (2000), and Cottrell and Sick (2001).

---

[67] See Cottrell and Sick (2001).

E. Impact on Firm Value of Changes in Cash Flow Volatility: Real Options versus Risk Management Theories

The value of real options used to manage competitive foreign exchange exposure is driven by two underlying stochastic factors, real price risk and quantity risk. An increase in real price risk or quantity risk increases the volatility of domestic cash flow. Real option theory predicts a positive impact of increases in cash flow volatility on expected cash flows and firm value, whereas risk management theories predict the opposite effect[68] (see also chapter 5/section 5.5.1):

- *Real options theories*: emphasize the option properties of growth opportunities presented by exchange rate changes. An increase in the volatility of cash flows a firm would receive from new investments would make its real options more valuable[69].

- *Capital structure and risk management theories*: predict that increases in cash flow volatility affect negatively firm value. The costs of cash flow volatility in terms of firm value are discussed in section 6.1.1/chapter 6.

3.4.2 Valuation of Risky Foreign Currency Cash Flows - Standard Techniques

If the firm has no flexibility to change course when it acquires new information later on about the uncertainty, NPV is appropriate. Even for flexible firms, NPV valuation methods are relevant for two reasons: (i) real options may have no value, e.g., the firm's decisions over the valuation period may involve low uncertainty, (ii) NPV is the foundation for real option analysis: the present value of a project without flexibility constitutes the base case of the real option approach.

A. Adjusted Present Value versus Weighted Average Cost of Capital

The adjusted present value (APV) and weighted average cost of capital (WACC) methods are two methods for valuing real assets[70]. Both methods use as their starting

---

[68] This discussion is based on Shin and Stulz (2000).

[69] This would also increase equity volatility. Real option theory predicts a positive relation between equity volatility and firm value with valuable real options. See Merton (1974), Shin and Stulz (2000).

[70] Under the WACC methodology, a project is acceptable if it can pay the after-tax debt used to finance it and generate a better return on the equity invested. The *WACC* is defined as:

points the unlevered cash flows generated by the project, assuming that the project is financed entirely by equity. The APV method calculates the net present value (NPV) of the all-equity-financed project and adds the value of the tax and any other benefits of debt. It is a direct estimate of the increase in shareholders wealth. The WACC method accounts for any benefits of debt by adjusting the discount rate[71].

The WACC method is the most frequently used in practice, but the APV is a superior approach in some respects: (i) it calculates separately the value created by the project and the value created by the financing. Adjusted discount rate and WACC methods aggregate operational and financing cash flows and discount them at a single rate. (ii) it is easier to use when debt levels or tax rates change over time[72]. The drawback of the APV approach is that it requires a clear identification and evaluation of the financing and hedging decision side effects. For this reason, firms often prefer to only adjust the discount rate and otherwise follow the standard NPV methodology.

B. Valuation of Risky Foreign Cash Flows in Base Currency

The calculation of exposure measures relies on accurate domestic currency cash flow forecasts. It is based on[73]: (i) project or firm performance data at the time of exposure measurement including actual and budgeted costs, (ii) projected foreign exchange rates to determine the future and current value in domestic currency, (iii) projected interest rates to define discount rates for present value measures of future exposures.

When money and exchange markets are integrated, three methods can be used to calculate expected domestic currency cash flows[74]:

1) Discount first the foreign currency cash flows at the foreign rate of return that local investors would require for a similar investment, and then translate foreign-currency

---

$$WACC = \frac{E}{V}K_e + \frac{D}{V}K_d(1-T)$$

where E/V and D/V are the equity and debt financing proportions, K_e and $K_d(1-T)$ are the costs of equity and debt financing respectively, and where the cost of debt is, on an after tax base, the same as equity cost. The cost of equity can be estimated with the CAPM or APT or dividend-discount model. See Booth (1998), p.32, Demacopoulos (1987), p. 211.
[71] See Shapiro (1999), pp. 723-724, Grinblatt and Titman (2002), ch. 13.
[72] See Grinblatt and Titman (2002), p. 461.
[73] See Demacopoulos (1989), p. 102.
[74] See Sercu and Uppal (1995), pp. 587-590.

present value into domestic currency at the current spot rate. For example, a multinational corporations would (i) forecast cash flows in foreign currencies of subsidiaries, (iii) estimate the cost of capital based on comparables as discount rates, (iii) discount the foreign cash flows of subsidiaries at the foreign currency cost of capital, (iv) forecast exchange rates for the translation, (v) translate to the base currency of the company[75].

2) Foreign cash flows can be translated in base currency using the distribution of the future spot rates and then discounted to determine present value measures[76].

3) Translate into domestic currency using forward rates as the certainty equivalent of the future spot rate, then discount.

When money and exchange markets are not integrated (segmented), only the second method is applicable. Other aspects are important for valuing foreign cash flows:

Treatment of Inflation: based on the premise that shareholders are interested in the purchasing power of future returns for their consumption, the effect on cash flows is evaluated in real term. Cash flows must be treated consistently for inflation: (i) nominal cash flows should be discounted at nominal discount rates and real cash flows at real discount rates[77], (ii) nominal value should be adjusted with the use of an appropriate *consumption price index*. The index that matters from the perspective of shareholders should reflect costs of living conditions, and not the firm's activities related prices, which are relevant primarily for determining the competitive costs of the firm[78]. A consumption price index should be used to adjust nominal cash flows in real terms, but foreign cash flows can fluctuate in nominal terms as a result of other price indexes, e.g., because expected costs are affected by the volatility of input prices.

Calculation of Discount Rates: firm value is equal to the expected cash flows discounted at the expected rate of return investors require for cash flows of comparable risk. The international CAPM can be used as a model for risk-adjusting discount rates and value them in domestic currency[79]. The ICAPM model implies that diversifiable (systematic or market) risks should not be reflected in the discount rate but in the value

---

[75] See Demacopoulos (1989).
[76] See Demacopoulos (1989).
[77] See Demacopoulos (1989), p. 206.
[78] See Demacopoulos (1987), p. 216.
[79] See Solnik (1996), p. 140.

of expected cash flows. The beta used to measure the discount rate should only reflect non-diversifiable (unsystematic or unique) market related factors.

Variance-minimizing financial hedges reduce the covariance of cash flows with their beta (i.e. market trends), and therefore reduce the discount rate used in the present value computation. As such, they contribute positively to the value of the firm. The effect of exposure asymmetries on the discount rate is more ambiguous. The effect of real options is to make the covariance of cash flows with their beta (i.e., market trends) conditional on the exchange rate. As such it is impossible to find the opportunity cost of capital with standard NPV valuation methods because the risk of cash flow changes with the exchange rate (see also chapter 3/section 3.4.1, and chapter 5/section 5.5.1).

C. Capital Structure: Effects of Financing Decisions on Firm Value

Expected cash flow volatility associated with exchange rate uncertainty can affect firm value by changing either the discount rate or expected cash flows. The NPV rule assumes that project selection and financing decisions do not interact and treats projects as if they were all-equity financed. The lack of interaction between investment and financing decisions is consistent with the Modigliani-Miller (M-M) theorem: the decision on how to spend funds should not be affected by the way these funds are raised. The M-M Theorem implies that the sum of all future cash flows distributed to the firm's debt and equity investors is unaffected by capital structure in the absence of market imperfections, e.g. taxes or transaction costs. The M-M Theorem implies that exchange rate changes would affect the weights in the capital structure. If the cost of foreign currency debt financing changes, the cost of equity would also change so as to leave the weighted average cost of capital unchanged[80].

In practice, market imperfections exist and financing transactions, including foreign exchange hedging alternatives, have an impact on a firm's total cash flows for example by altering its tax liabilities since the interest tax deduction makes debt financing less expensive than equity financing, or because of bankruptcy costs. The impact of financing transactions on firm value affects the present value of costs and the firm's decision to hedge or not an exposure[81].

---

[80] See O'Brien (1998).
[81] See Demacopoulos (1989), p. 207.

A flaw of structural models of foreign exchange exposure is that they ignore the effects through the cost of capital and the effects through taxes. The effect through the tax rate can be important. For example, a foreign currency depreciation could not only reduce an exporter's cash flows, but also its taxable income. Each home currency unit lost because of this depreciation means that taxes paid are reduced[82]. Examples of exchange rate effects through the cost of capital include:

- *Direct costs associated with financing in foreign currency*: a firm's cost of capital generally rises when its domestic currency depreciates if there are costs associated with external financing. Such an increase in capital costs can reduce the value of a firm's existing operations and adversely affect its real investment opportunities. For a firm with a net long economic position in foreign currency, the benefits of a home currency depreciation may in this case be outweighed by the costs, and exposure could be negative[83]. An example of negative exposure due to foreign currency debt is given by the Asian countries that had been hit by the Asian financial crisis during 1997. Many Asian conglomerates had borrowed large amounts in foreign currency, which resulted in very large contractual exposures accompanied by high debt-equity ratios. When the Asian currencies lost their value against the US-dollar, these firms had difficulties in servicing their foreign debts. Moreover, several overseas projects which were expected to generate foreign currencies were underperforming[84].

- *Perceived riskiness of foreign currency claims*: the cost of capital can be influenced by the perceived riskiness of claims on firms and that perceived riskiness, relative to other firms, could be altered in the short run by heavy exposures in foreign currencies[85]. However, if exchange rate exposure is a priced factor, hedging may be rewarded with a lower cost of capital.

- *Effect through the capital account*: exchange rate changes also impact a country's capital account transactions, which in turn affect the pricing and availability of financial capital. These effects could be felt across financial assets denominated in a particular currency, when a prospective home currency depreciation leads to a rise

---

[82] See Stulz (2000), ch. 8, p. 27.
[83] See Froot and Stein (1991). See also The Economist, August 18th 2001, p. 50, for empirical evidence on the effect of the cost of capital on foreign exchange exposure.
[84] See, e.g., Giannetti (2002), p. 7.
[85] See Jacque (1981).

in all domestic interest rates, or across financial claims for a particular country[86]. These effects are also part of a firm's foreign exchange economic exposure.

- *Financial constraints, due to capital market imperfections, to fund the exercise of real options*: if capital markets are imperfect, the financing mix and hedging strategies affect a firm's investment choices and the efficiency of its operations. A higher foreign exchange exposure could increase the expected external foreign currency financing costs and lead to underinvestment and reduction in expected firm value (see chapter 6) [87].

3.4.3 Real Option Valuation of Risky Foreign Cash Flows

A. Real Option Valuation in Four-Steps

The present value of real options is one component of the value of a firm that one needs to calculate for exposure measurement. The derivation of the real option value can take place within four steps[88]:

1. Computation of *present value of the project without flexibility* using standard valuation techniques, e.g., APV or WACC.

2. Modeling the set of values that the underlying risky asset may take through time in an *event tree*: This involves estimating (i) the stochastic properties of the variables driving the volatility of the risky asset, e.g., real exchange rate/price and demand, (ii) the volatility of the rate of return.

3. Description of the payoffs from optimal decisions, conditional on the state of nature in a *scenario tree*. This requires putting decisions into the nodes of the event tree[89]. The decision to exercise a real option at a given period should be based on the value of the firm or project and not on the cash flow in that period[90].

4. Calculation of the *real option value* of the project with flexibility and determination of *optimal contingent plan*, by working backward in the tree (unless there is path

---

[86] See Levich (1998), p. 568.
[87] See Myers (1977) for the problem of debt overhang, Grinblatt and Titman (2002), pp. 564-565.
[88] See Copeland and Antikarov (2001).
[89] It is possible to have multiple decisions per node and payouts may include cash flows as dividends.
[90] See Copeland and Antikarov (2001), p. 152.

dependency) to obtain values at each node and to make optimal decisions. This uses the no arbitrage condition to conform to the law of "one price".

B. Valuation of Real Options under Real Exchange Rate/Price Risk and Demand Risk

Under uncertainty, a flexible firm must base its investment decisions on the ROV of its expected cash flows. Valuing real options under real exchange rate/price risk and quantity risk can be done within eight steps[91]: (1) *Exchange rate scenarios*: construction of a lattice or recombining scenario tree model of future exchange rate scenarios. (2) *Real option model:* development of a model of the firm's flexibility. (3) *Strategic and contingency planning*: definition of ex-ante as well as ex-post operating decisions (4) *Demand scenarios*: description of demand risk in multiple scenarios. (5) *Managerial flexibility model*: determination of a set of operating strategies and development of alternative operating flexibility models for each strategy. (6) *Lattice tree*: combination of operating policy and exchange rate scenarios are represented in a lattice tree. The corresponding operating flexibility models are solved for each system state, i.e., combination of operating policy an exchange rate scenario in the lattice tree. Scenarios on *real exchange rate/price risk* could incorporate assumptions about nominal prices adjustments through and exchange rate elasticity of prices or costs, or constraints in the form of demand requirement as well as capacity limits[92] (see section 3.5 on flexibility bounds). (7) *Stochastic dynamic program:* a stochastic dynamic program uses backward recursion to determine optimal investment policies. (8) *Option value of flexibility*: The difference between the base case or status-quo operating strategy and alternative (optimal) operating policies equals the option value of flexibility.

Since sunk costs incurred for exercising options, including foreign exchange losses from past exposures, are past and irreversible outflows, they cannot be affected by the

---

[91] This section draws from the ROV methodology proposed in Cohen and Huchzermeier (1999), pp. 3-4.
[92] See Cohen and Huchzermeier (1999), p.4. Pricing policy in terms of Exchange Rate Pass-Through can be used in simulation models of exposure estimation. CorporateMetrics suggests an approach to mapping home currency cash flows to exchange rates through price elasticity estimates. See CorporateMetrics (1999), pp. 43-45.

decision to accept or reject a project, and are therefore irrelevant to the ROV computation[93].

Two approaches can be used to calculate real option value[94]:

1. *Replicating portfolio approach*: this involves discounting expected cash flows at a risk-adjusted rate.

- *Twin security approach*[95]: by the law of one price, a replicating portfolio that is composed of shares of a twin security and a risk-free bond is formed. The replicating portfolio and the option should have the same present value since the payouts of the replicating portfolio and of the option must be identical. It is however generally not possible to find a priced security whose cash payouts in every state of nature over the life of the project are perfectly correlated with those of the project.

- *Marketed asset disclaimer (MAD) approach*[96]: this involves using the present value of the project itself, without flexibility, as the underlying risky asset as if it were a marketed security. This assumes that the present value of the cash flows of the project without flexibility is the best unbiased estimate of the market value of the project were it a traded asset.

2. *Risk neutral probability approach*[97]: this is an application of the *certainty-equivalent* (i.e. risk-neutral) method. The certainty-equivalent value of a real option is an estimate of the option's market value if it were traded. It assumes that shareholders have access to assets with the same risks characteristics (e.g., the same beta) as the capital investments being evaluated. A real investment opportunity is assumed to have a "double" in the form of a security or portfolio with identical risk. An investor would pay for a real option based on the project, the same as for an identical traded option written on the double. This traded option does not have to exist; it is enough to know it would be valued by investors, who could employ either the arbitrage or the risk-neutral

---

[93] See Brealey and Myers (2000), p. 123, Muralidhar (1992).
[94] See Copeland and Antikarov (2001).
[95] See Copeland and Antikarov (2001), pp. 90-93.
[96] See Copeland and Antikarov (2001).
[97] See Copeland and Antikarov (2001).

method. The expected rate of return of the double represents the cost of capital for the real investment and the discount rate for a DCF valuation of the investment project.

3.4.4 Quadrinomial Real Option Valuation with Real Price Risk and Quantity Risk

The quadrinomial approach can be used to estimate the real option value of cash flows whose volatility is driven by two correlated underlying stochastic processes. This method is appropriate to estimate two sources of uncertainty separately[98].

Foreign exchange competitive exposure implies that real option payoffs are based on the value of a real asset driven by two sources of uncertainties, real exchange rate/price risk and quantity risk. The presence of exposures asymmetries suggests that these two underlying stochastic processes are correlated. A quadrinomial approach with correlated uncertainties can be used in that case[99]. It is a two-variable binomial event tree that has four branches at every node[100].

The expected growth rate in real exchange rate is denoted by g_1 with standard deviation σ_1, and the expected growth rate in quantity by g_2 with standard deviation σ_2. Assuming risk-neutrality, their growth rates are equal to the risk-free rate. Therefore, the equations for the growth of price, P, and quantity, Q, can be written as:

[3. 3]
$$d\ln(P) = \left(r_f - \frac{\sigma_1^2}{2}\right)dt + \sigma_1 dz$$

[3. 4]
$$g_1 = \left(r_f - \frac{\sigma_1^2}{2}\right)dt$$

[3. 5]
$$d\ln(Q) = \left(r_f - \frac{\sigma_2^2}{2}\right)dt + \sigma_2 dz$$

[3. 6]
$$g_2 = \left(r_f - \frac{\sigma_2^2}{2}\right)dt$$

---

[98] See Copeland and Antikarov (2001) for a consolidated approach.
[99] See Copeland and Antikarov (2001), pp. 279-296.
[100] Based on Copeland and Antikarov (2001), pp. 284-296.

The growth rates follow an arithmetic Brownian motion with constant up and down changes of opposite sign $(u = -d)$. The quadrinomial combinations of the growth rate value of Q, $\Delta \ln(Q_0)$, and of P, $\Delta \ln(P_0)$ are:

1. $\Delta \ln(P_0) + u_1, \Delta \ln(Q_0) + u_2$

2. $\Delta \ln(P_0) + u_1, \Delta \ln(Q_0) - d_2$

3. $\Delta \ln(P_0) + d_1, \Delta \ln(Q_0) + u_2$

4. $\Delta \ln(P_0) + d_1, \Delta \ln(Q_0) + d_2$

A system of six equations and six unknowns can be solved for the risk-neutral probabilities and for the up and down movements:

[3. 7] $$E(g_1) = \left(r_f - \frac{\sigma_1^2}{2}\right)\Delta t = (p_{u1u2} + p_{u1d2})u_1 - (p_{d1u2} + p_{d1d2})u_1$$

[3. 8] $$\sigma_1^2 \Delta t = (p_{u1u2} + p_{u1d2})u_1^2 - (p_{d1u2} + p_{d1d2})u_1^2$$

[3. 9] $$E(g_2) = \left(r_f - \frac{\sigma_2^2}{2}\right)\Delta t = (p_{u1u2} + p_{d1u2})u_2 - (p_{u1d2} + p_{d1d2})u_2$$

[3. 10] $$\sigma_2^2 \Delta t = (p_{u1u2} + p_{d1u2})u_2^2 - (p_{u1d2} + p_{d1d2})u_2^2$$

[3. 11] $$\rho_{12}\sigma_1\sigma_2\Delta t = (p_{u1u} - p_{d1u2} - p_{u1d2} - p_{d1d2})u_1u_2$$

[3. 12] $$p_{u1u} + p_{d1u2} + p_{u1d2} + p_{d1d2} = 1$$

The risk-neutral probabilities for each of the possible states and the up and down movements (period volatilities for the two uncertainties) are expressed as:

[3. 13] $$p_{u1u2} = \frac{u_1u_2 + u_2g_1 + u_1g_2 + \rho_{1,2}\sigma_1\sigma_2\Delta t}{4u_1u_2}$$

[3. 14] $$p_{u1d2} = \frac{u_1u_2 + u_2g_1 + d_1g_2 - \rho_{1,2}\sigma_1\sigma_2\Delta t}{4u_1u_2}$$

[3. 15] $$p_{d1u2} = \frac{u_1u_2 + d_2g_1 + u_1g_2 - \rho_{1,2}\sigma_1\sigma_2\Delta t}{4u_1u_2}$$

[3. 16] $$p_{d1d2} = \frac{u_1 u_2 + d_2 g_1 + d_1 g_2 + \rho_{1,2} \sigma_1 \sigma_2 \Delta t}{4 u_1 u_2}$$

[3. 17] $$u_1 = \sigma_1 \sqrt{t}$$

[3. 18] $$u_2 = \sigma_2 \sqrt{t}$$

The present value of cash flows is calculated by multiplying the cash flows by the risk-neutral probabilities at each node and by dividing the result by the risk-free rate. The real option payoffs that reflect the optimal decisions at each node in the tree are valued by weighting them by their risk-neutral probabilities and discount at the risk-free rate.

Using the quadrinomial probabilities with correlation and Bayes' Law, the conditional binomial probabilities for the two uncertainties can be obtained. For example, the conditional probabilities for the quantity going up given that the real exchange rate is up or down are[101]:

$$p(Q_u | P_u) = \frac{p(Q_u \cap P_u)}{p(P_u)} \qquad\qquad p(Q_u | P_d) = \frac{p(Q_u \cap P_d)}{p(Q_d)}$$

Positive correlation would result in greater probability on the extreme values and as a result an increased volatility of the project[102]. This corresponds to a curvilinear (concave/convex) foreign exchange exposure profile.

3.5 Foreign Exchange Exposure with Bounded Flexibility

3.5.1 Value-Maximizing Strategic Behavior with Full Flexibility

A. Value-Maximizing Pricing Behavior

The decision to exercise a real option at a given period should be based on the value of the firm and not on the cash flow in that period[103]. What matters is the expected effect of exercising real options on the exposure of firm value. Suppose an exporter who faces an exchange rate pass-trough decision[104]. Pricing flexibility is an important factor contributing to foreign exchange exposure, since it affects the sensitivity of markups to

---

[101] See Copeland and Antikarov (2001), p. 294.
[102] See Copeland and Antikarov (2001), p. 294.
[103] See Copeland and Antikarov (2001), p. 152.
[104] This concept is defined in section 3.6.3.

exchange rate changes in the short term and adjustments in quantities in the long term. Because a profit-maximizing firm sells only where the demand is elastic (*elasticity of demand greater than 1*), changes in the nominal foreign price leads to more than proportional changes in nominal foreign cash flows[105]. As such, the *value-maximizing* strategy is to:

- fully pass-through (in the short term) an appreciation of the foreign (destination market's) currency, in order to increase market shares (in the long term). The domestic profit margins are unchanged (short term) with higher market share[106]. In practice, firms often set prices to increase market shares even when this results in negative profits, by pursuing predatory pricing, that is, deliberately making losses with anti-competitive intent[107].

- *not* pass-through a depreciation of the foreign currency, in order to keep its market shares. This implies lower (short term) profit margins and same (long term) market shares.

The exposure would be symmetric under some assumptions about demand elasticities. This strategy is value-maximizing: suppose that the firm keeps its foreign price at the same level after the foreign currency appreciation. The Law of One Price implies that *in the long term*, the firm will be forced to pass-through the foreign currency appreciation. The higher profit margins in the short term would result in lower long term market shares. For an elasticity of demand higher than *1*, this strategy is not value-maximizing (see discussion in chapter 4).

However, a firm could be a *profit-margin* maximizer for example because it is *financially pressed*. The firm would pass-through appreciations and leave foreign prices unchanged after depreciations. This behavior would correspond to the optimal

---

[105] A profit-maximizing firm sells only where demand is elastic (> 1) ensuring that prices are positive. See Levi (1994), p. 40. Constant elasticity of demand is the special case where elasticities are independent of the price. Elasticities increase with price for demand schedules less convex than a constant elasticity schedule, e.g., linear demand. See Goldberg and Knetter (1996), p. 16.

[106] An established empirical result is that relative prices affect the quantity exported, but that they do so with a lag. See, e.g., Krugman and Baldwin (1987). There is often a long delay, perhaps of more than a year, before consumers and producers adjust to changes in prices. See The Economist, A Faded Green, Dec 4th 2003.

[107] See Economic Focus: Preying on Theory, The Economist July 10th 1999, p. 88, for theoretical arguments supporting the possibility of predatory pricing.

strategy if the elasticity of demand were smaller than *1*, and would also convexify the exposure profile of firm value.

B. Market Share Expansion Objective and Value-Maximization

In so-called "customer markets", firms have a stock of customers who only gradually respond to price changes[108]. In a customer market, the pricing decision is a dynamic optimization problem since the current price affects the customer stock and future revenues[109]. It is value-maximizing to tradeoff current profit margins for future market shares if the firm sells where the elasticity of demand is greater than *1*. The elasticity of demand is function of consumers' switching costs. Because of imperfect information or/and adjustment costs, customers cannot immediately switch to the firm with the lowest price. These switching costs can be seen as the adjustment costs paid by customers to exercise an option implicitly purchased to the firm.

A model examines the pricing behavior of exporters with market share expansion objectives[110]. In a duopoly model, the second-period demand and profit depends on the first-period market share, λ. Because the price in the first-period affects the customer stock, and hence future revenues, the pricing decision is a dynamic decision problem[111]. To maximize the present value of profits in domestic currency, π, the firm chooses its first-period price, p, taking the foreign competitor's first-period price, p^*, as given:

[3. 19] $$\pi = s_1 \pi_1(p, p^*, s_1) + \delta s_2 \pi_2(\lambda(p, p^*, s_2))$$

where π_1 and π_2 are the first and second period profits in foreign currency, s_1 and s_2 the first and second period prices of foreign currency in terms of the domestic currency, and δ the discount factor. Second-period profits are a function of its first-

---

[108] The original customer market model is due to Phelps and Winter (1970). Applications to the open economy include, e.g., Froot and Klemperer (1989).

[109] See Gottfries (1994), pp. 2-3.

[110] The original model is from Froot and Klemperer (1989). This simplified presentation of their model is from Koutmos and Martin (2003), pp. 367-368. See also Clark et al. (1999), pp. 254-255 and 260-261, Knetter (1994), Krugman (1987), Marston (1990).

[111] A second established empirical result is that relative prices affect the quantity exported, but that they do so with a lag. See, e.g., Krugman and Baldwin (1987). If quantities respond to price changes with a lag, firms should take account of the lags when they set prices and assess their foreign exchange exposure.

period market share. The first-order conditions, after applying simplifying assumptions, emphasize that firms may trade-off the marginal cost of investment in first-period market share, $\partial\pi_1/\partial p$, for marginal return on this investment that is received in the second period, $(\partial\pi_2/\partial\lambda)(\partial\lambda/\partial p)$:

[3. 20] $$\frac{\partial\pi}{\partial p} = s_1\left[\frac{\partial\pi_1}{\partial p} + \left(\frac{\partial\pi_2}{\partial\lambda}\right)\left(\frac{\partial\lambda}{\partial p}\right)\right]$$

For example, a low exchange rate pass-through in the first-period after depreciations would lead to a high $\partial\pi_1/\partial p$ and a relatively lower $(\partial\pi_2/\partial\lambda)(\partial\lambda/\partial p)$. Competitive disadvantages can eventually affect the market share of firms. The effect on exposure is as follows:

- *exporter's currency depreciates*: the exporter lowers the foreign currency price in order to build market share, i.e., the domestic price stays at the initial level.

- *exporter's currency appreciates*: it protects market shares by holding constant the foreign currency price and accepting lower margins, rather than allowing it to increase according to the Law of One Price, especially if it thinks the currency will weaken again[112].

There is pervasive empirical evidence that some German, Japanese, U.K., and U.S. firms choose to defend market share and not to pass-through adverse changes in exchange rates[113]. This suggests that they price-to-market, and that relative export prices between different markets are affected by nominal exchange rates[114].

---

[112] Dynamic optimization can arise because of firms' different profit maximizing horizons. Ohno (1990) shows in a simulation analysis that ERPT is inversely related to the length of firms' planning horizons.

[113] See Knetter (1993). There is evidence supporting that exporters in large economies such as Germany, the U.S. and Japan can pursue policies of price discrimination. See Knetter (1997), who analyzes the law of one price for 37 German seven-digit export categories in the 1973-1987 period and find that exports to Japan are systematically more expensive than exports to the U.S. market. The magnitude of that premium ranges from 10-45 percent.

[114] Some evidence indicates German and Japanese exporters have a greater propensity to PTM than do US exporters, which more fully pass-through movements in the dollar. See Krugman (1987), Giovannini (1988), Knetter (1989), Knetter (1993), Ohno (1989), Kasa (1992), Marston (1992). The German automobile industry has been reported to exhibit more PTM when its domestic currency is appreciating. See Knetter (1994). See Knetter (1989), Knetter (1993) for evidence that German exporters adjust their profit margins to stabilize dollar-prices on goods exported to the United States.

3.5.2 Effect of Volume Constraints on Expected Firm Value and Exposure

A. Exposure Profile with Volume Constraints

The value of a real option may depend on a probability distribution of cash flows/firm value that is truncated. Bounds on flexibility can explain (i) negative real options payoffs: volume constraints imply that a higher quantity risk reduces expected firm value, (ii) exposure asymmetries caused by constrained rather than discretionary strategic behavior. Capacity constraints/marketing bottlenecks models give insights on the effect of flexibility bounds. The objective of these models is to examine the effects of exchange rate fluctuations on pricing (pricing-to-market) and profit margins. Interpretation of volume constraints models in terms of profits/firm value is necessary with regard to foreign exchange exposure. Volume constraints affect the firm's value-maximizing strategy. For example, for a firm that is long on foreign currency:

After a depreciation of the domestic currency, if it is costly for the firm to expand sales rapidly because of binding volume constraints, it will only pass-through to the point where demand equals capacity. Volume constraints provide an incentive to stabilize destination price and output. A bottleneck occurs "when a firm is unable to respond to increase in demand because of low distribution intensity"[115]. There may be substantial costs of entry, expansion, and exit that force producers to absorb exchange rate fluctuations in their mark-ups instead of passing them on to consumers as prices change[116]. The domestic currency price will increase until more capacity or marketing distribution is put in place[117]. The beneficial effect of a depreciation on firm value will be relatively smaller than with no flexibility bounds.

After a depreciation of the foreign currency, a firm that cares primarily about market shares and firm value will keep foreign prices at the same level. Since a depreciation of the foreign currency implies a contraction rather than an expansion of demand, the flexibility bound is asymmetric[118].

---

[115] See Baldwin (1988) for a "capacity constraints in distribution networks" model. See also Knetter (1992), p. 14., Levi (1996). See Gil-Pareja (2000), Krugman (1986). Krugman (1987). p. 63, Kadiyali (1997), p. 440.

[116] See Dixit (1989).

[117] Thus, Pricing-to-Market will be observed until capacity expands sufficiently to meet the demand.

[118] That is, the exchange rate pass-through is higher than for foreign currency appreciation, thereby implying less Pricing-to-Market.

By doing so, the adverse effect of an appreciation is relatively higher than the beneficial effect from a depreciation:

- *Reduction of expected mean firm value*: bounds on quantity flexibility truncate the probability distribution of profits and skew negatively the firm value distribution. The effect on firm value distribution depends on the persistence of the bound. For foreign exchange exposure measurement, one needs to determine the time frame within which the firm cannot react by adjusting production and sales volumes. The firm could be "locked in" through contractual or strategic commitments extending in the future and not be free to react immediately.

- *Exposure profile truncated*: because the quantity flexibility is asymmetric, the exposure is asymmetric. The truncated right tail of the cash flow distribution makes exposure asymmetric. The firm is relative more exposed to exchange rate appreciations as a result. At the exchange rates at which the bound is expected to become effective, depreciations have no beneficial effects on cash flows. The downside exposure of firm value is greater if the firm pass-trough exchange rate appreciations. This focus on short term profitability would be justified if for example the firm were financially pressed.

Typically, the hypothesis of exposure asymmetries has been justified by volume models of cash flow determination. If it is costly for exporting firms to expand sales rapidly, foreign currency prices will not fall much when the foreign currency appreciates. The asymmetric exchange rate pass-through leads to *asymmetric profit margin sensitivities* (higher for foreign currency appreciations) [119]. However, the focus on the sensitivity of profit margins is not what ultimately matters for economic exposure measurement. Finally, although we supposed quantity risk to be endogenous to the exchange rate, it could be determined by other factors.

Capacity constraints and market share building models lead to opposite predictions on pricing behavior and exposure. Table 3.3 above shows that in a market share model, more pricing-to-market (PTM) may be observed during appreciation of the exporter's currency, whereas quantity restrictions models predict the opposite.

---

[119] Overall, empirical results on this issue are sparse and far from definitive. Coughlin and Pollard (2000) find that U.S. import prices rise more due to a depreciation than they fall due to an appreciation, i.e., pass-through effects are relatively larger during dollar depreciations than dollar appreciations.

Table 3. 3 Exporter's Pricing Policy and Effect on Expected Firm Value and Real Option Value

	Home currency depreciation	Home currency appreciation	Effect of higher quantity risk on: i. expected firm value / ii. real option value
Volume Constraints	ERPT low PTM high	ERPT high PTM low	i. lower expected firm value ii. negative effect
Market Share Objective	ERPT high PTM low	ERPT low PTM high	i. higher expected firm value ii. positive effect

B. *Illustration: Bounds on Strategic Flexibility from Marketing Bottlenecks*

We examine the reported pricing behavior of *German luxury car exporters* to the U.S. market during the 1970s – 1980s and the effect on their short and long term exposures. For most of the period 1975-1987, German exporters to the U.S. experienced large US$ appreciations.

Marketing bottlenecks in the early 1980s: empirical evidence suggests that they did not pass-through the US$ appreciation[120] in the early 1980s, because they had inadequate U.S. distribution facilities and could not have supplied the increased demand that lower U.S. prices implied[121]. Instead of passing through the increases in DM profit margins to their U.S. customers in the form of lower US$ prices, they kept them. Some firms even raised their foreign prices in that situation[122]. By pricing-to-market, luxury German cars became far more expensive in the U.S. than in Europe during the 1980-84 dollar appreciation[123].

Loss of market shares after the mid-80s: but they passed-through the subsequent US$ depreciation after the mid-80s by increasing their US$ prices, which prevented their profit margins from falling in the short term. As a result, prices of these cars in the U.S.

Other empirical studies on asymmetric pricing include Mann (1986), Kreinin et al. (1987), Marston (1990), Goldberg (1995), Kadiyali (1997).
[120] Krugman (1987), p. 49, reports that European luxury automobiles raised their prices in U.S. dollar terms during that period despite huge declines in European currencies against the dollar. See also Levi (1996), p. 340., Knetter (1994), Clark et al. (1999), p. 251.
[121] See Knetter (1994).
[122] See Krugman (1987), p. 49, Froot and Klemperer (1989). Kasa (1992), p. 2. reports that during the strong dollar of the mid 1980s prices of upscale German automobiles were as much as 30-40 percent higher in the United States than in Europe.
[123] See Krugman (1987), p. 49.

again became closer to those abroad[124]. The lack of pricing-to-market (incomplete pass-through) was reported to have hurt German firms in the high quality end of the market during that period. Porsche, BMW and Mercedes had experienced large decreases in market shares, in part due to new Japanese entrants in the high-quality segment of the market[125].

The interpretation in terms of exposure can be made as follows:

- *Period of US$ appreciation in the early 1980s*: the marketing bottleneck reduced their ability to exploit upside demand potentials and increase expected firm value. The value of their real option to adjust prices was reduced. The marketing bottleneck put a bound on their flexibility to pass-through, and by reducing their firm value exposure to the beneficial US$ appreciation, also reduced their expected firm value. Also, a higher pricing flexibility/degree of pass-through *during this period* may have helped preventing the subsequent entry of Japanese competitors during the US$ depreciation after the mid-80s.

- *Period of US$ depreciation after the mid-80s*: by passing-through, they protected their short term profits, but eventually lost market shares. But they probably would have been better off in the long term by pricing-to-market more rather than passing-through the US$ depreciation (the effects on exposure of a firm's strategic interactions with its competitors are discussed in chapter 4).

3.5.3 Value of Bounded Flexibility and Types of Flexibility Bounds

A. Effect of Higher Quantity Risk on Option Value

The common assumption is that under uncertainty, the value of real options is always positive, but that the price one has to pay for it often exceeds its value[126]. Financial option pricing theory states that an increase in the variability of the underlying stochastic process increases the option value, i.e., the ratio of option price at which it is exercised to the strike price increases with exchange rate volatility. Similarly, the value of real options is generally assumed to be positively related to the volatility of the cash

---

[124] See Froot and Klemperer (1989).
[125] See Gagnon and Knetter (1994).
[126] See, e.g., Copeland and Antikarov (2001).

flows of its underlying real asset. By reducing the firm's downside risk exposure, real options should therefore have a positive impact on firm value and shareholder value[127]. This supposes that flexibility has the effect of positively skewing firm value distribution and gives long real options. Foreign exchange exposure will be higher (lower) to beneficial (adverse) exchange rate changes.

This is not always the case. The value of a real option can be negatively affected by an increase in the volatility of the cash flows of its underlying. Here, the volatility of the cash flows generated by the underlying asset is driven by real exchange rate/price risk and quantity risk. With bounds on volume flexibility, a *higher quantity risk can reduce the value of an option*. For example, increased demand risk may lead to lower expected sales. Volume constraints can limit a firm's ability to capture upturns of market demand. The demand distribution is truncated and "with more downside risk because of a higher probability to have to fulfill lower levels of demand with lower profit"[128]. "Expected sales will decrease due to an increase in downside risk while the upside is truncated"[129]. This is because a higher quantity risk implies a higher probability for the constraint to become effective. A higher volatility of demand uncertainty can therefore reduce the option value[130].

B. Types of Flexibility Bounds

The argument in the context of sales and distribution constraints is equally applicable to other types of flexibility constraints (see table 3.4 below).

The exposure is asymmetric at the exchange rates at which these bounds on flexibility are expected to become effective. Bounds on flexibility can arise from (i) constraints on the supply side, (ii) constraints on the demand side, (iii) financing constraints on investments (see chapter 6/6.3.2), (iv) government interventions (see chapter 4/ 4.2.2.3).

---

[127] See, e.g., Amram and Kulatilaka (1999).
[128] See Cohen and Huchzermeier (1998), section 21.2.3.
[129] See Cohen and Huchzermeier (1998), section 21.2.3.
[130] "Increases in the volatility of demand uncertainty lead to a reduced option value of stochastic recourse". See Cohen and Huchzermeier (1998), section 21.2.3.

Table 3. 4 Constraints on Supply/Demand Side Dynamics

Production capacity constraints	▪ limited access to input. ▪ limited manufacturing/production capacity. ▪ adjustment costs in production. ▪ adjustment costs in prices.
Marketing bottlenecks	▪ sales constraints. ▪ distribution constraints.
Managerial constraints	▪ inertia and internal managerial opportunism[131]. ▪ imperfect information: limited ERPT could reflect evidence of short run price rigidity, for example because of firms being imperfectly informed about competitors' prices and exchange rates when they set their prices[132].
Financing Constraints	▪ credit constraints: ability to raise external capital to fund investments might be endogenous to the exchange rate.

3.6 Types of Real Options and their Effects on Foreign Exchange Exposure

Real options' payoffs are function of the flexibility to make operating adjustments through: (i) adjustment in quantities, e.g., output flexibility, (ii) adjustment in relative costs, e.g., production location flexibility, (iii) adjustment in relative prices of outputs, e.g., pricing flexibility. Changes in real costs/revenues structure influence the real value effects of unexpected nominal exchange rate changes.

Generic types of real options include switching options, growth options (options to expand), abandonment options[133]. Other types of operating flexibilities relevant to foreign exchange exposure can be interpreted as real options. The option to pass-through exchange rate changes onto consumers (pricing flexibility), and the option to enter/exit foreign markets.

3.6.1 Switching Options

3.6.1.1 Process and Product Flexibility to Switch

I. Types of Switching Options

---

[131] See Rangan (1998), p. 220, Lee and Solt (2000), p. 6.
[132] See Gottfries (1994).
[133] See Carter et al. (2003), pp. 10-14, Shapiro (1999), p. 358.

"Switching options are *portfolios of American call and put options* that allow their owner to switch at a fixed cost between two modes of operation"[134]. A firm could have switching options as a result of a production *process flexibility* based on flexibility in cost structure. Over time, this optimizes the marginal production or procurement costs function, and raises expected cash flows and firm value. This entails relative cost savings that reduce costs exposure. For example, flexibilities in the firm's cost structure can be in the form of[135]:

- **Procurement flexibility**: for example in the form of *purchasing flexibility to switch input sources across borders*, allowing firms to expand purchases of inputs from suppliers in countries with relative low currency values and reduce purchases from other suppliers. A firm currently purchasing inputs from a domestic supplier is implicitly long call on domestic currency (long put foreign currency) that gives the right to switch to the foreign supplier. Conversely, if the firm currently purchases from a foreign supplier, it implicitly has a long put on domestic currency (long call foreign currency) that can be exercised to switch to the domestic supplier[136].

- **Production flexibility**: this can be in the form of (a) *production location switching flexibility* giving a firm the flexibility to move production from one country to another based on the prevailing exchange rate, (b) *flexibility to vary capacity utilization* giving the possibility to vary the capacity utilization of plants located in different countries depending on the prevailing exchange rate, (c) *flexibility to switch to a production technology which is less/more intensive in a foreign factor of production:* as the domestic currency depreciates, a firm would switch to a production technology which is less intensive in foreign factors of production, whereas when the domestic currency appreciates, it would make more intensive use of the foreign factors.

Strategies that can minimize expected production costs through production flexibility include: (i) building excess capacity in numerous locations, (ii) adopting technologies that employ low fixed costs, to enable the firm to cease production in a

---

[134] See Copeland and Antikarov (2001), p .12.
[135] The terminology of process flexibility and product flexibility is from Trigeorgis (2002), p. 7.
[136] See, e.g., Carter et al. (2003), pp. 11-12.

location at little cost when changes in the exchange rate warrants it[137], (iii) having the possibility to outsource production[138].

Product flexibility to switch comprises the flexibility to switch sales between markets for final products, the flexibility to enter/exit markets, and so forth.

II. Switching Option on Production Location: An Illustrative Case

A. Flexibility Effect on Costs Exposure

We examine the effect on exposure of a firm having the flexibility to switch between production locations. A German firm is assumed to sell its output in its domestic market and incur revenues in euro (€). It has production capacity in both Germany and the United States that gives it the right to pay a fixed exercise price (adjustment costs) to switch between the two production facilities[139]. The investment made in the U.S. production facility can be interpreted as an option premium. It is assumed that the firm is exposed only on the costs side.

Figure 3. 11 Switching Option as a Function of the Exchange Rate[140]

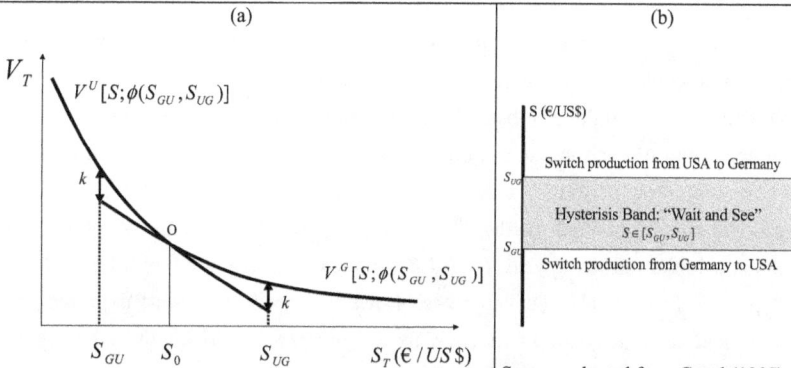

(a)

Source: adapted from Mello et al. (1995), p. 34.

(b)

Source: adapted from Capel (1997), p. 102.

---

[137] See Booth (1996), p.18.
[138] See, e.g., Kogut and Kulatilaka (1994), Mello et al. (1995), Capel (1997), Rangan (1998).
[139] This example is an interpretation in terms of real options of the model of multinational firm of Mello et al. (1995), pp. 30-37.
[140] Reference to Mello et al. (1995), p. 34, though the interpretation is different.

The value of the firm is a function of the operating policy chosen and of the prevailing exchange rate (state of nature). Figure 3.11 below represents the exposure profile of firm value at time T. $V^U(S;\phi)$ and $V^G(S;\phi)$ denote the domestic currency (€) value of the firm when currently producing in the U.S. and when producing in Germany, respectively. The firm value function when producing in Germany $V^G(S;\phi)$ is negatively sloped, because it includes the value of flexibility and the value of expected saving from closing down the U.S. production facility[141]. Similarly, the slope of the curve $V^U(S;\phi)$ is convexified by the firm's flexibility. An operating policy of the firm is defined by the two switching exchange rate values, $\phi(S_{GU},S_{UG})$. The exchange rate S_T is the price of the US\$ in terms of €. Depending on the prevailing exchange rate, the German firm sources its production either from the U.S. in US\$, or from Germany in €.

B. Stochastic Dynamic Programming

At a given period of time, the German firm can be pursuing either of the two following strategies: (i) production costs incurred in U.S. requiring payment in US\$, (ii) production in Germany implying costs in €. We make the following assumptions[142]:

- *Valuation and planning horizon*: there is a four-period planning horizon. The production cycle is of one period, which means that the adjustment lag between a switching production decisions and the ensuing actual production is one period. At the beginning of each new period, one obtains an estimate of production costs for the four coming periods. At the beginning of the first period ($t=0$), estimated productions are obtained for the 2nd, 3rd, and 4th period and for the 5th period, and similarly in the following year. $t = 0,1,2,3$, indicate the beginning of the 1st, 2nd, 3rd, 4th periods respectively. To value cash flows, we need to forecast expected cash flows and then discount them back to the present at a risk-adjusted weighted average cost of capital (WACC). The time value of money is not taken into consideration for simplicity, i.e., the cost of capital is assumed to be zero.

---

[141] See Mello et al. (1995), p. 32.
[142] Numerical example based on Capel (1997), pp. 104-106.

- *Quantity produced and real costs*: the quantities produced at each period are of 100 units. This implies that the *real* costs of producing in Germany at a given period is 100. The *switching costs k* amount to € 25.

- *Exchange rate process over the planning horizon*: parity of real € and US$ costs is assumed at the beginning of the initial period. The real exchange rate *S* is equal to 1 at the beginning of *t=0*. The exchange rate behavior and uncertainty is described with a binomial process with an equal probability of appreciation of 10% and of depreciation of 10%. Over the planning horizon the exchange rate can follow eight different paths over the next three periods, that is, between the beginning of the 1st and the beginning of the 4th period.

The two event trees in figures 3.12 represent the cash flows of the two modes of operation. *Because of the path dependencies*, the nodes of the event trees cannot represent the value of costs but the cash flow of cost given the mode of operation in that state of nature[143].

The states of nature are represented by the values taken by the exchange rate.

- The mode of operation production in Germany becomes relatively better when the US$ appreciates: $S_T(€/US\$) \uparrow$. If the firm is currently producing in the U.S., a US$ appreciation makes U.S. production more expensive and lowers the value of the firm. Thanks to the production flexibility, the firm can escape these rising variable costs by moving production to Germany after paying the switching cost *k*. If the exchange rate falls again the firm can shift production back to the U.S.

- The mode of operation production in U.S. becomes relatively better when the US$ depreciates: $S_T(€/US\$) \downarrow$.

If the firm is currently producing in Germany, it has a long put on the US$ written at the money, whereas if it is currently producing in the U.S., it has a long call on the US$[144]. The put option gives the right to use the foreign real assets (U.S. production facility), whereas the call gives the right to sell the foreign real asset. The firm can shut down the German production facility to switch to U.S. production by exercising the

---

[143] See Copeland and Antikarov (2001), p. 180.
[144] The long put on the US$ is equivalent to a long call on the €. The long put on the € is equivalent to a long call on the US$. See Shapiro (1999), p. 179.

put. Restarting operations in Germany can be done by exercising the call. This reduces the value of expected domestic costs over time.

Figure 3. 12 Event Tree with Cash Flows (a) when Initial Production Facility in Germany, (b) when Initial Production Facility in U.S.

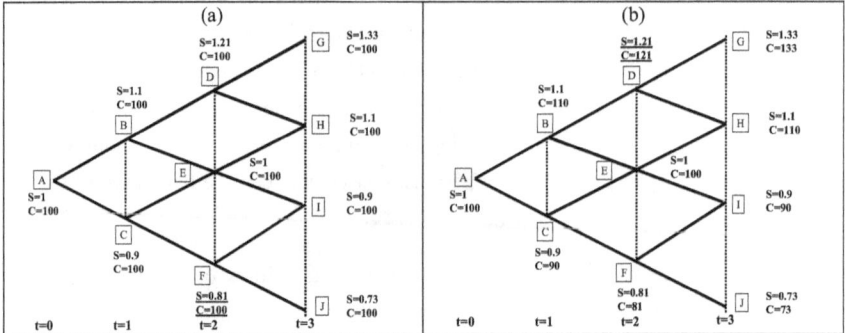

Optimal Execution of Switching Option: Costs Minimizing Decision-Making

It is worth switching when the present value of the cost of producing in one location is smaller than the present value of the cost of producing in the other one. The optimal action depends on the exchange rate, but also on the mode of operation that the firm was in when it entered a state of nature. Because of the exposure path dependency, the current production framework depends on previous exchange rate values[145]. When the exchange rate lies within the bounds of the two switching points, $S \in [S_{GU}, S_{UG}]$, the firm may be producing either in Germany or in the U.S., depending upon the past history of the exchange rate movements. Path dependencies imply that the optimal decision at each period depends on two aspects: (1) where the firm was producing before, (2) the prevailing exchange rate.

Path dependency implies that we use a backward dynamic programming process – one that is both backward and forward looking. The stochastic dynamic programming procedure used in the calculations is the same as the procedures used to determine the value of an American option. Table 3.5 shows the net present value of costs at

---

[145] See Copeland and Antikarov (2001), p. 180 for a discussion on switching options and path dependency.

$t=0,1,2,3$ depending on the path followed and the optimal switching behavior to pursue for each possible sequence of states of nature. The determination of cost-minimizing decisions at $t=1,2,3$ involve the following steps. First, the solution of the lattice is solved backward, starting from $t=3$: we calculate optimal decisions for the last period ($t=3$) for all possible exchange rates and for the two production strategies with which the firm may have entered the period. Since quantities equal to 100 units, the *real* costs of producing in Germany at a given period are 100. Cost-minimizing decisions for all states are obtained by comparing the costs of continuing the existing strategy to the costs of switching to the other strategy. Second, having obtained the best decisions at $t=3$, those at $t=2$ can be determined and so on.

Table 3. 5 Cost-Minimizing Decisions on Production Location

Nodes	S	Existing strategy	Real € costs of continuing existing production strategy		Real € costs of switching to alternate production strategy (k=€25)
			Cost-minimizing decisions at t=3		
G	1.33	G	100	<	133+25=158
H	1.10	G	100	<	10+25=135
I	0.90	G	100	<	90+25=115
J	**0.73**	**G**	**100**	**>**	**73+25=98**
G	1.33	U.S	133	>	100+25=**125**
H	1.10	U.S	110	<	100+25=125
I	0.90	U.S	90	<	100+25=125
J	0.73	U.S	73	<	100+25=125
			(Expected) cost-minimizing decisions at t=2		
D	1.21	G	100+0.5(100+100)=200	<	121+25+0.5(125+100)=263.5
E	1.00	G	100+0.5(100+100)=200	<	100+25+0.5(110+90)=225
F	**0.81**	**G**	**100+0.5(100+98)=199**	**>**	**81+25+0.5(90+73)=187.5**
D	**1.21**	**U.S**	**121+0.5(125+110)=238.5**	**>**	**100+25+0.5(100+100)=225**
E	1.00	U.S	100+0.5(110+90)=200	<	100+25+0.5(100+100)=225
F	0.81	U.S	81+0.5(90+73)=162.5	<	100+25+0.5(100+98)=224
			(Expected) cost-minimizing decisions at t=1		
B	1.10	G	100+0.5(200+200)=300	<	110+25+0.5(200+225)=347.5
C	0.90	G	100+0.5(200+187.5)=293.75	<	90+25+0.5(200+162.5)=296.25
B	1.10	U.S	110+0.5(200+225)=322.5	<	100+25+0.5(200+200)=325
C	0.90	U.S	90+0.5(162.5+200)=271.25	<	100+25+0.5(187.5+200)=318.75
			(Expected) cost-minimizing decisions t=0		
A	1.00	G	100+0.5(293.8+300)=396.9	<	100+25+0.5(322.5+271.3)=421.9
A	1.00	U.S.	100+0.5(322.5+271.3)=396.9	<	100+25+0.5(293.8+300)=421.9

Source: adapted from Capel (1997), p. 106. C stands for the production costs, S for the exchange rate, G for Germany. The € costs of the production location decisions that minimize expected costs are underlined.

At each node, decisions are based on two questions[146]: (i) assuming we have been in U.S. production mode at the previous state, would we stay in the U.S. or would we switch to Germany and pay the switching cost?, (ii) assuming we have been in Germany production mode at the previous state, would we stay in the Germany or would we switch to the U.S. and pay the switching cost? We can discount the expected cash flow costs along the event tree for both modes of operation and get a corresponding tree with the present values. The present value of costs at each stage of nature is equal to the expected value of costs discounted at a risk-adjusted discount rate plus the costs in the current period $C_{US/E}$. For example, the calculation for the present value of costs $PV_{US/E}$ at point E in figure 3.12 (b) is:

$$PV_{US/E} = \frac{p \times PV_{US/H} + (1-p)PV_{US/I}}{(1+WACC_{US})} + C_{US/E}$$

where p and $(1-p)$ are the objective probabilities for up and down movements. The optimal decision at each period t and at each knot is based on three scenarios, depending on the prevailing exchange rate and the previous production location:

(1) *Inertia*: the exchange rate has to cross the thresholds S_{GU} and S_{UG} before switching becomes optimal. The hysterisis band is delimited by these two switching points. This band is characterized by inertia, meaning that the firm will not undertake any operative measures. Within $[S_{GU}, S_{UG}]$, the exposure moves along $V^U(S;\phi)$ or $V^G(S;\phi)$, depending on the current production location.

(2) *Large Exchange Rate Depreciation* - € depreciates against the US$ to a level higher than S_{UG}: if the firm is currently producing in Germany, it keeps its production there. If it is currently producing in the U.S., it exercises its call on US$ and shifts production to Germany. The call places a ceiling on the costs in US$ relative to the costs in €. The optimal decision at node D in figure 3.12 (b) is:

$N_{US/D} = MIN(PV_{US/D}, PV_{G/D} + C_{UG}) = MIN(238.5, 200 + 25) = 225 \Rightarrow$ *switch to Germany*

with $N_{US/D}$ indicating the minimum costs at node D and C_{UG} the switching cost. Figure 3.13 below shows the calculation of the present value of costs at node B when the firm

---

[146] See Copeland and Antikarov (2001), p. 182.

initially produces in the U.S.[147]. In $t=2$, if $S=1.21$, the German firm exercises its call option and switches production to Germany. The knot at which $S=1.21$, $PV_{G/D} + k = 225$ corresponds to S_{UG}. The real option is more valuable "when the correlation between marginal costs in the two countries is decreasing, the standardization of products is high, switching costs are low, and exchange rate uncertainty is high"[148].

Figure 3. 13 (a) Call Payoff and (b) Present Value of costs at node B when Initial Production Facility in U.S.

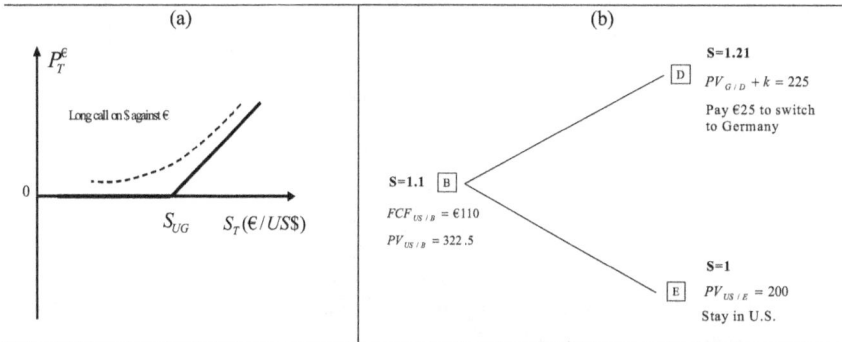

The option to switch production to Germany is like a call option. If the investment is now or never, the call's payoffs are shown by the solid line. If the investment can be postponed, the call option is valuable even if the project NPV is zero or negative[149]. When the firm gives up its option to wait, it can no longer take advantage of the volatility of the project's future value.

(3) *Large Exchange Rate Appreciation:* € appreciates against the US$ to a level lower than S_{GU}. If the firm is currently producing in the U.S., it will keep its production there. If it is currently producing in Germany, it exercises the put on the *US$*, and shifts its production to the U.S. Figure 3.14 (a) shows the calculation of the present value of costs at node C when the firm initially produces in Germany. The firm exercises its put and switches production to the U.S at $t=2$, when $S=0.81$. The knot at

---

[147] For example, $PV_{US/E}$ is the present value at node E when producing in the U.S. p is the probability of the exchange rate taking the values 1.33 or 1.1 at $t=3$. The *WACC* is assumed here to be zero and the FCF at E is 100. Therefore, $PV_{US/E} = (0.5 \times 110 + 0.5 \times 90) + 100$.

[148] See Kogut and Kulatilaka (1994), Capel (1997).

[149] See Brealey and Myers (2000), p. 626.

which $S=0.81$, $PV_{US/F} + k = 187.5$ corresponds to S_{GU}. The put places a ceiling on the costs in € relative to the costs in US$. The optimal decision at node F is as follows[150]:

$$N_{G/F} = MIN(PV_{G/F}, PV_{US/F} + C_{GU}) = MIN(199, 162.5 + 25) = 187.5 \Rightarrow switch\ to\ U.S.$$

Figure 3. 14 (a) Present Value of costs at node C when Initial Production Facility in Germany, (b) Put Payoff.

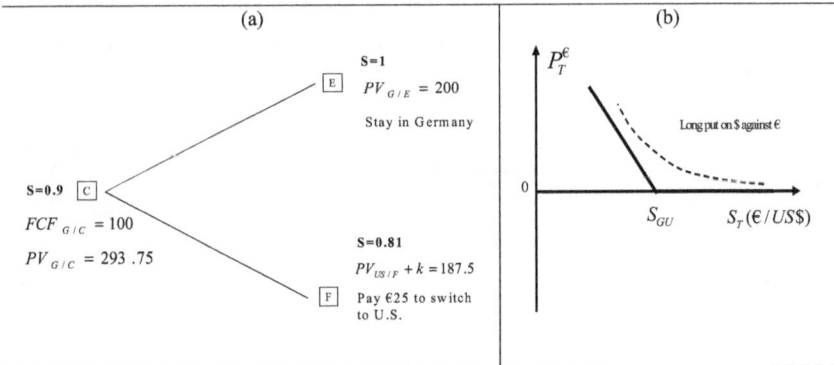

Figure 3.14 (b) shows the payoffs of the put implicitly owned by the firm when currently producing in Germany.

C. Contingent Planning and Exposure Asymmetries Measurement

A treasurer with domestic and foreign production sites could give the production department guidelines to switch to home currency costs if the real exchange rate is above a certain value, and to turn to foreign currency costs if it is below a value, and to keep the prevailing strategy if the exchange rate fluctuates between these two thresholds[151]. Here, the operating managers could give the production guidelines to switch production from USA to Germany if the real exchange rate is above S_{UG}, to turn to US production if it is below S_{GU}, and to stick to the prevailing strategy as long as the real exchange rate fluctuates between these two values. See figure 3.11 (b) above. To account for exposure asymmetries, contingent plans must be integrated into exposure measurement.

---

[150] If the firm continued to use German inputs, the costs would be €199. By switching, the costs are reduced to €187.5 [=0.81x100 + 25+0.5(90+73)].

[151] See Capel (1997), pp. 101-102.

D. Skewness of Costs Value Distribution and Exposure Asymmetries

The firm's exposure is affected by the distribution of foreign currency costs. As for an importer, the exposure profile is negatively sloped. For evaluating the effect of the switching option in terms of exposure asymmetries, we need to examine how the costs distribution in each period and the value distribution of costs at the beginning of the valuation period ($t=0$) are affected. Figure 3.15 below shows that the long call reduces the right tail of the costs value distribution, while the long put increases the left tail of the distribution. The expected value of costs is reduced. The effect is to increase the firm's exposure to €/US$ depreciation and reduce the exposure to €/US$ appreciation, and to positively skew the firm value distribution.

Figure 3. 15 Distribution of Costs Value

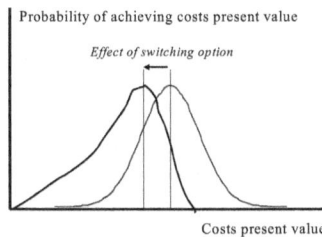

By reducing downside risk, investing in costs flexibility raises expected cash flows and firm value. Exchange rate volatility has therefore a positive effect on firm value[152]. The costs flexibility makes firm value volatility dependent on the exchange rate and implies heteroskedasticity of the conditional variance of firm value.

(i)   *Exposure of periodic cash flows is truncated:* the switching option truncates the costs distribution and the profits distribution, and makes it dependent on the current production location and on the exchange rate[153]. For example, if the firm is initially in the U.S., the costs exposure to the US$ is truncated (terminated) at S_{UG}.

---

[152] For example, the present value of costs PV_{US} when producing in the U.S. is equal to € 396.9.

[153] See Mello et al. (1995), p. 31.

(ii)   *Exposure of firm value at t=0* is convex and changes dramatically at the trigger points S_{GU} and S_{UG}. The distribution of the net present value of costs at *t=0* is skewed with a shorter left tail[154].

Since firm value reflects all future cash flows, small exchange rate changes can induce large changes in firm value.

3.6.1.2 Exit and Entry Options

Market entry modes can be in the form of foreign direct investments (FDI), wholly owned subsidiaries, joint venture, exporting, licensing[155]. The effect of exchange rate changes on decisions to enter/exit foreign markets can be analyzed using real option valuation techniques[156]. Exchange rate uncertainty has an effect on decisions to enter/leave foreign markets, because such decisions imply investment/disinvestment projects that entail an irreversible cost, can be postponed, and is contingent on the exchange rate.

Figure 3. 16 Switching Entry/Exit Option

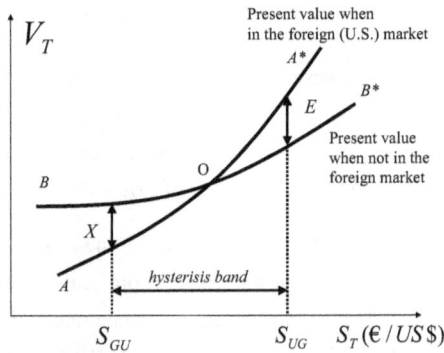

Figure 3.16 above shows the exposure profiles of a German firm contemplating entering/exiting the U.S. market, with S_T the exchange rate level and V_T the present

---

[154] The sunk cost *k* does not affect valuation calculations. See Brealy and Myers (2000), p. 123.
[155] See Shapiro (1999).

value of future cash flows. The exposure is path dependent, it depends on past exchange rates and on the firm's location when it enters period T:

- *German firm currently in the U.S. market (exposure AOA*)*: a US$ depreciation makes it less profitable to sell in the U.S. market. The firm's flexibility to leave the U.S. market is like a *long put on the US$*. However, even if revenues from U.S. sales are outweighed by the costs of producing the good, the German firm might continue selling in the U.S. market if the savings from leaving the market do not exceed the exit cost X. This hysterisis band where the firm does not act is delimited by the thresholds exchange rates S_{GU} and S_{UG}. The option to exit the U.S. market has a low value if the sunk costs to exit X is high and the cost E to re-enter is high.

- *German firm currently outside the U.S. market (exposure BOB*):* If a firm wants to enter or re-enter the market, it has to pay the entry costs E, for example the costs of hiring new labour. In that case, the firm is *long call on the US$*.

Exposure path dependencies associated with hysterisis imply that once the firm has entered/exited the U.S. market, the firm's current and future cash flow distributions are affected. The width of the hysterisis band depends on the *sunk costs* to exercise the option and on the *risk of exchange rate mean reversion*: exchange rate volatility creates an incentive to pursue a "wait and see" attitude[157]. The firm will wait for a more favorable exchange rate before entering, and will remain in the market for a more unfavorable exchange rate, the greater the perceived future uncertainty of the exchange rate[158]. The exposure is asymmetric at the thresholds S_{GU} and S_{UG}, at which the options are expected to be exercised.

Alternatively, the German firm could face the threat of entry of a foreign competitor in its domestic market. The German consumers' option to switch their purchasing to imported goods would be for the German firm like having written a put on the import-competitor's currency[159].

---

[156] See Dixit (1989a).
[157] Several studies have used option pricing methods to explain why Japanese firms did not leave the US market when the Japanese yen appreciated against the US-dollar in the 1980s. See comments in Sercu and Uppal (1995), p. 677.
[158] See Krugman (1989).
[159] See Sercu and Uppal (1995), p. 182.

3.6.2 Abandonment Options

Abandonment or termination options are American *put* options that give the right to rid oneself of a risky real asset, at a fixed price and for some liquidation value[160]. Long puts on foreign currency make possible abandoning a foreign exchange exposure by selling an underlying foreign real asset[161]. It can give the opportunity to stop negative cash flows by closing a foreign operation/subsidiary and re-deploy resources to more profitable investments, by giving an exporter the right to abandon selling in a foreign market, and so forth. The exercise price can be for example the sales value of a domestic plant and equipment and the set up costs of a new production facility in a foreign country. The switching option examined in section 3.6.1.1 can be interpreted in terms of abandonment option. If the € depreciates against the US$, the German firm continues producing domestically, whereas if the € appreciates, the firm exercises the option to abandon the domestic production facility and start producing in the U.S.

Figure 3. 17 (a) Exposure with Abandonment Option, (b) Present Value of Abandonment Put

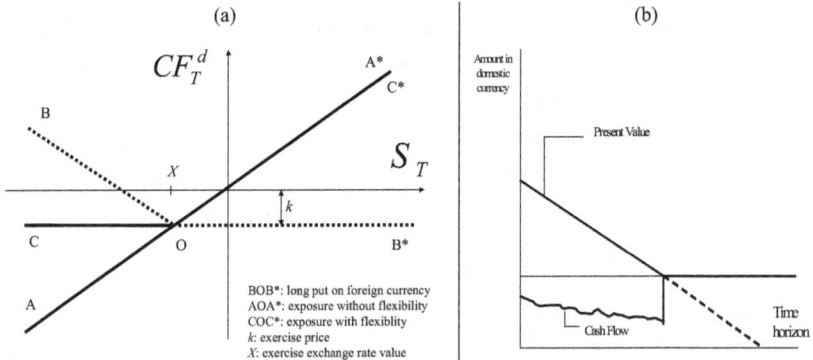

Source: adapted from Copeland (2001)[162]

Figure 3.17 (a) shows the effect on exposure of an abandonment option. The put is exercised at *X*. The put's payoff is positive for $S_T < X$. By eliminating large downside

---

[160] See Copeland and Antikarov (2002), p. 12.
[161] See, e.g., Aabo (1998).
[162] Adapted from T. Copeland, Trends in Valuation, NIVRA, Amsterdam, June 1, 2001 by Monitor Company Group, L.P.

risk, the abandonment option truncates the lower tail of the cash flow distribution and trims the event tree at the period the option is exercised. The distribution of firm value is skewed with a shorter left tail and with an increased mean value. As a result, the exposure profile is asymmetric at X. Figure 3.17 (b) shows that the abandonment put is exercised when the present value of the remaining cash flows falls below the liquidation value.

3.6.3 Exchange-Rate-Pass-Through Options

The literature on pricing has given little attention to two areas: (i) the option characteristic of pricing flexibility, (ii) the relationship between pricing flexibility and foreign exchange exposure.

3.6.3.1 Currency of Determination and Risk Sharing

A. Option to Exchange-Rate-Pass-Through and Cash Flow Volatility

The concept of exchange-rate-pass-through (henceforth, ERPT) provides a metric for assessing a firm's strategic pricing behavior[163]. It indicates how a firm alters the *nominal* foreign currency price of its good, to *pass through to customers changes in costs* due to currency movements. ERPT is commonly defined as the elasticity of the local-currency prices of imported goods with respect to the exchange rate. If we assume a firm exporting to a foreign country, with P_t the foreign-currency price of the product, and S_t the exchange rate measured as the price of one foreign-currency unit in terms of this firm's home currency, the (instantaneous) pass-through of the exchange rate change to the export price in foreign currency is given as[164]:

[3. 21]
$$\eta = -\frac{\partial P_t/\partial S_t}{P_t/S_t} = -\frac{\partial p_t}{\partial s_t}$$

where the lower-case letters denote logarithmic values, i.e. $x = \ln X$. ERPT is related to the concept of a product's currency of determination in a given market, which is the

---

[163] See Bodnar (1999). The term "strategic pricing" refers to long term corporate objectives, whereas "tactical pricing" refers to short term measures, such as giving discounts.
[164] See Kumakura (2001), p. 3.

currency in which the product's price is stable[165]. Because it affects domestic *real price risk* and involves an adjustment cost which is irreversible, that can be delayed, and that is contingent on the exchange rate, the flexibility to pass-through can be interpreted as a real option. Table 3.6 below highlights the relation between ERPT and currency of determination for the case of an exporter that has a long position in foreign currency.

Table 3. 6 Exchange-Rate-Pass-Through and Currency of Determination

$\eta = 1$	*Full ERPT*: local currency prices move in proportion to the exchange rate. ▪ risk is transferred to consumers, who bear all the exchange rate effect. ▪ equivalent to *indexing* the price in local currency to foreign exchange changes[166] or invoicing in domestic currency[167].
$\eta = 0$	*No ERPT*: no adjustment in local currency prices. ▪ all risk is retained by the firm[168]. ▪ currency of determination is unambiguously the local currency[169]. ▪ In perfectly competitive local markets, the price is independent of the exchange rate.
$0 < \eta < 1$	*Partial ERPT*: partial adjustment in local currency prices. ▪ *risk-sharing*: risk shared between the firm and consumers[170]. ▪ likely under imperfect competition if relative costs or the elasticity of demand are affected.

Typically, real options are associated with costs or quantity flexibilities. For example, export flexibility gives an exporter the flexibility to endogenously increase sales. The associated short term pricing decisions that lead to increased sales is generally not examined. It is possible to interpret the flexibility to adjust *nominal* foreign currency prices as a real option based on the following reasons:

---

[165] See Section 2.4 in chapter 2, O'Brien (1998), p. 6.

[166] See O'Brien (1998), p. 5, Milley (2000).

[167] See Levich (1998).

[168] It is supposed that export prices are invoiced in foreign currency. For example, the currency of determination of Merck's pharmaceutical products, a US drug company, is the local currency in which they are sold, since their prices are held fixed in local currencies. See Lewent and Kearney (1990).

[169] An example is the US firm Vulcan Materials Co. Since the currency of determination of metals is generally the US dollar in all markets, the currency of determination for Vulcan's products is US dollars. See Gardner and Shapiro (1984), pp. 6-17, O'Brien (1997), pp. 5-7.

[170] See O'Brien (1998), p. 6, Milley (2000). This would be possible if for example foreign competitors have hedged foreign exchange or they are "buying" market share. Partial ERPT is probable due to local competition.

(1) *setting price is not equivalent to setting quantity in imperfect information*: operating decisions regarding the "capacity planning" depends on the international pricing decisions[171]. Setting price is not equivalent to setting quantity in imperfect information. If competitors' prices and demands were known to the firm, choosing price would be equivalent to choosing the quantity exported. But if the firm is imperfectly informed about market conditions when it takes its decisions, setting price is not equivalent to setting the quantity[172].

(2) *adjustments in the nominal foreign price affect the domestic real price*: imperfectly competitive firms have the flexibility to adjust their domestic real prices by modifying their foreign nominal prices. They have some power to segment and price discriminate between national markets.

(3) *pricing adjustments are partially irreversible, can be delayed, and are contingent on the exchange rate:* adjustment costs in prices explain the partial irreversibility. Periodically adjusting prices is costly, in terms of the direct costs associated with changing price lists, as well as the indirect costs associated with damaging consumer goodwill/firm's reputation[173].

The extent to which prices and markups are related to exchange rate changes depends on industry and destination specific factors like the degree of market segmentation (whether the market is integrated or separated with barriers to arbitrage), product substituability (whether the product is homogenous or differentiated) and industry competitive structure. There is a negative relation between ERPT and exposure. A high ERPT narrows the distribution of cash flows (figure 3.18).

The ability to pass-through adverse exchange rate movements onto local prices provides a natural hedge, a "reduction in variability of cash flows that come from the normal way the firm does business"[174]. As a result, "the exchange rate exposure of a

---

[171] See Huchzermeier (2001), section 5.
[172] See Gottfries (1994) for a discussion on the industrial organization issue of whether firms compete in prices or quantities.
[173] See Brown (2001), p. 421.
[174] See Levich (1998), p. 584. This depends on the elasticity of demand. For instance, the demand for commodity goods, such as textiles and metals, is quite sensitive to price changes. In contrast, the prices of higher value products that are less sensitive to price increases, can be more easily protected in terms of the exporter's currency. See Klitgaard (1996).

monopolistic firm with the ability to pass its increases in costs through to customers may be small and undetectable" [175].

Figure 3. 18 Exchange Rate Risk with High and Low Exchange-Rate Pass-Through

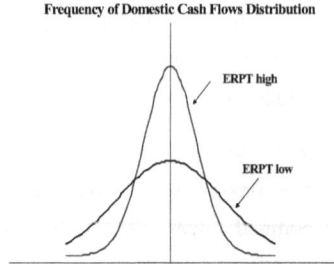

Frequency of Domestic Cash Flows Distribution

ERPT high

ERPT low

B. Tradeoff between Current Profit Margins and Future Market Shares

A monopolistic firm with some market power faces a market determined trade-off of price and quantity. After an appreciation of the euro (€) relative to the US$, a German exporter to the U.S. would have to decide how much to pass-through the US$ depreciation onto the U.S. customers:

- *No ERPT*: it could lower the € price so that the US$ price remains unaffected. The US$ price and volume sold in the U.S. market remain unchanged, but the markup of price over cost in € is reduced.

- *Full ERPT*: it could keep the € price unchanged by completely passing through the US$ depreciation to U.S. consumers. The profit margin would be unchanged, but the volume of sales would likely subsequently drop, leading to a lower level of profits[176].

- *Partial ERPT*: it may lower its profit margins to absorb only part of the exchange rate change, thereby passing-through only part of the appreciation to the importer's

---

[175] See Levich (1998), p. 584.
[176] Lessard and Lightstone (1986) distinguish the effect on the quantities sold (market share effect) from the effect on profitability (profit margin effect).

price. Both the € price and U.S. sales falls[177]. With either complete or partial pass-through the effect on profit margin is negative.

On the other hand, a US$ appreciation presents the German firm with desirable choices. It can either (i) increase its markup by maintaining the US$ price (no ERPT): the € price rises, while the US sales are unaffected, raising the profit margins; or (ii) decrease the US$, hoping to increase market share (full/partial ERPT): with full ERPT, the € price remains constant while US sales rise, raising profit margin. With partial ERPT, the € price and the US sales both rise.

3.6.3.2 Price Commitment versus Price Flexibility

A. Exchange-Rate Pass-Through and Foreign Exchange Exposure

A model of duopoly examines the relation between ERPT and exposure[178] (calculations in Appendix B). An exporter produces with domestic and imported inputs and competes in a foreign market with a foreign import-competing firm with sales only in the foreign market and with only domestic costs[179]. The *foreign consumers' preferences* over the differentiated goods in the foreign market are represented by the CES utility function:

[3. 22] $$U(q_1, q_2) = [\alpha q_1^\rho + (1 - \alpha) q_2^\rho]^{1/\rho}$$

where $U(.)$ represents the consumers' utility function, q_1 the quantity of the exporter's product sold in the foreign market, q_2 the quantity of the foreign import-competing firm's product sold in the foreign market. The extent to which foreign consumers favor the exporter's goods in consumption is given by α, a preference weighting parameter, which represents the nominal expenditure share allocated to the exporter's goods. The industry structure is captured by ρ, a parameter measuring the substitutability between

---

[177] The extent of the change in profits when pass-through occurs is determined by the elasticity of US demand for the foreign product. In the extreme case of perfectly inelastic demand, the profits of the foreign firm are unaffected.

[178] See Bodnar, Marston and Dumas (2002). The objective of this model is to determine the relationship between pass-through behavior and exposure. But this model does not investigate the effects of industry structure on exposure. Industry structure in this model is exogenous to exchange rate changes. See Marston (2001), p. 150. The structural model of exposure above, is, to our knowledge, the only one that has been directly empirically tested.

[179] The firm is engaged in quantity competition with the other firm, so it treats prices as exogenous.

the two products, with competitive industries defined as industries with high substitutability. By assuming differential degree of substitution across the goods, we can examine ERPT and exposure elasticities for various degrees of industry competitive structure.

An expression for the *ERPT elasticity* shows the channels that transmit the effect of exchange rate changes to prices:

[3.23]
$$\eta_1 = -\frac{d \ln p_1}{d \ln S} = (1 - \gamma)(1 - \rho\lambda)$$

with $\gamma = Sc_1 / (c_1^* + Sc_1)$ the fraction of marginal costs due to foreign currency-based inputs, and λ, the market share of the exporting firm in the foreign market. The impact of a higher product substitutability is to moderate the pass-through of exchange rate changes into foreign currency prices, because the increase in substitutability raises the elasticity of demand faced by the exporter and smaller price changes are thus necessary to achieve the new profit maximizing level of sales in the foreign market:

[3.24]
$$\frac{d \eta_1}{d \rho} = -\lambda(1 - \gamma) < 0 \qquad \text{if} \qquad \gamma < 1$$

An expression for the *exposure* can be written as:

[3.25]
$$\delta = \frac{d \ln \pi_1^*}{d \ln S} = \underbrace{1}_{\substack{CONVERSION \\ EFFECT}} + \underbrace{(1-\gamma)\rho(1-\lambda)}_{\substack{MARKET \\ SHARE \\ EFFECT}} + \underbrace{\frac{(1-\gamma)\lambda\rho^2(1-\lambda)}{[1-\rho(1-\lambda)]}}_{\substack{PROFIT \\ MARGIN \\ EFFECT}}$$

ERPT and exposure are related, since they both depend on industry structure. ERPT and exposure are both function of (i) firm's competitiveness (cost ratio), (ii) industry competitive structure (substituability), and (iii) market power (market share). These aspects define the firm's supply and demand conditions in the foreign market and determine the firm's pricing flexibility.

This expression permits to separate the full impact of the exchange rate change on profits into three different effects: (1) a *conversion effect*, (2) a *market share effect* representing the change of the share of total expenditures accruing to the exporter, (3) a *profit margin effect* representing the impact of the change in the exchange rate on the domestic-currency profit margin of the exporter. The market share and the profit margin effects combined represent the competitive effect. This competitive effect arises because the two firms have costs in different currencies. The exposure elasticity is always greater than one, since the first two terms together are greater than one and the third term, the profit margin effect, is also positive if the exporter uses some domestic inputs, that is, if $\delta < 1$. Thus, the competitive exposure of a random foreign currency cash flow will be relatively *greater than* the contractual exposure of a fixed foreign currency cash flow[180]. This corresponds to a curvilinear exposure (concave/convex).

When the US\$ depreciates, a more competitive industry reduces the value of the long put and decreases the degree of ERPT. The ability to preserve the value of the ERPT put option will depend on the firm's ability to segment the markets and successfully price discriminate. A more competitive industry leads to a lower ERPT because of the firm's reduced ability to preserve the value of its ERPT option. The firm will lose substantial market shares if the industry is very competitive. For a given level of market share, the exposure is affected positively by an increase in product's substitutability:

[3. 26] $$\frac{d\delta}{d\rho} = (1-\gamma)(1-\lambda)\frac{(1-\rho)^2 + 2\lambda^2\rho^2 + \lambda\rho(4-3\rho)}{[1-\rho(1-\lambda)]^2} > 0 \qquad \text{with } 0 < \rho,\ \lambda < 1$$

Since ERPT is negatively related to product's substituability, ERPT is negatively related to exposure. As substituability increases, keeping market share fixed, ERPT is lower and exposure higher[181].

B. Pricing Flexibility and Foreign Exchange Exposure Asymmetries

Asymmetric exposures have been explained by the asymmetric sensitivity of profit margins as a result of asymmetric ERPT behavior. However, the discussion from a risk management perspective should be in terms of asymmetric effects on profits and firm value. The cash flow and value implications of ERPT decisions depend on the

---

[180] See Bodnar et al. (2002), p. 212.
[181] There is evidence that ERPT varies both across and within industries. See Yang (1997), Coughlin and Pollard (2000). The hypothesis that industries with less competitive market structure have higher ERPT is supported. A study of the effects of exchange rate fluctuations in the (formerly) G7 countries has reported that real home currency appreciations have adversely affected traditional sectors to a greater extent than high-tech sectors in part because traditional sector firms are more likely to be price takers and are less able to insulate themselves from the effect of exchange rate appreciation. See Burgess and Knetter (1996).

elasticity of demand/industry structure. Changes in real prices lead to more than proportional changes in real cash flow/quantity because the *elasticity of demand is greater than 1* for a profit maximizer.

- Passing-through foreign currency appreciations is like a *long call* if the elasticity of demand is higher than *1*. The firm does not benefit from higher profit margins in the short term but in the long term, firm value is increased.

- Passing-through foreign currency depreciations protect profit margins in the short term. But this strategy is not value-maximizing if the elasticity of demand is greater than *1*. This is like a *long put*.

The exposure is asymmetric depending on the pricing behavior and assumption about elasticities.

C. Price Commitment versus Price Flexibility

Invoicing in domestic currency protects the firm against adverse exchange rate changes, but eliminates the possibility to exploit beneficial exchange rate changes. Invoicing in domestic currency can be viewed as a *natural hedge*. The tradeoff between the benefit of setting a natural hedge and having flexibility is discussed in chapter 6.

An other issue is the choice between price commitment and flexibility in setting prices under exchange rate uncertainty. *Price commitment* means that firms set prices before the exchange rate uncertainty is resolved, whereas *pricing flexibility* means deferring setting price until exchange rates are known[182]. Pricing flexibility has relatively more value under high exchange rate volatility.

Exchange rate volatility determines the *risk of exchange rate mean reversion* and the option value-of-waiting[183]. If an exchange rate change is expected to revert, the costs related to both the price change and the corresponding quantity adjustments may not be justified.

---

[182] See Chang and Lapan (2001).
[183] See Dixit (1989), p. 634.

- *exchange rate change is considered temporary and likely to be soon reversed*: there is little incentive for adjusting local currency prices and sales volume. Therefore, the response may be to completely absorb the exchange rate change in the profit margin. For example, in response to an adverse exchange rate change, the firm would hold market share and preserve customer relations, at the expense of short-run margins.

- *exchange rate change is considered permanent*: in response to a large and persistent exchange rate change, firms are more likely to change their prices rather than adjust their profit margins, since adjustments of supply, or expanding or contracting production and distribution, may be justified[184].

The value of the ERPT option increases with exchange rate volatility since a higher exchange rate uncertainty increases the value of deferring action and the profitability of maintaining price flexibility. As such, the exercise of the ERPT option implies that ERPT is usually negatively related to the variance of the exchange rate, since "the worse the quality of the signal coming from an exchange rate change, the less likely the firm will make a pass-through decision"[185].

Volkswagen in the 1970s for example made operating adjustments that had the effect to increase its pricing flexibility in the U.S. market[186]. Volkswagen had achieved its export prominence on the basis of low-priced, stripped-down, low maintenance cars. The appreciation of the DM against the US$ in the early 1970s, however, effectively ended VW's ability to compete primarily on the basis of price:

- In the short run Volkswagen had to decide to what extent it should change the US$ price of its cars, trading off sales volume against profit margin[187].

---

[184] See Froot and Kemplerer (1989), Kasa (1992).
[185] See Friberg (1998), p. 4. Consequently, ERPT should be greater and exposure lower in countries where fluctuations in exchange rates have displayed greater persistence, and in countries where exchange rate has been less volatile. See McCarthy (2000), p. 5.
[186] See Shapiro (1999), p. 352, Sercu and Uppal (1995), p. 489.
[187] "In the 1970's Volkswagen's profits from exports to the US were severely affected by the fall of the US$ from DEM/US$ 4 to about DEM/US$ 2". See Sercu and Uppal (1995), p. 489. "The company lost more than $310 million in 1974 alone attempting to maintain its market share by lowering prices. To compete in the long run, VW was forced to revise its product line and sell relatively high-priced cars to middle-income consumers, from an extended product line, on the basis of quality and styling rather than cost". See Shapiro (1999), p. 352. It has been argued that VW should have used US$

- In the longer term, VW had little pricing flexibility to pass-through the US$ depreciation. VW could manage its exposure only by developing new differentiated products with lower price elasticities of demand and by establishing production facilities in lower-cost nations[188].

The duration of the exposure was determined by its operating flexibility to make structural changes to support a policy of higher ERPT.

3.6.4 Growth Options

The value of growth options is function of the firm's "perceived ability to develop new profitable projects"[189]. Growth options are the "opportunities a firm may have to invest capital so as to increase the profitability of its existing product or to expand into new products or markets"[190]. A firm could acquire growth options to manage its foreign exchange exposures for example by:

(a) *Setting up a foreign subsidiary*: establishing a subsidiary in a foreign country would make it easier to introduce a new product in the local market. This would give the firm a growth option to expand its product line at a later point in time[191]. In the future, the firm could respond to unexpected favorable exchange rate fluctuations by expanding into the foreign market. At the time of the initial investment, the firm should assess the value of the option to expand into other products or into other markets[192]. This growth option can be interpreted as a long call on the foreign currency. The expansion will take place if the increase of the project's present value is larger than the expected additional investment.

(b) *Investing in product cycle flexibility:* investing in a shorter product cycle time gives a growth option to boost competitiveness from compressing the time it takes to bring new and improved products to market. Higher productivity flexibility could help a firm mitigate the effect of exchange rate induced changes in competitiveness

---

financing in proportion to its net dollar cash flow from U.S. sales. This strategy would have cushioned the impact of the DM appreciation. See Sercu and Uppal (1995), Shapiro (1999), p. 360.

[188] "Volkswagen's long run problem was to decide whether to continue competing in the US market, and if so, whether or not it should move production from Germany to the US, or to Latin-America". See Sercu and Uppal (1995), p. 489.

[189] See Grinblatt and Titman (2002), p. 392.

[190] See Shapiro (1999), p. 790.

[191] See Carter et al. (2003), p. 14.

[192] See Kogut (1983), p. 48.

through changes in relative prices. For example, it has been reported that "during the late 1980s and early 1990s, despite the strength of the yen and the D-mark, Japanese and German firms made impressive gains [in productivity] against their American competitors, not least in the car industry"[193]. This growth option can be interpreted as a long put on the foreign currency.

3.6.5 Global Supply Chain Network

A. Portfolio of Real Compound Options

Because of their foreign operation's network or supply chain network, multinational corporates *(MNCs)* own a portfolio of real options[194]. An *MNCs'* operating flexibility can be viewed as a "portfolio of real compound options that are exercised in response to the demand, price and exchange rate contingencies faced by firms in a global supply chain context"[195]. Like learning options, compound options are options on options whose value is contingent on other options[196]. The value drivers of compound option value include[197] (i) "stochastic recourse", e.g., to postpone distribution logistics decisions until after the uncertainty of the exchange rate is resolved. "Stochastic recourse can depend on either exchange rate/price scenarios, demand scenarios, or both", (ii) "the ability to make multiple resource deployments, e.g., expand/contract production capacity within a global manufacturing and distribution network"[198].

In figure 3.19 an *MNC* could exercise one of its 12 options by adjusting its global configuration in response to an exchange rate shock. The value of operational flexibility in a global supply chain network can be exploited through (i) global coordination, (ii) transfer pricing, (iii) knowledge transfer[199].

The multiple options may interact rather than being value additive. The value of a portfolio of options is generally less than the sum of separate or independent option values. For example, the "presence of a later option can enhance the value of the

---

[193] See The Economist, August 18th 2001, p. 50.
[194] See Cohen and Huchzermeier (1998), Huchzermeier (2001).
[195] See Kogut and Kulatilaka (1995).
[196] See Copeland and Antikarov (2001), p. 163.
[197] See Cohen and Huchzermeier (1998), section 21.2.
[198] Several studies on multinational corporates *(MNCs)* performance have documented that *MNCs* build value by increasing the flexibility of their operating networks. See, e.g., Kogut (1983), Dunning and Rugman (1985).
[199] See Cohen and Huchzermeier (1999), p. 1.

underlying asset for a prior option, while exercising an earlier option may alter the scale of (and in the case of the option to abandon, may extinguish) a later option"[200].

Figure 3. 19 Supply Chain Network and Operational Flexibility[201]

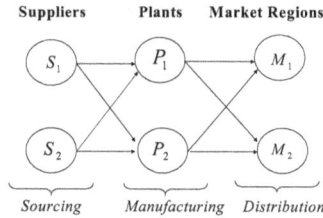

3.7 Financial Flexibility Options and their Effects on Foreign Exchange Exposure

3.7.1 Interaction between Real Options and Financial Flexibility Options

A. Relevance of Financial Flexibility Options for Economic Exposure

Theoretical studies generally assimilate economic exposure to the exposure of operating cash flows and typically ignore financial flexibilities in a firm's financial structure. A reason is that models of exposure typically examine the exposure of a single-period cash flow and ignore the fact that current asset/liabilities will ultimately be reflected into cash flows. But over a valuation period, one cannot ignore the economic relevance of contractual exposures. Although contractual foreign cash flows are converted with nominal exchange rates, they are then adjusted for inflation for economic exposure measurement. Financial flexibility can be interpreted as *financial flexibility options* and can be valued with option pricing methods[202].

B. Interaction between Real Options and Financial Flexibility Options

Although financial flexibility options make nominal adjustments, they have real effects. Of interest in terms of exposure asymmetries is the interaction between

---

[200] See Trigeorgis (2002).
[201] See Shi (2003), p. 27.
[202] See Muralidhar (1992), Trigeorgis (2002).

financial flexibility options and real options. To evaluate this interaction, one needs to understand the interdependency between corporate investment and financing decisions[203]. The following examples clarify this aspect:

- *Strategic pricing behavior in imperfect capital markets*: an exporter who is financially pressed could pass-through relatively more foreign currency depreciations, so as to limit adverse profit margins effects in the short term, although this may not be value-maximizing and may have adverse consequences on future market shares[204].

- *Tradeoff between natural hedges and operating flexibility*: natural hedges, e.g., through foreign debts, can reduce the firm's operating flexibility (see chapter 2/2.4.4, chapter 6/6.3.3).

- *Interaction between financial hedging and real options*: financial hedges and real options can be used in a complementary way. As such, financial hedges can increase the effect on firm value of operating flexibility (see chapter 6/6.3.2).

- *Agency costs* can create a link between financial policy and production decisions[205].

- *Risky debts* can lead to underinvestment[206] and make the exercise of real options less likely.

3.7.2 Capital Structure and Financial Flexibility Options

Adjustments in financial structure affect exposure through cash flows or the cost of capital. In imperfect capital markets, the cost of capital depends on the capital structure. A firm can change its mix of debt and equity to reduce the cost of capital and its exposure[207].

---

[203] This is noted for example by Trigeorgis (2002), p. 18.
[204] See Gottfries (1991). See also section 3.5.2.
[205] See Mello et al. (1995).
[206] See Myers (1977).
[207] "An increase in debt capacity of the firm results in tax shields that have some value, because interest is tax deductible. The value of the tax shields is a function of the corporate and stockholder personal tax rates". See Demacopoulos (1987), p. 207.

A. Flexibility in Corporate Tax Liability

Flexibility in tax jurisdiction implies that a multinational firm can mitigate tax differentials and influence the costs of leverage by shifting income and/or tax shields across subsidiaries. The flexibility to shift profits to favorable geographical tax jurisdiction can lower the global tax liability and increase a firm's value[208]. This option could involve several forms of funds transfer[209], such as *sale-and-lease-back* arrangements, *transfer-pricing* adjustments, *cross-guarantees of subsidiary debt*, or a variety of other mechanisms. These types of cross-borders measures could make difficult the assessment of a firm's exposure to a particular currency.

B. Contractual Financial Flexibility

Multiple currency price lists. A company's cash flows may vary non-linearly with changes in exchange rates when contracts with embedded optionality are used. A firm offering *multiple "currency price lists"* for its products or services would have a nonlinear exposure, because it would implicitly grant an option to its customers[210]. Dual currency pricing for example, is used in situations where the provider has given the customer the option to pay in one of two different currencies[211]. By doing so, the firm has implicitly written a put option to the customer, without receiving a premium.

Bond with asymmetric payoff. We consider a second example of a financial contract with asymmetric payoff that could be a source of exposure asymmetries[212]. We assume a U.K. company that issued bonds giving the holder, at maturity T, the choice between £ 10,000 and € 20,000. If the holder is a U.K. investor, he would view such a bond as a £ 10,000 bond plus a call on € 20,000 at the exercise price $X=£/€$ 0.5. The investor receives £ 10,000, but has the right to exchange the £ 10,000 for € 20,000. By doing so, the issuing U.K. company has implicitly written a call option to the bondholder. The company could then hedge itself against potential losses by buying a call that offsets the implicit call it has written.

---

[208] See, e.g., Muralidhar (1992), ch. 2., for an option pricing model valuing tax flexibility under exchange rate uncertainty.
[209] See Kogut (1983), p. 46, Sercu and Uppal (1995), pp. 635-637, Singh and Hodder (2000), p. 854.
[210] See Giddy and Dufey (1995), p. 55.
[211] Dual currency pricing is also used in situations where a customer has requested a price for a service or product in low currencies. See Milley (2000), p. 3.
[212] This example is from Sercu and Uppal (1995), p. 183.

Contractual negotiation flexibility: a firm could be given the possibility to renegotiate the terms of its contracts. For example, it could get a price discount from a foreign supplier if the currency of the supplier has depreciated substantially against the firm's currency[213].

C. Financial Management Flexibility in Timing

Flexibility in frequency of cash flows: for example, during the Asian financial crisis in 1997 that began in Thailand, Avon Products, an American cosmetics firm, decided to reduce currency risk "by having the Asian units remit earnings weekly instead of monthly"[214].

Flexibility in debt redemption: foreign exchange exposure can play a role in debt-denomination decisions[215]. For instance, an exporter that "sells to a foreign market and that diminishes its exposure by means of a foreign currency loan. If real exchange rates change so that at some future date it is no longer profitable to sell on the foreign market, the firm ends up having foreign currency costs and no foreign currency revenues (if the loan does not allow for accelerated redemption)"[216]. After an exchange rate change, a firm with financial flexibility could "restructure the firm's long-term financing to include a component of foreign currency assets or liabilities that permanently alter the firm's financial exposure"[217].

3.7.3 Hedges with Asymmetric Payoffs

Since exposure is by definition an after-hedge measure, financial hedging with asymmetric cash flows payoffs and asymmetric hedging behavior make exposure asymmetric:

---

[213] See Shapiro (1999), p. 363.
[214] See Shapiro (1999), p. 363.
[215] See Giddy (1994), pp. 480-483.
[216] See Capel (1997), p. 103.
[217] See Levich (1998), p. 595. Adjusting the currency, tenor and mix of debt can be used to manage economic exposures. This can provide protection for exposures that are relatively constant through time but it is less effective for variable exposures. But the flexibility to make such changes ex-post provides a non-linear hedge.

(a) *Use of financial hedging instruments with asymmetric payoff:* exposure can be asymmetric as a result of asymmetric financial hedging. Currency options for example, would convexify the exposure profile by reducing the left tail of the cash flow distribution, but at the expense of a reduction in the mean cash flows reflecting the option premium[218].

(b) *Exposure management based on aversion to downside risk:* risk managers' asymmetric perception of risk could explain asymmetric hedging strategies. Exposure management may not be based on a general aversion to exchange risk but on an aversion to downside exchange risk. It has been argued that the likelihood and magnitude of an unfavorable outcome rather than the variances of the company's market value or cash flows should be the concern of risk management[219]. As such, risk managers may perceive risk in terms of outcomes entailing a loss rather than in terms of the dispersion of outcomes. For this reason, exchange rate changes that have adverse effects on firm value could be managed, while beneficial changes are left unmanaged. The result of this asymmetry in attention paid by managers to positive and negative changes would make foreign exchange exposure larger to beneficial changes than to adverse ones.

(c) *Poor risk management:* although a firm could be hedging its exposure, poor risk management could result in a concave exposure profile. If the firm is unable to protect against adverse exchange rate movements and unable to exploit favorable movements, then the firm will have a piecewise concave exposure[220].

(d) *Selective hedging:* financial hedges can be put in place because of unexpected as well as anticipated exchange rate movements, that is, a treasurer could hedge with a view or without a view on future exchange rates. Firms could hedge only positions for which they expect a currency loss while leaving open positions for which they expect a currency gain[221]. Such selective hedging strategies would make a firm's exposure asymmetric.

---

[218] See Jorion (1997), p. 279.
[219] See Stulz (1996).
[220] See Andren (2001).
[221] See Brown and Khokher (2000), Glaum (2000), Glaum (2001).

4. Asymmetric Foreign Exchange Exposure and Strategic Real Options

Exposure asymmetries reflect a firm's real options and financial flexibility options. The underlying of a real option is a real tangible asset, e.g., a foreign production plant or a business unit. The uncertainty of a real option's underlying is generally assumed to be *exogenous*, whereby it is meant that the actions of the firm associated with the exercise of options have no influence on the uncertainty of the expected cash flow from exercising the option and undertaking a project.

For oligopolists, the uncertainty of the underlying cannot be assumed exogenous. Typically, the actions of a firm implied by the exercise of real options affect the actions of its competitors and other market participants, and consequently the nature of the uncertainty the firm faces. In the foreign exchange exposure literature, this endogeneity can be related to the notion of *indirect exposure*. The uncertainty of the underlying of a *strategic real option* is endogenously determined, that is, it is influenced by the actions of the firm and other market participants over the valuation period.

This chapter examines the effects on exposure of strategic real options. Two related issues are also examined. First, other factors, e.g. macroeconomic or political risks, can affect a firm's foreign cash flow volatility and as a result its foreign exchange exposure. Second, a firm might be engaged in different activities with differently exposed cash flows. Portfolio effects influence a firm's overall cash flows exposure. The plan of this chapter is as follows. Section 4.1 discusses the "indirect exposure" of oligopolists in terms of real options and economic rent. Section 4.2 and 4.3 assess the effects of strategic real options on exposure. Section 4.4 examines the portfolio effects that characterize a firm's overall exposure profile.

4.1 Indirect Foreign Exchange Exposure and Shared Options

4.1.1 Industry Structure and Indirect Foreign Exchange Exposure

A. Indirect Foreign Exchange Exposure

Strategic real options imply that the behaviour of other market participants makes the uncertainty of the firm's real options endogenous. In imperfectly competitive markets, the possibility arises for strategic behavior. Whereas in perfect competition, market constraints dictate that the firm's only decisions are whether and how much to produce, in imperfect competition, firms must assess the likely response of competitors, consumers, and foreign governments to their range of possible actions[1]. The implication is that a firm can be indirectly exposed through its strategic interactions with other market participants, and that exposure asymmetries should be viewed as resulting from "strategic real options"[2].

- *Direct exposure*: a firm can make operating adjustments to manage the effects on firm value resulting from exchange rate changes. The exposure resulting from a firm's activities and operating responses, such as switching between different production locations or between export markets is called "direct exposure"[3].

- *Indirect exposure*: in an oligopolistic industry, a firm's exposure depends not only on how it is affected and reacts, but also on how its competitors, customers, and suppliers are affected and react. The exposure resulting from these indirect effects is called "indirect exposure"[4].

Table 4.1 below shows that a chain view encompassing these interrelations is necessary to have a complete view of a firm's competitive exposure. A firm would prefer to sell its products and earn profits in markets with strong currencies, and incur sourcing and production costs in markets with weak currencies. Direct exposure is associated with these direct effects. Other things equal, a firm is better off as a real exchange rate change strengthens its customers and suppliers, and weakens its competitors. Moreover, a firm would indirectly benefit when the position of its competitors deteriorates, when its suppliers are enjoying healthy markets, and when an exchange rate change benefits its customers, as shown in the lower part of the table[5].

---

[1] See, e.g., Varian (1999).
[2] Strategic options are generally defined as the "future opportunities that are created by today's investments", whereas real options are defined as "the subset of strategic options in which the exercise decision is largely triggered by market-priced risk, a risk that is captured in the value of traded security". See Amram and Kulatilaka (2000), p. 10. In other studies, the term "strategic real options" is used. See, e.g., Sparla (2001).
[3] See Pringle and Connolly (1993).
[4] See Pringle and Connolly (1993).
[5] See Pringle and Connolly (1993), Levich (1998), pp. 570-571.

Table 4. 1 Channels of Exposure to Foreign Exchange Risk - Direct and Indirect Exposures

	Home Currency Strengthens	*Home Currency Weakens*
Direct Economic Exposure		
Sales Abroad	Unfavorable - Revenue worth less in home currency terms	Favorable - Revenue worth more
Sources Abroad	Favorable - Inputs cheaper in home currency terms	Unfavorable - Inputs more expensive
Profits Abroad	Unfavorable - Profits worth less	Favorable - Profits worth more
Indirect Economic Exposure		
Competitor that sources abroad	Unfavorable - Competitor's margins improve	Favorable - Competitor's margins decrease
Supplier that sources abroad	Favorable - Supplier's margins improve	Unfavorable - Supplier's margins decrease
Customer that sells abroad	Unfavorable - Customer's margins decrease	Favorable - Customer's margins improve
Customer that sources abroad	Favorable - Customer's margins improve	Unfavorable - Customer's margins decrease

Source: Pringle and Connolly (1993), p. 66.

Theoretical predictions on exposure and real options generally neglect indirect exposures. Direct exposure has been examined in *partial equilibrium* and static models, and typically considered the case of a monopolist[6]. The prediction that a falling domestic currency promotes the competitiveness of exporting and import-competing firms and has an adverse effect on importing firms is based on this type of analysis. In contrast, *general equilibrium* models suggest that the sign of exposure often turns on assumptions about consumers' demand shifts and the strategic behavior of competitors[7]. The message of these models is twofold: (i) an oligopolist's exposure cannot simply be inferred from its sector of activity (i.e., from whether it is long/short in foreign currency), (ii) whether an oligopolist benefits or suffers following an exchange rate shock cannot be determined analytically and is an empirical question.

---

[6] See, e.g., Shapiro (1975), Hodder (1982), Levi (1994). Some studies, e.g., Shapiro (1975), developed oligopolistic models, but since they did not consider firms' reoptimization after an exchange rate shock, their treatment was actually analogous to the case of a firm under monopoly.
[7] These models incorporate demand-side effects and the effect of firms' reoptimization after an exchange rate change. See, e.g., Choi (1986), Luehrman (1990), Luehrman (1991), Marston (2001).

B. Insights and Limitations of Exposure Models with Strategic Interactions

A *Cournot duopoly* model illustrates the importance of industry structure and strategic interactions between firms as determinants of foreign exchange exposure[8]. This shows the complexity of determining the demand and cost derivatives necessary for estimating the exposure of imperfectly competitive firms. An exporting firm's exposure is determined by the relative importance of a competitive effect resulting from the strategic interaction between the firm and its competitor, and a conversion effect resulting from the necessity to convert the firm's foreign currency cash flows. When these two effects have opposite signs, the exporter's exposure can be negative, meaning that it could be adversely affected by a home currency depreciation.

This model consists of a domestic country (Germany) and a foreign country (US), and two firms, one based in each country. A euro-based German exporter (firm 1) and a local American firm (firm 2) compete in the US market. Both firms are assumed to sell only in the US market. Each firm manufactures its products only in its domestic country; the German exporter has costs based in euro and the foreign US firm in US\$. The German exporter produces q^1 units of its goods at a price in US\$ of p^1, while the local US firm produces q^2 units at a price in US\$ of p^2. The goods produced by the firms are assumed to be heterogeneous so that substituability between the goods can play an explicit role. The firms' inverse demand functions take the general form[9]:

[4. 1] $\qquad p^1 = D^1(q^1, q^2)$ $\qquad\qquad D_1^1 < 0$

[4. 2] $\qquad p^2 = D^2(q^1, q^2)$ $\qquad\qquad D_2^2 < 0$

The two firms' demand functions are tied together by the two goods substituability ($D_2^1, D_1^2 < 0$). $C^1(q^1)$ is the total cost function for the exporting firm measured in euro

---

[8] This "non-cooperative Nash equilibrium in quantities" model has been developed by Marston (2001), based on the model of duopoly from Dixit (1986), pp. 108-115. According to Dixit, "any model with heterogeneous products becomes unwieldy once more than two firms are introduced". Other Cournot models of exposure can be found in Luehrman (1990), Bodnar (1999), pp. 15-16. The interpretation of the term "general equilibrium" usually implies models with interaction between competing firms and consumers. See, e.g., Bodnar (1999), p. 15. However, this can have a different meaning in this context. Knetter (1992), p. 5, says that this type of analysis is "partial equilibrium in nature in that the producer's actions are assumed to have no effect on the exchange rate".
[9] The quantity competition model is more conveniently solved using inverse, rather than direct demand functions (the latter of which relate output to prices in the two markets). See Marston (2001).

and $C^2(q^2)$ the total cost function in dollars for the US firm. Profits in each firm's own currency can be stated as:

[4. 3] $\qquad \pi_1^{\epsilon} = sq^1 D^1(q^1, q^2) - C^1(q^1)$

[4. 4] $\qquad \pi_2^{\$} = q^2 D^2(q^2, q^1) - C^2(q^2)$

where s is the €/US\$ exchange rate. A firm is assumed to believe that the other firm's output is linked to its own by a "conjectural variation" relation:

[4. 5] $\qquad dq^j / dq^i = v^i(q^1, q^2) \qquad j, i = 1 \ or \ 2, \ with \ j \neq i$

Given the firms' conjectural variations to allow for possible interaction between the decisions of the two competing firms, the first-order conditions for profit maximization are obtained by setting the perceived marginal profits equal to zero[10]:

[4. 6] $\qquad \dfrac{\partial \pi_1^{\epsilon}}{\partial q^1} = s[D^1(q^1, q^2) + q^1 D_1^1 + q^1 D_2^1 v^1] - C_1^1 = 0$

[4. 7] $\qquad \dfrac{\partial \pi_2^{\$}}{\partial q^2} = D^2(q^1, q^2) + q^2 D^2 + q^2 D_1^2 v^2 - C_2^2 = 0$

The firms *simultaneously* maximize their profits by choosing the quantity of output to produce and let the market determine the price. From equation [4.6], we see that the perceived marginal revenue of the exporter, M, measured in US\$, is expressed as $M = D^1(q^1, q^2) + q^1 D_1^1 + q^1 D_2^1 v^1$. The second-order and stability conditions are given in appendix D.

The duopoly equilibrium is defined by the pair of first-order conditions [4.6] and [4.7]. Using comparative static methods, we can examine the effects of a depreciation of the euro, $ds > 0$, on the duopoly equilibrium. A shift in the exchange rate change parameter will affect the firms' optimum production decision as defined by the first-order conditions. In order to derive an expression for these exchange rate effects, we differentiate the first-order conditions with respect to output[11]:

---

[10] Since the conjectural variation term was used when differentiating profits, [4.6] and [4.7] are the "perceived marginal profits". See Dixit (1986), p. 108. The first-order conditions for firm 1 implicitly defined q^1 as a function of q^2, and similarly for firm 2.

[11] Dixit (1986), p. 111, defines this expression in general term to allow for the possibility to examine the effect from other parameters, such as "demand and cost shift, tax and other policy instrument, or a prior-stage decision variable like capacity or advertising that affects this period's costs and demand".

[4. 8]
$$\begin{bmatrix} R_1^1 & R_2^1 \\ R_1^2 & R_2^2 \end{bmatrix}\begin{bmatrix} dq^1 \\ dq^2 \end{bmatrix} = \begin{bmatrix} -Mds \\ 0 \end{bmatrix}$$

where R_j^i is the derivative of the *ith* firm's first-order condition with respect to the output firm j, and Mds is the shift in the euro value of the perceived marginal revenue M at a given (q^1, q^2)[12]. Since the US local firm is not exposed "directly" to the exchange rate, $R_1^2 dq^1 + R_2^2 dq^2 = 0$. The firms' output adjustments in response to the exchange rate change can be derived from [4.8][13]:

[4. 9]
$$\begin{bmatrix} dq^1 \\ dq^2 \end{bmatrix} = \frac{1}{R}\begin{bmatrix} -R_2^2 & R_2^1 \\ R_1^2 & -R_1^1 \end{bmatrix}\begin{bmatrix} Mds \\ 0 \end{bmatrix}$$
with $R = R_1^1 R_2^2 - R_2^1 R_1^2$

which can be rewritten as $dq^1 / ds = -R_2^2 M / R$ and $dq^2 / ds = -R_1^2 M / R$. $dq^1 / ds > 0$ if the stability conditions are verified, and the sign of dq^2 / ds depends on the sign of R_1^2. Using the reaction function expressions below, the solution to [4.8] is[14]:

[4. 10]
$$\begin{bmatrix} dq^1 \\ dq^2 \end{bmatrix} = \frac{-1}{R}\begin{bmatrix} R_2^2 & R_1^1 r_1 \\ R_2^2 r_2 & R_1^1 \end{bmatrix}\begin{bmatrix} Mds \\ 0 \end{bmatrix}$$

From these effects of the exchange rate on (q^1, q^2), the effects on prices and profits can be obtained. It can be shown that in the general duopoly case, the exchange rate depreciation adversely affects the profits of the US firm, but has an indeterminate effect on the exporter's profits (see appendix D). The first-order condition for firm 1 implicitly defines q^1 as a function of q^2, as expressed in the firm 1's reaction function. Firm 2's reaction function is defined in a similar manner. From [4.8] and [4.9] the slopes of the two reaction functions are given by[15]:

[4. 11] $r_1 = -R_2^1 / R_1^1$

[4. 12] $r_2 = -R_1^2 / R_2^2$

Given the stability conditions $R_1^1 < 0$ and $R_2^2 < 0$, the reaction functions are downward sloping if and only if R_2^1 and $R_1^2 < 0$. The products being "strategic substitutes" verifies

---

[12] Since the German exporter has costs denominated in euro, it has only a revenue exposure.
[13] See Dixit (1986), p. 112.
[14] See Dixit (1986), p. 112.
[15] See Dixit (1986), p. 110.

this property[16]. By assuming that marginal revenue would fall, the negatively sloped reaction function is viewed as the "normal case" in Cournot oligopoly [17]. Whether the German exporter will be adversely or positively affected by the depreciation, depends on the industry structure in the US market. The form of industry structure will characterize how the two firms behave strategically in the US market. Under *Cournot competition*, since each firm takes the other firm's output as given, the conjectural variations terms equal zero ($v^i = 0$) and the sign of R_j^i depends on $M = D^1(q^1, q^2) + q^1 D_1^1$[18]. Expressions for the foreign exchange exposures of the firms are given by:

[4. 13]
$$\frac{d\pi_1^{\epsilon}}{ds} = q^1 D^1(q^1, q^2) - \frac{sq^1 D_2^1 MR_2^2 r_2}{R} \qquad \text{if} \quad r_2 < 0$$

[4. 14]
$$\frac{d\pi_2^{\$}}{ds} = \frac{-q^2 D_1^2 MR_2^2}{R} < 0$$

These exposure expressions are more complex than in the monopoly case examined in chapter 2, and depend on marginal costs and price elasticities of demand, both direct elasticities and cross-elasticities. Unlike in the case of monopoly, demand and supply behavior have an impact on exposure independently of the initial level of export revenues. The US firm is exposed indirectly through its competition with the German firm, although it does not trade internationally. As in the general duopoly case, the profits of the US firm fall following a depreciation of the euro. The exposure of the German exporter is non-linear, that is, it depends on the exchange rate level. The profits of the German firm rise as long as the reaction function of the foreign US firm

---

[16] Two goods are strategic substitutes if a rise in one firm's output lowers the marginal profit of the other firm. See Bulow et al. (1985), Marston (2001), p. 157, Luehrman (1989), p. 229, Tirole (1990), pp. 207-208. A study on the oligopolistic market of automobile in Switzerland found that in most cases, "automobiles from different source-countries are strategic complements". See Gross and Schmitt (2000), p. 106. For a discussion on the role of the strategic subsituability/complementarity concept in international pricing, see Clark et al. (1999), pp. 260-262.

[17] This condition was assumed by Hahn (1962). In the general case of non-Cournot competition, positively-sloped reaction functions are possible, and it is possible that the output of the foreign firm can rise rather than fall when the euro depreciates (see appendix D). Luehrman (1990) shows that bimarket duopolists' reoptimization following an exchange rate shock has effects on firm value with ambiguous signs and generally significant magnitudes.

[18] The conjectural variation term that is included in the first-order conditions could allow for possible interaction between the decisions of the two competing firms under other industry structures. See Marston (2001), pp. 160-163, and next section.

is negatively sloped $r_2 < 0$ [19]. Exposure measurement for an imperfectly competitive firm necessitates forecasting endogenous demand shifts and competitors' reactions.

Comparison with Other Forms of Industry Structures

This model can be used to examine other forms of quantity competitions. Firms facing Cournot competition are relatively more exposed than monopolists. This is the result of a lower ability to pass-through exchange rate changes into prices. An other reason is that it should be easier for a monopolist to hedge, since its exposure is proportional to its initial revenue in foreign currency and therefore easier to forecast (see chapter 2). Other forms of competition can be examined in this model of duopoly[20].

(a) *Stackelberg leadership by the German exporter* (quantity leadership): the German exporter dominates in the sense that it formulates its profit-maximizing output decision only after taking the output responses of the foreign firm into account, while the foreign firm pursues a myopic Cournot strategy[21]. The exposure of the German exporter will be smaller than for the case of Cournot competition[22]. In the case of Cournot competition, both firms *simultaneously* optimize their profits. A Stackelberg firm, in contrast, can incorporate the effect of its competitor's strategic behavior on its exposure, before making profit maximizing production decisions. This information advantage, compared to the Cournot case, reduces the firm's exposure, since the degree of uncertainty related to its foreign currency cash flows is lower (quantity risk lower)[23].

(b) *Stackelberg follower*: the German exporter's exposure is still lower if the *U.S. firm is a Stackelberg leader* (at least as long as $r_2 < 0$). Since a firm that acts as a Stackelberg leader can mitigate the impact of exchange rate fluctuations on its profits by optimally adjusting to exchange rate changes in the output, market

---

[19] If demand curves are non-linear, positively-sloped reaction functions are possible. See Marston (2001), p. 157. However, in the case of a constant elasticity demand, there is no ambiguity. Profits of the exporting firm rise in response to the depreciation of the euro. See Marston (2001), p. 160.

[20] See Marston (2001), pp. 160-163.

[21] In the model above of Marston (2001), that means that the exporter takes into account the foreign firm's output decision by setting its conjectural variations parameter equal to the slope of the foreign firm's reaction function. See Marston (2001), pp. 160-161.

[22] It can be shown that in this case, the exposure of the exporter is the same as for a monopolist. See Marston (2001).

[23] The Stackelber model can be examined as a sequential game. See Varian (1999).

leaders should have lower competitive exposures. The exposure of the German firm is smaller when it is a leader than a follower.

(c) *Consistent conjectures:* if both firms take the other firm's output response into account in their profit-maximizing decisions *(consistent conjectures),* their exposures will again be lower than if they pursue a Cournot strategy, and this result holds independently of whether the other firm acts as a Stackelberg leader or not[24].

This type of models suggests that for exposure measurement, one needs to know the:

- *Effects on profits and firm value of strategic interactions.* Accordingly, the value of operating flexibility should be influenced by strategic interactions. In most forms of imperfect competition we need to assess the likely response of competitors, consumers, and foreign governments to the firm's range of possible actions.

- *Timing of operating adjustments,* which depends on the dynamic interaction between the firm and competitors' strategic behavior.

Measuring exposure is complex for oligopolists, since it requires that they be capable of predicting competitors' responses to their own actions. Except under restrictive conditions, these models find indeterminate exposure signs. A reason for this limitation is that to determine the sign of exposure, we need to be more specific about the distribution of foreign currency cash flows and measure exposure in terms of value rather than of single-period cash flows. Real options models can describe and value the strategic flexibility that lead to these adjustments.

4.1.2 Economic Rent and Distribution of Industry Value

A. Economic Rent

Expected cash flows from an investment project can be decomposed into two components: (i) cash flows necessary to obtain a return equal to the cost of invested

---

[24] Krugman (1987), p.62, argues that a relevant model for issues of prices and exchange rates "would be one in which firms produce differentiated products and probably engage in Bertrand competition". See Fridberg (1998) for a Bertrand model of exposure. However, the Bertrand model is often rejected because it predicts that firms in industries with a small number of firms never succeed in setting a market price that makes profit. It has been shown that with appropriate modifications to the Bertrand model, the Cournot predictions will prevail. See Tirole (1990), Harris (1996), p. 92.

capital and (ii) economic rents[25]. The difference in competitive settings is accounted for by adjusting the expected economic rents[26]: for a *monopoly*, expected economic rents are constant. For *perfect competition* firms, assuming initial rents, they are expected to decline exponentially with entry until the return on the project is equal to its cost of capital. In a *duopolistic* setting, rents evolve according to the competitors' actions. The implication is that real options value and exposure asymmetries depend on a firm's degree of control over the economic rents resulting from exchange rate changes. For example, the threat of an entrant would be expected to reduce the economic rent from a favorable exchange rate change and reduce the value of its pricing flexibility.

By modifying a firm's competitive position, exchange rate changes present firms with the possibility of higher or lower economic rents. A firm would want to maximize the strategic opportunity created by a favorable exchange rate change, and minimize the loss from an adverse exchange rate change. But in oligopoly, the exposure profile of a flexible firm is not necessarily convex, since firms compete for the value generated by the industry. An exchange rate change is beneficial in the sense that a firm is in a better position to appropriate the industry value, but this is its strategic decisions that will determine if this translates into more revenues from the industry's consumers and into firm value enhancement.

B. Endogenous Uncertainty of Real Options' Underlyings

Despite the importance of strategic interactions, under the standard real options approach, agents formulate optimal exercise strategies in isolation and ignore competitive interactions. The firm's and competitors' actions are treated as exogenous[27], meaning that competing firms do not recognize each other's optimizing behavior and adjust their actions accordingly. For example, a competitor would enter the market and reduce the abnormal rent over time no matter what the firm does. The firm, on the other hand, would optimize its competitive response to a predetermined competitor's action. The interdependencies between the firms' decisions are not

---

[25] "Economic rent is defined as those payments to a factor of production that are in excess of the minimum payment necessary to have that factor supplied". See Varian (1999), p. 403.
[26] See Varian (1999), pp. 403-406, Huisman and Kort (1999), Boyer et al (2004), p. 6.

considered although a firm's exercise of real options may affect the actions of its competitors, and consequently the nature of the exchange rate uncertainty that the firm faces[28].

An implication of strategic competition is that it is critical to examine exposure asymmetries in a dynamic and strategic framework. Some operating responses could be valuable in a static environment, but not if they are adjusted for the possibility of competitors' reactions.

C. Proprietary and Shared Options

In an oligopolistic setting, the effect of a strategic real option on exposure depends on how its value is shared among market participants. The resulting benefits of a strategic investment can be *proprietary* or *shared*. Proprietary options imply that the firm has full control over the value of its option. After an exchange rate change, the option value is shared among market participants according to how they interact strategically. Two examples clarify this notion (see also section 4.3.2.1):

(a) *Value of exchange-rate pass-through options shared with customers*: a firm supplying inputs to a firm in a foreign market could partially pass-through foreign currency depreciations into higher foreign currency prices. By only partially passing along some of the adverse effect of the depreciation to its corporate customer, the firm would implicitly give a part of the value of its pricing option to its customer. The firm would prefer to keep the entire option value, but it might not be able to do so if the demand is elastic and consumers' costs to switch to a competitor are low. If the consumer switches to a competitor, then the option value is completely destroyed.

(b) *Value of growth options shared with the government*: in response to an exchange rate change, a firm might decide to exercise a growth option to expand into a foreign market. However, at the same time, the foreign government could decide to increase import tariffs. This situation can be interpreted as the firm having to share

---

[27] Typical assumptions underlying real options analysis comprise *exclusive* rights to invest in a project (e.g., government licenses, monopolies, patented products).

[28] See Copeland and Antikarov (2001), pp. 111-112.

the value of its growth option with the foreign government. The government takes a portion of the firm's option value in the form of tariff revenues.

The distribution of a firm's options value between the firm and other market participants is function of how each of them is able to take advantage of the competitive changes in the industry induced by an exchange rate shock. In an oligopolistic setting, the distinctive aspect of a firm's exposure asymmetries is that it is determined by (i) the competitive forces that drive the behavior of all market participants in the industry, and (ii) the firm's corporate strategy given these competitive forces. This suggests that a corporate manager should link exposure measurement to strategic planning.

D. Option Value of Waiting and Strategic Exercise of Options

While partial equilibrium real options models emphasize that a valuable option to wait leads firms to invest only at large positive net present values (NPV), the impact of competition drastically erodes the value of the option-to-wait and leads to investment at very near the zero NPV threshold[29]. Having to share the value of a real option, as a result of market forces, affects the option value of waiting. As noted earlier, the real options valuation method is applicable when (i) the future is uncertain, (ii) the investment decision is irreversible, fully or in part, (iii) the firm holding the investment option has the ability to delay. In an oligopolistic setting, the third condition needs to be re-evaluated, since competition influence not only project value, but also investment timing. The ability to hold an option by delaying an investment is affected by the actions of other firms. For example, postponement may imply a loss in the expected value of the project due to anticipated competitive entry. This expected erosion of economic rents would give an incentive to invest early. The effect of real options exercise rules on foreign exchange exposure is discussed in section 4.2.3.2.

---

[29] See Grenadier (2002).

4.1.3 Strategic Real Options and Markets Segmentation

A. Competitive Market Forces and Short Options

To a large extent, foreign exchange exposure results from departures from Purchasing Power Parity (PPP). The Law of One Price (LOP), which also applies to a basket of goods, "implies that the exchange rate is determined so that PPP holds"[30].

Real exchange rate changes affect a firm's competitiveness and trigger the exercise of real options. Typically, the exchange rate will revert ex-post to its PPP value. This mean reversion is explained through arbitraging forces in the goods market. These forces can be interpreted as resulting from the firm having short real options positions. For example, a country's currency appreciation could induce the entry of foreign firms. However, the magnitude of this economic rent to foreign firms is not permanent. Typically, the LOP would imply that consumers could switch to local firms that can now import the good at a lower price because of their currency's appreciation. The local consumers' option to buy imported goods is for the foreign firm like being the writer of a put.

B. Market Power and Preservation of the Real Option Value

The exercise of any type of real options can attract counter actions from competitors, e.g., in the form of production reallocation. This is especially the case for the option to exchange rate pass-through (ERPT). The effects of pricing actions on firm value are "difficult to determine, because they are the most likely to attract counter actions from competitors"[31].

Suppose a German exporter to the U.S. market. Figure 4.1 above illustrates the effect of various degrees of ERPT on the German firm's exposure profile at a future date T, with S_T the exchange rate[32]. AOA^* traces the firm's cash flows under a scenario of low ERPT, BOB^* represent the exposure profile under a scenario of high ERPT. The slope of the BOB^* curve indicates a lower exposure. The slope of the curves at point O measures the exposure at an initial exchange rate level ("base" case).

---

[30] See Stulz (2000), ch. 8, pp. 18-19.
[31] See Damodaran (2004-a), p. 28.
[32] See Levich (1998), p. 583.

Figure 4. 1 Law of One Price and Short Term/Long Term Exposure[33]

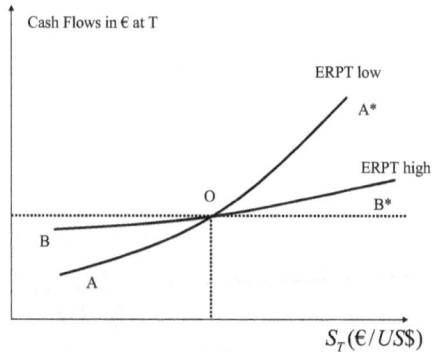

Under *monopoly*, the German exporter has a high degree of control over the value of its real options. For certain, it would like to keep its US$ price at the same level after US$ appreciations and pass-through US$ depreciations. The exposure profile of a monopolist has a "kinked" shape (*BOA**) resembling that of a call option contract with a trigger exchange rate at *O*.

If the uncertainty of the underlying of the ERPT option is endogenous, the exposure profile is more complex. In *imperfect competition*, e.g., oligopoly, the exercise of the ERPT option can attract counter actions by competitors:

Depreciation of the euro ($S_T(€/US\$)$ ↑): a high degree of ERPT is value-maximizing (assuming an elasticity of demand greater than *1*). The ERPT option is like a *long call* option and convexifies the exposure profile of firm value. A high ERPT is consistent with competitive forces associated with the LOP[34].

Alternatively, suppose no ERPT. The firm may however come under pressure to reduce its US$ price because of competitive forces associated with the LOP[35]. A U.S. importer could purchase the good in Germany and sell it in the U.S. The U.S.

---

[33] Source: Levich (1998), p. 584. See Levich (1998), pp. 583-585 and 602-603 for a scenario analysis of an exporter's exposure under various degree of exchange rate pass-through leading to such an exposure profile with a kinked shape.

[34] ERPT, PTM, and LOP are related. The higher the ERPT, the smaller the deviation from LOP. Firms ability to price discriminate between national markets is evidence of market segmentation that prevent arbitrage of goods according to the LOP. Evidence of PTM behavior explain departures from the LOP. See Goldberg and Knetter (1996).

[35] See Levich (1998), p. 583.

consumers' option to buy imported goods is for the German firm like being the *writer of a call on the US$*. The German firm sells an implicit right to the U.S. consumers that give them the option to switch to U.S. importers. The German firm's ability to segment the U.S. market and price discriminate (price-to-market) will determine the exchange rate level at which the call is exercised[36]. In the long term, PPP may hold and the economic rent disappear. But during the exchange rate reversion to its PPP value, the firm makes periodic profits. As such, the exposure of present value of cash flows at T is convex.

Appreciation of the euro ($S_T(\text{€}/US\$) \downarrow$): pricing flexibility gives the firm a long put on the US$. But the payoff of this put will be reduced if competitors retaliate, e.g., by lowering their US$ prices.

The importance of markets segmentation suggests that firms' strategies toward barriers to entry are important determinants of exposure. This example shows the necessity of analyzing exposures in a dynamic framework. Corporate strategies are pursued to preserve or gain economic rents resulting from changes in competitive positions associated with exchange rate changes.

4.1.4 Foreign Exchange Exposure Profile with Strategic Real Options

At each decision node in an event tree, decisions to exercise real options are based on the *expected value at each period* - not on the cash flow that period - by discounting the expected cash flows that period until the end of the project/terminal value[37]. But financial hedges often need to be based on cash flow measures of exposure. One thus needs to evaluate both the exposure of periodic cash flows and of their value.

The competitive effect, i.e., the exchange rate sensitivity of local currency cash flows, results from endogenous changes in competitiveness. The competitive effect can be seen as resulting from three interrelated effects:

- changes in the competitive position: short put/long call.

- firm's strategic responses: long put/call.

---

[36] The degree of global market integration affects the "proportion of product market cash flows that non-domestic firms can contest". See Luehrman (1991).

- other market participants' strategic responses: short or long call/put.

We have noted in chapter 2 that a competitive (non-linear) effect arises also for fully inflexible firms, through a marginal cost effect. By analogy to the concept of direct/indirect exposure, a distinction can be made between long/short options. Figure 4.2 shows the exposure of a firm with a long foreign currency position. In addition to a (non-linear) competitive effect, exposure has a linear component from having to convert risky real foreign cash flows with a nominal exchange rate. This linear component is like a long forward on foreign currency and results from (i) the effect on the ex-ante amount of foreign cash flow, (ii) the volatility of foreign cash flow unrelated to the exchange rate volatility. For example, this amount could depend on the probability of winning a bid in foreign currency. If the probability of the bid's success is independent of the exchange rate, the slope of the linear curve AOA^* will be affected by the uncertainty of the bid.

Figure 4. 2 Cash Flow Exposure Profile with Strategic Real Options

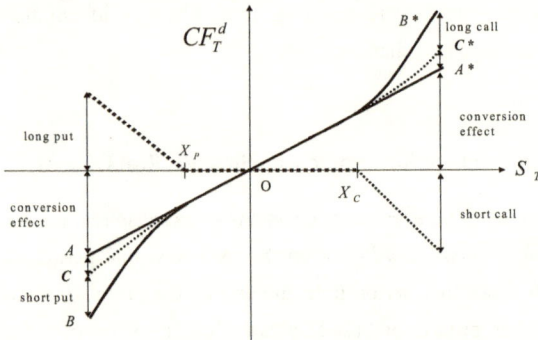

The endogeneity of the uncertainty of a real option's underlying can have the following effect:

- *Negative value of flexibility*: ex-post adjustments in the industry affect the expected value of a real option. Strategic competition can erode or make the value of real options negative. The value of a real option can be negative *independently* from the amount paid as option premium.

---

[37] See Copeland and Antikarov (2001), p. 152.

- *Negative exposure*: if short options more than offset the competitive effects associated with long options and competitive effects through costs (*AC* and *A*C**), the sign of the exposure can be negative. In other terms, exposure is negative if the competitive effect more than offset the linear effect. As such, strategic real options could explain the intertemporal instability of a firm's exposure sign.

4.2 Dynamic of Strategic Real Options and Foreign Exchange Exposure Asymmetries

4.2.1 Strategic Determinants of Real Options

The valuation of asymmetric foreign exchange exposures needs to be done based on the firm's overall strategy and based on all factors affecting the firm's competitiveness. The reason is as follows. An important difference on a firm's exposure of currency derivatives and operating measures is that the use of currency derivatives modifies the firm's foreign exchange exposure, whereas the use of operating instruments affects the firm's *overall exposure profile*. This has two implications: (i) *ex-ante*, strategic measures not implemented for managing foreign exchange exposure also have an effect on foreign exchange exposure, (ii) *ex-post*, the operating response to unexpected exchange rate changes is tied to the firm's overall exposure and overall corporate strategy. The value of strategic real options and asymmetric foreign exchange exposures depend on overall strategic considerations which in turn depends on all factors of competitiveness, not only real exchange rates.

4.2.1.1 Industry Competitive Forces and Market Participants' Behavior

In imperfectly competitive markets, the possibility arises for strategic behavior, in the sense that a firm "attempts to gain advantages over its competitors even at some short run cost to itself, presumably because of expected gains from increasing market share (economies of scale) or market power (driving competitors out of business)"[38]. Whereas in perfect competition, market constraints dictate that the firm's only decisions are whether and how much to produce, in imperfect competition, firms must assess the likely response of competitors, consumers, and foreign governments to their

---

[38] See Bodnar (1999), p. 6.

range of possible actions[39]. The notions of production "strategies" or pricing "strategies" are only sensible for a firm operating in an imperfectly competitive environment.

The term "operating flexibility" does not presume any implication in terms of firm value. This simply says that the firm has the ability to make some changes in the firm's operating structure. Adjustments made in the firm's operating structure in response to unexpected exchange rate changes may or may not have an impact on firm value. In the previous chapter, we examined how operating flexibility can create value by influencing the firm's cash flows distribution under exchange rate uncertainty. The effects on firm value of these real options can be influenced, even destroyed, by the behavior of other market participants. Therefore, in order to identify sources of exposure asymmetries and their likely effects on firm value, one needs to consider two aspects, which can be examined within a real option analytical framework:

(i)   *Endogenous interactions between the exercise of real options by the firm and by other market participants*: this implies assessing how market participants interact dynamically over the exposure valuation period.

(ii)   *The value effects of the firm's strategic real options on its foreign exchange exposure:* this implies assessing the implications of corporate strategies on the value of standard real options.

Measuring the exposure of oligopolists necessitates the evaluation of how the other market participants' real options, proprietary or shared, interact among them and with the firm's real options. This evaluation needs to be based on an analysis of the competitive forces driving the industry. We need to identify the factors that determine the type of operating flexibility (competitors and suppliers), behavioral flexibility (consumers), and policy flexibility (government). For example, a firm might wish to estimate its elasticity of demand of consumers having the option to switch to a competitor. But if the consumers expect the competitor to increases its prices if they switch, thereby destroying the value of their switching option, they might stick with the

---

[39] "Most firms that participate in international activities are in fact, large. They tend to have some market power and have the ability to partially segment the markets in which they sell products. Product differentiation and geographic and legal barriers to arbitrage tend to permit discrimination across markets and increase the market power of firms in the industry". See Knetter (1992), p. 18.

same firm. This shows that we need to understand the strategic real options of all market participants in a dynamic context.

A. Drivers of Market Participants' Behavior

Real exchange rate changes modify a firm's competitive position. This will affect the firm's ability to generate future cash flows. If the firm possesses real options, it can control to some extent this competitive effect on future cash flows. A firm's flexibility offers options to either mitigate or exploit the effect of the change in competitive position on future cash flows. In oligopoly, the value of these options reflects strategic choices based on the competitive forces driving the behavior of market participants in the industry. To a large extent, the real options value of oligopolists depends on how a firm can strategically influence the quantity or price setting of competitors and pre-empt competitive entry.

Since exposure is affected by all the factors influencing the firm's competitiveness, measuring foreign exchange exposure requires an *industry analysis*. For example, for assessing competitors' pricing flexibility, one needs to assess their ability to adjust their global production configuration, possibly through product differentiation, changes in product sourcing and plant location, foreign direct investment, and so forth[40]. A strategic analytical framework used to analyze the competitive forces that drive the interactions between market participants within an industry identifies "five forces" (figure 4.3 below)[41]. These five forces capture the influence of the factors affecting a firm's competitive position and the value of its strategic options. All the factors that define the industry competitive structure determine to some extent *how* firms are affected by exchange rate changes.

---

[40] See, e.g., De Meza and Van Der Ploeg (1987), Dixit (1989b), Miller and Reuer (1998). Miller and Reuer (1998) provide empirical evidence that foreign direct investments (FDI) reduce exposure. "The firm may also alter the product in some way, perhaps to make the demand less price-sensitive, or even to withdraw from the market. If a firm can develop highly specialized, differentiated products, e.g. leading to a patent, like a pharmaceutical product that no other firm produces, Steinway pianos, Harley Davidsons, the demand will be less sensitive to currency risk. If a firm produces a homogenous, standardized commodity like steel, or wheat, or oil, demand will be very elastic because of the existence of many substitutes".

[41] Known as "Porter's Five Forces Model". See Porter (1980), pp. 3-33, 187. The importance of this type of analysis for exposure measurement is discussed in Demacopoulos (1989), pp. 50-62, Miller (1992), pp. 316-320, Brandenburger and Nalebuff (1996), p. 17, Aabo (1999), essay 1, p. 46.

1. The threat of entry of new competitors

The threat of entry of new competitors makes exposure asymmetric at the exchange rate at which the threat is expected to become effective. The entry would reduce the firm's profitability and increase the value of an implicit option sold by the firm to consumers (see section 4.2.2.2). Since the behavior of the new firms may be hysteretic, meaning that they would stay in the market after the exchange rate shock is dissipated, this threat can significantly affect expected cash flows and exposure. In this case, exposure asymmetries would depend largely on the industry's barriers to entry, and on the firm's strategic measures to defend these barriers to entry.

Figure 4. 3 Competitive Forces Driving an Industry and a Firm's Competitive Position[42]

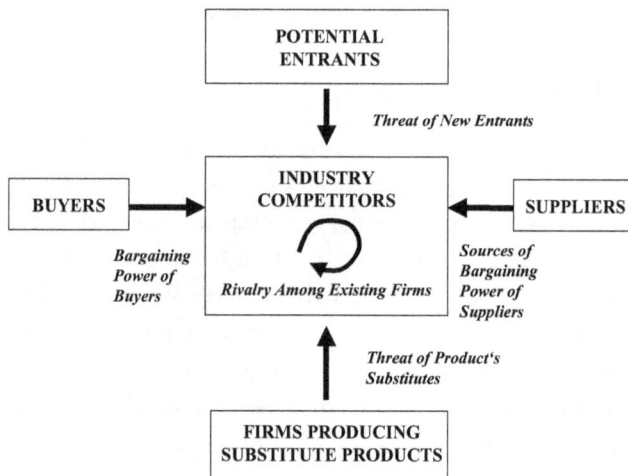

Source: adapted from Porter (1980), p. 4 and p. 187.

2. The power of buyers

Exposure could be asymmetric at an exchange rate at which consumers are expected to switch to a competitor. Buyers can influence the competition with their requirements and negotiating power. This influence is likely to be high where there are a few, large players in a market, e.g., the large grocery chains. The bargaining power of buyers is

---

[42] See also Brandenburger and Nalebuff (1996), p. 17, Demacopoulos (1989), p. 51.

determined by the cost of switching between suppliers, brand identity, buyer information, the existence of substitute products, price sensitivity, product differences[43]. For example, the elasticity of demand affects a firm's ability to pass-through exchange rate changes to consumers.

3. The power of suppliers

The suppliers of the firm's inputs provide the various inputs in the production process, including labor, materials, equipment, management and finance. Input prices are dependent on the prices set by suppliers in domestic and international markets and on the negotiating power of these suppliers. The competitiveness of the firm is thus linked to the competitiveness of the industries of its suppliers in costs and technologies. A firm's exposure could be asymmetric because of the indirect influence of their suppliers' pricing flexibility.

4. The threat of substitutes for the product

The appreciation of a firm's domestic currency could for example induce its consumers to switch to imported substitutes. How an international trading firm invests in developing new competitive advantages that are transferable overseas and that are not easily replicated by the competition will therefore also influence its competitive exposure. The threat of products' substitutes is determined by the relative price performance of substitutes, switching costs, buyer propensity to substitutes, new type of products, new technologies[44].

5. Competitive rivalry

The factors that drive the competition among existing rival firms can have an important influence on a firm's exposure. How a firm and its competitors find new sources of competitive advantage in response to exchange rate changes affect a firm's exposure. Competitive rivalry is likely to be high when new entrants are likely, when there is a threat of substitute products, and when suppliers and buyers have an influential

---

[43] See Demacopoulos (1989).
[44] See Brandenburger and Nalebuff (1996), p. 17.

position on the firms' operations. For this reason, competitive rivalry is in the center of the diagram[45].

This shows the importance of building risk management into the way a company does business[46]. As a result of the evolution of managing risks in a strategic framework, an increasing number of companies are linking the management of risks, such as exchange rate risk, and the strategic planning and budgeting processes. Strategic risk management implies that risk management is tied to the strategic planning process, and ensures that risk management is aligned with overall business strategy[47].

An industry competitive analysis is necessary in scenario analysis. Probabilities are attributed to events, such as the likelihood that consumers may switch to a competitor's product or the possibility that a foreign competitor enters the market at some exchange rate. Information on a firm's expected strategic response to exchange rate changes can be obtained from *contingency plans*. When making scenario projection about the future exchange rates, a firm often makes contingency plans for various possible future exchange rates[48]. This planning involves developing several plausible currency scenarios, analyzing the effects of each scenario on the firm's competitive position, and deciding on strategies to deal with these possibilities[49].

---

[45] See Demacopoulos (1989). Factors affecting rivalry among existing firms: (1) Industry growth: fixed costs/value added, product differences, switching costs, diversity of competitors, exit barriers, (2) Concentration and balance: intermittent overcapacity, brand identity, informational complexity, corporate stakes. See Brandenburger and Nalebuff (1996).

[46] Since the measurement of competitive exposure requires an understanding of these possible adjustments, "finance managers need to supplement their knowledge of credit and foreign exchange markets if they want to capture the essence of foreign exchange risk. This requires data on the firm's degree of flexibility to change markets, product mix, sourcing, and technology. Some of these information, such as whether cost changes will be passed on to the customer can be obtained from the marketing manager, or from the executives involved with purchasing, marketing, and production". See The Economist Intelligence Unit (1992).

[47] "Strategic risk management calls for a close connection between risk assessment and strategic planning, and the information output of the strategic plan is part of the information input of the foreign exchange risk exercise and vice versa". See CFO Research Services (2002).

[48] See Sercu and Uppal (1995), p. 509.

[49] See Shapiro (1999), p. 358.

B. Effect of Competition on the Value of Strategic Real Options

Figure 4.4 below shows the channels through which competitive factors can affect economic profitability and the value of strategic real options. A manager estimates exposure based on a perception of other market participants' strategic behaviors. For example, the price per unit could be expected to decrease because of the threat of entry of a competitor. Or price competition between firms in a local market could be expected to erode the profitability of an exporter by reducing price-cost margins and reduce the value of its ERPT option. The effects of these factors need to be viewed in dynamic over the estimation period.

Figure 4. 4 Industry Competitive Forces and Economic Profitability[50]

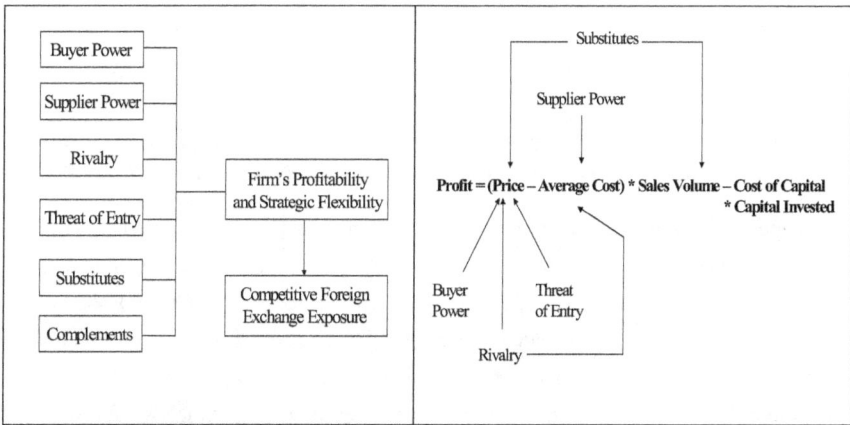

The five forces model emphasizes the role of strategic interactions in explaining the industry's profitability. The unit of analysis is the industry[51]. But for exposure measurement, an analysis at the firm and macroeconomic level is also necessary. One missing aspect for example is that government interventions could alter the industry competitive environment.

---

[50] Varian (1999), pp. 326-327, defines economic and accounting profits.
[51] See Porter (1980).

4.2.1.2 Investments in Flexibility and Firm's Competitiveness

A. Exposure Time-Variation as a Result of Investment in Flexibility

Investments in flexibility could be made for the direct purpose of managing foreign exchange exposure, or indirectly through unrelated strategic investments. Corporate strategies are formulated based on the competitive forces in the industry. Analytically, the effects of corporate strategies on exposure should be viewed in two phases: (i) ex-ante phase: investment in flexibility. Investments in flexibility are sometimes interpreted as implementing pre-emptive operating measure, or implementation of real hedges. However, the interpretation in terms of investment in flexibility is better suited to understand the sources of exposure time-variation[52]. To a large extent, exposure is time-varying because of the strategic investments that affect the firm's operating flexibility to respond to exchange rate changes. (ii) ex-post phase: flexibility to make ex-post adjustments. Real options value investment in this type of flexibility which is source of exposure asymmetries.

B. Sources of Firms' Competitive Advantages and Strategic Investment in Flexibility

Strategic real options are acquired through investments in flexibility. What types of strategic investments could convexify an oligopolist's exposure profile by creating real options? To answer that question, a corporate manager needs to identify the sources of competitive advantages that can be exploited to enhance the value of the firm's flexibility to respond to exchange rate changes. Understanding the types of strategic investments that affect foreign exchange exposures is also essential for formulating hypothesis in empirical analysis. Since corporate strategies are important determinant of *how* exchange rate changes affect a firm's value, this highlights the firm-specificity of a firm's exposure.

A firm's sources of competitive advantage need to be viewed in dynamic since they are constantly shifting, and can be divided into three categories[53]:

---

[52] For example, strategies about export intensity could change over time. Miller and Reuer (1998), p. 495, measure export intensity as net export intensity, i.e., exports less imports divided by total sales.
[53] See Grinblatt and Titman (2002), pp. 424-425.

Barriers to Entry and Sunk Costs

The exercise of a strategic option can attract counter actions from competitors. The value of a strategic option thus depends on the firm's ability to segment markets and preserve the erosion of its economic rent as a result of competitors' actions. By exploiting product and factor markets imperfections, a firm can pursue strategies to defend and optimize the value of its strategic options.

Setting barriers to entry would prevent competitors from eroding profits by destroying the value of the firm's strategic options, and would allow the firm to earn excess returns for longer periods of time[54]. For that reason, strategic risk management is likely to generate the most value for firms that operate in highly volatile exchange rates environment with substantial barriers to entry.

Strategies aimed at increasing barriers to entry could lead to increases in the cost of entry by restricting the access to distribution channels, by engaging in pricing deterrence strategies, by setting up legal constraints such as patents or regulation, and so forth[55]. For example, the threat of entry of a new (either local or foreign) competitor makes exposure asymmetric[56]. Setting barriers to entry will increase the sunk expenditures that are necessary to be paid by competitors to exercise their entry options and preserve the value of the firm's option[57]. In other terms, setting barriers would increase the hysterisis band where there is no entry/exit of competitors.

Economies of Scale and Market Share

Per-unit production costs decline with the scale of production, thus making producers of large quantities of a good more efficient than small producers[58]. As such, high economies of scale are a kind of barrier to entry that can restrict entry into an industry. Typically, higher market shares affect a firm's exposure by increasing its market power

---

[54] See section 4.1.2.
[55] Entry barriers against new entrants depend on "economies of scale, brand identity, capital requirements, proprietary product differences, switching costs, access to distribution, proprietary learning curve, access to necessary inputs, low-cost product design, technology ladder position, high-tech vs. low-tech, government policy, e.g. new competition laws, expected retaliation from competitors, the high or low cost of entry". See Brandenburger and Nalebuff (1996).
[56] See sections 3.6.1.2 and 4.2.2.1.
[57] Large capital expenditures required for entry that are not sunk are not a barrier to entry.
[58] See Grinblatt and Titman (2002), pp. 424-425.

and pricing flexibility[59]. High economies of scale would give a firm with large market shares a sustainable advantage to manage its foreign exchange exposure.

Economies of Scope

Economies of scope arise when a certain product or service can be supplied more efficiently by a firm that makes a related product. "Economies of scope manifest themselves in the superior knowledge, marketing system, or production technology that are required only by first producing a related product" [60]. For example, strategies in:

- *research and development (R&D)* intensity could lead to increased production efficiency/productivity, that would make the firm more profitable and less exposed[61].

- *marketing*: for example, investing in *product differentiation* or in *customer relations* to reduce costs associated with changes in prices[62] would increase pricing flexibility[63] and the ability of the firm to manage its exposures[64].

- *product sourcing and plant location, foreign direct investment, acquisitions and divestitures*, would affect the flexibility of a firm to use its global production configuration[65].

---

[59] See Bodnar et al. (2002).

[60] See Grinblatt and Titman (2002), pp. 424-425.

[61] See, e.g., Miller and Reuer (1998).

[62] See Oxelheim and Wihlborg (2002), p. 13.

[63] "Market segmentation and increasing demand rigidity implies that the price of a company can differ from the price of competitors without causing significant changes in demand. This can be achieved by differentiating products or having long-term relationships with customers". See Goldberg and Knetter (1996).

[64] However, it has recently been observed that the ability to pass on the effects of a stronger currency has been waning in recent years around the world. An explanation is that the increasingly integrated global economy has eroded companies' pricing power. See The Economist, A faded green, Dec 4th 2003.

[65] See, e.g., De Meza and Van Der Ploeg (1987), Dixit (1989b), Miller and Reuer (1998). Miller and Reuer (1998) provide empirical evidence that foreign direct investments (FDI) reduce exposure. The firm may also alter the product in some way, perhaps to make the demand less price-sensitive, or even to withdraw from the market. If a firm can develop highly specialized, differentiated products, e.g. leading to a patent, like a pharmaceutical product that no other firm produces, Steinway pianos, Harley Davidsons, the demand will be less sensitive to currency risk. If a firm produces a homogenous, standardized commodity like steel, or wheat, or oil, demand will be very elastic because of the existence of many substitutes.

Because all those factors of corporate competitiveness affect the operational ability to respond to exchange rate changes, they are determinants of a firm's exposure.

C. Illustrative Historical Case

Japanese car exports to the U.S. market during the 1990s illustrate how different types of real options interact in practice and can be used in complementary ways across national markets. Despite an appreciating yen against the US$ during the first half of the 1990s, Japanese automakers selling vehicles in the U.S. have managed to maintain strong export sales growth to the US market. As the yen strengthened, these cars faced fierce price competition in the US market, and Japanese automakers could have been induced to raise their US$ prices to maintain profitability in yen, with a risk of losing market shares. Their strategy was to keep their prices in US$ relatively constant. They priced-to-market, by not passing-through (at least not fully) the US$ depreciation to US consumers. The Japanese exporters generally maintained the US$ price of their cars in an effort to maintain market share, with the immediate consequence of reducing their yen profit margins. The Japanese firms had initially entered the US market with low-price economy cars that appealed to the mass market. The strategy of cutting the yen price of exports was in part pursued by:

(a) *Marketing strategies*: shifting production from economy to higher-value cars[66]. Japanese automakers started exporting luxury cars, such as Lexus and Acura, with lower price elasticity of demand[67]. The demand for mass-market cars is more sensitive to price changes because US customers can easily switch to non-Japanese suppliers when a rise in the yen pushes the US price of Japanese exports higher. In contrast, the prices of higher value cars are less sensitive to price increases, and can be more easily protected in terms of yen.

(b) *Production strategies*: Japanese exporters were helped in their efforts to lower export yen prices by steep declines in the cost of imported materials, and by lowering wages, cutting profit margins, and boosting productivity[68].

---

[66] See Klitgaard (1996).
[67] See Shapiro (1999).
[68] See Klitgaard (1996), p. 2.

(c) *"Cross-national" exchange rate pass-through*: their efforts to maintain export growth to the US market was also indirectly helped by charging relatively higher prices to Japanese consumers[69]. The possibility that an exporter could pass-through to domestic consumers exchange rate changes affecting its competitiveness in foreign markets highlights that a firm's exposure to a currency actually can be determined by the industry structure of multiple markets and cross-country strategies.

On the other hand, the fall in the US$ made import-competing US car makers more competitive[70].

4.2.1.3 Real Options and Corporate Strategy

A firm's real options and therefore foreign exchange exposure depend on a firm's overall strategic objectives. To illustrate, we discuss how ERPT options are related to corporate strategy.

A. Firm's Overall Strategic Objectives and Exercise of Real Options

The effect of pricing flexibility on foreign exchange exposures depends on how firms are expected to strike the balance between profit margins (current profits) and quantity adjustments (long term expected profits) over time[71]. There are two basic ways for a firm to pursue its pricing strategy[72]: (i) it can decide to be a *volume leader*, reducing price and hoping to increase volume sufficiently to compensate. For this strategy to work, the firm needs a cost advantage over its competitors, to prevent predatory pricing that may make all firms in the sector worse off; (ii) alternatively, it can attempt to be a *price leader*, increasing prices and hoping that the effect on volume will be smaller. "From a value maximization standpoint, we can examine which approach yields the

---

[69] "To prevent the risk that a foreign firm will use high home-country prices to subsidize a battle for market share overseas, firms often invest in one another's domestic markets". This strategy is called "cross-investment". See Shapiro (1999), p. 684.

[70] Conversely, when the US$ appreciated during the early 1980s, hit an all-time high in 1985, that helped Japanese automakers and hurt import-competing U.S. companies. Japanese car makers could lower the dollar price of cars sold in the U.S., and still receive the same amount of Yen as before.

[71] The firm could achieve these two conflicting goals through hedging. See chapter 6.

[72] See Porter (1980), Damodaran (2004-a).

higher value and use that approach. In doing so, however, it is critical that we not assume a static environments and consider the actions that the firm's competitors would take in response to the firm's actions"[73]. Figure 4.5 below illustrates how pricing and exposures are influenced by multiple strategic factors[74]. The strategic pricing response is not solely determined by exchange rate uncertainty considerations[75]. Competitive symmetry refers to the role of strategic interactions with competitors.

Figure 4. 5 Export Pricing Strategic Flexibility and Foreign Exchange Exposure

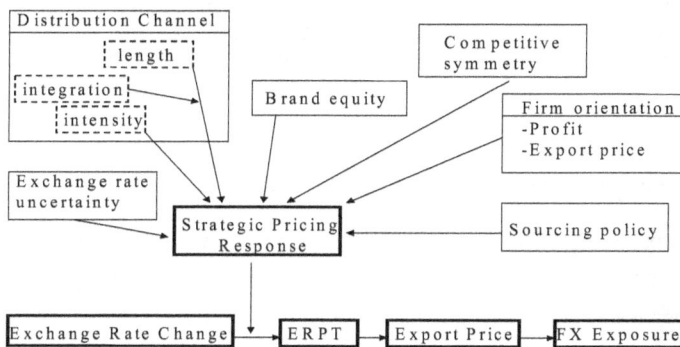

Source: adapted from Clark, Kotabe, and Rajaratnam (1999), p. 253.

ERPT decisions are function of overall strategic objectives that may or not be related to the exchange rate change, and that may have conflicting purposes. Table 4.2 lists the most common pricing objectives of industrial firms, which could have an influence on the price response of firms to exchange rate changes[76]. Because firms may have more than one pricing objectives at a time, and pricing objectives may be changing,

---

[73] See discussion in Damodaran (2004-a), p. 17, based on Porter (1980).

[74] Porter (1990), p. 49-50 and pp. 640-642 argues that "firms engaging in differentiation strategies have more sustainable competitive advantages than cost leaders under conditions of currency volatility". Miller and Reuer (1998), p. 496, argue that "product differentiation in „higher-order" advantages, e.g., proprietary technology, unique product characteristics, or brand reputation, strengthens the firm's capability to pass through to customers changes in costs due to currency movements".

[75] Brown (2001), p. 422, argues that "larger strategic decisions, such as expansion into new markets and location of manufacturing facilities, are based primarily on other factors. Once a major strategic decision has been made, the decisions regarding foreign currency and risk management are undertaken, e.g., functional currency and hedging strategies".

[76] Pricing strategies pursued for other reasons than in response to exchange rate changes would "indirectly" affect foreign exchange exposure, by changing the firm's cash flow distribution and total risk profile. However, only the linear, conversion effect would be modified.

according to the conditions both within and outside the firms' environment, the effect of pricing on exposure is likely to be complex and time-varying. For example, there are instances of negative ERPT behavior that have been reported[77], or of firms pursuing predatory pricing "by deliberately making losses with anti-competitive intent"[78].

Table 4. 2 Pricing Objectives of Industrial Firms

Target profit	Survival in the long-run	Meet customers requirements
Target ROI[79]	Maximum current profit	Value to the customer
Target sales volume	Maximum current revenue	Segmentation pricing
Target market share	Price similarity with competitors	
Sales stability	Price stability in the market[80]	

Source: Tzokas (2000), p. 194.

4.2.2 Real Options and Interactions between Market Participants.

We examine several cases to convey the complexity of how the interactions between market participants affect a firm's real options and exposure. An oligopolist needs to interpret and value the flexibility of other market participants, and assess how it affects its options and exposure.

4.2.2.1 Threat of Entrant and Consumers' Options

A. Endogenous Changes in Market Structure

A1. Threat of New Competitor in a Firm's Exporting Market

---

[77] "On January 5, 1994, the dollar was worth 113 Yen, while by April 19, 1995, it was worth only 80 Yen. This represented a 34% appreciation of the Yen against the dollar. For instance, the suggested retail price of a large-screen SONY Trinitron actually fell by 15% in the U.S. between 1994 and 1995". There was a negative ERPT of exchange rates to imported goods prices. See Goldberg and Knetter (1996), p. 2.

[78] See Economic Focus: Preying on Theory, The Economist July 10th 1999, p. 88, for theoretical arguments supporting the possibility of predatory pricing.

[79] The return on investment is "generally, the book income as a proportion of net book value". See Brealey and Myers (2000), p. 1071.

[80] For instance, partial ERPT has been shown to arise as a result of firms seeking to maintain local currency price stability rather than maintain constant margins in home currency terms. See Krugman (1987).

Exposure Profile and Exposure Elasticity

Exposure asymmetries can be the result of expected endogenous changes in market structure. At some exchange rates trigger points, the nature of the market structure could change and with it the nature of the exposure[81]. Figure 4.6 below assumes an exporter that sells in a foreign market. V_T^1 traces the present value of the exporter's cash flows under a scenario of low competitive foreign market structure, V_T^2 under a scenario of highly competitive industry, S_T indicates the exchange rate level. At the beginning of the period T, the firm is assumed to be on V_T^1. The slope at the point O measures the exposure at an initial exchange rate level, S_T^0, corresponding to a "base" case. The slope of V_T^1 (lower degree of competition) is higher than of V_T^2 (high degree of competition), but the exposure on V_T^1 is lower than on V_T^2.

Figure 4. 6 Exposure Profile with Changes in Market Structure (Firm Initially on V_T^1)

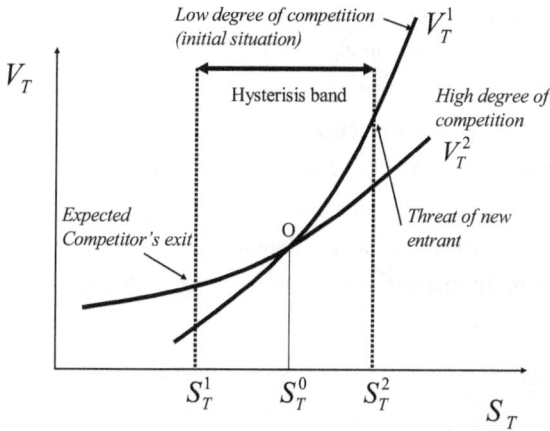

However, the slope of V_T^1 is higher than for V_T^2, although we know from our previous analysis that a firm operating in a more competitive industry should be relatively more exposed[82]. The slope of the exposure profile is $\Delta V_T / \Delta S_T$, but the exposure is defined

---

[81] Booth (1996), p. 9., shows in a microeconomic model that in that case, the firm's ex-ante profit function will be a piecewise non-linear function of the exchange rate.
[82] The difference between this exposure profile representation and the former ones is that formerly, is that we assumed a given industry structure. Here, the two exposure profiles correspond to two different degree of pricing flexibility or elasticity of demand.

by the *elasticity* $[(\Delta V_T / V_T)/(\Delta S_T / S_T)]^{83}$. A higher degree of industry competition has a stronger effect on the *level* of profits than on the amount by which profits *change*[84].

For example, assuming that the firm is on V_T^1 when it enters period T, the foreign currency appreciates, the effect of a more competitive industry structure is to reduce profits relatively more in level than in difference. The slope of the exposure profile is smaller, whereas the exposure elasticity is higher. Because of the change in industry structure, the beneficial effect from the depreciation on the level of V_T is larger than on ΔV_T, so that $\Delta V_T / \Delta S_T$ is smaller and $[(\Delta V_T / V_T)/(\Delta S_T / S_T)]$ higher, and the level of V_T is lower under a high degree of competition.

Treat of Entry and Consumers' Options

From the exporter's perspective, a real appreciation of the foreign currency increases its expected profits. But the increase in the profits rate in the foreign market could also serve as an incentive for new foreign competitors to supply the foreign market[85]. Suppose that the exporter's current profile is V_T^1. The competitor enters the market if an exchange rate change is large enough to make expected profits outweigh the cost of exercising the real option X $(X > S_T^2)$. The entry costs involved might include marketing expenditures or the establishment of a distribution network[86], and are expected to recur if the firm exit and re-enter the market. More competition increases price competition and forces down profit margins[87]. The final increase in the exporter's profit margin,

---

[83] See Varian (1999), pp. 266-267.
[84] By analogy to comment in Bodnar et al. (2002).
[85] "The demand curve facing a given firm would become more elastic as more firms produced more and more similar products. Thus entry into an industry by new firms with similar products will tend to shift the demand curves facing existing firms to the left and make them flatter". See Varian (1999), p. 450.
[86] See Baldwin (1998), Dixit (1989). See Tirole (1990), pp. 307-308 or Varian (1999), pp.353-354 for a detailed definition. These might also include the cost of information about demand conditions abroad, the costs of establishing a distribution network, or the search costs of identifying local bankers and transport companies. See Bernard and Wagner (1998), p. 6.
[87] The entry of the new competitor shifts down and makes more elastic the firm's demand curve. However, if the shock is small, there will be a movement along the curve. See Aabo (1999), p. 47.

and as a result its exposure, will thus be smaller than had no entry taken place[88]. The firm's exposure corresponding to the new industry structure is V_T^2.

From the perspective of the exporter, the entry option of the competitor can be viewed as the foreign consumers having an option to buy from a new competitor. This is *like the exporter selling a put on the foreign currency to the foreign consumers*[89].

In the next period, if the foreign currency depreciates and returns to its initial level, these firms may decide to stay in the market because of the entry sunk costs. There is a gap between the entry and exit conditions, because firms are willing to defend sunk-cost investments undertaken to establish foreign market share by accepting lower profitability when exchange rates move adversely. Because of the firms' hysteretic behavior, the decrease in firm value is relatively higher when the foreign currency depreciates than the increase in firm value when the foreign currency appreciates by a same magnitude. In terms of exposure, this means that the firm will be relatively less exposed to the beneficial foreign currency appreciation in the initial period than to the adverse foreign currency depreciation in the following period.

The exposure is affected in several ways: (i) the exposure is asymmetric at the trigger exchange rate values at which competitors are expected to enter the market, S_T^1, and exit the market, S_T^2. The firm shifts to an other exposure profile for large exchange rate changes. Small exchange rate changes within the hysterisis band cause no changes in market structure, while large exchange rate changes do; (ii) the exposure is path dependent. Hysterisis implies that large exchange rate shocks can have persistent real effects[90]. The exposure in two years could depend on whether a new competitor has entered the market in the previous year; (iii) the exposure experience intertemporal shifts. Hysterisis causes persistent changes in market structure. The exposure path dependencies resulting from this hysteresis effect can explain the large shifts in exposures that have been observed in empirical studies.

---

[88] A profit-maximizing monopolisito firm always produces where its elasticity of demand is elastic (greater than one).
[89] Payoffs resulting from entry can be analyzed in a game of entry deterrence. See Varian (1999), pp. 503-505.
[90] Within the hysterisis band, exposure depends on past exchange rates, and on the prevailing industry structure. These two path dependencies, the change in industry structure, and the dependence of exposure on previous exchange rates, can be integrated in estimation methods using simulation. See Aabo (1999), essay 4, pp. 45-53, for a simulation example of exposure estimation including the hypothesis of the threat of entry of a new competitor that display hysteretic behavior.

A2. Threat of Consumers Switching to an Import-Competitor

A firm's domestic customers could have the flexibility to switch to imported goods. Customers in a domestic market can switch to foreign suppliers when an exchange rate change decreases the domestic price of foreign imports. Foreign firms could start supplying the local market at an exchange rate $S_T = X$, where X is the exercise price. From the perspective of the local firm, the option of the consumers to buy imported goods is like being a *writer of a put option on the importer's foreign currency*[91], with exercise price X or alternatively a short call on the domestic currency. Selling a put means that the firm is forced to buy the importer's currency at X when the consumers' option is in-the-money ($S_T < X$), thus incurring a loss. Figure 4.7 shows that the cash flows can be viewed as the payoffs from a put option at maturity T, P_T^{HC}, P_T^{FC}. That makes the firm's exposure asymmetric at the threshold X and concave.

Figure 4.7 (a) Writing a Put Option on the Import-Competitor's Currency to Foreign Consumers, (b) Writing a Call Option on the Domestic Currency to Foreign Consumers[92]

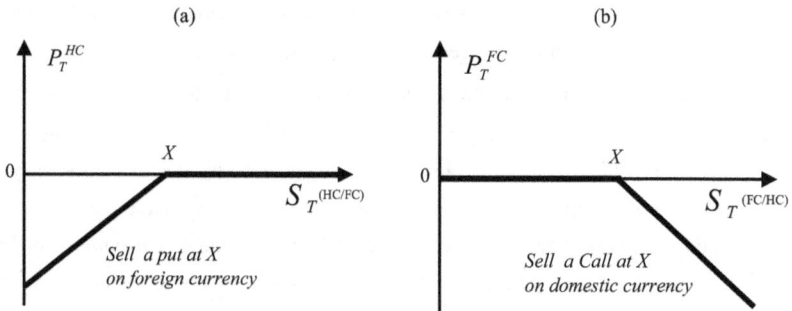

Figure 4.6 in the previous section can also be interpreted as the exposure profiles of a local firm subject to the threat of entry of foreign competitors. The short put on foreign currency forces the firm to buy at X when $S_T < X$, thus incurring a loss. The short call forces the firm to sell at X when $S_T > X$, thus incurring a loss.

---

[91] See Sercu and Uppal (1995), p. 182.
[92] Only the expiration value is displayed, and not the profit or loss from a particular strategy. See Sercu and Uppal (1995), p. 172.

An example that illustrates this situation and the notion of currency of determination is given by the German automobile manufacturers which exported to the United States in the early 1990s, and which benefited from a relatively stronger yen that hampered their Japanese competitors in the US market. The German exporters had an economic interest in the US market that was equivalent to a short US$/¥ position, and some companies are believed to have hedged by buying dollars against yen[93].

From the perspective of the German firms, the situation was like having written a put on ¥ against US$ to the U.S. consumers. The higher the relative depreciation of the ¥ against US$, the higher the deterioration of the competitive position of German firms in the U.S. market. As such, an hedging strategy of long put on the ¥ against the U.S.$ made sense.

A3. Firm with Full Export Flexibility

Assume a firm with a real option to switch sales between national markets in response to unexpected exchange rate fluctuations. Figure 4.8 shows that under exchange rate uncertainty and export flexibility, a firm has an asymmetric exposure profile[94]. A firm is assumed to have the flexibility, conditional on the realization of an unexpected exchange rate change, to sell either to its domestic market, at a price, P_d, denominated in domestic currency, or to a foreign market at a price, P_f, denominated in foreign currency. The domestic and foreign markets are assumed to be segmented. Arbitrage transactions are either impossible or unprofitable, thereby creating departures from the Law of One Price. Under full export flexibility, the firm's export decision is to sell the entire output to the foreign market if the realized exchange rate is sufficiently favorable ($SP_f > P_d$), or to sell exclusively in the domestic market if $SP_f < P_d$. The firm is indifferent between selling to either market if the Law of One Price hold ($SP_f = P_d$).In practice, because of sunk costs, X would correspond to an exchange rate higher than the exchange rate at which there is parity in sales revenues.

---

[93] See DeRosa (1996), p. 112.
[94] See Wong (2001) for a microeconomic model. See also Sercu and Uppal (1995), pp. 181-183.

Figure 4. 8 Foreign Exchange Exposure Profile with Export Flexibility as a Real Call Option[95]

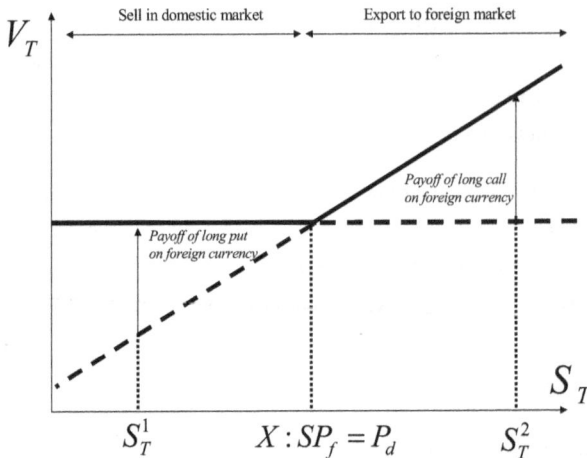

A firm's option to export is similar to being long call on the foreign currency which is exercised if the exchange rate is sufficiently high ($S > P_d/P_f$)[96]. The put implies that the firm sell at X when $S_T<X$, thus making a gain. The call implies that the firm buys at X when $S_T>X$, thus making a gain.

If the domestic price is so low that it is never optimal to sell in the domestic market, then the real option held by the firm is said to be *deeply out-of-the-money* and has zero option value of waiting. The firm receives the downside protection from selling in the domestic market at the certain domestic price P_d, and enjoys the upside potentials from exporting to the foreign country at favorable realizations of the exchange rate. The state-contingent export rule convexifies the firm's exposure profile, and can be viewed as giving it either a long call on the foreign currency or a long put on the domestic currency option like feature. It is this convexity which induces the firm to produce more when the foreign market is made accessible.

The greater the exchange rate volatility, the more likely large beneficial departures from the Law of One Price will occur, and consequently the higher the potential gains

---

[95] See Wong (2001), p. 170.
[96] See Sercu and Uppal (1995), pp. 181-186, Wong (2001), pp. 167-169.

from international trade. On the other hand, the equally higher likelihood of adverse exchange rate changes does not offset these potential gains since the firm may choose to give up export. The export flexibility reduces downside risk. At the exchange rate at which the foreign currency cash flow distribution is truncated, the exposure to the foreign currency terminates. Exposure convexity in the exchange rate reflects a positive effect of high exchange rate volatility on the expected firm value.

This exposure could be hedged by writing a financial call against the potential foreign currency export revenue. This short financial call means that the firm would sell the uncertain future gains for immediate cash, which could be appropriate for example if the firm is currently financially pressed[97].

A4. Exposure Profile with Strategic Real Option: Example

Figure 4. 9 Exposure Profile with Export Flexibility, Threat of New Entrant, and Expected Government Intervention

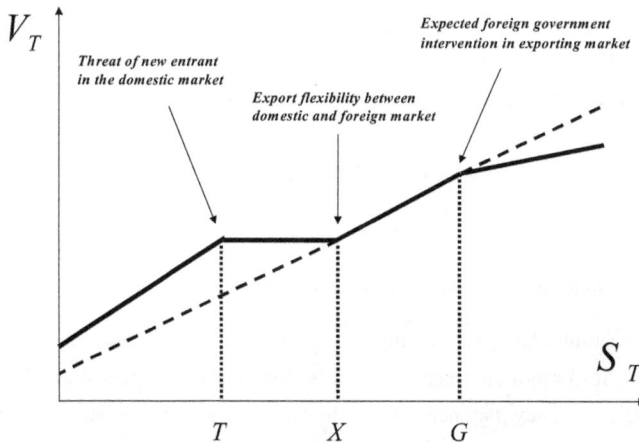

---

[97] See Sercu and Uppal (1995), pp. 181-182, Adam-Mueller and Wong (2001), p. 14. By writing call options, the firm creates a conditional obligation to deliver foreign exchange.

To convey the potential complexity of the exposure asymmetries of oligopolists, we consider a firm that sells both in its domestic market and exports to a foreign market, and that is subject to three sources of asymmetries (figure 4.9 above):

(i)   Threat of new entrant in the *domestic* market: the possibility that domestic consumers switch to a foreign import-competitor is like the firm selling a put on foreign currency at the exercise price T (selling a call on the domestic currency).

(ii)   Export flexibility between domestic and foreign market: the firm is long call on foreign currency with exercise price X (long put on domestic currency).

(iii)   Expected foreign government intervention in exporting market: the foreign government intervention can be viewed as the firm having written a call option on the foreign currency to the government with exercise price G (written a put on domestic currency).

B. Consumers' Asymmetric Response to Exchange Rate Changes

A firm's exposure can be asymmetric as a result of the flexibility in decision making of consumers. We saw that consumers have an implicit option to switch between firms. Other explanations can be given to the possibility that consumers respond only passively to small changes, but react quite dramatically to large exchange rate changes, or differently between appreciations and depreciations:

Foreign Exchange Accounts Receivable with Substantial Default Risk

Large depreciations have the potential to increase credit risk and the burden of debt denominated in foreign currencies. A firm's customer or supplier may *risk to default* on a foreign currency payment if his home currency depreciates and makes the payments more expensive in local currency. Such default risk will affect a firm's exchange rate exposure if the firm's customers or suppliers are affected by currency movements. The firm will be affected through this "indirect exposure"[98]. As only exchange rate movements from a certain magnitude and in one direction, i.e., either

---

[98] See Pringle (1995).

appreciations or depreciations, will hurt the firm performance and possibly causing default, the resulting exposure is asymmetric[99].

Income/Wealth Effects

A firm's exposure could also be asymmetric as a result of an income effect. Large changes in the real exchange rate result in substantial changes in relative prices, and as such, they influence the relative purchasing power of a consumer's currency. For instance, the appreciation of a country's currency may increase the wealth of its consumers, to the benefit of the firms serving them[100]. When the consumer's home currency appreciates substantially, this lead to an increase in the purchasing power of their home currency. Not only will this lead to a relative increase in the purchase of foreign goods, but through an *income effect* of the increased purchasing power of domestic residents it may also lead to an increase in both foreign and domestic purchases[101]. Such an *income effect of consumers* may mitigate the negative influence of a large appreciation on a domestic exporter that also has sales in its domestic market. The exposure profile will be convexified by this income effect.

An example of a firm that has been affected through its customers' exposure is Laker Airways, a UK firm whose base currency was British pounds (£), and whose activities were essentially domestic. Laker Air had been successful in flying British vacationers to the US at a time when the £ was relatively strong. However, Laker Air was affected when the US$ appreciated relative to the £. The increased cost of a trip to the US lead British tourists to reduce the use of the airline[102]. British consumers, and indirectly Laker Air, were negatively exposed to the US$. The situation of Laker Air was like it had written a real call on US$ to the British consumers. The identification of this exposure might then have led them to hedge financially by buying a financial call option on the US$.

---

[99] See Stulz (2000), ch.8, Holmes and Maghrebi (2002), p. 2.
[100] Choi (1986) shows in a partial equilibrium monopoly model that explicitly derive exposure in terms of output and input demand elasticities, that if exchange rate changes are included in the consumer's demand function, the sign of exposure is undetermined.
[101] See Bodnar (1999), p. 17, Froot and Stein (1991).
[102] See O'Brien (1997), pp. 7-8.

C. Interaction with Input Suppliers

The examples examined above illustrate how the evaluation of a firm's sources of exposure asymmetries and currencies of determination necessitate an analysis of factors such as the location of a firm's competitors, their foreign operations and strategic behavior, the entry/exit of firms not only in its output markets, but also in its input markets. Changes in the location of a firm's suppliers, of the suppliers of a firm's competitors, the entry of new suppliers in the input market, which are expected to occur at some distinct exchange rate, would make the firm's exposure asymmetric. Two examples illustrate this point.

- *Change in inputs market structure*: the market structure in a firm's input markets could be endogenous to the exchange rate. A firm's input market could become less competitive because of the exit of some firms. A less competitive input market would result in a relatively limited access to alternative sources of inputs and costs sourcing. The firm's competitive position and exposure could be affected by this limited operating flexibility, and be asymmetric at the exchange rates at which these suppliers are expected to leave the market.

- *Strategic behavior of input suppliers*: the asymmetric pricing behavior of suppliers could make a firm's exposure asymmetric. Although the pricing literature focuses on the role of market structure on an exporter's revenues, the same conclusions can be drawn for non-contractual cash flows on the cost side. The pricing behavior of international suppliers having market power positions allowing them to practice price discrimination across national borders and currencies, can affect a firm's noncontractual costs' exposure. Legal barriers, quotas, tariffs and other institutional reasons make it possible that some of a firm's suppliers can segment their markets and charge different price across markets[103]. Because of a relatively smaller and less competitive input markets, resulting in relatively limited access to alternative

---

[103] "The variability of costs facing a firm sourcing its inputs from an international supplier will tend to be lower from price discriminating sources. The firm that sources inputs from price discriminating environments will have higher exposure, due to the higher prices it has to pay, compared to competitive environments, but will also have reduced variability of its cash flows due to foreign exchange rate changes. In other words, part of the firm's foreign exchange risk, that is, part of the variability of its cash flows, is traded off with the higher price it pays to the price discriminating producer". See Demacopoulos (1989), for an analysis of the foreign exchange exposure of non-contractual costs in the U.S. construction industry.

sources of inputs and costs sourcing, a firm's competitive position and exposure could be affected from this limited operating flexibility.

4.2.2.2 Real Option Preemption and Value Effects of Government Interventions

Country risk analysis examines the "economic and social factors that contribute to the general level of risk in the country as a whole"[104]. Country risk includes factors such as price controls, interest rate ceilings, trade restrictions[105]. These government imposed barriers to the smooth adjustment of the economy to changing relative prices could also be source of exposure asymmetries, because these government interventions are likely to be function of the exchange rate level. Governments are likely to intervene only to relatively large real exchange rate changes, and differently to real exchange rate appreciation and depreciation. As a result, the government interventions will dramatically affect a firm's exposure for a certain range of exchange rates only, and make them asymmetric. At the exchange rate values where governments are expected to intervene, firms' exposure profiles will be characterized by trigger points, at which the nature of the exposure changes dramatically[106]. Government interventions could be directly targeted towards the industry, the result of general macroeconomic policy, such as trends in bilateral and multilateral trade, or be firm-specific[107]. Government policies can affect the demand/supply conditions of the firm's input and output markets. Some of the reasons why government may intervene asymmetrically in response to exchange rate changes comprise:

(a) Trade Policies

We saw that a firm can interpret the expected effects of government interventions in terms of real options. For instance, government interventions in an exporter's foreign market is like the exporter writing a real call option on foreign currency to the government. A firm's option to enter a foreign market (long call on foreign currency)

---

[104] See Shapiro (1999), p. 755.
[105] See Shapiro (1999), p. 758.
[106] Booth (1996), for example says that it is frequent in Canada and formally demonstrate this in a microeconomic model. In his model, non-linearities in the exposure function are generated by the fact that market structure is endogenous to exchange rate changes.
[107] See Shapiro (1999).

could be preempted by trade restrictions imposed by the foreign government (short call on foreign currency). See Figure 4.10 below. Notations are similar than in the previous section.

Figure 4. 10 Preemption of Exercising Option to Export from Threat of Trade Restrictions[108]

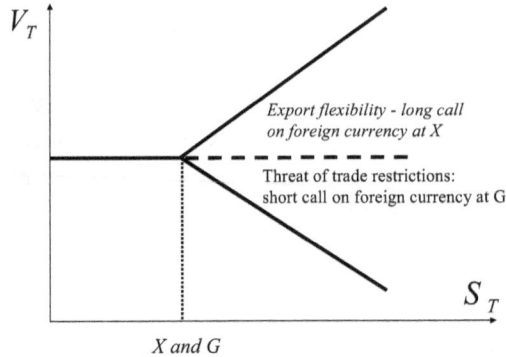

Trade policies comprise: (i) *direct assistance*: for instance, governments' interventions to assist industries that are suffering from increased import competition are likely to take place for large exchange rate changes only. A government could also institute subsidies to key export industries in response to a home currency appreciation but allow these exporters to benefit from currency depreciations[109]. A government is also more likely to provide foreign aid on the basis of a stronger home currency, when the change is large[110]; (ii) *protectionist policies*: large changes in exchange rates could cause governments to consider protectionist policies in the form of tariffs or non-tariff barriers such as quotas; (iii) *price controls*[111] will affect asymmetrically a firm's exposure, since they are likely to become effective for either depreciations or appreciations.

---

[108] This is the expiration value, not the profit or loss from a particular strategy. Sercu and Uppal (1995), p. 172.

[109] See Griffin and Stulz (2001), pp. 21-22, Brander and Spencer (1985). When in the early 1990s Daimler-Benz in Germany took over MBB, the German government offered an exchange rate guarantee for the revenue accruing in US dollars from the Airbus division of MBB. See Broll et al. (1999), p. 17.

[110] See Demacopoulos (1989), pp. 54-55, for examples of government providing foreign aid in the international construction sector.

[111] Lewent and Kearney (1990) explain that this is the case at Merck, as U.S. based pharmaceutical company.

(b) Exchange Rate Policies

Exchange rate volatility increases the real option waiting value because of the higher risk of mean reversion. The exchange rate mean reverting behavior can be affected by government interventions. When assessing the likely permanence of an exchange rate change, a move back toward equilibrium is considered more permanent than an exchange rate movement away from equilibrium, that is, one that is moving out of step with inflation[112]. In practice, "many of the latter, or disequilibrium, exchange rate moves, can be attributed to government interference in the foreign exchange markets. On the other hand, the adjustments back toward equilibrium are usually associated with free-market forces"[113].

Exchange rate policies can be in the form of *competitive depreciations:* the government could promote competitive depreciation to suit domestic economic interest[114]. Or in the form of *currency controls* that may also become more likely to be imposed at some specific exchange rate values[115].

(c) Policies on Capital Flows

These policies influence the degree of segmentation between national capital markets and influence firms' exposures through their cost of capital. Tax breaks could be offered for new foreign investments, controls on capital flows could be placed, and so forth[116].

(d) Monetary and Fiscal Policies

Since this is real exchange rate shocks that affect a firm's competitivity, the rate of inflation matters. This is determined in part by the country's monetary and fiscal

---

[112] In other terms, real exchange rate movements that narrow the gap between the current rate and the equilibrium rate are likely to be longer lasting than are those that widen the gap. See Shapiro (1999), p. 346.

[113] See Bishop and Dixon (1992), p. 346.

[114] However, large depreciations have also the potential to increase credit risk and the burden of debt denominated in foreign currencies. See Holmes and Maghrebi (2002), p. 2.

[115] See Demacopoulos (1989), p. 23.

[116] See Bodnar (1999), p. 17.

policy, through its effect on the quantity of money or interest rate[117]. The correlation of exchange rate changes with interest rate risk, for example, could create a nonlinear structure[118]. The government policies could be source of correlation between interest rates and exchange rate that could itself be function of the exchange rate. In that case, we could find that interest rates are non-linearly related to the exchange rate, because of monetary policies taking effect for some particular range of exchange rate values. As a result, the exposure would have trigger points at these exchange rate levels.

These government policies can play a critical role in determining how effectively a country will deal with external shocks, such as exchange rate risk. A country can cope with exchange rate changes if policies promote timely internal and external adjustment, as is manifest in relatively low inflation rates and small current-account deficits[119]. This could affect firms' foreign exchange exposures. Furthermore, a firm's exposure can be affected not only by the policies of its local government, but also by the policies of foreign governments. In order to assess a firm's foreign exchange exposure, it is thus useful to determine the relative susceptibility of the countries that are involved in the firm's trades, to these exchange rate shocks.

4.3 Corporate Strategy and Valuation of Asymmetric Foreign Exchange Exposures

Two aspects need to be assessed for measuring the effects of strategic real options on a firm's foreign exchange exposure: (i) calculation of the *real option value,* and (ii) derivation of the *optimal exercise rule* under various industry structures.

4.3.1 Firm's Control over the Value of Real Options

The industry structure determines a firm's degree of control over the value of its real options. There are few actions undertaken in response to exchange rate changes that increase value without any qualifiers. In most cases, the net effect on value will be a function of how competitors and other market participants react to a firm's actions. The

---

[117] See Shapiro (1999), pp. 757-758.
[118] See Stulz (2000), ch. 8, p. 40, Greene (2000).
[119] See Shapiro (1999).

exercise of a real option could be found to create value in a static analytical environment, but not if competitors' reactions are taken into consideration. It is thus critical that foreign exchange exposures be examined in a dynamic environment that considers the actions that the firm's competitors would take in response to the firm's actions. For measuring the influence of real options on foreign exchange exposure, a corporate manager needs to evaluate the degree of control that the firm has over the value effect of its real options. Actions that create value can be categorized both on *how quickly* they create value and *how much control* the firm has over the value creation[120]:

(a) "Actions where the firm has *considerable control* over the outcome and where the payoff in terms of value creation is *immediate*": for example, "eliminating new capital expenditures that are expected to earn less than the cost of capital" [121], or changing the ratio of foreign to domestic currency debts[122].

(b) "Actions that are likely to create value in the *near or medium term* and where the firm still continues to exercise *significant control* over the outcome": for example, "increasing the reinvestment rate or marginal return on capital or both in firm's existing business" [123].

(c) *"Actions that would create value in a static environment, but might not if competitors react by matching or beating the firm"*: for example, "increasing reinvestment rate or marginal return on capital or both in new business", or "changing pricing strategy to maximize the product's profit margins and turnover ratio" [124]. The effects of pricing actions on value are difficult to determine, because they are the most likely to attract counter actions from competitors. Passing-through exchange rate changes into foreign currency prices to increase margins may not work as a value enhancement measure if competitors react and change prices as well. Conversely, a firm that reduces prices to increase sales may find its competitors cutting prices in response, and end up with lower margins and lower sales.

---

[120] See Damodaran (2004-a), pp. 27-28.
[121] See Damodaran (2004-a), p. 28.
[122] See Levich (1998), p. 595.
[123] See Damodaran (2004-a), p. 28.
[124] See Damodaran (2004-a), p. 28.

A decomposition of the return on capital (*ROC*) on a project into margin and turnover ratio components gives some insights on the value effect of pricing decisions. The *ROC* on a project can be written as a function of its after-tax operating margin and its turnover ratio, where t is the tax rate and *EBIT* the earnings before interest and taxes[125]:

$$ROC = EBIT\ (1\text{-}t)/\ Sales\ *\ Sales\ /\ Capital$$

$$= After\text{-}tax\ Operating\ Margin\ *\ Capital\ Turnover\ Ratio$$

The destruction of the real option value would imply a normal distribution of foreign currency cash flows and a linear foreign exchange exposure. In that case, the standard DCF-based valuation method can be used instead of the ROV method. This implies that in a setting where there are strategic advantages to acting quickly and seizing the advantage over one's rivals (first-mover advantage), the use of a *standard* real options valuation method could cause a firm to miss strategic opportunities that would affect its competitive position.

4.3.2 Strategic Real Option Exercise Rules

Exposure measures need to incorporate the payoff value and exercise rules of these real options. In an oligopoly, the options exercise rules of a firm and its competitors are endogenously determined.

A. Emergence of Strategic Real Options Models of Exposure

Structural models of exposure and real option models are complementary. Structural models of exposure are generally cash flow based and examine strategic interactions in a static framework. However, the implications of the option-like nature of the investments that underlie operating responses to exchange rate changes are not examined. This makes these models not directly relevant for risk management, whose concern is shareholder value. Real option theory offers a more adequate framework for examining the costs and benefits of operating adjustments from a risk management perspective. Real option analysis helps discount the effect of exchange rate uncertainty on firm value and determine the value of a strategy in dynamic over the valuation

---

[125] See Damodaran (2004-a), p. 17.

period. But real options models have originally been developed for capital budgeting purposes either in a single firm settings with an exogenous price process or under monopoly, and not for describing risk exposures under oligopolistic industry structure. The integration of these two approaches gives insights into the real options value of oligopolists and make structural model of exposure relevant for risk management studies[126]. But for establishing operational rules that are relevant for the problems practitioners confront in actual conditions, heuristic, rather than formal theoretical models need to be devised[127].

4.3.2.1 Optimal Strategic Behavior with Proprietary and Shared Options

It is often viewed that corporations with the flexibility to adjust their production and operations to exchange rate changes, benefit, in relative competitive terms, from higher volatility because their competitors are slower to respond to currency changes[128]. However, strategic considerations also dictate the real option exercise timing. The interactions of a firm's options may positively or negatively interact with other market participants' options. For example, the decision to exercise one option may affect the exercise policy and incremental value of other additional options[129].

The value of the strategic investment and the optimal competitive strategy (e.g., to invest now or wait) depends on the following aspects[130].

- **Proprietary or shared option**: whether the resulting benefits of the investment are *proprietary* or *shared*. If a firm has a proprietary option, its exercise will be damaging to competitors, while if a firm has a shared option, its exercise will have benefiting effects on competitors. An aspect that determines whether the

---

[126] "Dynamic game theory is potentially a powerful analytical tool for valuing strategic real options and determining real options optimal exercise thresholds as a sequence of actions across the life of a project. Game theory can model different market structures from monopoly through duopoly, oligopoly, and perfect competition". See Fudenberg and Tirole (1992) for a detailed treatment of dynamic games, and Copeland and Antikarov (2001), pp. 349-351, and Huisman (2001), for an application of game theory to real option analysis.

[127] See, e.g., Kulatilaka and Perotti (1999) for a Stackelberg real options model, and Kogut and Kulatilaka (1999) for a discussion on heuristics and formal theory.

[128] See Giddy and Dufey (1995), p. 56.

[129] See Sercu and Uppal (1995), p. 677.

[130] See Trigeorgis (2002), pp. 13-15.

option is proprietary or shared is whether the goods are substitutes or complementary[131].

- **Contrarian or reciprocating behavior of competitors**: whether competitive reaction is *contrarian* (opposite to the action of the investing firm) or *reciprocating* (similar to the action of the investing firm)[132]:

Contrarian Competitor

(a) *Proprietary option*: the firm can improve its competitive position at the expense of its competitor by committing to an early investment (aggressive) strategy. The competitor's contrarian reaction implies for example that it will retreat and cut its market share under quantity competition as the firm expands its own market share[133].

(b) *Shared option*: the firm should follow a flexible "wait and see" strategy rather than subsidizing an aggressive competitor while itself paying the full cost, since the option exercise would also benefit the competitor, who would respond aggressively[134].

Reciprocating Competition

The above can be reversed under reciprocating competition.

(a) *Proprietary option*: it may make better sense to wait or not invest since the benefits are proprietary and will hurt a competitor who will retaliate, for example by entering into a price war[135].

---

[131] The Cournot model examined in section 4.1 suggested that, e.g., after a depreciation an exporter increases quantity and induces competitors' to (i) increase quantity (complementary goods) which reduces the long call payoffs, (ii) decrease quantity (substitution goods) which increases the long call payoffs. After an appreciation: exporter reduce quantities, but competitors either (i) increase quantity which reduces long put payoffs, or (ii) decreases quantity which increases long put payoffs.
[132] See Trigeorgis (2002), pp. 13-15.
[133] See Trigeorgis (2002), pp. 13-15.
[134] See Trigeorgis (2002), pp. 13-15.
[135] See Trigeorgis (2002), pp. 13-15.

(b) *Shared option*: the optimal strategy might be to invest early but not aggressively, since the benefits are shared and will benefit a competitor who will reciprocate when treated nicely[136].

4.3.2.2 Strategic Option Value of Waiting and Shared Options

A. Optimal Dynamic Competitive Strategy

The real option value to delay can be offset by the "convenience value" of possessing an operating project[137], which could be in the form of a first-mover or second-mover advantage or collusion. Dynamic multi-stage games examine how strategic interactions can lead to several types of equilibria, such as *preemption equilibria* or *tacit collusion equilibria*[138], and give indications on the real options payoffs under various forms of competition:

(a) *First-mover advantage*: a first-mover advantage could give a firm a higher option payoff if it acts first rather than second. The threat of preemption could reduce the option value of waiting. If a firm is preempted, a portion of the rents is lost depending on the relative strength of the rival[139]. Assume a firm with an option to enter a foreign market. A foreign currency appreciation would make it profitable to enter, but a high risk of exchange rate mean reversion would make it valuable to wait. Meanwhile, a competitor could enter the market, which could then preempt the firm's entry. A first-mover might be able to set barriers to entry, especially if consumers have high switching costs and that building market shares is valuable. In that case, the decision to delay the entry would reduce or even destroy the value of its option.

(b) *Second-mover advantage*: information spillovers may give a second mover advantage. In some cases, it might be preferable, for information advantage, to wait and see what an other firm does before acting[140].

---

[136] See Trigeorgis (2002), pp. 13-15.
[137] See Cottrell and Sick (2001).
[138] See Fudenberg and Tirole (1992), pp. 126-128 and p. 155.
[139] "Investing prematurely would result in a suboptimal prisoner's dilemma situation. Each of the two firms, being afraid that it may be preempted by the other and loose all, would rush to invest prematurely, rather than wait which may be the preferred outcome". See Trigeorgis (2002).
[140] See Trigeorgis (2002).

(c) *Cooperative strategy*: a firm could collaborate rather than try to gain a competitive advantage over its rivals. A joint venture for example may enable two firms to better appropriate the flexibility value from waiting by coordinating and jointly optimizing against exchange rate uncertainty[141].

B. Illustration: Effects on Exposure of Strategic Competition in Export Pricing

A German firm (G) and a Japanese firm (J) export strategic *substitutes* to the U.S. market[142]. Each firm is assumed to be market-share performance-oriented, and incurs all costs in its respective domestic country. Bilateral exchange rates are independent. Costs of the Japanese and German firms are fixed in domestic currency terms at some arbitrary level. The firms have no influence on the costs of inputs but have pricing flexibility on their supply side. After an exchange rate change, the effect of a firm's pricing on its profit margins and value depends on the strategic interactions with the other firm. Each firm must take account not only of its rival's actions, but also the rival's reaction to its own behavior. Competition in export pricing can erode profitability by reducing price-cost margins in the short term and affecting competitiveness and firm value over the long term. Figure 4.11 below illustrates the strategic interaction in export pricing.

The two firms have real options to pass-through the exchange rate changes to the U.S. consumers. The value of the strategic options, the optimal exercise strategy of the two firms, and the effect on their exposures depend on whether:

- the resulting benefits of the investment associated with exercise of the option are *proprietary* or *shared*: if the real option of G is proprietary (shared), its exercise hurts (benefits) J. With market share expansion objectives, a firm's price increase benefits the competitor.

- the competitive reaction is contrarian or reciprocating[143]: this depends on the bilateral and cross exchange rates and corporate strategies. For example, a firm can

---

[141] This would avoid the prisoner's dilemma. See Trigeorgis (2002).
[142] This example is partially based on Clark et al. (1999), pp. 260-261. Clark et al. however do not use this framework for the purpose of analyzing asymmetric exposures and strategic real options.
[143] See Trigeorgis (2002).

maximize its profit margins because it is financially pressed, whereas its competitor pursues a market share expansion strategy.

Figure 4. 11 Strategic Interaction in Export Pricing

	€/US$ up	€/US$ down	
	(I)	(IIa)	(IIb)
¥/US$ down	Japanese exporter's margin narrow German exporter's margin widen	€/¥ up	€/¥ down
	(IIIa)	(IIIb)	(IV)
¥/US$ up	€/¥ up	€/¥ down	German exporter's margin narrow Japanese exporter's margin widen

Source: adapted from Clark, Kotabe, and Rajaratnam (1999), p. 261.

A firm's exchange rate pass-through behavior can be complex in practice, for example because of (a) *predatory pricing*: firms can pursue predatory pricing "by deliberately making losses with anti-competitive intent"[144] and have negative pass-through behavior, (b) *"cross-national" exchange rate pass-through*: for example, an exporter selling both in a foreign market and its domestic market could pass-through exchange rate changes to its *domestic* consumers (see section 4.2.1.2).

Cell I: ¥/US$ down - €/US$ up:

1) G lowers p^s: The *resulting benefits* of the investment by G in a lower p^s are *proprietary*. The option of G is *damaging to* J. With the uncertainty of the option's underlying exogenous and an elasticity of demand greater than *1*, the value of G increases. The benefits in terms of firm value of exercising this option is damaging to

---

[144] See Economic Focus: Preying on Theory, The Economist July 10th 1999, p. 88, for theoretical arguments supporting the possibility of predatory pricing.

J. J could have the following reaction (the same effect would arise if G keeps p^s at the same level):

- Contrarian behavior: J increases p^s $ so as to protect profit margins in ¥. The contratian reaction of J implies that it retreats and cut its market share as G expands its market share. The reaction of J increases the value of the option of G and the exposure of G to exchange rate depreciations (ϵ/US ↑). The *optimal strategy for G* is to reduce foreign prices early to improve its competitive position at the expense of J.

- Reciprocating behavior: J lowers p^s if it highly values long term market shares[145] (negative pass-through). The reaction of J reduces the value of the option of G and the exposure of G to exchange rate depreciations. The *optimal competitive strategy*: is to wait or not invest.

2) G increases p^s (negative pass-through): flexibility of negatively passing-through is a shared option. The resulting benefits of the investment in higher p^s is shared with and benefits J.

- Contrarian behavior: J lowers p^s. The reaction of J reduces the value of the option of G and the exposure of G to exchange rate depreciations. The *optimal competitive strategy* is to have a flexible "wait and see" strategy.

- Reciprocating behavior: J increases p^s. The reaction of J increases the value of the option of G and the exposure of G to exchange rate depreciations. The *resulting benefits* of the investment by G to increase p^s are *shared* and benefits J. The optimal competitive strategy is to invest early but not aggressively

The situation is identical but reversed in cell (IV) [146].

---

[145] This could be enabled by combining other types of operating flexibility, e.g., the Japanese firm could increase its domestic prices, in order to pursue an aggressive pricing policy in the U.S. market.
[146] In the empirical literature, hypothesis of asymmetries based on corporate pricing *implicitly* assume that the firm is a monopoly. A typical hypothesis would be that the German firm's exposure is asymmetric because it pursues a market share expansion strategy. In that case when the exchange rate €/US$ goes up, the firm would pass-through the dollar appreciation into lower prices in US$. On the

Cell II: ¥/US$ down - €/US$ down: G has a shared option

Both the German and the Japanese firms have depreciating revenue streams in US$. G increases p^s. J could have the following reaction:

- Contrarian behavior: J lowers p^s. The reaction of J reduces the value of the option of G and the exposure of G to exchange rate appreciation ($€/US\$ \downarrow$).

- Reciprocating behavior: J increases p^s. The reaction of J increases the value of the option of G and the exposure of G to exchange rate appreciations.

Unless the cross exchange rate ($€/¥$) remains unchanged, one firm will gain a comparative advantage in relatively greater margins. In cell (IIa), the ¥ strengthens against the €, and the G is hurt less than the J. G gains a relative advantage over the J. At a time when both firms would like to increase the price of their products in the US to regain margins, G needs to do so the least. G might leverage its relative advantage by refusing to raise its price, or even by lowering it. In cell (IIb), the situation is reversed.

Cells (IIIa) and (IIIb): ¥/US$ up - €/US$ up: both firms experience increases in their revenues from the U.S., implying higher profit margins. The behavior of the ($€/¥$) will determine which firm realizes a comparative advantage. In cell (IIIa), the German firm has a comparative advantage, whereas in cell (IIIb), the Japanese exporter has[147]. If the German firm lowers its US$ price in order to undercut the Japanese competition in the U.S. market, Japanese exporters may not benefit from a ¥ depreciation against the US$.

4.3.3 Hysterisis and Exposure Intertemporal Instability

Firm market value exposure time-variation across estimation sub-periods is supported in virtually all empirical studies. Given that most determinants of foreign exchange exposure can reasonably be expected to be time-varying this is not astonishing. What is more difficult to explain is the nature of this exposure instability. The distribution of

---

other hand, when the exchange rate €/US$ goes down, the firm would not pass through the dollar depreciation.

[147] The case with strategic complements can be inferred by analogy. See Clark et al. (1999), p. 261.

exposure estimates is often observed to systematically *shift back and forth from positive to negative* over the sample period, and the magnitude of these shifts in the distribution of exposure coefficients over sub-periods seem surprisingly large[148]. These shifts have been reported to appear "too large and too sudden to be explained by structural changes in the firm's cash flow sensitivities or market structures"[149].

Temporal shifts of the exposure sign can be explained by changes in real activities, i.e. the exercise of real options. Operative measures create a fundamental change in the way a firm does business and thus a long-lasting (hysteretic) effect on foreign exchange exposure. Exposure asymmetries generate persistent effects which affects the temporal behavior of exposure:

(a) *Changes in sector of activity*: exposure time variation could be the result of a firm engaging in different activities. This could reverse the slope of the exposure profile. An empirical study has formally tested for constant foreign exchange exposures, and finds evidence that firms had switched from being net exporters to being net importers or vice-versa across the estimation sub-periods[150].

(b) *Setting up/closing foreign operations (growth option/abandonment option)*: the foreign exchange exposure of a company's subsidiary could have a sign different from the main company (see Appendix B). The exposure of a foreign subsidiary can offset the exposure of company and make the exposure negative.

(c) *Shifts in production location can explain shifts in exposure profile over time*: the switching option examined previously shows that the German firm's exposure to the €/US$ exchange rate can change in a persistent way over time. The exposure

---

[148] By negative exposure, it is meant that firms with a net long economic position in foreign currency will benefit (suffer) from an appreciation (depreciation) of their home currency, while firms with a net short economic position in foreign currency will suffer (benefit) from an appreciation (depreciation) of their home currency.

[149] See, e.g., in Bodnar and Wong (1999).

[150] Allayannis (1997), e.g., tests for constant foreign exchange exposures across different sub-periods. This study examines trade data for US manufacturing industries between 1978 and 1990 and reveals that approximately 43 percent of the US manufacturing industries have switched during this period from being net exporters to being net importers or vice-versa. He concludes that exposure time variation is driven by the monthly share of imports and exports and argues that the lack of significant evidence of foreign exchange exposure documented in the literature is due to the assumption that exchange-rate exposure is constant. Overall, most studies show that the relation between exchange rate changes and stock price returns is not stable over time. Bodnar and Wong (1999), Choi and Prasad (1995), Ibrahimi et al. (1995), Williamson (1996), for example, have found evidence of changing signs. However, most of their coefficients were insignificant. An exception is Glaum et al. (2000) who find unstable but significant exposures.

profile differs whether the firm is currently located in Germany or in the U.S. At a given period of time, the firm can switch production location and move to a different exposure profile. The change in exposure profile can be persistent because of the hysteretic effects associated with the operating adjustment. Because of hysterisis, exercising the option has persistent effect on exposure. Hysterisis makes the exposure of periodic cash flows path dependent. Switching costs explain why companies don't switch to alternative suppliers when the quality and the prices are better. In the example above, the exposure of the German firm to the €/US$ will shift from negative to being insignificant. Exposure asymmetries reflect also the possibility that exposure be truncated, e.g., by exercising switching or abandonment options.

Exposure intertemporal behavior can be explained by changes in behavior of other market participants (indirect exposure), e.g., changes in government policy regime, or changes in hedging policies. The same explanations can be given for time path of cash flow exposure over the valuation period.

4.4 Firm's Overall Exposure Profile and Portfolio Effects

The contribution of exchange rate risk to the firm's total risk reflects the relative importance of foreign exchange risk. An overall view of corporate and foreign exchange exposure must take two aspects simultaneously into account:

- *Portfolio effects on each cash flow component*: this implies recognizing the impact of business and political risk factors on foreign currency cash flows, and therefore on the exposure and value of the project and firm.

- *Foreign exchange exposure netting effect over the firm's various cash flows*: the "effects on the various cash flows of the firm should be netted over product lines and markets to account for diversification effects where gains and losses could cancel out. The remaining net loss or gain is the subject of economic exposure management"[151]. For example, a firm with *multicurrency cash flows would* (i) define cash flows by currency of denomination, (ii) forecast currency rates for the

---

[151] This aspect is discussed in Giddy and Dufey (1992), p. 13.

translation of future cash flows. This analysis will reveal the extent of unmatched inflows and outflows in multiple currencies[152].

The NPV and ROV rule is consistent with the *value additivity principle*, which states that the value of the firm is equal to the sum of the value of the firm's projects and other assets[153]. This implies that the analysis of exposure of cash flows from a project can be applied to the overall exposure of the firm.

4.4.1 Exposure Asymmetries and Factors of Foreign Cash Flow Volatility

4.4.1.1 Factors of Foreign/Local Currency Cash Flow Volatility

A. Interdependency of Exposures

Domestic currency values of foreign currency cash flows are affected by (i) changes in exchange rates and the resulting differentials between projected and actual exchange rates, (ii) changes in the foreign currency based cash flows and the differentials between projected, i.e., estimated, and actual foreign currency cash flows[154].

The impact of changes in foreign cash flows can contribute negatively or positively to a firm's exposure. The effect of exchange rates may be negligible after partialling out the effect of other factors. For example, changes in interest rates and exchange rates could have a simultaneous but differential impact on future cash flows. The causality of these effects must be assessed over the valuation period. The endogeneity of other factors of foreign cash flow uncertainty to the exchange rate create exposure asymmetries:

(a) *Default risk of foreign exchange accounts receivable/payables*: contractual foreign cash flows are not fully risk-free. Contractual exposures can be truncated and asymmetric at some exchange rates if the contractual foreign cash flows are subject to exchange rate related default risk. Contractual foreign exchange exposure is affected by a firm's own default risk and of its consumers, but also indirectly by the

---

[152] See Demacopoulos (1989), p. 87.
[153] See Brealey and Myers (2000), Damodaran (2004-a), pp. 4-8.
[154] See Demacopoulos (1989), p. 83.

endogenous risk of default of its suppliers and competitors[155]. Large depreciations have the potential to increase credit risk and the burden of debt denominated in foreign currencies[156]. Foreign exchange exposure can thus be related to interest rate exposure, since interest rates influence credit risk.

(b) *Default risk and strategic real options*: the exercise of strategic real options can trigger reactions from competitors that can lead to a firm to default. For example, a competitor might purposely lower its prices after an exchange rate change in an attempt to drive a highly leveraged firm out of business[157]. By doing so, a firm could bankrupt its more highly leveraged rival and force it to exit the market. The firm's foreign exchange exposure is asymmetric at the exchange rate at which such threat is likely to become effective.

(c) *Risk of derivative market illiquidity*: the possibility of hedging future exposures could be hampered by a reduction in the derivative market liquidity[158].

(d) *Foreign investments decisions based on exchange rates*: a future investment could be made only if the exchange rate reaches a certain value[159].

B. Typology of Factors of Foreign Cash Flow Volatility

The volatility of foreign cash flows in nominal terms is driven by a variety factors (table 4.3). The effect on the volatility of nominal foreign cash flows would then affect exposure, for example:

- *Country/macroeconomic policy risk*: risk of foreign cost overrun due to a risk of increase in the price of foreign inputs, e.g., because of a possible new tax policy, such as sales or value-added tax[160].

---

[155] The role of a firm's financial structure can be assessed with metrics such as the degree of leverage, debt-to-equity ratios, long-term debt ratio. The long-term debt ratio can give indication on a firm's probability of financial distress. Firms with higher long-term debt ratio tend to face larger expected costs of financial distress. "However, multinational firms with greater financial leverage are also more likely to hedge and hence may be less exposed to exchange rate risk". See He and Ng (1998), p. 741.

[156] See Holmes and Maghrebi (2002), p. 2, Stulz and Williamson (1996).

[157] See Grinblatt and Titman (2002), p. 609.

[158] See Giannetti (2002), p. 12, for an account of such event for Asian firms during the Asian financial crisis in 1997.

[159] See Stulz (2000), ch. 17, p. 4.

[160] Based on Demacopoulos (1989), pp. 83-85.

- *Business risk source*: risk that inputs may not be available from a given foreign supplier at the time of purchase[161], and that it might have to be purchased from a supplier an other country. A budget overrun could be realized.

Table 4. 3 *Typology of Risk Factors Affecting the Volatility of Foreign Cash Flows*

Business risks (Operating risk).	risks that the "corporation willingly assumes to create a competitive advantage and add value for shareholders", e.g., technological innovations, product design, marketing[162].
Strategic risks	risks that result from "fundamental shifts in the economy or political environment", e.g., , political risk, expropriation and nationalization[163].
	• *Industry factors of competitiveness*: change in competitive patterns can be driven by both internal changes in the resource base of a company, e.g., innovations from internal R&D, and by external changes in the environment, e.g., changes in government regulation. Exposures to strategic moves by competing firms may be important for assessing foreign exchange exposure. "The price of foreign competitor's exports may be interrelated with movements in real exchange rates. Other variables that may have an impact are the price of inputs, input supply, product demand risks, substitutes, domestic competitor's goods, technological state"
	• *Political and social risks:* political and government policy variables may affect business and "could have significant inverse relations with the value of a country's currency"[164]. Political risks reflecting actions of government agents, or country risks resulting from macro- and microeconomic policies and developments,
Financial risks	risks that relate to possible losses in financial markets, e.g., movements in exchange rates[165].
	• *Market risks:* "include *basis risk*, which occurs when relationships between products used to hedge each other change or break down, and *gamma risk*, due to non-linear relationship".
	• *Credit risks*: "arises when counterparties are unwilling or unable to fulfill their contractual obligations". The default risk of foreign customers, for example, could depend on the value taken by future exchange rates.
	• *Liquidity risks:*" takes two forms: (1) *market/product liquidity*: "arises when a transaction cannot be conducted at prevailing market prices due to insufficient market activity", and (2) *cash flow/funding*: "refers to the inability to meet cash flow obligations, which may force early liquidation, thus transforming "paper" losses into realized losses".

---

[161] Based on Demacopoulos (1989), pp. 83-85.
[162] See Jorion (1997), p. 3.
[163] See Jorion (1997), p. 4, Miller (1992), p. 321.
[164] See Miller (1994), p.10.

4.4.1.2 Competitive Interest Rate and Price Exposures

Interest rate and price exposures are also competitive exposures. As with foreign exchange exposure, what matters is the real effects of changes in interest rate and nominal prices[166].

A. Economic Interest Rate Exposure

Corporate competitiveness can be affected by changes in relative interest rates:

- *Competitive exposure of costs of borrowing*: debt service is usually the single largest source of interest rate risk for non-financial firms[167]. Financial assets are exposed if there is a net asset or liability position in financial assets that differs from that of its competitors. If there are deviations from real interest rate parity, stating that expected real interest rates on similar loans or investments in two countries should be the same, then firms with their financing in countries with low real interest rates will be at a relative cost advantage[168]. Interest rate differences among countries could be a source of interest rate driven competitive advantages for its firms, since the costs of borrowing to a large extent is determined by the domestic interest rates.

- *Competitive exposure of investments: effect on investments, costs, and revenues:* interest rate fluctuations are related to the economy business cycles, and they influence investment through the cost of capital. Deviations from real interest rate parity put firms with investments in countries with low real interest rates at a relative cost disadvantage.

- *Competitive exposure of revenues: firms are indirectly exposed* through other market participants. A firm will face interest rate exposure if the cost of financing is

---

[165] See Jorion (1997), pp. 14-16.

[166] Real interest rates are "expressed in terms of real goods, i.e., nominal interest rate adjusted for inflation". See Brealey and Myers (2000), p. 1070.

[167] See Eiteman et al. (2000), p. 288. Highly levered firms have a higher expected cost of financial distress and are thus more vulnerable to interest rate risk.

[168] The interest rate exposure of financial assets can be assessed with "duration" measures. This shows that the debt maturity affects the interest rate sensitivity of a firm's cash flows. See Jorion and Khoury (1996), p. 73-121, Grinblatt and Titman (1998), pp. 787-837.

an important component of the purchase price of its products[169]. Similarly to firms, the costs for consumers' borrowing is determined to a large extent by the domestic interest rates, a higher domestic interest rate leads to higher savings and to lower consumption and demand, and vice versa. For this reason, firms with sales in countries with low interest rates may have a competitive advantage on their revenue side.

C. Foreign Exchange Exposure and Price Exposure

Distinction between Contractual Foreign Exchange Exposure and Inflation Exposure

The real exchange rate index used for measuring the exposure of non-contractual cash flows incorporates inflation exposure. For contractual cash flows, one needs to treat separately foreign exchange exposure and inflation exposure. Nominal contractual cash flows are converted with a nominal exchange rate, and then adjusted for inflation. As such, the economic exposure of nominal cash flows should be viewed as resulting from both nominal exchange rate uncertainty and inflation uncertainty[170]. It would be incorrect to say that the foreign exchange exposure of contractual cash flows increases with the horizon, because of inflation. The inflation exposure can be important for long term contractual cash flows (common in the construction sector[171]).

Competitive Foreign Exchange Exposure and Price Risk

Foreign exchange exposure is affected by price fluctuations through two channels, (i) the price indexes used to adjust the nominal exchange rate used for conversion, (ii) the price indexes that affect nominal foreign cash flows. For examples, costs are often

---

[169] For example, an automobile or home appliance manufacturer may experience a fall in demand as interest rates rise, because many customers finance the purchase of these "big-ticket" items. See Levich (1998), p. 567. Since cars are durable goods, we would expect that the firm would be exposed to the level of interest rates.
[170] Accordingly, the *risk* of a position that is nominal should not be attributed to exchange rate risk but to inflation risk". See Copeland and Weston (1992), pp. 814-815.
[171] There is also increasing difficulty to hedge as the timing of the cash flows goes beyond the near future. See Demacopoulos (1989), p. 48.

exposed to the US-dollar, since *commodity prices risk*, such as oil prices, are generally denominated in US-dollar[172].

4.4.2 Project Portfolio Selection and Corporate Diversification

In a world of perfect markets, diversification should be made by the firm's shareholders. The security portfolio selection methodology can be adapted to assess the diversification effect of a firm's projects. Several differences limit the analogy to security portfolio selection: "unlike the stock market, where securities are flexibly bought and sold over time, a firm's projects cannot practically be sold or abandoned, once the firm makes a commitment to them. International project abandonment can be equivalent to permanently writing off a country's market"[173].

A. International Corporate Diversification

At the firm level, a firm can "reduce its exposures by allocating optimum proportions of its operations in countries and projects that complement each other towards reducing total market exposure, i.e., business, political and exchange rate risk, and its impact on domestic currency returns". At a project level, it can "pursue currency of revenue and cost denominations that specifically reduce the foreign exchange exposure and its impact on domestic currency returns"[174].

A firm may have a portfolio of projects. These projects have individual and portfolio / risk profiles. "Similarly to security based portfolios, which can be changed by selling and buying securities, the existing firm's project portfolio can be changed through (i) addition of new projects, (ii) exercise of abandonment options in-progress projects. The firm has to decide how to select new projects on the basis of their interaction with existing project portfolio"[175].

---

[172] The majority of commodity trade takes place in three groups. (1) soft commodities like wheat, soya and sugar, (2) metals, ranging from precious metals to construction materials, (3) energy, predominantly oil and gas. See Moore (2003), p.1.
[173] See Demacopoulos (1989), p. 182.
[174] See Demacopoulos (1989), p. 184.
[175] See Demacopoulos (1989), p. 185.

B. Correlation between local market risk and exchange rate risk.

The expected value and variance of a firm's portfolio of multiple current projects M can be written as[176]:

[4. 15] $$E(V) = \sum_{i=1}^{M} s_i \cdot E(P_i)$$

[4. 16] $$\sigma^2(V) = \sum_{i=1}^{M} w_i^2 \cdot v[s_i \cdot E(P_i)] + 2 \sum_{\substack{i,j=1 \\ i \neq j}}^{M} w_i \cdot w_j \cdot \rho_{TPij} \cdot \sigma_T[E(P_i)] \cdot \sigma_T E[E(P_j)]$$

where:

ρ_{Akl}	coefficients of correlation between activities k and l, where the subscript A implies activity correlation
$\rho_{P_{ij}}$	project coefficients of correlation
$E(P_i)$	expected return in foreign currency from project i
$E(P_j)$	expected return in foreign currency from project j
σ_T	total individual country / project risk, including foreign market and foreign exchange risks
$v[\cdot]$	variance operator
s_i	exchange rate
V	value of portfolio of projects
w_i, w_j	probabilities

Expression [4.16] shows that the risk of cash flows in domestic currency depends on (i) *foreign market risk* that covers the variability of foreign currency project cash flows, (ii) *foreign exchange risk* that covers the variability of foreign exchange rates used in translating foreign cash flows in domestic currency. The correlation between the exchange rate and market movements indicates the contribution of exchange rate risk to total market risk[177].

---

[176] See Demacopoulos (1989), p. 186.
[177] See Demacopoulos (1989), p. 186.

PART TWO:EMPIRICAL EVIDENCE AND RISK MANAGEMENT IMPLICATIONS

5. Stock Market's Valuation of Foreign Exchange Exposure Asymmetries: Evidence from German Corporations

In part one, we have examined the asymmetric effects of unexpected exchange rate changes on firm value through variables in products markets, such as market shares, prices. In this chapter, we test the hypothesis of exposure asymmetry based on financial data. First, we test the hypothesis of asymmetry for a sample of German corporations. Second, we discuss to what extent the theoretical predictions on exposure asymmetries can be tested with stock market data. Third, we give explanations for our findings based on economic theories as well as on methodological shortcomings. We conclude with a discussion on the relevance of stock versus flow exposure measurement methods. The discussion focuses on the suitability of these methods to handle exposure asymmetries. Section 5.1 lays the hypothesis on exposure asymmetries based on the theory in part one. In sections 5.2 to 5.4, we empirically test the hypothesis of exposure asymmetries. Section 5.5 discusses several hypothesis for our findings. Throughout, we review the empirical issues and findings discussed in the finance literature[1].

5.1 Theoretical Predictions on Asymmetric Foreign Exchange Exposures

This section formulates hypothesis of exposure asymmetries, based on the theoretical analysis of part one. These hypothesis will be tested for the US-dollar exposure of German firms' stock returns.

---

[1] Other empirical studies on asymmetric exposures with threshold effects include Kanas (1995), Miller and Reuer (1995), Di Ioro and Faff (1999), Andren (2001), Bradley and Moles (2001), Aabo (2002), Koutmos and Martin (2003), Carter et al. (2003), test the hypothesis of asymmetric exposure profile. Bartram (1999), Bartram (2002), Priestley and Odegaard (2002) test for the more general hypothesis of curvilinear exposures.

5.1.1 US-Dollar Exposure of German Corporations

A. International Orientation of German Firms

German firms are expected to be significantly exposed to the US-dollar. The first reason is that *Germany is a very open economy*. Most studies of exchange rate exposure have been undertaken on U.S firms and rarely find significant measures of exposure. The foreign exchange exposure of German firms seems to be particularly interesting to investigate, since Germany is a relatively more open economy than the U.S. or Japan, and international trade accounts for a large part of its economy[2]. Although German firms have recently become more like U.S. multinationals in their reliance on overseas production, they remain much more export-oriented than firms in the United States[3]. German firms are therefore likely to be more exposed to exchange rate fluctuations than are firms in the U.S. and Japan[4].

B. Important Trading Activities in US-dollar

The second reason is that *a large number of German firms have important trading activities in US-dollar*. The US-dollar exposure of German Corporations is our primary interest. The degree of exposure, however, which refers to the percentage change in firm value in response to a one percent change in exchange rate, cannot uniquely be inferred from the extent of international trading done in a currency. For example, a purely domestic firm may be more exposed to the €/US$ than a German exporter to the U.S. if it is affected by import-competing American firms. However, there is evidence that the €/US$ is, for German firms, both a major currency of denomination and of determination. In the press, the US dollar is often viewed as a primary currency of

---

[2] The export plus import to GDP ratios during the period 1988 to 1998 was for Germany of about 49%, for the U.S. 21%, and 19% for Japan. See Dahlquist and Robertsson (2001), p. 6.

[3] Business cycles upturns in Germany have often been largely driven by exports. For instance, while German GDP increased by 1.8% per year from 1993 to 1997, German exports increased 7.0% per year over the same period, accounting for all the increase in aggregate output. See Bernard and Wagner (1998), p. 1.

[4] Friberg and Nydahl (1996) in an empirical study including Germany, established a positive relationship between stock market exposure to exchange rates and the openness of a country. They found this result for 10 out of 13 industrialized countries in the post Bretton-Woods period. Moreover, recent studies show much more evidence of exposure in industries and firms outside the U.S. See, e.g., Bodnar and Gentry (1993), He and Ng (1998), Glaum et al. (2000), Dominguez (2000), Dominguez and Tesar (2001).

determination of the stock value of German corporations[5]. Furthermore, there is empirical evidence that adjustments of the DM/US$ exchange rate toward its purchasing power parity value seem not to have taken place in the post-Bretton Woods era[6].

Based on the sector of activity, it is generally expected that large German firms should be highly positively exposed to the €/US$ (DM/US$), since they are generally net exporters to the U.S. market. In a survey, the majority of non-financial German firms (55%) reported that their operations typically generated net inflows in US$, whereas 19% of these firms generated net outflows in US$, and 26% did not have significant cash flows in US$[7].

C. Large International Manufacturing Companies

A third reason is that *Germany has large international manufacturing companies.* Some sectors are expected to be more exposed. If the conversion component of exposure dominates the competitive component, German firms with large trading activities in US$ should be relatively more exposed. For that reason, industrial companies are generally assumed to be more exposed to changes in exchange rates than trade and service companies. The automobile and transportation sector, chemical industry, pharmaceutical industry, machinery & industrials sector, retail & consumer, software & technology sectors, electronic equipment, engineering are manufacturing industries that are known to be mainly exporting sectors or directly exposed to strong foreign competition. On the other hand, banks, insurance, retail and food, support services are mainly service industries whose activities are largely oriented towards the domestic market and face little foreign competition[8].

---

[5] See, e.g., McLannahan and P.F. Larsen, 2004, Out for the Count: the reaction of Europe's auto manufactures to the sinking dollar provides an object lesson for other sectors, CFO Magazine, Feb. 17.
[6] See Juselius and MacDonald (2000).
[7] See Glaum (2000), pp. 46-47.
[8] See Lucke (1998), p. 2-3, DIW Foreign Trade, for data on Germany's leading export industries.

5.1.2 Hypothesis on Exposure Asymmetries

We test the hypothesis that the US$ exposure of German corporations is asymmetric to appreciation/depreciation.

A. Overview of Theoretical Predictions on Exposure Asymmetries

Table 5.1 below summarizes the hypothesis on exposure asymmetries. The interpretation is as follows:

- *Columns:* the total of firms in columns (1) and (3) are exposed to depreciations of their domestic currency. Firms in column (1) have positive exposures, firms in column (3) negative exposures.

- *Rows:* the total of firms in rows (4) and (6) are exposed to domestic currency appreciations. Firms in row (4) have positive exposures, firms in row (5) negative exposures.

Table 5. 1 Hypothesis on Foreign Exchange Exposure Asymmetries

Appreciations $\Delta e_t < 0$	Depreciations Home Currency against Foreign Currency: $(\text{€}/US\$) \uparrow$ $\Delta e_t > 0$			
	$\gamma_i^d > 0$	$\gamma_i^d = 0$	$\gamma_i^d < 0$	
$\gamma_i^a > 0$	(A) Linear exposure	(B) Asymmetric exposure	(C) __	(4) % of firms positively exposed to home currency appreciation
$\gamma_i^a = 0$	(D) Asymmetric exposure	(E) No exposure	(F) Asymmetric exposure	(5) % of firms insignificantly exposed to home currency appreciation
$\gamma_i^a < 0$	(G) __	(H) Asymmetric exposure	(I) Linear exposure	(6) % of firms negatively exposed to home currency appreciation
	(1) % of firms positively exposed to home currency depreciation	(2) % of firms insignificantly exposed to home currency depreciation	(3) % of firms negatively exposed to home currency depreciation	

Source: adapted from Miller and Reuer (1995), p. 24. and Andren (2001), p. 19.

Firms in cells (A) and (I) have symmetric exposures: a flexible firm can also have a linear exposure. A firm's operating flexibility has no value if there is no uncertainty, or if its value is destroyed by competitors. Alternatively, the symmetry could reflect the stock market valuing contractual exposures.

Firms in cell (E) have no significant exposure for both appreciation/depreciation. Exposures in cells (G) and (C) are unlikely: cell (G) corresponds to firms that benefit from any exchange rate movements. A hedging position referred as a "straddle"[9] is unlikely to be feasible because of the associated high costs. In cell (C), firms would lose whatever the exchange rate movement.

Four cells reflect exposure asymmetries: (B), (D), (F), (H). The interpretation for German firms *with long positions in US$* is given in table 5.2 below.

Table 5. 2 Types of Exposure Asymmetries

(B)	no exposure to US$ appreciation / adverse exposure to US$ depreciation.
	<ul><li>*Strategic competition/short real call*: firms cannot exploit beneficial US$ appreciations.</li><li>*Government interventions/short real call:* threat of government intervention limit upside potential in profits.</li><li>*Bounds on volume flexibility:* e.g., production constraints, marketing bottlenecks can make the value of real options negative.</li><li>*Entry/exit of competitors with hysteretic behavior.*</li><li>*Asymmetric risk perception of investors:* investors value relatively more downside risk.</li><li>*Poor currency risk management:* adversely affected by US$ depreciations but fail to realize any symmetric benefit when the US$ appreciates.</li></ul>
(D)	beneficial exposure to US$ appreciation / no exposure to US$ depreciation.
	<ul><li>*Real call options*: e.g., export flexibility.</li><li>*Long currency call options* to hedge exposures.</li><li>*Market share expansion* strategy with positive long term value effects (if elasticity of demand greater than 1).</li></ul>
(F)	adverse exposure to US$ appreciation / no exposure to US$ depreciation.
	<ul><li>*Short call position*: e.g. competitors exploit more aggressively US$ appreciations.</li></ul>
(H)	no exposure to US$ appreciation /beneficial exposure to US$ depreciation
	<ul><li>*Long currency put options* to hedge exposures.</li></ul>

---

[9] See Sercu and Uppal (1995), p. 184.

B. Effect of Real Exchange Rate/Price Risk and Quantity Risk on Expected Firm Market Value

- *Relatively higher exposure to beneficial exchange rate changes* - cells (D) and (H): a higher degree of uncertainty increases mean firm value. For example, in cell (D), risk neutral firms benefit from uncertainty, and are less exposed to downside risk. This implies that an increase in exchange rate volatility would increase shareholder wealth.

- *Relatively higher exposure to adverse exchange rate changes* – cells (B) and (F): a higher degree of uncertainty decreases mean firm value. Risk neutral firms are harmed by volatility.

- *Linear exposure*: no effect of uncertainty on mean firm value.

A crucial but plausible assumption for our interpretations is that the stock market has a long term view and assesses the exposure of firm value. There is evidence that investors have *long time horizons* and base to a large extent their valuation on future growth prospects[10]. This hypothesis is important. For example, a German exporter to the U.S. pursuing a strategy of market share expansion could have expected cash flows negatively affected by uncertainty, but expected firm value positively affected. Moreover, real options' value might be higher at long horizons, because the present value of sunk costs is lower[11].

C. Sectors of Activity, Industry Structure

We examine the exposure of German corporations in the DAX and MDAX indexes. What hypothesis can be made on the *degree of exposure, i.e.,* percentage change in firm value in response to a one percent change in exchange rates, and *the direction of exposure*, i.e., whether a firm gains or loses from a change in exchange rate? Table 5.3 below shows the typical exposure predictions based on the sectors of activity in which firms operate.

---

[10] "The view of the world embodied in the DCF model is (1) investors in companies are diversified, (2) have long time horizons, (3) care only about market risk". See Damodaran (2003-a), p. 17.

[11] See Muralidhar (1992).

A majority of German DAX and MDAX corporations have long position in US$ (see previous section) and should have positive exposures. The effect of an appreciation of the DM or euro (€) negatively affects the value of German firms. But these predictions are unambiguous for firms operating in simple industry competitive structures (perfect competition, monopoly) or with mostly contractual cash flows. In contrast to non-financial firms, financial firms (banks and insurance companies) are expected to be linearly exposed, since their cash flows are mostly contractual.

Table 5. 3 Effects of an Appreciation of the Home Currency (€) on the Value of Industries

Activity	Sign of Effect
Non-traded goods producers	(+)
Exporter	(-)
Importer	(+)
Import competitor	(-)
User of internationally-priced inputs	(+)
Foreign operations	(-)

Source: Bodnar (1999), p. 315.

We saw that for the following reasons, whether a firm benefits or suffers following an exchange rate shock cannot be determined analytically and is eventually an empirical question:

- *Firms having foreign operations or being engaged in various activities.*

The impact of exchange rate movements on a firm's value may be particularly difficult to predict if the company participates in activities with off-setting exposures or has foreign operations. The profitability of a foreign subsidiary may be enhanced by the same rate movement that reduces the return on exports from the home plant. As a result, an exporter with subsidiaries in foreign countries could have a negative exposure[12].

---

[12] Williamson (2001) gives the example of GM and Ford selling in Europe. However, the case of the automobile industry might be a special case.

German firms have become more like multinationals over the years, operating in oligopolitic markets. For that reason, we could observe a positive exposure in the early sub-samples, as most large German firms were involved in exports, and conflicting signs in more recent periods, as firms have become more like multinationals with foreign operations. For the same reason, we may expect firms to have become less exposed over the years, since firms can be expected to use their production network to insulate themselves against exchange rate uncertainty. Such hypothesis are difficult to test empirically. A first reason is that stock markets have also become more efficient over the years, and as a result, a relationship between stock returns and exchange rates should have become easier to detect. A second reason is that a deteriorating ability to pass-through exchange rate changes caused by trade globalization has been observed in empirical studies[13].

- *Strategic interaction between the firm and other market participants*[14].

Typically, firms in less competitive industries are expected to be relatively less exposed. Monopolists have exchange rate pass-through (ERPT) options and should be less exposed than firms in highly competitive industries, which are price takers and therefore less able to insulate themselves from the effect of exchange rate changes. There is some evidence that differences in market structures play a role in explaining cross-sectional exposure differences, because of the different pass-through ability observed across and within industries[15]. However, the nature of these differences is likely to be more complex for oligopolists.

We saw that the magnitude and sign of the exposure of oligopolist cannot be determined analytically. The effect of strategic real options on exposure turns on key assumptions about consumers' demand shifts, government policies, and the strategic

---

[13] See The Economist, A Faded Green, Dec 4th 2003, and chapter 3.
[14] Since exposure is by definition an after-hedge measure, negative signs could be the result of "finance managers trying to enhance their companies' incomes by maintaining and even increasing the foreign exchange exposure. In that case, the treasury or risk management department is considered as a "profit center". But whatever the concern, corporate users tend to be hedgers rather than speculators". See DeRosa (1996), p. 7.
[15] See Burgess and Knetter (1996), Yang (1997), Clifton (1998), Coughlin and Pollard (2000).

behavior of competitors[16]. This applies to most corporations in the DAX index, which operate in "strategic industries" with oligopolistic structures, where a few firms dominate the industry, e.g., the automobile sector and pharmaceutical sector[17].

Because of these indirect exposures, international trading firms are not necessarily more exposed than purely domestic firms, and firm's currencies of determination can be different from their currencies of denomination. For example, a domestic German firm could be exposed to the €/US$, through U.S. competitors importing to the German market. There is empirical evidence supporting the hypothesis that oligopolists are to a large extent indirectly exposed through competitive effects rather than based on their sectors of activity. A study found that the greatest exposure may actually exist for those purely domestic firms that suffer import competition in the domestic market. The same study shows that only those exporting firms with a very large percentage of foreign sales will have exposure close to that of the firm facing import competition[18]. Also, a recent study suggests that there is actually little evidence of a systematic link between exposure and trade[19]. This may reflect the fact that those "firms most engaged in trade are also the most aware of exchange rate risk, and therefore are the most likely to hedge their exposure"[20].

The exposure of German firms to the €/US$ with long position in US$ could also be negative because of *offsetting effects through the cost of capital* or because of the offsetting *effect of other factors on foreign cash flows*, e.g., macroeconomic, business, political factors. The impact of changes in these factors on cash flows can be substantial and contribute negatively or positively to a firm's exposure. In some cases it may offset the impact of the exchange rate changes[21].

---

[16] "All multinational corporates are oligopolists. Oligopoly and multinationality have been linked via the notion of market imperfections. These imperfections can be related to product and factor markets or to financial markets". See Shapiro (1999), pp. 679-681.

[17] See Luehrman (1990), p. 226.

[18] See Booth (1996).

[19] Dominguez and Tesar (2001) examines if firms that engage in trade are more vulnerable to exchange rate risk and find that " what little evidence there is of a link suggests that firms that engage in greater trade exhibit lower degrees of exposure.

[20] See Dominguez and Tesar (2001).

[21] See Demacopoulos (1989), p. 83.

D. Time Stability of the Exposures of Stock Returns

Virtually all empirical studies find exposure estimates that are time-varying and that shift back and forth over time between positive and negative values. We saw that exposures intertemporal instability can be caused by:

- *exercise of long real options*: can persistently modify a firm's operating structure and accordingly its exposure profile through hysteretic effects, e.g., exposure to the €/US$ could shift over time because of the exercise of switching options[22]. The large DM/US$ exchange rate swings that have historically been observed support this possibility[23].

- *exercise of implicit short real options*: sold to consumers or the government.

- *exercise of financial flexibility options*.

- *changes in foreign cash flow volatility from changes in market conditions*, e.g., interest rates, political factors, and so forth.

Whereas with the *exercise of a real option*, a firm would move to a different exposure profile curve, an *investment in flexibility* to acquire a real option would change the shape of the exposure profile curve.

Finally, although the hypothesis of exposure asymmetries is tested in *time series* regressions, interpretations should be cross-sectional in nature. It is common to view exposure being asymmetric in the sense that the "financial performance impact of a foreign currency appreciation may not be offset by the currency's depreciation"[24]. However, the "true" exposure corresponds to the coefficient of a *cross-sectional* regression across scenarios of future exchange rates at a given point of time[25].

---

[22] If the euro appreciate against the US$, a German exporter to the US could have the option to shut down production facilities in Germany and start producing in the US. See Mello et al. (1995).

[23] See Engle and Hamilton (1990).

[24] See Miller and Reuer (1995), p. 2.

[25] In one of the pioneering paper on the regression approach for exposure measurement, Adler and Dumas (1984) show that the exposure coefficient from a cross-sectional regression is obtained "by the financial manager first positing future states of nature regarding cash flows, exchange rates, and their respective probabilities". See also Sercu and Uppal (1995).

5.1.3 Hedging Effects

German corporations typically focus their risk management activities on contractual exposures and use primarily linear hedging instruments. The nonlinear component of foreign exchange exposures is rarely hedged[26]. Table 5.4 below shows that the objective of hedging is for most German firms to manage accounting earnings. Figures on US corporations are presented for comparison. While U.S. companies focus on managing cash flows (with accounting earnings as a close second), German companies focus on managing accounting earnings (with cash flows as a more distant second). Neither U.S. of German companies seem to focus on balance sheet accounts or firm value[27].

Table 5. 4 Most important objective of hedging strategy (percentage)

	Accounting Earning	Cash Flows	Balance Sheet Accounts	Economic Risk Firm Value
Germany	55	34	7.4	12
USA	44	49	0.9	8

Source: Bodnar and Gebhardt (1998).

Firms' exposures could be asymmetric because of hedging instruments with asymmetric payoffs. However, surveys on hedging practices reveal that most German firms use hedging instruments with linear payoffs, which are relatively more appropriate for hedging contractual exposure[28] (table 5.5 below).

Table 5. 5 Importance of FX Instruments in the Derivative Market (in percentage)

	OTC Forwards	Futures	OTC Swaps	OTC Options	Exchange traded options	Structured Derivatives	Hybrid Debt
Germany	75.5	4.3	13.8	18.1	0.0	1.1	0.0
USA	56.8	8.0	9.1	18.2	1.1	6.8	1.1

Source: Bodnar and Gebhardt (1998).

Since the bulk of firms' value comes from transactions not yet completed, using linear hedging instruments is a very incomplete strategy to hedge economic exposures[29]. As such, it is reasonable to assume that substantial (after-hedge) exposures should be

---

[26] See Bodnar and Gebhardt (1999), Bodnar et al. (1998).
[27] See Bodnar and Gebhardt (1998).
[28] See Glaum (2000), Bodnar and Gebhardt (1998).
[29] See Giddy and Dufey (1992).

observed in our tests. Figure 5.1 indicates the extent to which German firms hedge their exposure to the US$. A minority of firms attempt to hedge fully their exposures.

Figure 5. 1 Hedge Ratio of German Firms' Exposure to the U.S. Dollar

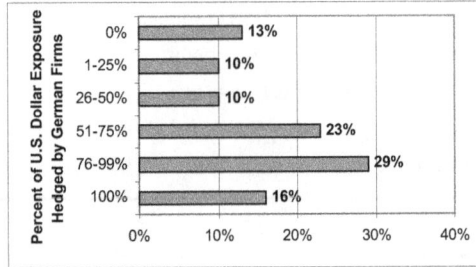

Source: Glaum (2002), p. 118.

Many German corporations *hedge selectively* their exposures, in the sense that their view on the evolution of future exchange rates influences their decision to hedge[30]. This should make them relatively more exposed to beneficial exchange rate changes. Figure 5.2 below shows the hedging practices of German corporations.

Figure 5. 2 Hedging Practice of German Corporations

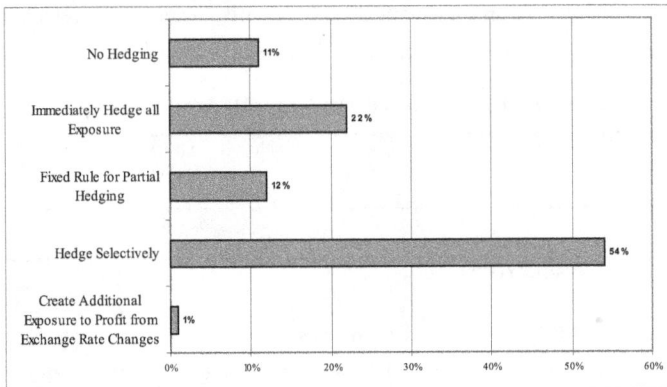

Source: Glaum (2002).

---

[30] The majority of German firms follow a "selective hedging" strategy, with the larger German firms being more likely to use forecasts in their exchange risk management decisions. See Glaum (2000), Glaum (2001).

5.1.4 Stock Markets' Valuation of Foreign Exchange Exposure Asymmetries

The asymmetries of equity exposures depend on how the stock market values the real options and financial flexibility options of firms[31]. In efficient capital markets, investors change the firm's current market value by an estimate of the change in present value of cash flows resulting from an exchange rate change. Equity returns are proxy for changes in total firm value. Equity volatility should be close to firm volatility for firms with low leverage[32].

A. Economic Exposure and Shareholder Wealth Creation

From an economic perspective, what should matter to a firm is the ability to generate real cash flows for *shareholders' wealth maximization*. Real cash flows are what shareholders, the legal owners of the firm, need for their consumption. This implies that foreign exchange exposure influence firm valuation. What should matter to managers is economic exposure, that is, the extent to which the value of the firm – as measured by the present value of its expected cash flows – will change when exchange rates change. An implied *normative* statement[33] is that equity valuation by the stock market should be based on the firm's ability to generate real cash flows rather than on accounting earnings.

Stock market efficiency implies that the stock market is able to see through accounting statements and values the firm's ability to generate cash flows. As a result, company's stock market capitalization should be closely linked to its discounted cash flow value. This means that "if we project how much cash a company will generate and discount it at a rate which reflects risk, then the stock market's and the DCF valuation of the company should be close"[34]. We should note that management does not necessarily

---

[31] For example, the Japanese automakers established production in the U.S. after a depreciating US$ following a peak in the middle of the 1980s. Williamson (1998), using the stock market approach, shows that the announcement of plans for U.S. production and the actual beginning of production in the US made the US$ exposure for most Japanese automotive companies insignificant.
[32] See Shin and Stulz (2000), p. 20.
[33] A statement is *normative* (rather than *positive*) in the sense that it is a recommendation based on economic theory, although it is not necessarily applied in practice. Normative statements refer to "what ought to be and are usually derived from an assumption about how the world behaves", whereas positive statements refer to "what is, was or will be, it is commonly referred to as an appeal to the facts". See Lipsey (1969), p. 4.
[34] See, e.g., Copeland et al. (1994).

know the expected performance of its company better than the stock market does. Analysts get information from sources other than management, e.g., customers, suppliers, competitors[35].

B. *The Stock Market Approach of Foreign Exchange Exposure Measurement*

Firm value is not observable, it has to be estimated. "Calculation of firm value based on DCF methods can be difficult, given the high uncertainty surrounding forecasted cash flows and the need to make appropriate assumptions regarding the discount rate and time horizon for a firm's operations"[36]. Analyzing cash flows directly avoids having to assume that financial analysts correctly make the link between exchange rates and the market value of the firm, but it requires more detailed information.

Equity value is obtained by substracting the value of loans, minority interests, preference stock and other non-equity financing to the firm's economic value. Market efficiency implies that rather than estimating exposures based on DCF methods, it is possible to measure exposures based on market valuation of shareholder equity. A possibility is to estimate a firm's aggregate foreign exchange equity exposures with observable stock returns. In an efficient equity market, a change in a firm's equity value would be reflected in the stock price[37]. This suggests that the market value of a firm's equity as proxied by its stock price can be used as the dependent variable in a regression to estimate exposure.

5.2 Empirical Design

5.2.1 Selection of Firms, Industries, and Currencies

The selection of firms and industries to test the hypothesis of exposure asymmetry is based on the following considerations. Selecting industries and firms that are presumed to operate in strategic industries. Large German corporations in the DAX index generally operate in oligopolistic markets, where firms' exposure is expected to be

---

[35] Managers might not have the resources in terms of time and employees to do that. This aspect is discussed in Copeland (2001-b), p. 6.
[36] See Miller (1994), p. 15.
[37] See Miller (1994), p. 15.

determined to a large extent by the behavior of other market participants. Automobiles and steel are often mentioned as industries whose competitors are affected by exchange rate changes[38]. For this reason, the exposure of DAX firms is of primary interest for evaluating exposure asymmetries. As a matter of comparison, the exposure of the MDAX firms is also evaluated. They are listed in Appendix H.

5.2.2 Stock Market Approach: Regression Equations and Hypothesis Tests

A. Stock Market Regression Approach

Estimating equity exposures is done most easily in a regression framework. Under this assumption, the exposure can be determined from the elasticity of firm value with respect to the exchange rate, which in turn could be obtained from a regression of a firm's stock returns on an exchange rate change variable. This approach, which only requires the researcher to obtain historical market data, greatly simplifies the estimation of exchange rate exposures and gives rise to the possibility of large-scale empirical studies on exchange rate exposure[39]. In this "top-down" approach, finance managers analyze directly the statistical relationship between the selected measure of firm value and currency values, without having to quantify the underlying mechanisms through which currency fluctuations affect firm value. This "reduced-form" approach offers a parsimonious way in terms of data required to estimate exposure[40].

Three research areas are related:

(a) The literature on *whether foreign exchange rate risk is a "priced factor"* in the stock market. Tests of whether the exchange rate is a priced factor in the stock market examine whether exchange rate movements affect expected (ex ante) stock returns.

---

[38] See Luehrman (1991), p. 626.
[39] This type of approach is sometimes assimilated to "external measures" of financial price risk or "market-based measures", as they rely on values obtained in the market. See Smithson et al. (1995) p. 137.
[40] Suggested by Adler and Dumas (1984). For a discussion on the shortcomings and advantages of structural models versus reduced-form models, See Dixit (2000), pp. 3-4.

(b) The literature on the *foreign exchange exposure of foreign investments in stocks*. That would concern, for example, a German investor who would have invested in US stocks, in US-dollar, and who would want to repatriate its gains in euro.

(c) The literature on measuring *corporate economic foreign exchange exposure*, based on the assumption that stock prices are good proxies for firm value. If stock markets are efficient, measuring the effect of unexpected exchange rate changes on corporate performance is equivalent to evaluating whether *shareholders benefit from exchange rate changes* by examining the relation between stock returns and exchange rate changes[41]. This is the subject of this study.

Since we are concerned only with whether exchange rate news affect ex-post stock returns as opposed to expected (ex ante) returns, our tests differ from tests of whether the exchange rate is a "priced factor" in stock market returns. Even if investors don't value the impact of exchange rate changes on firm value, we could still find a systematic relationship between stock prices and exchange rate changes. "Regardless of whether exchange rate exposure is a priced factor that influences expected returns, exchange rate changes can systematically affect realized returns since they provide information about economic conditions"[42].

The Original Regression Model

The most basic regression model estimates foreign exchange equity exposures by regressing the firm's stock returns on the percentage change or return of exchange rate[43]:

[5. 1] $r_{it} = \alpha_i + \gamma_i \Delta e_t + \varepsilon_{it}$ $t = 1, ..., T$

where r_{it} is the change in the value of the firm, measured by the rate of return on the ith company's stock, α_i, a constant term, representing the part of the value of the firm

---

[41] A distinction between the explicit relation of exchange rates and corporate performance, and the relation of exchange rates and stock returns, is made for example in Forbes (2002).
[42] See Bodnar and Gentry (1993), p. 33.
[43] See Adler and Dumas (1984), Adler and Simon (1986), Hodder (1982). In this regression, a firm's foreign exchange exposure is meant to be for a given operating and financial structure, although, in practice, a firm's operating and/or capital structure are likely to change through time. See O'Brien (1997), p. 46.

that is uncorrelated with the exchange rate. Δe_t is the rate of change in a multilateral or bilateral exchange rate, measured as the home currency price of the foreign currency. A positive value for Δe_t indicates a home currency depreciation (long exposure). The regression should be run in real terms, with real exchange rates and inflation-adjusted stock returns. Because this specification is appropriate only if changes in stock prices and exchange rates are essentially unanticipated, it usually assumes that exchange rates and stock returns follow a random walk process. Empirical evidence suggests that it is reasonable to assume that exchange rates and stock returns behave randomly, at least at short and medium horizons[44]. ε_{it} is a disturbance term that captures the residual risk[45]. γ_i is the exposure coefficient. γ_i is sometimes called the "total exposure" elasticity of firm i[46] or the "forex beta". γ_i represents the part of the value of the firm that depends on the exchange rate. Exposure is positive or long (negative) if a(n) depreciation (appreciation) of the home currency results in an increase (decrease) in the firm value. If the regression is conducted in levels, γ_i can be interpreted as the exposure measure (in foreign currency), and exchange rate changes times this exposure yield the exchange rate gain/loss. If conducted in logarithms or returns, γ_i corresponds to an elasticity measure[47]. This elasticity indicates the firm's average exposure over the estimation period as a percentage of the firm's market value. The regression allows us to decompose the change in the value of the firm into two parts, a part that is linearly exposed to the exchange rate, which is given by γ_i, and a part that is uncorrelated with the exchange rate, $\alpha_{it} + \varepsilon_{it}$. Even if a firm has a large and statistically significant foreign exchange exposure coefficient, this does not necessarily mean that exchange rate risk is an important determinant of the firm's overall risk. What matters eventually for risk management is the percentage of total cash flow or firm value variability that is due to currency fluctuations. Accordingly, the most important parameter, in terms of its impact on exposure management policy, is the regression R^2.

---

[44] See, e.g., Meese and Rogoff (1983). In some cases, it may be necessary to adjust the exchange rate index to account for autocorrelation. See, e.g., Allayannis (1996).

[45] "Because the value of the firm will be influenced by factors other than the exchange rate, that are not included in the model, then such a regression will not give an exact fit between the value of the firm and the exchange rate, and will contain an error term. If these factors are uncorrelated to the exchange rate, a regression's residual would express the quantity that is uncorrelated with the exchange rate and has zero mean". See Sercu and Uppal (1995), pp. 499-502.

[46] See Bodnar and Wong (1999).

[47] See Lardaro (1993), p. 365.

There is an important shortcoming with this econometric specification. The exposure coefficient γ_i picks up all covariance between the value of the firm and the exchange rate[48]. All sources of correlation of firm value with the exchange rate affect the exposure coefficient. The effect that is predicted by structural models and that we want to measure is the average value effect of the present value of cash flow changes *caused* by exchange rate movements. However, stock returns and exchange rates are jointly endogenous. Because the link measured by regressions must be interpreted as correlations, and not as causal relationships, the empirical model [5.1] may be misspecified because all sources of correlation of firm value with the exchange rate affects the γ_i coefficient, and not only the direct effect of exchange rate changes on stock prices. Total exposure can reflect several effects:

(1) the estimate of the average value effect of the present value of cash flow changes caused by exchange rate movements. This is the effect that is predicted by the microeconomic and industrial organization models of exposure examined in part one.

(2) the non-exchange rate related phenomenon that affects either cash flows in home currency or valuations and are spuriously correlated with the exchange rate variable. While a portion of this latter part will be idiosyncratic effects that cannot be controlled for directly, a portion of this effect will include "macroeconomic" effects that influence the valuation of all firms, such as changes in the risk free rate or the market risk premium, or other non financial factors such as investor sentiment[49].

(3) exchange rate related phenomenon that affect either cash flows in home currency or valuations and are not spuriously correlated with the exchange rate variable. This is because stock returns and exchange rates are both endogenous variables. No causal link is presumed between stock returns and exchange rate changes. Empirical studies implicitly assume partial equilibrium in the sense that exchange rate changes are considered exogenous to the value of a firm in the regression. It is a reasonable assumption for a single firm or industry. Causality should flow from exchange rates to stock prices, at least from an industry point of view. If the industry is a small part of a country's activity in the international economy, the exchange rate depends

---

[48] Notice that a small covariance is not the same as a small exposure.

[49] See Bodnar and Wong (1999).

much more on events in other industries than on events in the industry under consideration[50]. However, this hypothesis that the exchange rate is exogenous to stock returns does not imply that exchange rate and stock returns are not endogenous to other economic factors. The degree of association between stock returns and exchange rate changes may be determined simultaneously by underlying factors in the economy. This is a problem that afflicts all empirical studies of exchange rates and competitiveness[51].

Shocks of different origin can have very different effects on exchange rates and the rest of the economy. For example, an appreciation of the currency that results from a demand shock such as an investment boom might have a different effect on equity values than does an appreciation that results from a monetary contraction[52]. Moreover, the effect of shocks can differ according to whether the shocks are anticipated or unanticipated. As the nature of the shocks that are dominant at any point in time changes, the exposure coefficient will change. The average covariability might not be measured with any precision at all in these circumstances. To clarify this methodological issue, we envisage several cases:

(a) *Spurious Correlation.*

Suppose the exchange rate is correlated with the interest rate. Further, assume that stock returns are affected by interest rates and not by exchange rates. A regression of stock returns on exchange rates will then appear significant, even though there is no relationship between them, due to the correlation between the exchange rate and the interest rate[53]. For another example, suppose a German firm exports to Canada. A researcher does not know this and thinks instead that it sells to the U.S[54], and estimates a regression of stock return on the change in the €/US$ exchange rate. In this case, the

---

[50] See Allayannis (1996). This means that exchange rate changes are exogenous to the firm's decision making process. Change in the values of the firm's choice variables do not affect exchange rates, i.e., $ds_i/dx_i = 0$, where x_i is any choice variable of the firm for currency i, such as the markup/price or quantity of output of the firm. See Demacopoulos (1987), p. 166.

[51] Luehrman (1991), p. 643, points out to this methodological issue.

[52] See Cumby (1994), p. 63. Dornbush (1994).

[53] This example is provided by Stulz and Williamson (1996).

[54] Example adapted from Stulz (2000), ch. 8, pp. 35-36. Alternatively, a treasurer could identify incorrectly that one of its currency of determination is the US$, when it is the CAN$.

firm's sales to Canada would affect the regression coefficient of the firm on the €/US$ exchange rate because the €/Canadian dollar is correlated with the € /US$ exchange rate. As a result, we might conclude that the firm is exposed to a € /US$ exchange rate when it is not because it is exposed to a risk factor that is correlated with the currency used in the regression. Furthermore, if the correlation is not stable, we could conclude incorrectly that the exposure is time varying.

(b) *Exposure Dependent on the Nature of the Macroeconomic Shocks Affecting the Economy.*

The fact that both stock prices and exchange rates are endogenous implies that the nature of their relation depends on the nature of the macroeconomic shocks affecting the economy[55]. In other terms, "the degree of correlation between endogenous variables such as stock prices and exchange rates depends on the nature of the shocks affecting the economy"[56]. The stock market expectation about future economic growth, and the effect of monetary policy can affect the relation between stock prices and exchange rates. This could lead to negative exposures, which would contradict the prediction of traditional international trade models:

- *Expectation about economic growth*[57]: although changes in exchange rates and stock prices indeed often move in the opposite direction, this is not always so. Optimism about the economic growth prospects in a country often drives up both the exchange rate and stock prices. "Almost without exception, the stock market turns down prior to recession and rises before economic recovery"[58]. Stock values are based on corporate earnings, and the business cycle is a prime determinant of these earnings[59]. A country's currency is expected to appreciate from the increase in capital inflow. More generally, an exogenous decline in home country competitiveness would cause both a country's domestic currency to depreciate and

---

[55] This problem was mentioned as early as in Jorion (1990), but has not been subject to much further discussion. See however Luehrman (1991).

[56] Jorion (1990), p. 333.

[57] For an account the relation between economic growth and stock returns, see Siegel (1998), p. 129-131.

[58] See Siegel (1998), p. 172.

[59] See Bodie et al. (1998), ch. 12.

its stock prices to decline, thereby leading to a negative relation between stock returns and exchange rate[60].

- *Effect of monetary policy*: exposure coefficients estimated from regressions may probably also not be invariant to a change in the monetary policy regime. One might find that stock returns increase following a home currency depreciation simply because this depreciation is associated with an expansionary monetary policy that promotes higher economic activity from which all firms benefit[61]. Such an outcome would be predicted if one were to use a typical exchange rate determination model[62]. In this case, the exposure might just reveal the simultaneous impact of monetary factors on exchange rates and stock returns. For example, it is expected that a central bank tightening credit and raising interest rates will cause the value of its country's currency to rise. On the other hand, stock prices are expected to fall, as rising interest rates lower the value of stock.

This shows that some macroeconomic factors are likely to affect firms' foreign exchange exposures in opposite direction. For example, the combined effects on exposure of the stock market's anticipation about the economic growth and of changes in interest rates are ambiguous theoretically. The interaction of these two opposite effects on stock returns, will determine whether stock increases or decreases. Since both monetary and real factors drive exchange rate and stock movements, it is not surprising that the stock and currency markets often move independently of one another[63].

If these macroeconomic influences, which are relevant for firm value, are to any degree correlated with the exchange rate over the estimation period, they will influence the total exposure estimates and make difficult their interpretation in terms of the cash flow models of exposure that we examined earlier. Finding a significant exposure coefficient would not necessarily mean that stock returns are significantly affected by exchange rate movements, but possibly that other factors explain the correlation. Correspondingly, a hedge ratio based on this exposure measure would be imprecise.

---

[60] This possibility is mentioned by Luehrman (1991), p. 643.
[61] See, e.g., Dornbush (1976), Jorion (1990), Griffin and Stulz (2001).
[62] See, e.g., Dornbush (1976).
[63] In empirical studies, wee should thus try to identify periods when monetary developments/goods-market development have dominated the behavior of the currency. This has been suggested by Jorion (1990), p. 338.

However, these macroeconomic effects that are common to all firms should affect firms differentially. This effect should fall out when considering the relative exposures as opposed to the absolute exposure, and cross-sectional variation should be observed in the association between stock prices and exchange rates[64].

The Augmented Regression Model

To estimate the sensitivity of the firm's equity to the exchange rate only, one would therefore have to estimate the regression *controlling* for these other sources of risk on "total" exposure elasticities that affect the firm's equity and are correlated with the exchange rate. To deal with the very low explanatory power of the exchange rate for stock returns[65] and to control for these macroeconomic effects that are common to all firms, one method that is typically used in most studies is to add a stock market portfolio variable in the regression. The market portfolio is proxied by a stock market index[66]. Because the market return explains a substantial amount of the typical firm's stock return variation, its inclusion reduces the residual variance of the regression, thereby improving the precision of the residual exposure estimates[67]. This shows that there are factors which have more influence on stock returns than variations in exchange rate. This should also make the resulting residual exposure estimates more stable across horizons and sub-periods. The exchange rate exposure of firm i, γ_i, is now defined as the correlation between the firm's stock market returns and the changes in the exchange rate, conditioned on the average stock market rate of return. The alternative specification, called an *"augmented regression model"*, is written as:

[5. 2] $$r_{it} = \alpha_i + \beta_i r_{mt} + \gamma_i \Delta e_t + \varepsilon_{it}$$

where r_{it} is the stock market return of firm i over period t, β_i the beta of the firm with respect to the market portfolio (firm's systematic risk), r_{mt} the return on a market

---

[64] See Jorion (1990).

[65] Bodnar and Wong (1999) for example document that this modification of the model works to reduce some of the puzzling features of the total exposure estimates.

[66] If the correlation of this "macroeconomic" effect with exchange rates could be modeled, it would be possible to adjust the total exposure estimates to remove this impact. However, previous research has not been able to identify a consistent relation between observed proxies such as interest rates or market risk premiums for these "macroeconomic" impacts on firm value.

[67] Most empirical studies report that the domestic market index seems to have a much more powerful effect of stock returns than exchange rates. See Connolly et al. (2000).

portfolio, γ_i the "residual" exchange rate exposure elasticity of firm i from this modified regression, and Δe_t the exchange in the exchange rate. This equation is generally preferred by researchers, as it explains significantly more of the total variation in firms return and it can be motivated as an extension of the market model[68]. The definition of the exposure coefficient from equation [5.1] is now different. This modified exposure coefficient γ_i measures the exchange rate exposure elasticity of the firm as the residual difference between the firm's total exposure elasticity and the market's exposure elasticity adjusted by the firm's market beta. For this reason, γ_i is called the *"residual exposure elasticity"* of the firm[69]. The estimated "residual" exposure elasticity will differ from the "total" exposure elasticity whenever the market portfolio has a non-zero exposure to the exchange rate. Because of this, the interpretation of having "zero" exposure will not mean the same thing across these two measures if the market has a non-zero exposure. A zero "residual" exposure implies a firm has the same "total" exposure as the market portfolio. One puzzling aspects is that, although the inclusion of a market index seems to be crucial, many studies find little differences between estimates based on regression with and without the market portfolio variable. In practice, the coefficients of exchange rate exposure estimated by [5.1] and [5.2] are highly correlated[70].

The regression coefficient can be related to some exposure determinants in two-steps *regressions*. Several determinants of exposure have been investigated to explain the time pattern of the exposure distribution, such as industry structure as reflected in mark-ups[71], strategic factors[72], foreign sales[73].

---

[68] See Smithson et al. (1995), page 143. Empirical work using this approach includes Jorion (1990) Khoo (1994), Bodnar and Gentry (1993) and Amihud (1994), Allayannis (1995), Bodnar and Wong (1999).
[69] See for example Bodnar and Wong (1999).
[70] See, e.g., Jorion (1990).
[71] See Allayannis and Ihrig (1999).
[72] See Miller and Reuer (1998). However, there is an important limitation to this empirical inquiry for the German case, as Glaum et al. (2000) remark: "research into the determinants of German corporations' exchange risk exposure is hampered by the fact that German financial accounting standards do not require firms to report detailed information on their geographical business segments or on their hedging activities. Thus, consistent data on the importance of foreign activities (e.g. overseas sales, assets, or profits) or the degree to which exchange rate risks are managed is not readily available."
[73] See Jorion (1990). One empirical problem is that "the definition of foreign sales may differ across companies, which can create measurement errors when examining the cross-sectional differences in economic exposure".

Augmented Market Model for Capturing Exposure Asymmetries

Choosing an empirical model is a theoretical decision and should not be based solely on the shape of a graph of the data. Since computer programs have no understanding of the economic context of the empirical analysis, the equations that fit the data best are unlikely to correspond to economically meaningful models, and we won't be able to interpret the best-fit values of the variables, and the results are unlikely to be useful for data analysis. We need to pick a model based on our understanding of economic theory[74].

Because of the presence of exposure asymmetries, the firm's ex-ante profit function will be a piecewise non-linear function of the exchange rate. Industry structure should vary at some "break points" that make the exposure function asymmetric. We should observe certain thresholds for exchange rate, and the slope of the exposure profile should change at some distinct milestones[75]. In order to test the hypothesis of exposure asymmetry, we thus need an empirical method that can account for these threshold effects that may occur at some trigger exchange rate values.

This hypothesis of threshold effects allows for piece-wise linear approximation[76]. A type of suitable model is classified as a piece-wise linear regression that can account for potential non-linearities in the exposure function[77]. The model used to account for the possible asymmetric effects of currency appreciation and depreciation on firm value is a regression with dummy variables, whereby the time series sample is partitioned according to the sign of exchange rate movement[78].

We extend the augmented regression model by including two dummy variables to measure separately the effect of exchange rate appreciations and depreciations:

[5.3]
$$D_t^d = \begin{cases} 1 & |\Delta e_t > 0 \\ 0 & |\Delta e_t \le 0 \end{cases} \qquad D_t^a = \begin{cases} 0 & |\Delta e_t \ge 0 \\ 1 & |\Delta e_t < 0 \end{cases}$$

---

[74] See discussion in Kennedy (1996), p. 77 and pp. 85-86.
[75] The threshold values are called "knots" in the econometrics literature. See Greene (2000), p. 324.
[76] See Holmes and Maghrebi (2002), p. 4.
[77] See Greene (2000), ch. 8 for a description of this method in the context of nonlinear regressions, or Pyndick and Rubinfeld (1991), pp. 117-119.
[78] The hypothesis of asymmetry has also been tested using cointegration analysis, see Kanas (1996), curvilinear function, see Miller and Reuer (1995).

where a stands for appreciations of the home currency, and d depreciations. Dummy variables are a convenient means of building discrete shifts of the function into a regression model. The regression model with the exchange rate variable multiplied by its two dummies is written as:

[5. 4] $$r_{it} = \alpha_i + \beta_i r_{mt} + \gamma_i^a D_t^a \Delta e_t + \gamma_i^d D_t^d \Delta e +_t \varepsilon_{it}$$

where α_i is a constant term, r_{im} is the return on the market portfolio, r_{it} is the rate of return on the ith firm's stock, Δe_t the contemporaneous exchange-rate change, and ε_{it} is the idiosyncratic error term which is assumed to follow a normal i.i.d process, i.e. $\varepsilon_{it} \sim i.i.d.N(0, \sigma_\varepsilon^2)$, a white noise disturbance term[79]. The regression parameter β_i measures exposure to market movements, and the coefficient γ_i^a measures residual exchange rate exposure to exchange rate appreciation, while the coefficient γ_i^d measures the residual exposure to exchange rate depreciation. Exchange rate is stated as the home currency price of the foreign currency, so that a positive value for Δe_t represents a home currency depreciation, and a positive value of γ_i^d implies that a depreciation of the home currency leads to an increase in firm value. We have no a priori expectation regarding the value of the intercept. Because we use the firm's stock return as a proxy for changes in firm value, we evaluate the elasticity of the firm value to exchange rate changes. We investigate the possibility that stock returns react asymmetrically to currency appreciations and depreciations. Support for this type of asymmetry would be evidenced by different exposure coefficients when foreign currencies appreciate than when they depreciate.

The null hypothesis is that exchange rate exposure is symmetric, i.e., $H_0 : \gamma^a = \gamma^d$ against the alternative hypothesis that exposure is asymmetric, i.e., $H_1 : \gamma^a \neq \gamma^d$. Asymmetry implies different exposure coefficients when foreign currencies appreciate than when they depreciate. Expressing the dependent variable as the rate of return to shareholders results in a model which is invariant to changes in the size of the firm over time. Estimated parameters are also comparable across firms[80].

---

[79] The i.i.d. returns model is assumed to hold for all variables in the regression. However, this model needs not be the right one. See Stulz (2000), ch. 7, ch. 8, p. 35.
[80] See Miller (1994), p. 16.

Model [5.6] is used to estimate the exposure of German corporations to the DM/US-dollar, respectively to the €/US$. The purpose of including a market portfolio index is to deal with two aspects: (1) due to the low explanatory power of exchange rate changes, the inclusion of the market index should lead to a reduction of the residual variance of the regression and to a *reduction of the omitted variable bias*[81]. Without the market portfolio, the residuals from estimation are often poorly specified in terms of autocorrelations and heteroskedasticity. For example, the effects of interest rate risk should be captured to some extent by the market factor, because they feed into the market return. But the problem of omitted variables is only reduced, not solved[82]. (2) The second reason for including a market index factor is to *isolate the direct effect* of exchange rates on stock returns, by purging the exposure coefficient from other sources of correlation between stock returns and exchange rates. If these factors are in any way correlated to the exchange rate during the estimation period, and these correlations are not captured well by the market portfolio, then the interpretation of the exposure coefficient can be meaningless. Finding a significant exposure coefficient would not necessarily mean that firm's cash flows are significantly affected by exchange rate movements, but possibly that other factors may explain the correlation between stock returns and exchange rate changes.

The inclusion of a market portfolio variable leaves at least two issues unsolved: (a) *Idiosyncratic effects*. These other sources of correlation could be macroeconomic, but also due to idiosyncratic factors that affect stock returns and are correlated to exchange rates. The exposure coefficient is not purged from the effect of idiosyncratic factors on the correlation of exchange rates and stock returns. If these effects explain a large portion of firm's stock returns and are important relative to macroeconomic factors, then large scale studies may be complicated. (b) *Offsetting effects of macroeconomic factors captured by the market index.* To include all the macroeconomic factors in one variable might be too much of a simplification, due to offsetting effects between significant variables. The stock market index may be too aggregate a measure. The

---

[81] Omitted-variable bias: the missing information pollutes the estimated correlation between the two variables examined.

[82] Because of ommited variables, the detection of a statistically significant asymmetry could be caused "by depreciating or appreciating exchange rates trying to compensate (in a statistical sense) for the missing independent variables". See Aabo (2002), p. 14. The result of omitted variables can be exchange rate exposure coefficients that are "biased to such a degree that they are fundamentally flawed". See Greene (2000), p. 334-337. This specification bias, that arises because the true return generating process is not known, can even result in sign reversal. See, e.g., Lardaro (1993), p.430-431.

reason for the puzzling results found in empirical studies might be that the macroeconomic factors included in that control variable are not well isolated, because of how the market portfolio is constructed. For these reasons, we also include macroeconomic variables directly into the regression as an other way to control for these macroeconomic effects and to test the robustness of our results.

5.2.3 Data Characteristics and Sample Periods

I. Description of Data

A. Individual Firms

The sample consists of the German companies that were quoted in the DAX 100 index in 2002 for the period from January 1973 to September 2002, taken from the *Datastream International* database. The DAX 100 consists of the "Blue Chip" German firms included in the DAX 30 and the MDAX[83]. The DAX 30 comprises the 30 largest German publicly-traded corporations[84], and the MDAX comprises 70 "middle-sized capitalization" German corporations[85]. As we measure the perception of investors of firm's exposure, it is appropriate to select Blue-chip companies that have information content in the stock prices that are high and based on intense scrutiny from investors and analysts[86].

When constructing the sample, most studies on U.S. firms were interested in isolating a set of firms which were most likely to be affected by exchange rate changes, that is, with large international activities. The rationale for this is that companies that have an international activity are at least exposed to contractual exposure, which is expected to

---

[83] The DAX (Deutsche Aktienindex) and the MDAX (Mid-cap-DAX) are computed by the German stock exchange (Deutsche Börse AG). For a description of these indices, see Deutsche Boerse (2001).

[84] Size is one of the selection criteria for membership in the DAX 30 index. Large companies may be more likely to have international business and thus large exposures, but there may be also economies of scale for corporate risk management. The relationship between firm size and exposure has not been clearly identified in the empirical studies. Doukas et al. (1999) and Simkins and Laux (1997) find a negative relationship between firm size and exposure. He and Ng (1998) find a positive relationship.

[85] For a detailed description of the various indices, see Beike and Schluetz (1999), ch. 2 and 3.

[86] The current DAX index was introduced on July 1, 1998. The index includes the 30 German stocks, which have the highest turnover volume and market capitalization among the stocks traded in the Frankfurt Stock Exchange (Deutsche Börse AG). The DAX index can be considered as the German counterpart of the U.S. Dow Jones Industrial index. Both indexes represent more than one half of the total market capitalization in their respective exchanges. See Cheung and Westermann (2000), p. 4.

play an important part in economic exposure. Studies on German firms usually inferred that, as Germany is a very open economy, most firms should be strongly affected by exchange rate movements[87]. However, the degree of economic exposure might not be clearly positively linked to the degree of involvement in international trade. Some studies find that exposure varies systematically with foreign sales and firm size[88] but other studies argue that exposure is not related to foreign sales, firm size, or other international activities[89]. Import-competing domestic firms that have no international activities might also display large exposures. Therefore we include firms and industries with various degree of involvement in international activities, and with various industry competitive structures. Mostly non-financial firms are taken into consideration. Non-financial firms deal relatively more with non-contractually fixed cash flows and should thus display more significant economic exposures. In addition, the financial services firms might pursue different purposes when using derivative products, making results not directly comparable with those of non-financial firms. The list of the firms included in the sample as well as their corresponding sector of activity is presented in the Appendix H. A final remark is that there is little difference between using excess returns (returns over the risk-free rate) and simple returns, since the variation in interest rates is relatively small compared to the variation in exchange rates. Most studies use simple returns[90]. It is possible that this may bias the estimates of exposure in more recent years in the sample[91]. Moreover, to the extent that much of our analysis focuses on the variance of stock returns rather than on their mean values, the main results are not particularly vulnerable to the traditional survivorship bias[92]. The stock prices are adjusted for dividends and capital changes[93]. Adjustments for share

---

[87] See, e.g., Glaum et al. (2000).

[88] See, e.g., He and Ng (1998) for Japanese firms, Bodnar and Wong (2000) show that large U.S. firms have more exposure, even after controlling for the level of foreign sales.

[89] See, e.g, Dominguez and Tesar (2001), who use a sample of eight countries (not including the U.S.) and 2'387 firms.

[90] Brooks and Catao (2000), p. 7, include only post-merger companies, dropping companies that go into the merger. In the case of the merger between Mercedes-Benz and Chrysler, for example, their data cover Daimler-Chrysler but not Mercedes-Benz and Chrysler individually in the period leading up to the merger.

[91] Survivorship bias, meaning that only firms surviving over the full sample period are covered. No doubt this bias is important, especially in the context of global shocks such as the Asian crisis. But it is most likely offset at least in part by the fact that the data omit a large number of small firms where the risk of bankruptcy is greater. See Brooks and Catao (2000), p. 7.

[92] See Brooks and Catao (2000), p. 7.

[93] See Deutsche Börse (2001), Guidelines to Deutsche Börse's Equity Indices, Version 4.2, pp. 23-27. See also Sauer (1991), pp. 6-10.

splits are made[94]. Liquidity is an elusive concept, thus a lot of measures can be found in the literature. Daily number of shares traded as a proxy for liquidity[95]. Liquidity of the stock market is heavily concentrated in the first segment (Amtlicher Markt) and within this segment in the continuous market, while the periodic market only captures a very low percentage of the total trading volume[96]. The stocks not included in the DAX 100 sample accounts on average for less than 10 percent of the total trading volume[97].

B. Industries

Exposure will also be measured for industry sectors' indices. The Deutsche Börse computes nine "Sector Indices" for the DAX 100 companies. The base date is 12.30.1987[98]. The appropriate degree of aggregation can be a matter of concern. There is a potential problem of broad definitions leading to heterogeneous firms being placed in the same industry. It is possible that the failure to find low degree of exposure at the industry level is caused by individual firms' exposure canceling out each others. However, our choice is justified. First, more detailed sub-division of the industry classification can be examined by comparing the sector indices of the DAX 100 and of the CDAX[99]. This could be useful to investigate findings of different exposures' behavior at the individual firm's level. Second, it makes the results at the individual firms' level and at the industry's level directly comparable, and investigation of possible averaging-out effects within a given index less problematic. See Appendix H

---

[94] See Deutsche Börse (2001), Guidelines to Deutsche Börse's Equity Indices, Version 4.2, pp. 27-28. See Brealy and Myers (2000), p. 372.
[95] See Goeppl et al. (1995), p. 3.
[96] See Goeppl et al. (1995), p. 5. They find that continuous trading in the first segment is about 97 percent of overall trading, leaving only a small percentage to the periodic markets in the first to third segement.
[97] See Goeppl et al. (1995), p. 5.
[98] See Deutsche Börse (2001), Guidelines to Deutsche Börse's Equity Indices, Version 4.2, p.9.
[99] In the less aggregated sector classification of the CDAX, "Automobile & Transportation" is further subdivided into Automobile, and Transportation and Logistics, "Chemicals & Pharma" into Chemicals, Pharmaceutical & Healthcare, "Machinery & Industrials" into Basic Resources, Industrials, Machinery, and "Retail & Consumer" into Consumer Cyclical, Food & Beverages, Media, Retail[99]. Of course, during the period under consideration for our analysis, the composition of the industry sectors' indices have been to occasional modifications, with companies deleted or added to the indices. For a list of a list of the "deleted companies" and "new companies" in the sectors' indices, see Deutsche Börse (2001), DAX 100, p.4, and Deutsche Börse (2001), Guidelines to Deutsche Börse's Equity Indices, Version 4.2, p.7.

for a list of firms by sector of activity. Table 5.6 below indicates the number of firms per sector of activity in the DAX 100. Data are from the *Datastream International* database[100].

Table 5. 6 DAX 100 Firms per Sector of Activity[101]

DAX 100 Sectors	Number of DAX 30 Firms	Number of MDAX Firms	Number (and %) of DAX 100
Automobile & Transportation	6	8	14
Banks & Financial Services	4	7	11
Chemicals & Pharma	5	11	16
Construction	0	4	4
Insurance	2	2	4
Machinery & Industrials	4	20	24
Retail & Consumer	3	13	16
Software & Technology	3	5	8
Utilities & Telecommunication	3	0	3

Sources: Adapted from Börsen-Zeitung Nr. 179, 17. September 2002. Guidelines to Deutsche Börse's Equity Indices, August 2001.

Industry return indices from *Datastream* are value weighted so that the largest firms in the industry are given the greatest weight in the index[102].

C. Market Portfolio

In a perfectly integrated world, the relevant market portfolio would be the world market portfolio. For international asset pricing models, the financial integration evidence suggests that the relevant benchmark portfolio for measuring international

---

[100] "Sector allocation is determined according to the respective company's main source of turnover. Should this have changes in an individual case, the company in question can be removed from one sector and admitted to another at the next chaining" . See Deutsche Boerse (2001), p. 8.

[101] As of 17. September 2002 in the Börsen-Zeitung Nr. 179.

[102] See Dominguez and Tesar (2001), p. 4. Value-weighted market returns are dominated by large firms that are more likely to be multinational and/ or export oriented and are more likely to experience negative cash flow reactions to home currency appreciations than other firms. Therefore, including the value-weighted market return in an exposure test not only removes the standard macroeconomic effects, but also the more negative cash flow effects of larger firms. This would likely bias tests toward finding no exposure. See Bodnar and Wong (1999).

risk should be a global market index[103]. In contrast, studies on multinational firm stock returns reveal that the firm's home country index generally dominates global market indices in explaining individual firm returns[104]. Thus, studies that directly analyze the impact of domestic and global factors on individual stock returns seem to find results that are in contrast to the financial integration, one global index, asset pricing model. However, recent findings report that the percentage of the total movements in share prices that is explained by changes in global factors, as opposed to country-specific ones, seems to have increased substantially during the 1990s[105]. A recent study suggests that regional indices have greater influence on individual stock returns than global indices [106]. For European countries such as Germany regional factors seems to be even more important than domestic factors[107].

Because of the mixed empirical evidence, we allow for the possibility of at least partial segmentation in capital markets, and also control for the returns on the local stock market[108]. Our empirical strategy is to use the CDAX as a measure of the overall domestic stock market movement, and to test the robustness of the results with the results of the multivariate model with macro risk factors[109]. If strong differences are found, we will investigate the impact of other market indexes on our regression's results. Data are from the *Datastream International* database.

D. Exchange Rates

All data are from *Datastream International*. For the short-term interest rates for Germany, Japan, and the US, the middle rate of the 3-month Eurocurrency interest rate were used. The long-term interest rates variables consists of the yields on long-term

---

[103] See Harvey (1998), Bekaert and Harvey (1995).
[104] See Jacquillat and Solnik (1978), Eun et al. (1991).
[105] The correlation between changes in American and European share prices has risen from 0.4 in the mid-1990s to 0.8 in 2000. See Brooks and Catao (2000). See also The Economist, Economic Focus: Dancing in Step, March 22nd 2001, p. 106.
[106] Connolly et al (2000) find that, consistent with increasing integration of European markets, European index exposure is larger than home country exposure for many European countries including Germany.
[107] See Connolly et al. (2000).
[108] See Ferson and Harvey (1993). For a discussion on the role of domestic and international factors for the valuation of Multinational firms, see for example Solnik (1996), p. 228-229.
[109] The CDAX is a broad value-weighted stock market performance index available for Germany.

10-year German, Japanese, and US bonds. For the inflation rates variables for Germany, Japan, and the US, consumer-price indices are used[110].

(1) *Real versus nominal exchange rate index*

From a theoretical point of view the changes in exchange rates considered should be real rather than nominal. However, two aspects motivate the use of nominal changes:

■ *Inflation available with time lag*: using the real exchange rates would assume that inflation rates are instantaneously observed, as these inflation rates are necessary for calculating the real exchange rates[111]. Such an instantaneous observation is not possible in real life. Using the real exchange rate would assume that financial markets instantaneously observe the inflation rates that are necessary for calculating the real exchange rate. "Since nominal exchange rates are readily observable, it is less demanding to assume that the markets correctly measure nominal exchange rates[112].

■ *High correlation between nominal and real exchange rates*: over short time intervals changes in nominal exchange rates are highly correlated with changes in real exchange rate. Among the industrialized countries month-to-month changes in exchange rates show little correlation with month-to-month changes in relative purchasing power parities[113]. There is little difference between using nominal and real exposure, since the largest percentage of variation comes from exchange rates and not from inflation. Moreover, studies that have used both nominal and real exchange rate change have not found significantly different results[114].

For these reasons, nominal changes in exchange rates are used in our regressions. Moreover, for developing countries in general, real exchange rate variability is considerably lower than nominal exchange rate variability, because the covariance between nominal exchange rate changes and inflation differentials is highly negative[115].

---

[110] The European Central Bank (ECB) targets consumer prices and the Stability and Growth Pact is aimed at avoiding divergences in consumer prices among the countries in the Euro area. See Andren and Oxelheim (2001), p. 4.
[111] See Bodnar and Gentry (1993), Dornbusch (1976).
[112] See Bodnar and Gentry (1993), p. 33.
[113] See Mussa (1979).
[114] See Jorion (1990), p. 334, Booth and Rotenberg (1990), p.14, Amihud (1994), p. 51, Choi and Prasad (1995), p. 80.
[115] Recall that

We should note that the inclusion of price variables results in having real exchange rates.

(2) *Anticipated versus unanticipated exchange rates*

Firms are affected by unanticipated changes in exchange rates. From a theoretical point of view the considered changes in exchange rates should be unanticipated as anticipated changes are already reflected in the stock prices.

There is evidence of random walk behavior of exchange rates in the medium term. Isolating the unanticipated part from the expected part of exchange rate changes would require a model of exchange rate behavior. A monetary model of exchange rate determination has been sometimes used for that purpose[116]. An other possibility is to estimate a model to account for possible autocorrelation in the exchange rate index[117]. However, that would suppose that stock market investors believe that firms are capable to use these models of exchange rate determination to forecast "out-sample" exchange rates. However, it is well known that neither models of exchanges based macroeconomic fundamentals such as the monetary model, nor models of exchange rates based on the forecast of market participants as embodied in the forward rate or survey data can explain exchange rate movements significantly better than a random walk model for the post-Bretton Woods period[118], at least in the short and medium term. This is a confirmation of the findings that the current exchange rate performs just as well in predicting the future exchange rate than estimated models at a one to twelve month horizon[119]. Error correction terms can explain exchange rate movements significantly better than a no change forecast[120] but only for long-term prediction horizons[121]. For short term prediction horizons fundamental models forecast no better than a random walk model. Exchange rate is an asset price which is influenced by expectations about future realizations of the exchange rate itself as well as other

---

$$Var(\Delta e_t) = Var(\Delta s_t) + Var(\pi^*_{t,t+n} - \pi_{+n}) + 2Cov(\Delta s_t, \pi^*_{t,t+n} - \pi_{+n}).$$

Where e is the real exchange rate, s the nominal exchange rate, π (π^*) the inflation rate in the home foreign) country. The third term is highly negative for developing countries. See Coval (1998), March 30, p. 11.

[116] See, e.g., Gao (2000).
[117] See for example Allayannis (1996).
[118] See Meese (1990).
[119] See Meese and Rogoff (1983).
[120] See Chinn and Meese (1995) and Mark (1995).
[121] However, this result has been challenged by Berkowitz and Gioganni (1998).

fundamentals[122]. The strength of the correlation between exchange rates and other fundamental variables has been the subject of much empirical work. The findings suggest, among other things, that a large part of exchange rate fluctuations seem unrelated to fundamentals, and that estimated relations are not stable out of sample. Nevertheless, exchange rates are related to fundamentals. In the very short run (within a day, say) exchange rate changes are correlated with news about macroeconomic conditions. The relations are weak in monthly and quarterly data, where exchange rate fluctuations seem to be dominated by "noise", but become stronger again at longer horizons[123]. Thus, there is ample evidence that changes in the nominal exchange rates are largely unpredictable. Consequently, an attempt to divide the changes in the nominal exchange rates into anticipated and unanticipated changes shall not be made.

The standard regression specification assumes that exchange rates and stock returns follow a random walk process which implies that the actual changes in the exchange rates and stock returns represent the unexpected changes[124]. The random-walk assumption was employed for all variables, thus making all changes in the variables unexpected. This assumption can be tested by evaluating a series of time-series forecasts for the macro prices, showing the random walk to be a competitive assumption[125]. If the exchange rates indices do not follow a random walk but are autocorrelated, it is no longer true that the actual changes in the exchange rates represent the unexpected changes. In this case, it is necessary to use tests that correct for the presence of autocorrelation in the exchange rate indices. The residuals from the regression of the exchange rate index on its lagged change can be used.

There are also theoretical arguments for using the total variability of the independent variables rather than just deviations from expectations. Since managers are interested in how the variability of environmental contingencies affects corporate performance regardless of whether the variability is foreseen or not, it makes sense to specify models of economic exposure in terms of total variability of the independent variables. While defining economic exposure just in terms of unanticipated movements in the independent variables accommodates the properties of financial market hedging

---

[122] See Andren and Oxelheim (2001), p. 16.
[123] See Friberg and Vredin (1996), p. 12.
[124] See Adler and Dumas (1984), Jorion (1990), Amihud (1993).
[125] See Andren (2001).

instruments, such a definition is inconsistent with managers' concerns about the impact of both foreseeable and unforeseeable contingencies[126].

(3) *Bilateral versus multilateral exchange rate indexes*

Most of the studies in the literature use a trade-weighted exchange rate index to measure exposure. Collapsing all exchange rates into one multilateral exchange rate avoids the problem of multicollinearity that arises because many cross-exchange rates are fixed relative to each other, or nearly so. However, the problem with using a trade-weighted basket of currencies in exposure tests is that the results lack power if the nature of firm exposure does not correspond to the exchange rates (and the relative weights) included in the basket. Moreover, there is a possibility of estimation errors due to averaging-out effects. For this reason, it might be better in some cases not to use exchange rate indices and instead use bilateral exchange rates[127]. However, the use of exchange-rate indices might not be feasible if they are highly correlated. One possibility is to focus on one bilateral exchange rate[128]. Or focus on the currency(ies) of determination relevant for a particular firm or sector.

(4) *Data frequency*

Monthly data were used. In traditional studies of exchange rate exposure, end-of-month stock returns are related to end-of-month exchange rates. Conflicting opinions and results exist regarding the adequate frequency of data to be used: Using daily data (for share price and for exchange rate) might avoid the problem of averaging-out effects that could be produced with data of lower frequency[129]. This could lead to underestimation of exposure. On the other hand, this could lead to problems associated with nonsynchronous trading[130]. In addition, the existence of inefficiencies and time-consuming information processing could be expected to lead to short-run share-price fluctuations being independent of macroeconomic fundamentals[131]. Then, averaging of short-run mispricing in long-interval returns should lead to exposures converging to

---

[126] See Miller (1994), pp. 17-18.
[127] See Glaum and al. (2000) in order to prevent possible averaging-out effects, do not use exchange rate indices or monthly averages. Instead, they use daily changes of a single exchange rate. They concentrate on the German firms' exchange rate exposures to the US dollar.
[128] See, e.g., Glaum et al. (2000).
[129] See, e.g., Glaum et al. (2000) for a study favoring that argument.
[130] See Williamson (2001), p. 450.
[131] See Bartov and Bodnar (1994).

stable levels reflective of the true fundamental relationships[132]. Furthermore, if inflation is to be included in the assessment, monthly data is the shortest possible observation frequency[133]. In practice, changes intervals of three months are common[134].

II. Selection of Sub-Periods and Behavior of the DM/US$ and €/US$ Exchange-Rates

We select sub-periods based on the directional movement in exchange rates. We subdivided our base period into sub-periods when the DM/US-dollar exchange rate underwent episodes in which it seems to change dramatically. As the nominal and real exchange rates have been highly correlated in the post-Bretton Woods period, we have based our segmentation on the nominal exchange rate. Dramatic breaks in the DM/US-dollar exchange rate time series have been identified in a study using a Markov switching model[135].

Figure 5. 3 The DM/US-dollar exchange rate from Jan. 1974 to Dec. 2001

Source of Data: Datastream International, WHU Koblenz

---

[132] See Rees and Unni (1997).

[133] This point is stressed by Andren (2000), p. 27.

[134] See Bishop and Dixon (1992). With quarterly data, a total time span of five years would give sufficient degree of freedom.

[135] See Engle and Hamilton (1990). Glaum et al. (2000) also refer to this study for the segmentation of their base period. See Hamilton (1994), pp. 677-703 for modeling time series with changes in regime. Holmes and Maghrebi (2002) estimate exchange rate exposure with a Markow regime switching model.

The large swings displayed by the DM/US-dollar real exchange rate shown in figure 5.3 suggests that exposure could fluctuate greatly[136]. We also display the DM/Yen and the Yen/US-dollar exchange rates. Euros rates were established on December 31, 1998, at 1 Euro = 1.95583 DM. During the period 1999-2001, companies kept their books and carried on business in either their old currencies or in euro.

Figure 5. 4 The DM/Yen exchange rate from Jan. 1974 to Dec. 2001

Source of Data: Datastream International, WHU Koblenz

It is important in the stock market approach to have a view of the macroeconomic context in which firms operate. We briefly review here the main events that led to the large swings that the D-mark/US-dollar underwent. These developments should also be useful in understanding the factors that led to exchange rate and stock prices movements.

In *sub-period I* (1974:1 to 1979:1), generally there was an overall decrease in the value of the dollar from the breakdown of the Bretton woods system of fixed exchange rates until the beginning of the 1980s. This decrease was followed by an increase against the major currencies from the early to the mid 1980s (*sub-period II: 1980:1-1985:2*). In

---

[136] Empirical studies on the DM/US$ suggest that adequate adjustment toward PPP between USA and Germany seem not to have taken place in the post-Bretton Woods era. See Juselius and MacDonald (2000).

part, this was due to the high real interest rates and consequently large inflows of foreign capital. The high real interest rates were essential to finance the growing budget and trade deficits[137]. The appreciation of the US$ by nearly 50 percent in real terms over the 1980-1985 period coincided with an increase in the US merchandise trade deficit to nearly $160 billion in 1987. Some US exporters were hit heavily by this period of dollar appreciation, losing market share and profitability to foreign competitors. US auto companies appeared to allow their prices to rise parallel to Japanese prices during this period and therefore could not use the dollar's sharp depreciation over the 1985-87 period to gain market share and profits at the expense of foreign firms[138].

The US$ peaked in February 1985 and subsequently undertook a steep depreciation which was due to both the record size of the trade deficit in 1985 and coordinated international intervention through the Plaza Accord (*sub-period III: 1985:1-1987:6*). From the time of the Plaza Accords in 1985, in which the group of five industrial countries agreed to depreciate the dollar against other major countries, there was a decrease in the dollar value relative to other major currencies such as the D-Mark[139]. In contrast, the Yen to D-Mark exchange rate fluctuated around the initial levels for the entire sample period. The extent of the US$ appreciation in the period 1979 to February 1985is much smaller relative to the JPY than the ECU[140].

Around the 1987, fears were rising that the dollar had depreciated by too much. Intervention ensued that the dollar stabilized briefly. However, the depreciation continued in the final years of the 1980s (*sub-period IV: 07/1987-12/1998*). The period from the end of 1990 to the end of the sample is characterized by a more stable period of US$ rates. The extent of the average US$ movements in this period are small relative to earlier periods but the movements were still considerable, and the volatility is similar to the two earlier regimes. The ERM crisis in effect resulted in a movement

---

[137] See Priestley and Odegaard (2002), p. 10.
[138] See Amihud and Levich (1994), p. 2.
[139] "During the first half of the 80 decade, the U.S. dollar exchange rate nearly doubled (on an effective basis against major trading partners) and then fell by about half before the end of the decade". See Amihud and Levich (1994), p. V. "At the beginning of the 1980s, the dollar was worth roughly 1.7 German marks. By early 1985 it had risen above 3.3 marks, an increase of nearly 100% in its value relative to the mark, in sprite of the fact that U.S. inflation exceeded German inflation during this period. It then fell dramatically to less than 1.6 marks by late 1987. The changes in the yen/dollar exchange rate were nearly as large over this same time period". See Knetter (1992), p. 1.
[140] See Priestley and Odegaard (2002), p. 10.

from fixed to floating exchange rates, which might have lead to changed volatility patterns, and thus exposures, among macro prices[141]. Sub-period V (1999:1-2002:9) covers the Euro period.

Figure 5. 5 Monthly Returns on the DM/US-dollar

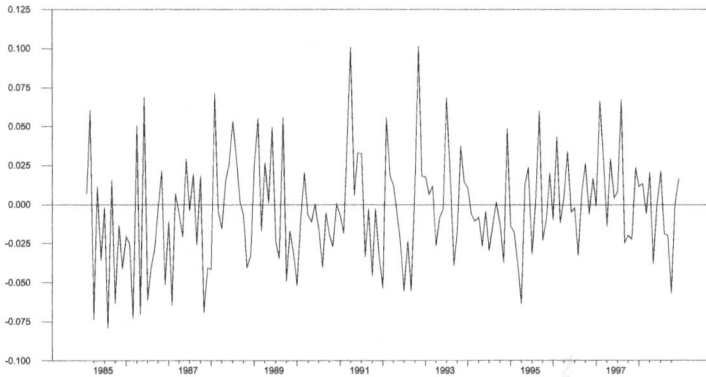

Figure 5.5 above shows the volatility of the monthly returns on the DM/US$ exchange rate. A feature is that exchange rate *volatility is clustered*, i.e. periods with low volatility are followed with periods with much higher volatility. As a result, the nature of the asymmetries in the estimated exposure profiles of flexible firms will be time-varying. When the exposure profile is asymmetric / non-linear, changes in exchange rate volatility induce changes in the extent to which firm value and shareholder wealth are affected by exchange rate uncertainty.

5.2.4 Results

A. Results of Augmented Regression, Exposure to the DM/US$ and €/US$

The estimations' results of exposures to the DM/US-dollar appreciation and depreciation for the DAX 30 firms and MDAX firms are presented in Appendix J. All summary tables of results have the same outline as the matrix table 5.1. The cells

---

[141] See Andren (2000).

present the percentage shares of significant coefficients for each combination of exposure to the DM/US-dollar appreciation and depreciation. We also provide a table that summarizes the results for the DAX30 and MDAX firms combined. Regressions are estimated by ordinary least squares (OLS) [142]. All significances are measured at 10% significant level. Standard errors are corrected for serial correlation and heteroskedascticity in error terms with the Newey-West method[143]. Multicolllinearity was assessed through bivariate and partial correlations[144], showing that multicolinearity should not constitute a problem. The statistical power of the regressions were measured by the adjusted R^2.

The majority of firms is not exposed to either currency appreciations or depreciations, and end up in the no-exposure cells (cells E). However, the percentage of significant coefficients is in general higher than in most empirical studies, but much lower than in a other recent study on German firms[145].

The firms that are significantly exposed to the US-dollar are exposed asymmetrically. Firms with significant exposures are either exposed to increases or decreases in the exchange rate. Some firms fall in cell (C) representing significant positive exposure to the DM appreciation against the US$, and significant negative exposure to the DM depreciation. But for almost all periods the majority of firms with significant exposure fall in cell (B), representing significant positive exposure to the DM appreciation against the US-dollar, but insignificant exposure to the DM depreciation. For all periods, DAX30 firms are relatively more exposed to the dollar than the MDAX firms, but their exposure pattern is relatively similar. Results are found to be relatively similar for the sectors' exposures.

Similar results have been found by other researchers. A recent study on European firms, including 88 German corporations, find that the highest percentage of European firms significantly exposed to the DM/US$ also falls into cell (B) although by a less clear majority. He makes, however, no further interpretation on this finding[146]. An other study, that surveyed non-financial UK firms finds that "in 1996, 33 percent of the firms

---

[142] Unit-root tests were performed for all variables with augmented Dickey-Fuller tests. All variables are stationary in returns.
[143] See Newey and West (1987). Also the RATS 4.0 manual.
[144] See Pindyck and Rubinfeld (1991), p. 86-88.
[145] See Glaum et al. (2000).
[146] Andren (2001).

had reported an increase in margin following sterling depreciation, whereas in 1997, the proportion of respondents reporting a reduction in export margins as a result of sterling appreciation was significantly higher at 46 percent, indicating an asymmetric currency effect. The results suggest that respondent firms were more exposed to the adverse effects of appreciation and less able to benefit from depreciation[147]."

B. Interpretation of Results

Assuming that German firms are in large majority export oriented, the evidence suggests that adverse *D-mark appreciation against the US-dollar affect negatively firms' market values to a much larger extent than beneficial changes.* When we find little evidence of significant exposure to D-mark depreciation, exposure estimates actually tend to be negative. The assumption of market efficiency implies that the stock market recognize that the expected value of German firms decrease when there is increased uncertainty of the €/US$ and of the future market conditions in the U.S. Based on our theoretical analysis, this pattern is consistent with:

(1) *Destruction of the value of real options by competitors for US$ appreciations* (see chapter 4/section 4.3.1).

(2) *Bounds on flexibility*: volume constraints may limit the firm's ability to capture upside demand potentials associated with *US$ appreciations* (see chapter 3/section 3.5.2).

(3) *Risk management theories*: predict negative effects of cash flow volatility (see chapter 3/section 3.4.1).

(4) *Hysterisis effects related to entry/exit of competitors*: an appreciation of the US$ could incite the entry of new competitors, which would put pressure on the firms' prices and profit margins. On the other hand, a depreciation of the US$ would not induce these firms to leave the market. The hysteretic behavior of the firms is explained by the sunk costs to be paid for re-entry. Hysterisis would make the German firm relatively more exposed to US$ depreciation (see chapter 4/section 4.2.2).

---

[147] See Bradley and Moles (2001).

(5) *Investors valuing relatively more adverse changes*[148]: minimization of lower tail outcomes could be the primary concern for investors (see chapter 3/section 3.7.3).

(6) *Firms manage poorly their currency risk* (see chapter 3/section 3.7.3).

(7) *Stock market inefficiencies:* exposure asymmetry might constitute "one of the complexities facing investors that may lead them to make systematic errors in assessing the relationship between firm's value and exchange rate changes"[149].

The evidence of piece-wise linear concavity suggests that an increase in the DM/US$ or €/US$ volatility will reduce shareholder wealth.

5.3 Macroeconomic Exposures

5.3.1 Interrelation of Macroeconomic Exposures

A. Selection of Macroeconomic Variables

The choice of these macroeconomic variables is derived from international equilibrium relationships (see Appendix F). Simple regressions cannot separate returns fluctuations that occur via changes in the discount rate from those that occur through changes in cash flows. However, the impact of exchange rate changes on cash flows could be reverted by the effect on interest rates[150]. Foreign exchange risks cannot be treated separately from interest rate risks since interest rates directly affect the company's shareholder value via the discounting of future cash flows, and possibly have an impact on the size of the cash flows too. Correlation between exchange rates and interest rates is expected, because interest rate changes affect international capital flows and hence exchange rates. Current and prospective exchange rate changes impact a nation's capital account transactions, which in turn affect the pricing and availability of financial capital. These effects could be felt across financial assets denominated in a particular currency, for example when a prospective US$ depreciation leads to a rise in

---

[148] Andren (2001) raises this possibility.
[149] Bartov and Bodnar (1994), p. 1761, for example briefly allude to this issue.
[150] See Froot and Stein (1991).

all US interest rates, or across financial claims for a particular country[151]. Because exchange rate changes result in changes in domestic prices as well as macroeconomic variables such as interest rates, they will also have an impact on firms that have no direct international activities[152]. By including price variables, the impact of real exchange rates on firm value will be evaluated. Expected GDP growth also seems to be relevant. However, we expect its effect to be captured by the interest rates as an indicator of expected economic conditions.

Because of the interrelation of these risk factors, movements in one exchange rate could be offset by other factors. Unexpected changes in interest rates and exchange rates could have a simultaneous but differential impact on future cash flows. For instance, one might find negative exposures in our historical data if a depreciation of the DM was offset by the Bundesbank increasing interest rates. This action, in turn, is typically associated with lower stock prices[153].

The selection of regressors is based on three requirements:

1. *Variables that are likely to influence a majority of firms*: multi-firms studies cannot easily deal with highly firm-specific variables, such as variables related to corporate strategies. We select variables that are relevant for a majority of firms. Most firms' stock prices are exposed to interest rate and inflation risks, which are expected to explain a large part of stock price variations and to be correlated to exchange rates[154].

2. *Variables that explain a large portion of stock price movements*: exchange rate changes have been reported to explain only a relatively small amount of the total variation in stock returns[155]. In practice, changes in firms' competitive position are generally reported to be caused by changes in market prices other than exchange

---

[151] See Levich (1998), p. 568.
[152] See Bartov and Bodnar (1994), p. 1758.
[153] One might find negative exposure if a depreciation of the German mark was offset by the Bundesbank increasing interest rates. This action, in turn, is typically associated with lower stock prices. Dahlquist and Robertsson (2001) find a negative average exposure for Sweden Stock returns for the period January 1988 to October 1992 and provide this explanation.
[154] These factors are representative of the "macroeconomic uncertainty". See Eiteman (2000).
[155] Griffin and Stulz (2000) focus on the economic magnitude of exchange rate exposure and find that exchange rate changes explain only a relatively trivial amount of the total variation in excess industry returns.

rates[156]. For that reason, the inclusion of other factors should reduce the omitted variables bias. As a result, the residual variance of the regression should be reduced and the precision of the exposure estimates improved.

3. *Variables that are correlated to exchange rates*, but this correlation should not be too high to avoid the problem of multicolinearity. Nominal exchange rates are relative prices of different national monies. As such, they should be affected by monetary policy and correlated with other variables that are affected by monetary policy. Monetary policy has immediate effects on exchange rates and short run nominal interest rates, partly through expectations about future policy. Monetary policy affects inflation with a lag. Nominal rigidities imply that these effects on nominal variables, in turn, are transmitted to real interest rates and real wages, at least temporarily[157].

The basic statistical requirement is that the "interdependence between exchange rates, interest rates, and inflation rates is neither too strong so as to create multicollinearity, nor so weak that the measuring of each variable separately is acceptable"[158].

B. Selected Country Variables and Data Description

Exposure to market risks is investigated by including currencies, interest rates, and inflation rates of Germany, the United States, and Japan. The USA and Japan are the two main non-European trading partner countries outside the European Union[159]. Furthermore, the US and Japan are the major senders and receivers of goods and capital to and from the EU. The US is by far the most important recipient of German foreign direct investment. Almost 25% of German foreign direct investment is in the US[160]. Moreover, many goods such as oil are internationally priced in US dollars[161]. Focusing on these two countries should capture the majority of global international

---

[156] See Stulz (2000).
[157] See Andren and Oxelheim (2001), pp. 15-16. Monetary policy can also affect aggregate output and employment in the short run.
[158] See Oxelheim (2002), p. 12.
[159] The main trading partners of Germany are France, the Netherlands, Italy, Belgium/Luxembourg, Great Britain, the USA, Switzerland, Austria and Japan. See Statistisches Bundesamt (1996), p. 297-299. See also Andren (2001).
[160] See Glaum et al. (2000), Deutsche Bundesbank (1997).
[161] See Bishop and Dixon (1992).

trade flows of German companies as well as international competitive relations[162]. However, we know that what matters for economic exposure are the currencies of determination and not of denomination. The German car industry for example, is probably also exposed to movements in the US-dollar/Yen exchange rates. If we find that the results from the two empirical specifications are not robust, this possibility will also be investigated. Empirical support for an asymmetric relationship between stock returns and inflation, and stock returns and interest rates also exist[163].

All data are from *Datastream International*. For the short-term interest rates for Germany, Japan, and the US, the middle rate of the 3-month Eurocurrency interest rate were used. The long-term interest rates variables consists of the yields on long-term 10-year German, Japanese, and US bonds. For the inflation rates variables for Germany, Japan, and the US, consumer-price indices are used[164].

C. Econometric Model Specification

We estimate the exposure to the US-dollar/D-mark with the inclusion of these other market risk factors. However, since the "true" model is not known, the exact consequences to using either the model with the market index or with other macro variables is also not known. And unless a comparison is made of the costs of misspecifications, it is not possible to say one specification is preferred to the other[165].

Monthly changes in each sample firm's stock price over the period 1973:1 to 2002:09 and over 5 sub-periods were regressed on monthly changes in these market risk factors. The model used to estimate asymmetric risk exposure to market factors increases and decreases for a firm or industry i at time t is given as[166]:

---

[162] Andren (2001) estimate firms' exposure for various European countries and use the German mark as proxy for the Euro during the pre-Euro era.

[163] Domian and Gilster (1996) find evidence that decreases in inflation expectations lead to stock price increases, whereas increases in expected inflation do not influence aggregate stock prices.
Bartram (2001) in a study on 490 non-financial German corporations finds strong evidence of asymmetric exposure of firm value to domestic interest rate risks.

[164] The European Central Bank (ECB) targets consumer prices and the Stability and Growth Pact is aimed at avoiding divergences in consumer prices among the counties in the Euro area. See Andren and Oxelheim (2001), p .4.

[165] A problem raised, for example, by Khoo (1994).

[166] See Andren (2001), p. 15.

[5. 5]

$$r_{it} = \alpha_i + \gamma_1^I D_{1t}^I \Delta e_{DM/US\$,t} + \gamma_1^D D_t^D \Delta e_{DM/US,t} + \gamma_2^I D_2^I \Delta e_{DM/Y,t} + \gamma_2^D D_2^D \Delta e_{DM/Y}$$
$$+ \gamma_3^I D_3^I \Delta i_{G,t}^s + \gamma_3^D D_3^D \Delta i_{G,t}^s + \gamma_4^I D_4^I \Delta i_{US,t}^s + \gamma_4^D D_4^D \Delta i_{US,t}^s + \gamma_5^I D_5^I \Delta i_{J,t}^s + \gamma_5^D D_5^D \Delta i_{J,t}^s$$
$$+ \gamma_6^I D_6^I \Delta i_{G,t}^l + \gamma_6^D D_{6t}^D \Delta i_{G,t}^l + \gamma_7^I D_7^I \Delta i_{US,t}^l + \gamma_7^D D_7^D \Delta i_{US,t}^l + \gamma_8^I D_8^I \Delta i_{J,t}^l + \gamma_8^D D_8^D \Delta i_{J,t}^l$$
$$+ \gamma_9^I D_9^I \Delta p_{G,t} + \gamma_9^D D_9^D \Delta p_{G,t} + \gamma_{10}^I D_{10}^I \Delta p_{US,t} + \gamma_{10}^D D_{10}^D \Delta p_{US,t} + \gamma_{11}^I D_{11}^I \Delta p_{J,y} + \gamma_{11}^D D_{11}^D \Delta p_{J,t}$$
$$+ \varepsilon_{it}$$

With the two dummy variables defined as:

$$D_{j,t}^I = \begin{cases} 1 | e_t > 0 \\ 0 | e_t \leq 0 \end{cases} \qquad D_{j,t}^D = \begin{cases} 0 | e_t \geq 0 \\ 1 | e_t < 0 \end{cases}$$

i is the interest rate risk factor measured by the percentage rate of changes in interest rate, i.e., $(r_t - r_{t-1})/r_{t-1}$ where r is the interest rate. e_t is the exchange rate risk factor measured by the percentage rate of change in currency exchange rate, i.e., $(e_t - e_{t-1})/e_{t-1}$ where s is the value of the DM in terms of the foreign currency.

Changes in stock price were regressed on monthly changes in exchange rates, on monthly changes in the short term German, Japanese, and US interest rates, on monthly changes in the yields on long-term German, Japanese, and US government bonds[167], on the monthly changes in the German, Japanese, and US consumer-price indices. The random-walk assumption was employed for all variables, thus making all changes in the variables unexpected.

This model tests the null hypothesis that exchange rate exposure is symmetric, i.e., $H_0 : \gamma^I = \gamma^D = \gamma$ against the alternative hypothesis that exposure is asymmetric, i.e., $H_1 : \gamma^I \neq \gamma^D$. The coefficients measure the sensitivity of the real return of firm i to a one percent unexpected change in macro price j, after controlling for movements in the other macro prices. Table 5.7 below summarizes the various effects that these macro risk factors can have on firm market value.

---

[167] If we use the percentage change (1+interest rate) instead of the percentage change in the interest rate themselves, the coefficient of the regression could be interpreted as "duration" measures. See Smithson et al. (1995), p. 144. A popular measurement method for interest rate risk is to use duration. Duration measures the percentage decrease in the market value of a series of cash flows, for one percentage increase in the (continuously compounded) per annum yield-to-maturity. The duration of a series of cash flows Ct, is a weighted average of the times-to-maturity of the individual cash flows, with the weights being the present values of each cash flow expressed as a fraction of the portfolio's total present value. See Sercu and Uppal (1995), pp. 479-482.

Table 5. 7 Possible Exposure Profile Resulting from Interest Rate Risk and Inflation Risk

	Increases in interest rates and consumer prices $\Delta e_{j,t}, \Delta i^s_{j,t}, \Delta i^l_{j,t}, \Delta p_{j,t} > 0$			
Decreases $\Delta e_{j,t}, \Delta i^s_{j,t}, \Delta i^l_{j,t}, \Delta$	$\gamma^I_i > 0$	$\gamma^I_i = 0$	$\gamma^I_i < 0$	
$\gamma^D_i > 0$	(A) Linear exposure	(B) Asymmetric exposure	(C) ___	(4) % of firms positively exposed to macro-price risk decreases
$\gamma^D_i = 0$	(D) Asymmetric exposure	(E) No exposure	(F) Asymmetric exposure	(5) % of firms insignificantly exposed to macro-price risk decreases
$\gamma^D_i < 0$	(G) ___	(H) Asymmetric exposure	(I) Linear exposure	(6) % of firms negatively exposed to macro-price risk decreases
	(1) % of firms positively exposed to macro-price risk increase	(2) % of firms insignificantly exposed to macro-price risk increase	(3) % of firms negatively exposed to macro-price risk increase	

Source: adapted from Miller and Reuer (1995), p24. and Andren (2001), p. 19.

5.3.2 Results

We check for the robustness of the results to additional explanatory variables. We consider the robustness of the exposure estimated to the inclusion of other explanatory variables. We then estimate the exposure of the DAX 30 firms and MDAX firms to the 11 macro risk factors using model [5.7]. Regressions are estimated by ordinary least squares (OLS)[168]. All significances are measured at 10% significant level. Standard errors are corrected for serial correlation and heteroskedascticity in error terms with the Newey-West method[169]. The statistical power of the regressions were measured by the adjusted R^2. Multicolllinearity was assessed through bivariate and partial correlations

---

[168] Unit-root tests were performed for all variables with augmented Dickey-Fuller tests. All variables are stationary in returns.
[169] See Newey and West (1987). Also the RATS 4.0 manual.

coefficients for the market risk factors[170], showing that multicolinearity should not constitute a problem. Exchange rates, interest rates, and inflation rates co-vary, but not perfectly so. There are indications of multicolinearity, but they are not strong enough to motivate any changes in the model specification. Most researchers appear to consider the value of 0.9 as the threshold beyond which problems are likely to occur[171].

The cells in the table of the appendix K, present the percentage shares of significant coefficients for each combination of exposure to a macro price increase and decrease. Again, we provide a table that summarizes the results for the DAX30 and MDAX firms combined. Results with model [5.5] are compared with those of model [5.4]. We then run again regression model [5.5] for the nine industry sub-indices of the DAX 100 to observe possible cross-sectional differences. We also provide results for all the individual DAX 100 firms, and categorize them per sector, according to the DAX 100 index sectors terminology. Estimates of exposures per sector are compared between those directly estimated with the sector indexes and those obtained by categorizing per sector the exposures of the firms taken individually. Summary of the results are presented in appendix L.

Before interpreting these findings further, we check the robustness of these results for the firms' exposure to the D-mark/US-dollar exchange rate by running regression [5.7]. Adding other macro risk factors significantly reduce the residual variance of our regressions. The results for model [5.7] provide further evidence that firms are not symmetrically exposed to the D-mark/US-dollar appreciations and depreciations. The proportion of firms significantly exposed to the D-mark/US-dollar exchange rate is substantially higher. Again, DAX30 firms are relatively more exposed than the MDAX firms. Exposures are rarelyP symmetric. There appears to be robustness in our results. The general pattern of asymmetric exposures is relatively similar for model [5.5] and the regression model [5.4]. However, the pattern of exposure that seemed to emerge with model [5.4] is now much more pronounced. A clear majority of firms that are significantly affected fall into cell (B), representing significant positive exposure to the

---

[170] See Pindyck and Rubinfeld (1991), p. 86-88.

[171] See Lardaro (1993), p. 453. Partial-correlation coefficient is given as $r_{i,j}^{partial} = \sqrt{t_j^2 / (t_j^2 + DF)}$, where t_j is the t-statistic for variable j=1,... in a regression of one market risk variable on the other market risk variables, and DF is the degrees of freedom of the t-statistic. See Andren (2000), p. 34.

D-mark (or Euro) appreciation against the US-dollar, but insignificant exposure to the D-mark depreciation[172]. Exposure should thus display a piecewise concave shape.

Euro effect on Exposure to the US-dollar

An other observation emerges from our results. The percentage share of German firms significantly exposed to the US-dollar seems to have decrease after the emergence of the Euro in comparison to *sub-period III (1985:1-1987:6)* and *sub-period IV (07/1987-12/1998)*. The only exception is for the DAX firms estimated with the simple regression [5.4]. This could be explained by a decrease in trade between the two countries, or the result of less competition from other Euro area firms in the US market. When we classify these firms per sector, this result is confirmed for firms in the sectors of Chemicals & Pharma, Automobile & Transportation, Banks & Financial Services, Construction, Machinery & Industrials, Software & Technology, Utilities & Telecommunication. The two exceptions are the sectors of Insurance, and Retail & Consumer (see table 5.8 below).

The increasing economic integration in Europe has affected cross-border activities by German and other firms. Also, since the introduction of the Euro, the volatility and the persistence of the German stock index have fallen significantly relative to those of the U.S. index. In the case of the Euro, the "US dollar value of the single European currency in 1999 displayed a much smaller variability than that of the DM in, say, 1998"[173]. "The volatility of the US dollar/Euro exchange rate in 1999 is much lower than that of the dollar/DM rate in, for example, 1998. The empirical evidence suggests that the volatility of the Euro exchange rate is much lower than that of the pre-1999 DM". The decline in exchange rate uncertainty can reduce the pricing uncertainty for German firms with overseas operations and for foreign investors[174]. The reduction in exchange rate uncertainty can lead to reduction in equity market uncertainty[175]. It is not the introduction of the euro per se, that would explain that result, but the economic

---

[172] Andren (2001) find very similar results for as sample of 88 German firms. He interestingly also finds that the highest percentage of European firms significantly exposed to the DM/US$ also falls into cell (B) although by a less clear majority. He makes, however, no interpretation on this finding.
[173] See Cheung and Westermann (2000), p.2.
[174] See Cheung and Westermann (2000), p.3.
[175] See Krugman and Miller (1993).

convergence caused by the euro, leading to purchasing power parity and real interest rate parity[176].

As for the other macro factors, we see that German corporations are exposed to a much less extent to the DM/Yen exchange rate than to the DM /US-dollar exchange rate. As expected, an increase in long term German bond yield affects many German firms' value negatively. An explanation is that there is substituability between investments on stocks and bonds, which affects corporate value through firms' costs of capital.

Table 5. 8 Percentage of DAX 100 Firms Significantly Exposed to the Euro (DM) / US$ Exchange Rate, per Sector of Activity- Model [6.2] – Sub-period IV and V

	Sub-period IV (7/87-12/98)			Sub-period V (1/99-9/02)		
Sectors of Activity	DAX30	MDAX	DAX100	DAX30	MDAX	DAX100
Automobile & Transportation	100%	100%	100%	50%	57.1%	76.9%
Banks & Financial Services	100%	25%	57.1%	66.7%	42.9%	50%
Chemicals & Pharma	100%	87.5%	92.3%	80%	54.5%	62.5%
Construction[177]	100^%	75%	75%	100%	25%	25%
Insurance	50%	50%	50%	100%	50%	75%
Machinery & Industrials	100%	80%	83.3%	33.3%	70%	65.2%
Retail & Consumer	100%	60%	69.2%	100%	84.6%	87.5%
Software & Technology	50%	100%	75%	75%	20%	44.4%
Utilities & Telecommunication	50%	100%	50%	33.3%	100%	33.3%

---

[176] See Andren and Oxelheim (2001), pp. 6-7.
[177] For a detailed analysis of foreign exposure in the construction industry, see Demacopoulos (1987).

5.4 GARCH Analysis

5.4.1 Exposure Asymmetries and Conditional Heteroskedasticity

A. Departures from Normality and Conditional Heteroskedasticity

Most studies that estimate foreign exchange exposure assumes that the error term is *i.i.d.* But we saw in chapter 3 that the effect of flexibility is to skew firms' cash flows and value distribution, and make their conditional variances function of the exchange rate (heteroskedastic). The possibility that the distribution of stock returns may not correspond to a normal distribution could explain time variation in risk.

The assumption of homoskedasticity is related to the assumption of normality. Assume that y_t denotes domestic cash flows, X_t is an exchange rate random variable that takes values x_t. The assumption that $Var(y_t/X_t = x_t) = \sigma^2$ is free of x_t is a consequence of the assumption that $D(y_t, X_t; \psi)$ is multivariate normal. $D(.)$ is the joint distribution of y_t and x_t, with ψ the parameters[178]. Regression disturbances whose variances are not constant across observations are heteroskedastic. The presence of conditional heteroskedasticity leads to inefficient parameter estimates as well as biased test statistics. By modeling the variance of residuals it may be possible to obtain more efficient estimators. Financial return data typically exhibit *volatility clustering*. The presence of such dependencies is due to conditional heteroskedasticity, which is the tendency of large changes to be followed by large changes in either direction[179].

B. GARCH Model

ARCH models[180] and GARCH[181] are designed to model and forecast conditional variances of residuals. The regression is stated as: $y_t = \beta' x_t + \varepsilon_t$ with $\varepsilon_t = u_t \sqrt{\alpha_0 + \alpha_1 \varepsilon_{t-1}^2}$, where u_t is distributed as standard normal. Conditioned on an

---

[178] See Spanos (1995), p. 372.
[179] There is an extensive body of literature, however, documenting second moment temporal dependencies in returns of speculative assets. See, e.g., Bollersev, Chou, and Kroner (1992), Tse (1998), Baillie and Bollersev (1989), Hsieh (1989).
[180] See Engle (1982).
[181] See Bollerslev (1986).

information set at time t, denoted Ψ_t, the distribution of the disturbance is assumed to be $\varepsilon_t | \Psi_t \sim N[0, \sigma_t^2]$, where the conditional variance is:

[5. 6] $$\sigma_t^2 = \alpha_0 + \delta_1 \sigma_{t-1}^2 + \delta_2 \sigma_{t-2}^2 + ... + \delta_p \sigma_{t-p}^2 + \alpha_1 \varepsilon_{t-1}^2 + \alpha_2 \varepsilon_{t-2}^2 + ... + \alpha_q \varepsilon_{t-q}^2$$

$$\sigma_t^2 = \gamma z_t$$

The model in [5.6] is a GARCH(p,q) model, where p refers to the order of the autoregressive part. The variance term depends upon the lagged variances and the lagged residuals. The conditional variance evolves over time depending on the parameter values and on p and q. The GARCH model can be rewritten in terms of polynomials in the lag operators:

[5. 7] $$\sigma_t^2 = \alpha_0 + D(L)\sigma_t^2 + A(L)\varepsilon_t^2$$

The conditions for stationarity is that $A(1) + D(1) < 1$. It has been shown that a GARCH model with a small number of terms appears to perform as well as or better than an ARCH model with many[182]. GARCH (1,1) is a popular model that generally works fairly well for financial returns. We model temporal dependencies via a GARCH (1,1) process given by ($y_t = \sigma_t \varepsilon_t$, $\varepsilon_t \sim NID(0,1)$):

[5. 8] $$\sigma_t^2 = \alpha_0 + \alpha_1 \varepsilon_{t-1}^2 + \alpha_2 \sigma_{t-1}^2$$

where α_0, α_1, α_2 are nonnegative fixed parameters. The degree of volatility persistence is measured by $\alpha_1 + \alpha_2$, and the unconditional variance, σ_t^2, is given by $\alpha_0 / (1 - \alpha_1 - \alpha_2)$. Existence of the unconditional variance requires that persistence is less that one.

GARCH models are non-linear. The parameters must be estimated by maximization of the likelihood function, which involves a numerical optimization. Typically, it is assumed that the scaled residual has a normal distribution. For normally distributed disturbances, the log-likelihood for a sample of T observations is[183]:

[5. 9] $$\ln L = \sum_{t=1}^{T} -\frac{1}{2}\left[\ln(2\pi) + \ln \sigma_t^2 + \frac{\varepsilon_t^2}{\sigma_t^2}\right] = \sum_{t=1}^{T} \ln f_t(\theta) = \sum_{t=1}^{T} l_t(\theta)$$

---

[182] See Bollerslev (1986). Comment in Greene (2000), p. 802.
[183] See Greene (2000), p. 803.

where $\varepsilon_t = y_t - \beta' x_t$ and $\theta = (\beta', \alpha_0, \alpha', \delta') = (\beta', \gamma')'$. Note that the constant term can be excluded in the *RATS* computer program that has been used for this analysis, since a constant has no effect on the solution of an optimization problem[184].

5.4.2 Results

Table 5.13 below shows the estimation results of the exposure of the DAX 30 corporations to the DM/US\$ and €/US\$ for sub-period V, using a GARCH (1,1) model. Unlike with the previous tests, no general pattern seems to emerge. This is not a priori inconsistent with theoretical predictions. We showed that the interaction between competitive effects and conversion effects can explain the intertemporal instability of exposure estimates. But it is difficult to discriminate between various theoretical explanations. As discussed in the next section, explanations can be given based on economic theories, but also based on methodological shortcomings. For example, the issue of the dependency of exposure estimates on the type of model specification used has been discussed in the literature[185].

Table 5. 9 Exposure to DM/US\$: DAX30 Corporations – sub-period V: GARCH (1,1).

			$\Delta e_t > 0$		
	$\Delta e_t < 0$	$\gamma_i^d > 0$	$\gamma_i^d = 0$	$\gamma_i^d < 0$	
$\gamma_i^a > 0$		(A) 0%	(B) 0%	(C) 8%	(4) 8%
$\gamma_i^a = 0$		(D) 8%	(E) 56%	(F) 8%	(5) 72%
$\gamma_i^a < 0$		(G) 8%	(H) 8%	(I) 4%	(6) 20%
		(1) 16%	(2) 64%	(3) 20%	

---

[184] See comment in Enders (1995), p.165.
[185] See Bodnar and Wong (1999).

5.5 Conclusions on Empirical Findings

Alternative explanations for our empirical findings may be grouped broadly within two categories:

(1) category of explanations consisting of hypothesis about *methodological shortcomings*, here those that are specific to the regression techniques employed.

(2) category of explanations consisting of *economic theories* that predict such results, or related to the industry environment assumed.

5.5.1 Explanations Based on Economic Theories

A. Discussion and Implications of Empirical Results

In part one, we have found that there exist strong theoretical arguments supporting the hypothesis of exposure asymmetries. In the empirical analysis, the percentage of German firms exhibiting significant exposures to the DM/US$ or €/US$ was small. There are several explanations possible for this result, which we have mentioned earlier. Many German firms are engaged in various activities with offsetting exposures, use hedging instruments, and so forth.

The German firms with significant exposures generally exhibited asymmetric exposure profiles corresponding to cell B (no exposure to US$ appreciation / adverse exposure to US$ depreciation) consistent with:

- *Strategic competition/short real call*: firms cannot exploit beneficial US$ appreciations. They face an erosion of exchange rate related economic rents because of competition.
- *Government interventions/short real call*: threat of government intervention limit upside potential in profits.
- *Bounds on volume flexibility*: e.g., production constraints, marketing bottlenecks can limit the firm's ability to capture upside movements in demand that could even make the value of real options negative.
- *Entry/exit of competitors with hysteretic behavior.*
- *Asymmetric risk perception of investors*: investors value relatively more downside risk.

- *Poor currency risk management*: adversely affected by US$ depreciations but fail to realize any symmetric benefit when the US$ appreciates.

The results are robust in the first two empirical specifications. Although we did not detect a pattern as clear as for the first two specifications in the results from the GARCH analysis, the hypothesis tests also could not reject the hypothesis of asymmetric exposures for a majority of the German firms that were significantly exposed. While there was limited evidence for asymmetric exposures, there was almost no evidence that German firms are exposed in a symmetric fashion. This finding challenges the symmetry assumption underlying the regression models used in most empirical studies.

We have interpreted and commented our results for each empirical specification separately in sections 5.2.4, 5.3.2, and 5.4.2. Additional comments have been made in the concluding chapter 7. We draw below several general conclusions from these empirical results. We emphasize again that although our estimates result from a *time series* analysis, a firm's exposure profile should be interpreted from a cross-section perspective. A firm's "true" exposure corresponds to the coefficient of a *cross-sectional* regression across scenarios of future exchange rates at a given point of time[186].

Real Option Effects on Foreign Exchange Exposure Profile

We find no evidence that real options convexify the exposure profile of German firms. The empirical evidence did not support the contention that German firms possess options allowing them to profit from movements in the value of the DM/US$ or €/US$ exchange rates. There is no evidence that German firms take advantage of exchange rate movements and limit the impact of detrimental movements. The inconsistency of our results with standard (i.e. in partial equilibrium and with full flexibility) real option theory might indicate:

(a) *Exchange rate fluctuations not viewed as a major source of risk, or opportunities offered by exchange rate fluctuations left unexploited.* Unlike currency options, the exercise of real options affects a firm's overall risk profile and the exercise

---

[186] See Adler and Dumas (1984), Sercu and Uppal (1995).

decision is not solely based on exchange rate uncertainty considerations. Foreign exchange rates are only one set of factors of uncertainty relevant to corporate strategists. Therefore, a concave foreign exchange exposure profile might indicate (i) that German firms have risk management strategies that deals relatively more with other risk than foreign exchange risk. Concerns about exchange rate fluctuations might be subordinate to other types of risk factors[187], (ii) possible unexploited opportunities for managing foreign exchange exposure through the use of real options[188]. Most German firms have been reported to manage their contractual exposures[189]. It might be evidence that the importance of the long term competitive effects of exchange rate fluctuations is not viewed as being a matter of concern for most German firms. The corollary is that the potential benefits of managing currency risk with real options might be overlooked.

(b) *Insufficient risk management expertise or capabilities.* German firms might simply not possess (or not have possessed over the estimation period) foreign exchange risk management capabilities allowing them to benefit on average from movements in exchange rates. Evidence on the currency risk management practices of German firms suggests that they may actually not attempt to manage long term competitive foreign exchange exposures[190].

(c) *Difficulty to capture upturns in market demands.* Because of flexibility bounds (e.g., marketing bottlenecks), threat of government interventions (e.g., anticipation of Plaza Accord in 1985), and so forth, German firms could have been unable to benefit from US$ appreciations. For example, there is evidence that German car makers experienced marketing bottlenecks in the US market in the early 1980s[191] (see chapter 3/section 3.5.2 B).

(d) *Globalization of markets of goods.* A higher competitive structure of the industries in which German firms operate might have eroded their operational ability to defend economic rent associated with exchange rate changes. For example,

---

[187] Brown (2001), p. 422, argues that "larger strategic decisions, such as expansion into new markets and location of manufacturing facilities, are based primarily on other factors. Once a major strategic decision has been made, the decisions regarding foreign currency and risk management are undertaken, e.g., functional currency and hedging strategies".

[188] These two arguments are suggested in Miller and Reuer (1998), p. 1190.

[189] See Glaum (2000).

[190] See Glaum (2000).

[191] See Krugman (1987), p. 49, Levi (1996), p. 340., Knetter (1994), Clark et al. (1999), p. 251.

strategic competition in the form of a threat of a competitor's entry with hysteretic behavior can substantially reduce a firm's real options value. It has also been observed that the ability to pass through the effects of a stronger currency has been waning in recent years around the world. An explanation is that the increasingly integrated global economy has eroded companies' pricing power[192].

(e) *Volatility of DM/US$ and €/US$ small relative to the cost of exercising a real option.* The volatility of the exchange rate needs to be of a certain magnitude relative to the cost of option exercise for the real options to be valuable and have a positive effect on firm value. However, the historical long swings in the DM/US$ exchange rate suggest the potential benefits of flexibility. Dramatic breaks in the DM/US$ exchange rate time series have been identified in a study using a Markov switching model[193] (see section 5.2.3 II).

Cash Flow Volatility, Equity Volatility, and Shareholder Wealth

Equity in a levered firm is a *call option on the value of the firm*[194]. "An increase in firm cash flow volatility that leaves expected firm cash flows unchanged increases equity value as well as equity volatility, thereby leading to a positive relation between equity volatility and shareholder wealth"[195]. Standard real options models predict that an *increase in cash flow volatility* will increase expected firm value and be *beneficial to shareholders*. This is what partial-equilibrium real option models under full flexibility predict. Increases in the volatility of cash flows that the firm would receive from new investments make real options more valuable and increase equity volatility. As a result, there would be a *positive relation between equity volatility and value* for flexible firms[196]. Interpreted in terms of competitive foreign exchange exposure, real option

---

[192] See The Economist, A Faded Green, December 4th 2003.
[193] See Engle and Hamilton (1990).
[194] See Black and Scholes (1973), Merton (1974). "The equity is a call option in the sense that if the shareholders pay off the debt at its face value at maturity, then they can keep the firm's assets; otherwise the assets will belong to the creditors". See Bodie et al. (1993), p. 571.
[195] See Shin and Stulz (2000), p. 1. In the *Black-Scholes* formula, the volatility of the return of an option increases as the value of the underlying decreases. As a consequence, "a decrease in firm value decreases the value of equity and increases the volatility of equity. There is a positive relation between changes in firm value and changes in the value of equity". See Shin and Stulz (2000), p. 18.
[196] See Shin and Stulz (2000), p. 1.

theory predicts that an increase in real exchange rate risk or quantity risk increases the volatility of cash flows and equity and has a positive impact on shareholder wealth.

Our results suggest however that cash flow volatility as a result of real price risk/exchange rate risk and quantity risk is costly in terms of expected firm value and is detrimental to shareholders. Our results are consistent with *capital structure and risk management theories*, which predict that increases in cash flow volatility affect negatively firm value[197]. "Greater cash flow volatility hurts shareholders, since, for a given leverage, it reduces the present value of the firm's tax shields from debt and increases the present value of costs of financial distress. An increase in cash flow volatility that increases equity volatility affects shareholders adversely by reducing their expected cash flows, so that there is a *negative relation between changes in equity volatility and shareholder wealth*"[198] (the costs of cash flow volatility in terms of firm value are also discussed in section 6.1.1/chapter 6).

Foreign Exchange Exposure Profile and Shareholder Wealth

"Stocks are claims on cash flows generated by real assets"[199]. If stock markets are efficient, measuring the effect of unexpected exchange rate changes on corporate performance is equivalent to evaluating whether shareholders benefit from exchange rate changes by examining the relation between stock returns and exchange rate changes[200]. We find no evidence that German firms can use real options under exchange rate uncertainty to improve their *corporate performance*, i.e., by increasing their ability to generate real cash flows. The corollary of this result is that an increase in exchange rate volatility will reduce shareholder wealth. German firms do not seem in a position to exploit exchange rate uncertainty for the benefit of their shareholders. Put it differently, there is no evidence of beneficial exchange rate related real options effects on shareholder returns and wealth.

---

[197] See Shin and Stulz (2000).
[198] See Shin and Stulz (2000), p. 2.
[199] See Solnik (1996), p. 146.
[200] A distinction between the explicit relation of exchange rates and corporate performance, and the relation of exchange rates and stock returns, is made for example in Forbes (2002).

Asymmetric Foreign Exchange Equity Exposure, Time-Varying Equity Risk, and the Cost of Capital

The intuition is that if exchange rate uncertainty has a detrimental effect on shareholder wealth, an increase in exchange rate volatility will result in a higher cost of equity and capital because of a higher currency risk premium. If a firm's foreign exchange risk is a *priced factor that influences expected stock returns,* the possibility of asymmetric exposures would have implications in terms of asset pricing methods. For example, in the *international CAPM,* investors determine their demands for each asset by a mean-variance optimization[201], which assumes a *linear* relation between expected return and the currencies' betas[202]. In other terms, the ICAPM assumes a symmetric risk/return trade off. An asymmetric exposure of the equity to the exchange rate would imply departures from normality of the currency premium distribution (that is, the currency risk premium would be function of the exchange rate level), and make irrelevant the mean-variance optimization framework that is based on the assumption that the asset returns' (normal) distribution can be fully described by its first two moments. The effect of real options is to make the covariance of cash flows with their currencies' betas (i.e., market trends) conditional on the exchange rate, thereby implying a non-linear relation between expected returns and the currencies' betas.

We saw in chapter 3/section 3.4.1 that departures from normality of the cash flows distribution implies that it would be impossible to calculate the opportunity cost of capital that is used to discount cash flows in a static NPV valuation approach[203]. It is impossible to find the opportunity cost of capital because the risk of cash flow changes with the exchange rate. An asymmetric equity exposure reflects a skewed equity distribution, and therefore a volatility of equity that is function of the exchange rate level. As such, the *equity volatility/risk varies over time with the exchange rate* (see also comments in chapter 3/section 3.3.2 A).

However, no conclusion can be made from our empirical results on whether and how foreign exchange exposure is a priced factor that influences expected stock returns. Our tests measure the effect of currency news on *ex-post* stock price movements and do not have as objective to assess whether currency risk is a priced factor in stock

---

[201] See Solnik (1996), p. 140.
[202] See Bodie et al. (1993), pp. 334-335.
[203] See Brealey and Myers (2000), p. 601.

market returns. The tests here are different from those that examine the *ex-ante* effect of currency movements on stock returns[204]. Regardless of whether foreign exchange exposure is a priced factor that influences expected stock returns, "currency changes can systematically affect realized returns since they provide information about economic conditions"[205].

Sensitivity of Exposure Estimates to Model Specification

Our difficulty in providing a specific theoretical explanation for our results reflects some inherent limitations of the empirical methodology adopted. This type of study has relatively little power to discriminate among economic models and theoretical interpretations. Furthermore, the empirical results obtained with three different econometric specifications suggest that model specification is an issue for the assessment of foreign exchange exposures. When moving from the bivariate to the macroeconomic approach, the results indicate a similar pattern of asymmetric exposures. However, when moving to the GARCH specification, the results reveal a different pattern of asymmetric exposures.

Empirical findings may only be meaningful with reference to a particular empirical model specification and for a particular time frame. This raises the question of what is the "right" empirical specification when making statements about the effect of an exchange rate change on a firm's performance and value[206]. The sensitivity of the exposure elasticity estimates to these various specifications of the empirical model need to be investigated[207].

---

[204] See comments in Tai (2004), p. 8.
[205] See Bodnar and Gentry (1993), p. 33.
[206] The role of model specification in exposure estimates is discussed for example in Bodnar and Wong (1999).
[207] Griffin and Stulz (2001) note that "one can never fully rule out the possibility that we measure exposure incorrectly". Sercu and Uppal (1995) notes, "it is important to keep in mind that the estimate of exposure that one calculates changes over time, and may not be very precise at a given moment." "However, this measure is useful -even if it gives us only an approximate indication of the sign and size of a firm's exposure - because it forces us to think about the way exchange rates affect the firm's operations."

B. Insights from Hypothesis of Exposure Asymmetries on Three "Puzzles" in the Empirical Literature

One contribution of this study was to explain theoretically some of the puzzling findings that have been reported in most studies, namely, low exposures, negative exposures, intertemporal stability of exposure with large shifts back and forth between positive and negative values. These characteristics can be justified based on the presence of exposure asymmetries.

The result of the theoretical research has been the general proposition that exchange rate changes affect the firm's cash flows, from which it follows that market values should also be affected. However, despite this strong theoretical prediction, empirical support is weak. These empirical studies are generally characterized by three puzzles that the hypothesis of exposure asymmetries can a priori explain:

1) Statistical Insignificance

Despite the ability to explain to a large degree the sources of exchange rate exposure, most empirical evidence shows that firms are either not systematically affected by foreign exchange rate changes or are only weakly affected. An explanation is that the stock market may not recognize the extent to which firms are involved in exchange rate sensitive activities[208]. It is a surprising finding, given the fact that investors often mention exchange rate changes as a factor of corporate performance. This result is also puzzling if we consider that large movements in exchange rates away from purchasing power parity have occurred during the post-Bretton Woods period[209], and that global competition across firms from different countries has intensified. Furthermore, these deviations in exchange rates have often lead to large movements in firms' price markups and profit margins[210]. But none of these empirical studies are directly based on an explicit model of firm-level behavior, so it is difficult to assess whether estimated exposures are too small or too large[211]. However, although estimates of exposure for individual firms, as well as industry portfolios, have tended to suffer from

---

[208] See Griffin and Stulz (1997).
[209] See, e.g., Froot and Rogoff (1995).
[210] See Knetter (1993), Froot and Klemperer (1993).
[211] An exception is Bodnar et al. (2002), who provide a benchmark for judging the size of the exposure coefficients.

low levels of statistical significance, tests have demonstrated sensible patterns of cross sectional variation. The exposure estimates usually vary across firms in a manner broadly consistent with the theoretical predictions of the impact of exchange rate changes on firms' cash flows and market value[212].

The first major empirical study using the regression approach can be found in a 1990 paper[213]. This empirical analysis of exposure examined the exchange rate exposure of 287 U.S. multinationals firms with large foreign operations and estimated this regression with data for 1971-1987 and found that only 15 firms had significant exposure coefficients. This is not strong evidence in favor of exposure because 15 is roughly the number of significant coefficients that one would expect by chance in a sample of 287[214].

2) *Temporal Instability*

A second general result in empirical studies is that the sign of exposure estimates are unstable over different sample sub-periods. Although it has been observed in many studies that firms with positive exposure are more prevalent than firms with negative exposure[215], the distribution of exposure estimates is also often found to systematically shift back and forth from positive to negative over the sample period[216]. Even when the coefficients of exposure are significant, their time series behaviors do not seem to be supported by theoretical models[217]. Moreover, these shifts in the distribution of exposure coefficients over sub-periods appear too large and too sudden to be explained by structural changes in the firm's cash flow sensitivities or market structures[218]. Temporal instability is not necessarily in contradiction with theoretical predictions.

---

[212] See, e.g., Jorion (1990), and Bodnar and Gentry (1993).

[213] See Jorion (1990). Jorion uses the augmented regression model to evaluate the exposure of U.S. multinational firms to the dollar price of a trade weighted basket of foreign currencies, and shows that the exposure to the price of a basket of foreign currencies systematically increases as a firm has more foreign operations.

[214] In other terms, this is slightly higher than the 5 percent expected to be obtained by chance.

[215] See, e.g., Bartov and Bodnar (1994).

[216] Most studies have shown that the relation between exchange rate changes and stock price returns is not stable over time. For example Bodnar and Wong (1999), Choi and Prasad (1995), Ibrahimi et al. (1995), Williamson (1996), have found evidence of changing signs. However, most of their coefficients were insignificant. An exception is Glaum et al. (2000) who find unstable but significant expsosures.

[217] See, e.g., Glaum et al. (2000).

[218] This is argued, e.g., in Bodnar and Wong (1999).

Here, a distinction is to be made between two issues. Temporal instability can be caused by economic reasons. In that case, the theoretical hypothesis on which empirical tests are based, may be too simplistic. A second possibility is flaws in empirical specifications, which may not efficiently isolate the direct effect of exchange rate on firm value.

3) *Negative Exposures*

Many studies find measures of exposure with unexpected signs. Typically, the distribution of exposure estimates tends to suggest that, for some periods, the average value of firms assumed to be mainly export oriented, increases with a home currency appreciation. Although, as we saw, this result is not necessarily at odd for oligopolistic firms operating in "strategic industries", it contradicts other studies that directly examined the effect of exchange rate changes on firms' profits instead of stock returns[219]. Since profits are a close proxy for cash flows that should be related directly to firm value, the divergence of these results is puzzling.

Except the common finding in most studies that measures of exposure are low and that cross-sectional differences between firms exist, other stylized facts are rare, and many studies find conflicting results between them. For instance, some studies find that exposure varies systematically with foreign sales and firm size[220]. Other studies, however, argue that exposure is not related to foreign sales, firm size, or other international activities, for similar samples[221]. These conflicting results suggest that, either we may not have sufficient information about the exact activities and operational structure of the firms that were examined, and in that case, we would be assuming wrong theoretical predictions for the exposure of these firms, or alternatively, the theoretical predictions themselves may be flawed because they are based on too simplistic models of exposure. In any case, these cross-sectional results suggest that foreign exchange exposure may be a firm-specific phenomenon, and that in practice, general theoretical predictions for a group of firms may not be possible.

---

[219] Clarida (1992), Hung (1992), Uctum (1996), for example, find that the annual profits of U.S. firms are positively related to dollar depreciations.
[220] See, e.g., He and Ng (1998) for Japanese firms, Bodnar and Wong (2000) show that large U.S. firms have more exposure, even after controlling for the level of foreign sales.
[221] See, e.g, Dominguez and Tesar (2001), who use a sample of eight countries (not including the U.S.), 2'387 firms.

5.5.2 Hypothesis about Methodological Shortcomings

A second set of explanation comprises empirical methodological aspects which are inherent to the regression approach based on historical market data. In the stock market regression approach, exposure coefficient could be negative because of (a) the underlying macroeconomic shock affecting simultaneously stock returns and exchange rates, (b) reverse causality between stock returns and exchange rates, (c) offsetting effects of other variables, e.g., an offsetting effect through interest rates, (d) inefficiencies of the stock market, (e) omitted variables.

Explanations for our finding may result from methodological shortcomings. The empirical literature suggests several explanations. Following the early research's inability to document a significant and theoretically consistent contemporaneous correlation between exchange rate changes and firm returns by using simple regression, several recent studies have tried to develop more elaborated estimation methods. Building on the basic regression approach described above, several empirical improvements have been proposed to solve this puzzle:

(1) *Successful corporate hedging*: a first group of studies is based on the presumption that empirical studies are unlikely to observe significant stock price effects because these firms are in fact not as exposed to exchange rate movements as they might appear to be at first glance. In other word, firms should be able to take financial or operational actions to mitigate exposure, both in anticipation of, and in response to, exchange rate changes. This also assumes that firms' hedging activities are known and impounded in stock prices by the stock market[222].

(2) *Experimental problems*: an other group of studies is based on the belief that even though firms are exposed to exchange rate changes, empirical studies are unlikely to document such exposure because of experimental problems. This belief is supported by the structural models of exposure discussed in part one. Examples of experimental issues that have been raised refer to the specification of the exchange rate indexes, to the market portfolio, to misspecifications in the OLS regressions, to potential drawbacks in the research designs, to the sample selection procedure, to the possibility of stock market inefficiencies.

---

[222] See Jorion (1990).

How to assess the relevance of these two set of explanations is a major challenge of the regression approach. We review below the empirical improvements that have been proposed in the finance literature. As we shall notice, the interdependence of the various explanations make it difficult to devise empirical strategies. An evaluation of the relevance and implications of these explanations requires a review of the premises involved, and of the interdependency of the assumptions underlying our interpretations. For interpreting the validity of each explanation, it is thus important to be aware of the previous assumption from which another is inferred. At a fundamental level, the relevance of the market value approach crucially relies on the premise of market efficiency.

Generally, empirical studies have proposed methodological extensions to explain the common findings of low significance of coefficients. Broadly, it is subject to debate whether these small coefficients are due to[223]:

- *Stock market inefficiencies*: exposure exists, but investors and stock analysts are unaware of it and do not efficiently adjust share prices in response to exchange rate changes.

- *The effect of hedging activities*: either there is a lack of corporate foreign exchange exposure, or firms have implemented measures to neutralize their currency exposure.

- *Empirical design*: experimental problems, measurement errors.

5.5.2.1 Stock Market Inefficiencies

A general theoretical proposition is that exchange rate changes affect firms' current and future cash flows, from which it follows that their market values are also affected. The aggregate foreign exchange equity exposures can in turn be estimated with actual

---

[223] Other types of investigations include examining the effect of exchange rates through a liquidity effect. Some papers suggest that asset liquidity affects a firm's value through its impact on the firm's expected return. A study considered the effect on a firm's value of exchange rate changes through its effect on the liquidity of a firm's shares and concludes that the impact of exchange rate volatility on market liquidity is however not a conduit by which stock values are affected. See Huang and Stoll (2001).

stock returns. By using market data in the estimation of exposure, we implicitly rely on the assumption that capital markets are efficient, and that share prices respond *instantaneously and appropriately* to unexpected exchange rate changes[224]. Under the hypothesis of efficient equity markets, movements in the firm's market value reflect the effect of any news, such as unexpected changes in exchange rates, on future profits[225]. Since there are plenty of indications in financial reports and the press that practitioners and investors generally believe that changes in foreign exchange rates can significantly affect corporate performance, we expect exchange rate changes to have at least a significant effect on stock returns even if the sign differs from theoretical predictions.

However, the assumption that the market is aware of the impact of the foreign exchange risk management process on an ongoing basis, may not be valid. More plausible is that the possibility that only general announcements by companies concerning their current operations include information relevant to foreign exchange risk. As a consequence, it may be more appropriate to interpret the estimation of the impact of exchange rate changes on a firm's market value as the stock market's *perception* of that exposure[226]. Two reasons could induce stock markets to make the link between firm value and exchange rate changes in an inaccurate way:

(a) Time-lag Hypothesis

Investors may not have access to relevant information on a timely basis. A hypothesis tested by several empirical studies is that stock prices react correctly, but only with a time delay. The lagged effect could be explained by the lack of information available to investors on a continuous basis. Characterizing the exposures of firms on a timely basis may be difficult for investors due to complexities associated with their determination. Without extensive knowledge of international pricing policies, strategic responses to exchange rates such as the changing markets, product mix, sourcing, and technology, foreign currency positions, currency hedging activity, or experience in estimating firm operations, investors may wait for the firm to release information about

---

[224] Capital markets efficiently impound the impact of exchange rate changes on the firm's performance into their stock valuation.
[225] See Bodnar and Gentry (1993), p. 33.
[226] Andren (2001), e.g., makes this distinction.

its actual performance before they adjust firm value in response to past exchange rate changes resulting in a delayed rather than contemporaneous relation[227]. The stock market would react only after the effects of exchange rate changes are disclosed in quarterly financial reports. This delayed response is attributed to analysts and the market not adequately modifying earnings forecasts during the quarter for the effect of the exchange rate change. This suggests that the market has difficulty determining the full impact of exchange rate changes in current and future cash flows and that the full impact of an exchange rate changes is not instantaneously revealed in stock returns as investors wait for the firm to reveal the full extend of these effects. Thus tests requiring contemporaneous relations may fail to find significant exposures even when they exist economically[228]. This may signify that there is a lag structure involved in the response of firm value to an exchange rate change[229].

Several empirical evidence suggest that the market is indeed slow to incorporate the full impact of exchange rate changes into firm value[230]. It has been documented that firms with large consistent impacts of exchange rates reported in financial statements have a predictable stock price reaction around the earnings announcement based upon the exchange rate change over the previous quarter[231]. This raises the possibility that the lack of evidence of a contemporaneous exposure is a special form of market inefficiency, namely, lagged adjustment.

---

[227] See Amihud (1994), Bartov and Bodnar (1994) Palia and Thomas (1997).
[228] Amihud (1993) considers the possibility of a lagged relation between changes in firm value and changes in the value of the US dollar for a sample of the 32 largest US exporters from 1982 to 1988. However, he finds little evidence of a relation between lagged monthly (or quarterly) changes in the US dollar on changes in firm value for these firms. Consistent with this view, Bartov and Bodnar (1994), Bodnar (1998) document evidence that a lagged change in the exchange rates significantly affects stock returns. However, He and Ng (1998) do not find this effect for Japan.
[229] With the inclusion of a lagged changes in exchange rates, equation [6.2] becomes $r_{it} = \alpha_i + \beta_i r_{mt} + \gamma_i \Delta e_t + \delta_i \Delta e_{t-1} + \varepsilon_{it}$ with δ_i representing the effect of lagged exchange rate changes on stock returns and the same notation for the other variables than in equation [6.2].
[230] See, e.g., Amihud (1994), Bartov and Bodnar (1994). Palia and Thomas (1997) document more conflicting results, with opposite signs for contemporaneous and lagged exchange rate effects.
[231] For a sample of US firms reporting foreign revenues, Bartov and Bodnar (1994) find no contemporaneous relation between quarterly exchange rate changes and stock returns but find that the lagged change in exchange rates is a statistically significant determinant. The study argues that investors fail to adequately incorporate the impact of exchange rate movements into stock returns.

(b) Information Unavailable or Too Complex

Since exposure asymmetries are relatively complex to assess, the stock market may find it difficult to assess them in an efficient manner. Exposure asymmetry might constitute "one of the complexities facing investors that may lead them to make systematic errors in assessing the relationship between firm's value and exchange rate changes"[232]. For that reason, investors may not be able to make the relation between firm value and exchange rate changes. Information about the level of economic exposure of a firm may not be as easily available to outside investors as it is to managers of the firm. It is plausible that managers of the firms have superior information about the firm's cash flows compared to that of the outside investors[233]. A reason is that the risk of exposing a weakness that can be exploited by competitors could prevent the firm to give shareholders a detailed analysis of the company's risk factors[234]. It may also be the case that investors simply cannot not fully understand the impact of exchange rates on stock prices. If capital markets were unable to assess correctly the impact, even with a time delay, then it would not make sense to use stock returns in our regressions. It would then be more appropriate to use cash flows instead of stock returns[235]. Analyzing cash flows directly avoids having to assume that financial analysts correctly make the link between exchange rates and the market value of the firm, but requires more detailed information that may not be available in all cases. This is the distinct feature of market value exposures as compared to measuring cash flows exposure[236]. Stock returns are a reasonable proxy for firm value only if they are highly correlated to the firm's cash flows.

A reason often mentioned why exposure estimates should be significant and of a particular sign is that the stock market seems to impound these exchange rate effects in stock prices. Evidence can indeed be found in the financial press that investors, analysts and finance managers are often seriously concerned about exchange rate risk. However, their concerns may not reflect an economic view of exchange rate risk. Since most treasurers have been reported to manage their contractual exposures, it is likely

---

[232] Bartov and Bodnar (1994), p. 1761, for example briefly allude to this issue.
[233] See Bartov and Bodnar (1994).
[234] See Oxelheim (2002), p. 25.
[235] In practice, regressions are often performed with both stock returns and cash flows for comparison. This is done, for example, at British Petroleum. See Smithson et al. (1995), pp. 115-116.
[236] See Andren (2001).

that their statements about exchange rate risk will be based on the contractual concept of exposure. Accordingly, analysts may also base their investment recommendations on contractual exposures.

5.5.2.2 Effect of Hedging

A important problem for explaining and assessing the relevance of exposure measures estimated with stock returns, is related to the inability to correctly identify the pre-risk management effect of exchange rates[237]. A firm's cash flows may be significantly affected by exchange rates but proper hedging may mitigate these effects and reduce the firm's exchange rate exposure. If these hedging activities are known and impounded in stock prices by the market, they will reduce the correlation between stock prices and exchange rates, and this may be one of the reasons why exposure estimates are often found to be insignificant in empirical studies.

However, it is generally assumed in empirical studies that a significant residual exposure should remain even after accounting for the possibility of hedging effects[238]. The reasons for this assumption comprise: (1) firms mostly hedge their contractual exposures with linear hedging instruments, and leave their competitive exposures unhedged, (2) competitive exposure is difficult to eliminate: quantity risk is unhedgeable and is difficult to avoid since future foreign currency cash flows are uncertain and have to be estimated. The exposures on which hedges are structured are difficult to predict. A firm may have a thorough understanding of how to hedge the effect of exchange rate movements on a stream of foreign cash flows but little knowledge of how foreign exchange movements will impact foreign demand and competition. For example, despite the importance of the elasticity of demand for assessing a firm's competitive exposure, it is actually rarely known in practice[239]. Moreover, competitive exposure is a real and long term exposure that cannot be fully mitigated by financial means.

---

[237] This difficulty is compounded if we consider not only intratemporal but also intertemporal hedging. See Adam (2002).
[238] Géczy, Minton, and Schrand (1997) and Allayannis and Ofek (1998) discuss the use of currency derivatives by multinational firms and its impact on firm value.
[239] See Levi (1996).

Empirically, it is difficult to assess to what extent firms are successful at insulating themselves against exchange rate risk. There are several difficulties with isolating this hedge effect:

(a) *Data availability on firm's hedging behavior*: a common problem is that no micro data are available about firms' hedging practices. This is the case for German firms, which are not required to disclose such activities.

(b) *Difficulty to find proxies for hedging behavior*: since generally not direct data are available about corporate hedging behavior, several empirical methods have tried to isolate the pre-hedge component of exposure with proxies. Several issues are associated with this approach:

- *Finding proxies for hedging behavior that are relevant for multi-firm studies*. Table 5.10 below describes three types of proxies.

- *Difficulty to test hypothesis with proxies*: if the stock market efficiency argument is valid, we may observe that large firms have higher equity exposures than small firms. Larger firms are more closely followed by analysts than small firms, so that a relation between stock prices and exchange rates could be more detectable[240]. This prediction is the opposite of what is inferred from the assumption that large firms have more incentives to hedge and should be less exposed. This shows the difficulty to test specific hypothesis based on proxies, and to evaluate the results of empirical tests. The premises of the hypothesis tested should be kept in mind when interpreting the results, since very often, uncertainties exist not only about the hypothesis tested, but also about the premises on which it is based. For example, the market value approach assumes that the use of derivatives by firms is impounded into stock prices, based on the premise that the hypothesis of stock markets efficiency holds.

---

[240] Doidge and Williamson (2000) examine this relation by focusing on the differential impact of exchange rates on stock returns for small and large firms with high and no foreign sales.

Table 5. 10 Proxies to Isolate the Hedging Effects

Firm size: larger firms, that have more access to risk management expertise, or that have economies of scale in hedging costs, are more likely to hedge than small firms, and as a result, should be less exposed. As such, firm size could be used as a proxy for hedging. The amount of hedging within an industry may also be endogenous since industries with inherently large exposures are the most likely to hedge through financial markets[241].

Long-term debt ratio: firms with higher long-term debt ratio tend to face larger expected costs of financial distress and hence have a greater incentive to engage in hedging activities[242]. This implies that the long-term debt ratio can be used to measure the probability of financial distress and can be used as a proxy for firms' hedging needs[243]. For this reason, multinational firms with greater financial leverage are more likely to hedge and hence should be less exposed to exchange rate risk.

Dividend payout ratio and quick ratio: corporations can mitigate expected costs of financial distress and agency costs by maintaining a larger short term liquidity position in terms of having a lower dividend payout ratio or a higher quick ratio[244]. Firms' liquidity is negatively related to hedging activities[245]. Firms with weak short-term liquidity positions or with high financial leverage have more incentive to hedge and hence should have smaller exposures.

(c) *Presence of other hedging effects.* Even if the hedging effect could be isolated, other offsetting effects could explain the lower significance of exposure estimates. Exchange rate affects the profitability of a firm through many channels that may offset each other, but the exposure measurement captures only the overall exchange rate effect. A firm could be insulated from exchange rate fluctuations through other means than financial or real hedging:

- *Internal financial techniques*: beside the external financial techniques of hedging, which include the use of forwards, futures, financial swaps and options and other derivatives, the internal financial techniques include netting[246], pooling and invoicing.

---

[241] See, e.g., Bodnar and Gentry (1993) , p. 36.
[242] See He and Ng (1998), p. 741.
[243] See, e.g., He and Ng (1998).
[244] See Nance et al. (1993).
[245] See Froot et al. (1993).
[246] Exposure netting consists in "offsetting exposures in one currency with exposures in the same or another currency, where exchange rates are expected to move in such a way that losses (gains) on the first exposed position should be offset by gains (losses) on the second currency exposure". See Shapiro (1999), p. 789.

- *Natural hedges*: it is difficult to assess the extent to which natural hedges mitigate firms' overall exposure, and there is no clear understanding of the factors which affect firm's decisions to use natural hedges versus financial hedges. Mitigating effects that should be taken into consideration for evaluating exposure estimates include:

  (a) *Offsetting exposures*: corporations that both source and sell in competitive international markets will be less sensitive to changes in foreign exchange rates than those firms engaged solely in importing or exporting.

  (b) *Foreign operations*: foreign operations can be used as a natural hedge for foreign sales. If firms hedge operationally through foreign operations, then firms with foreign assets should have less exposure than firms with no foreign assets after controlling for foreign sales. Parent companies of multinational corporations may allow individual business units to have large exposures but select a portfolio of business in which the exposures tend to cancel one another. A firm can diversify into multiple business segments in order to reduce its exposure to any one business segments. However, empirical studies usually assume that these types of international corporations should be strongly affected by exchange rate changes.

  (c) *Foreign currency denominated debt.*

The problem of assessing the extent of these effects can make the interpretation of exposure estimates difficult. Moreover, the perception of the stock market of corporate risk management activities may have historically varied. There is evidence that the stock market increasingly value firms' risk management activities. This implies that analysts could expect significant effects of exchange rate changes on firms' performance, but could believe that firms are able to successfully mitigate them and are as a result not exposed.

5.5.2.3 Empirical Design

(a) Timing Relation and "Reverse Causality" between Stock Prices and Exchange Rates

Reverse causality between stock prices and exchange rates "afflicts all empirical studies of exchange rates and competitiveness"[247], and could explain the negative exposure signs frequently observed in empirical studies. "Reverse causality" can be observed if there is an exogenous decline in home country competitiveness that would cause the home currency to depreciate. This would lead to an estimated coefficient representing a negative relation between stock returns and home currency depreciation. The reason is that the timing of the effect of the exogenous change in competitiveness will affect stock returns first, and only subsequently exchange rates[248]. This problem is not resolved with the inclusion of a market portfolio to control for macroeconomic factors.

The central hypothesis of the regression approach is that exchange rate changes lead stock returns, or, in other words, exchange rate changes are expected to give rise to stock price changes. This argument is based on the traditional trade approach suggesting that a real exchange rate appreciation tends to reduce the competitiveness of the domestic economy and therefore reduce domestic activity. An exchange rate change is expected to affect firms' foreign operations and overall profits, which would in turn affect their stock prices. However, as capital markets become more and more integrated, changes in stock prices and exchange rates may reflect more of capital movement than current account imbalance.

Such negative exposures can be explained by a "money demand model"[249]. In this model, real growth in the domestic economy leads to increased demand for the domestic currency through a traditional money demand equation. This increase in currency demand induces a rise in the relative value of the domestic currency. Because domestic stock prices are strongly influenced by real growth, this model justifies a

---

[247] See Luehrman (1991), p. 643.
[248] The direction of causality can differ from country to country, but also from period to period. This indicates that whether stock price movements Granger cause exchange rate volatility or vice versa is country and time dependent. Ramasamy and Yeung (2001) find for a sample of Asian stock prices, that stock price changes lead exchange rate changes in many cases.
[249] See Lucas (1982). See also comments on this model in Solnik (1996), p. 151.

positive association between real stock returns and domestic currency appreciation. The money demand approach predicts that an increase in domestic economic growth leads to a real currency appreciation.

Conversely, a negative real growth in the domestic economy will induce a general downward movement of the stock market that will motivate investors to seek for better returns elsewhere. The decrease in stock prices causes a reduction in the wealth of domestic investors, which in turn leads to a lower demand for money which pushes interest rates down. The lower interest rates cause capital outflows of funds (ceteris paribus), which in turn is the cause of currency depreciation[250]. Under this assumption, stock prices are expected to lead exchange rates with a negative correlation[251]. As barriers to capital movement have been gradually removed since the early 1990s, this possibility cannot be ignored[252].

(b) Omitted Variables

Regressions could be misspecified because of the omission of other variables. The effect of other market risk factors should to some extent be captured by the market index, because they feed into the market return. However, how well the macroeconomic factors included in that control variable are isolated depends on how the market portfolio is constructed.

Prior to the regression analysis, a fundamental analysis is needed to identify variable with potential economic explanatory power. Economic theory should be the foundation of and guiding force in a specification search. Two difficulties may arise: (1) since the

---

[250] Such logical deductions characterize so-called "portfolio approach" theories. See Granger et al. (2000).
[251] If a market is subject to the influences of both approaches simultaneously, a "feedback loop will prevail with an arbitrary sign of correlation between the two variables". See Granger et al. (2000), pp. 338-339. Granger et al. (2000) uses a Granger causality test and find for a sample of Asian firms, that in most markets, changes in stock prices lead that in exchange rates.
[252] "However, it is sometimes difficult to interpret the underlying fundamental economic relation based on those results. It is likely that the results may be generated from other structure relations, i.e., via interest rate parity condition or IS-LM related policies. For example, some recessionary shocks or unfavorable information on the country will cause a stock price decrease and an exchange rate depreciation. In this case the timing relation between the stock price and exchange rate will be generated from the relative efficiency of the stock market and foreign exchange market. In this case, both approaches may not play any role in generating the timing relation". See Granger et al. (2000), p. 352.

set of relevant variables may shift over time, the finance manager should follow up the process of identification continuously. (2) because of possible multicolinearity, only a selected number of variables could be included into the regression analysis.

Since the environmental contingencies relevant to explaining corporate returns to shareholders vary across industries and firms within industries, the explanatory power of any single model is likely to vary considerably across industries and firms. Hence, it is problematic to postulate a single set of regressors applicable to all firms in large scale empirical studies.

(c) Measuring Long-Run Foreign Exchange Exposures

Exposure measures depend on the length of the estimation period. The lack of a perfect long-term financial hedge may leave firms exposed to long-term exchange rate movements[253]. However, exposures could also be lower in the long run. Over longer period of time, firms have the ability to make real operating adjustments[254].

If financial markets are efficient, the effect of unexpected exchange rate changes should be widely known and immediately impounded in firms' market value. As a result, exposures should be independent of the horizon over which they are measured. For that reason, and similarly to the asset pricing literature, much of the empirical literature on foreign exchange exposure has used monthly data. However, if the stock market does not instantaneously impound the effect unexpected exchange rate changes into firm value, differences in the horizon of returns will have an influence on the characteristics of the exposure estimates. This hypothesis is investigated in "long-horizon regressions", and moving-window regressions or rolling regressions[255]. By increasing the estimation period interval, for example, from one month, to one year, to two years, and so forth, we may find that exposure is different in the long run[256].

---

[253] This is argued by Allayannis (1996), p. 7.
[254] See Froot (1993) for evidence that exposure to real exchange rate changes is lower at long horizons. The exchange rate pass-through might be also different in the long run. See Dwyer et al. (1993).
[255] See Glaum et al. (2000).
[256] The empirical results investigating this aspect are mixed. In support of a longer horizon view, some evidence suggests that the exposure of U.S. firms becomes much more detectable when the return horizon in extended out beyond 12 months. Chow, Lee and Solt (1997b) Chow, Lee and Solt (1997b) look at a measure of "total" exposure for a small set of 213 U.S. multinational firms and find a statistically significant relationship between stock returns and foreign exchange exposure. An other

A non-linear exposure is function of the exchange rate level. This means it varies with changes in real exchange rate. As such, the expected mean-reverting behavior of the exchange rate to its purchasing power parity value in the long run can affect exposure only if quantity risk and price risk are related. Otherwise, only foreign exchange risk is affected. A similar observation can be applied to the possible better ability to forecast exchange rates at long horizons.

(d) Sample Selection Procedure

Most of the literature examining exposure at the individual firm level is for US firms[257], and generally finds insignificant exposure estimates. A possible explanation is that many US firms may have little international activities and those that do may utilize operational and financial hedging to a greater extent than in other countries.

Studies attempting to estimate exposure of firms located in other countries than the US, primarily focus on industry portfolios[258]. These studies using industry portfolios may experience an aggregation problem. While it is interesting to compare exchange rate exposure across markets, using industry portfolios is not necessarily the best method. Firms within the same industry may be exposed to exchange rates but in offsetting directions which may lead to a low estimate of the exposure relation on the industry portfolio. Firms can also be involved in many activities with different exposures to exchange rates that change over time, causing the firm's exposure to fluctuate, or even switch signs[259].

---

study consider the impact of horizon issues in a variety of model specifications as well as for a much larger set of 910 firms and find more exposure at longer-horizon real exchange rate changes. Bodnar and Wong (1999). Griffin and Stulz (2000) find more exposure at longer-horizon real exchange rate changes. An other study on US firms reports significant long-term exposure. See Allayannis (1996). In contrast, other empirical evidence report that daily data provides better results of sensitivity than monthly data, but for banking institutions. Chamberlain et al. (1996). Differences in exposure estimates across return horizons may be due to different correlation between cash flows and exchange rates and/or different correlation between exchange rates and macro factors.

[257] Two exceptions are He and Ng (1998), and Williamson (2000), Glaum et al. (2000).

[258] See, e.g. Bodnar and Gentry (1993).

[259] Consistent with this argument, Williamson (2000) finds varying exposure for firms within the automotive industry and that the exposure is affected by a firm's foreign operations. To address this concern, Doidge and Williamson (2000) when grouping firms, allow for the influences of foreign sales, income, and assets.

An other study estimated an equation similar to equation [5.2] for industries in the United Sates, Canada, and Japan over the 1979-1988 period. The results show that exposure is significant in 22 of the 78 industries examined. Even though the exposure coefficient is not significant in many individual industries, a joint test that all coefficients are zero is strongly rejected. Moreover, the average size of the exposure coefficients tends to be larger for industries in Canada and Japan, which have smaller, more open economies, than in the United States. They used industry portfolios from the US, Japan, and Canada and find that the direction of exposure in certain industries is generally consistent with economic theory. Traded goods industries have more exposure than non-traded and Japanese and Canadian industries have more significant exposure than in the US[260]. An other study using a sample of 171 Japanese multinational firms finds significant exchange rate exposure for 25 percent of the firms. This finding contrasts the results found previously for US firms, but it is unclear whether these differences can be partly attributable to differences in methodology or sample selection procedures[261].

5.5.3 Discussion on the Stock Market Regression Approach

A major advantage of the stock market approach is its simplicity. There is no need for string of assumptions/guesses at parameter values, and no concerns about functional forms of equations are required. It depends on the stock market to have accurately evaluated firm's exposure. It assumes that the stock market is able to efficiently assess firms' foreign exchange exposures. All the complexities, such as elasticities of demand, strategic interactions, effect through consumers, and so forth, are assumed to be appropriately and fully incorporated into stock prices by the stock market. However, since exposure asymmetries are relatively complex to assess, the stock market may find it difficult to assess them. Exposure asymmetry might constitute "one of the complexities facing investors that may lead them to make systematic errors in assessing the relationship between firm's value and exchange rate changes"[262]. Several other methodological issues associated with this approach need to be taken into consideration:

---

[260] See Bodnar and Gentry (1993).
[261] See He and Ng (1998). Using quarterly cash flows data, Linck (1998) finds no significant impact of exchange rates on cash flows for a sample of US firms.
[262] Bartov and Bodnar (1994), p. 1761, for example briefly allude to this issue.

(a) *Depends on historic relation:* the major drawback of the regression approach is that exposures are assumed to be constant. For a treasurer, who has to use this measure of exposure for managing future exposures, this approach will be valuable only if past exposures are believed to remain similar in the future. However, company's activities might change and therefore exposures. If not, then he won't be able to apply the exposure coefficients as a hedge for hedging decisions in the future. Moreover, the perceptions of investors may change over time[263]. An other drawback is that exposure estimates are average values, with the following consequences:

- *Extreme values are average out.* Because the regression approach uses historical market data, exposure coefficients are an average value over a sample period, that will be valid only in normal conditions. It means that "breaking points" representing large unusual occurrences may lead to unexpected average estimates and false conclusions about a firm's exposure[264]. The regression historical approach, however, assumes normal business conditions, and only the effect of factors that systematically affect exposure can be detected. For unusual events, such as a one time government subsidy, regression analysis is inappropriate. This will be averaged out over the estimation period.

- *Exposure measure is meant to be for a given operating and financial structure.* However, the time series observations may come form an overall time period when the firm's operating structure and/or capital structure are significantly changing[265]. For a treasurer, an average value may not be informative if he is concerned mainly with large exchange rate changes.

- *Assume invariant hedging policies.* Regression analysis also requires that the firm followed the same hedging policies over the period and that the industry was characterized by a similar degree of international competition. For instance, if a firm followed a conservative hedging policy for several years and then an

---

[263] Moving window estimation of the model allows for time-varying exposures. See, e.g., Glaum et al. (2000). The major drawback of this approach is that the changing exposure might be caused by the new observation that is added to the window as well as by the one that drops out of the window. In the latter case the changing exposure was not triggered by new information. See Hallerbach and Menkveld (1999), p. 7.

[264] Peso problem occurs when a small probability of an unusual event is incorporated into the expectations of the market participants. If the data period fails to hold enough of these unusual events, statistical inference may be distorted. See Meese (1990).

[265] See O'Brian (1998).

aggressive risk-taking policy, we would not expect the stock return's response to be similar across the entire sample period.

(b) *Difficulty to identify appropriate estimation period:* although the market value approach assumes that the stock market is able to efficiently process and incorporate information about these aspects into stock prices, it is still important, for all the reasons mentioned, to correctly sub-divide the sample period under consideration. However, academic studies often lack the firm-specific information to properly segment their sample.

(c) *Data availability:* First, relevant data may be difficult to gather. A frequent challenge when using regression is obtaining sufficient historical data on market values and exchange rates for the analysis. Because firm structures and market conditions and characteristics may change, only a few years or relevant data may be available. A paucity of data may undermine the statistical significance of the results. A rule of the thumb sometimes recommended is that the analysis incorporates at least 36 observations[266]. Second, this approach is unsuitable for new firms. This implies that the regression approach is unsuitable for newly organized firms, newly privatized firms, or newly merged or reorganized firms for which there is no large sample or consistent observations. In the case of a de novo venture, however, data from a comparable business may constitute a reasonable approximation[267].

(d) *Complex non-linearities:* the usefulness of the linear regression approach is limited when the exposure depends on the levels of the risk factors. If exposure is non-linear, it will depend not only on variation, but also on the level of real exchange rates, which could make the choice of an appropriate estimation even more problematic. Regression methods may not be suitable to deal with complex non-linearities.

(e) *Determination of a firm's underlying exposure:* the term "underlying exposure" refers to an exposure measure that has not been hedged financially. In contrast, exposure estimates from regressions are after-hedge measures. Using these regression coefficients as hedge ratios requires an adjustment for the hedging effect. However, the interdependency of financial hedging and operating strategies makes the separation

---

[266] See Ramlochan (2001).
[267] See Levich (1998).

between underlying exposures and after-hedge measures ambiguous in theoretical analysis, and questionable empirically.

Despite all these shortcomings, regressions analysis remains useful because it is the only method available for large-scale empirical academic studies. In practice, in the rare example of firms having implemented such an approach, treasurers blend knowledge about basic business practices, such as pricing, with statistical analysis of market behavior to develop an understanding of the sensitivity of specific cash flows to currency movements[268]. For treasurers, a useful application of the regression technique is to examine market-based measures of exposures for the firm's major competitors. This exercise can provide useful insights into the nature of the competition and the structure of the industry. Examining competitor's exposures can be especially valuable if the firm is private and thus lacks the return data to estimate its exposures directly[269].

---

[268] Such an approach is typified by the approach of the pharmaceutical firm, Merck, in which a model of the firm's foreign currency cash flows is built. From this model the impact of various exchange rate changes on the operating decisions and financial performance of the firm can be estimated and optimal hedging decisions made. See Lewent and Kearney (1990).

[269] See Smithson et al. (1995), p. 144.

6. Hedging Asymmetric Foreign Exchange Exposures

Foreign exchange exposure asymmetries have implications in terms of risk management strategies. A common recommendation is to hedge asymmetric exposures with hedging instruments that have asymmetric payoffs such as currency options[1]. However, the selection of a hedging strategy should be based on a more sophisticated view of a firm's exposure. Given that asymmetric foreign exchange exposures are not only non-linear, but also uncertain, real, and generally of long durations, the elaboration of a risk management strategy can be highly complex. In this chapter, we address these issues and identify the factors that should be taken into consideration when assessing the optimality of a currency risk management strategy.

Several insights and recommendations emerge from our analysis. First, exposure asymmetries provide an economic rationale for hedging with currency and real options. However, minimum-variance hedges are generally not value-maximizing for asymmetric exposures. Value-maximizing risk management policies need to combine the use of strategic real options, derivatives, and financial flexibility options. For example, inter-temporal and intra-temporal hedges can be tailored with currency options in a consistent way with corporate investments and financing decisions, and with value-maximization. Second, the effect of foreign cash flow volatility on exposure may be due to other risk factors than exchange rates, and make irrelevant the use of currency derivatives for hedging foreign exchange exposures. The relation between real price risk and quantity risk gives indication on the factors of exposure uncertainty and the effectiveness of currency hedges. Third, the relative efficiency of natural hedges is function of a tradeoff between natural hedging effect and loss of flexibility value.

Section 6.1 examines the objectives of risk management in presence of exposure asymmetries. Section 6.2 presents variance-minimizing hedges, while section 6.3 examines value-maximizing risk management strategies based on strategic planning, currency hedges efficiency in presence of real exchange rate/price risk and quantity risk, and so forth.

---

[1] See, e.g., Kanas (1995), Booth (1996).

6.1 Foreign Exchange Exposure Asymmetries and Risk Management Objectives

6.1.1 Firm's Objective Function and Risk Management Objectives

A. Firm's Objective Function and Economic Exposure

Economic exposure is the exchange rate sensitivity of firm market value. In practice, firms can have one of the following three objective functions[2]:

- *Stock price maximization:* is the most restrictive of the three objective functions. It requires that "managers take decisions that maximize stockholder wealth, that bondholders be fully protected from expropriation, that markets be efficient and that social costs be negligible"[3].

- *Stockholder wealth maximization:* is "less restrictive than stock price maximization, since it does not require that markets be efficient"[4].

- *Firm value maximization:* is the least restrictive, since it "does not require that bondholders be protected from expropriation. For firms which are not publicly traded, the objective in decision making is the maximization of firm value"[5].

These objectives are not mutually exclusive. For example, "when a firm's actions (such as investing or financing) increase firm value, this will translate into increases in stockholder wealth and stock price if the more restrictive assumptions hold. Conversely, if an action increases the stock price, but the less restrictive assumptions do not hold, firm value may not necessarily be increased"[6]. A firm could directly hedge the stock price, firm value, or *intermediary targets* of value maximization such as cash flows. Only in the case of non-diversified stockholders the stock price may be a relevant parameter.

---

[2] See Prof. Aswath Damodoran's website at New York University (NYU), Stern Business School (http://pages.stern.nyu.edu/~adamodar).
[3] See Prof. Aswath Damodoran's website at NYU.
[4] See Prof. Aswath Damodoran's website at NYU.
[5] See Prof. Aswath Damodoran's website at NYU.
[6] See Prof. Aswath Damodoran's website at NYU.

B. Hedging Metrics and Timing of the Hedge

A manager dealing with a *sequence of foreign cash flows* over a valuation period faces two fundamental decisions[7]. First, whether to hedge at the time of analysis of the exposure, or to wait until the next time period to re-evaluate the exposure. Second, whether to hedge directly present values or the cash flows themselves. Value hedges minimize the variance of the terminal value in domestic currency by continuously hedging the present value of its foreign currency cash flows[8].

We consider four alternative hedging strategies:

Strategy 1 - long-term fixed cash flow hedge: immediately hedging all periodic cash flows over the planning horizon eliminates all exposure at the initial date. The maturities of the hedges increase over the valuation period. For example, an exporter would lay down a fixed hedge by selling forward today all the expected future foreign currency cash flows[9].

Strategy 2 - roll-over hedge: at some time intervals, the firm purchases a hedge that covers a determined horizon, e.g., each year the firm sells forward the next year's expected cash flow. The exposure is hedged progressively over time.

Strategy 3 - net present value (NPV) hedge: hedge today or in subsequent periods the NPV of its exposed assets minus exposed liabilities evaluated at prevailing market interest rates[10]. The objective is to minimize the covariance between the future firm value and the exchange rate.

Strategy 4 - real option value (ROV) hedge: hedge ROV today or in subsequent periods.

---

[7] See Demacopoulos (1987), p. 241. In the theoretical literature, the stylized single-period cash flow is the classic example for illustrating the use of futures and options as hedging instruments. See comment in Levich (1998).
[8] See, e.g., Kaplanis and Schaefer (1991).
[9] In February 2004, for example, during the long slide of the US-dollar against the euro, Porsche was reported to have hedged all its expected US-dollar revenues until July 2007. See McLannahan and P.F. Larsen, 2004, Out for the Count: the reaction of Europe's auto manufactures to the sinking dollar provides an object lesson for other sectors, CFO Magazine, Feb. 17. See also The Economist, 2004, Currency Hedging: Holding Back the Flood, Feb. 21st, p. 84.
[10] See Levich (1998), p. 592.

Assessing the relevance of a particular strategy raises several issues. How does the *intent of the hedge* determine whether cash flows or value should be managed? What is the *optimal timing* of cash flow hedges? In what way will exposure asymmetries influence the relevance of cash flow versus value hedges?

Cash Flow versus Value Hedge - Intent of the Hedge

In practice, there is no consensus on what risk management should try to achieve. Firms try to reduce fluctuations in reported earnings[11], cash flows or firm value[12]. A majority of the firms that hedge cash flow-related measures does not lay down present value hedges but hedge the cash flows themselves. Common arguments for financial hedging have a short-horizon perspective, for example minimizing systematic shareholder risks, achieving short-run tax, monitoring, and investment efficiencies[13].

The early finance literature recommended managing firm market value[14]. But the current view is that hedging adds value mostly through managing cash flows[15]. The optimal choice depends on the *intent of the hedge*. A firm may have various hedging objectives that cannot be pursued simultaneously. A hedge that minimizes the volatility of cash flows will not always effectively insure against longer-term changes in firm value, which is likely to be more important if there is concern about financial distress[16].

The implication is that although firm value is theoretically equal to the present value of expected future cash flows, the difference between the two objectives is not simply a matter of time frame and can reflect conflicting objectives. Managing the exposure of cash flows is not always an intermediate target for managing the exposure of firm value.

---

[11] Many companies list reducing earnings volatility as the main goal of their risk management efforts. The reason given is that investors prefer to see steady earnings growth, and punish companies that miss their numbers. See CFO Research Services (2002). However, there is evidence that investors value cash flows rather than earnings.
[12] A Wharton survey asked a pool of US companies to rank the importance of various risk management goals of using derivatives. The result was (i) managing volatility in cash flows: 49%, (ii) managing volatility in accounting earnings: 42%, (iii) managing the market value of the company: 8%, (iv) managing balance sheet accounts or ratios1%. See Marston et al. (1998).
[13] See Coval (1998).
[14] See, e.g., Adler and Dumas (1984).
[15] See, e.g., Froot et al . (1993), Froot (1994), Stulz (1996).
[16] See Grinblatt and Titman (2002).

Timing of Cash Flow Hedges

There are several advantages of rolling a hedge instead of setting a long horizon static hedge:

- *risk of opportunity costs of hedging is higher at long horizons*: there is a risk of opportunity cost if a firm hedges at the initial date and that the market subsequently moves to levels more favorable than the hedge rate. Buying financial hedging contracts today runs the risk that today's hedging price of the currency or of the currency volatility is extraordinarily high[17]. As such, the length of a hedging horizon may be limited by the perceived risk of opportunity cost[18]. The advantage of a rolling hedge is that the firm can gain from a more diversified draw. But this opportunity cost is not completely eliminated. Rolling hedge leaves the firm exposed to the risk that, by the time that the future foreign cash flows are recognized and hedged, the hedge rate has changed[19]. For example, locking-in at a forward rate may prevent future windfall gains[20]: selling a weakening currency far forward is dangerous when there is *exchange rate overshooting* and the currency value is subject to mean reversion. If the exchange rate changes direction, the weakening currency will gain value and hedgers will regret that they rushed to sell it forward[21].

- *locking-in at a hedge rate may be a source of competitive disadvantage*, e.g., locking-in at a forward rate could prove unfavorable if competitors have not hedged with similar forwards.

The choice of a rolling hedge can be imposed, since financial hedges can be unavailable at long maturities. Financial instruments have a fixed maturity that can be shorter than the firm's planning horizon. Liquid markets for most futures and options typically do not go much beyond 18 months[22]. Even if available, outside of swaps,

---

[17] See Levich (1998), p. 592.
[18] See Levich (1998), p. 591, Lidbark (2003), p. 2.
[19] See Brealey and Kaplanis (1995), p. 780.
[20] And, conversely, windfall losses.
[21] See Levich (1998), p. 592. Because exchange rates might overshoot after a shock and the real exchange rate might revert to its mean in the long run, it is possible for the nominal and real exchange rates to reverse course after an initial shock. See Dornbusch (1976).
[22] See Harris et al. (1996), p. 90.

most financial hedges become quite expensive over longer horizons[23]. But while swaps can provide an inexpensive way to construct a series of long-dated forwards, they require accurate assessment of future cash flows. As such, they are inappropriate to hedge asymmetric exposures, which can be highly uncertain.

Rolling hedges however can be very prohibitively in terms of trading costs. Typically, operational hedges are used to hedge competitive exposures for which financial hedging instruments are unavailable, illiquid, or too expensive[24].

6.1.2 Time Path of Cash Flow Exposures and Exposure Asymmetries

Foreign exchange exposure asymmetries imply that the need for financial hedging is related to the degree of operating flexibility. It is therefore important to evaluate financial hedges using exposure measures which account for a firm's operating flexibility to respond to exchange rate movements. A flexible firm is faced with a dynamic programming problem where future cash flows depend on the firm's future prevailing operating structure, which is function of the periodic distribution of exchange rates. Because real options make the amount to be hedged dependent on the exchange rate path, one needs flexible hedging instruments whose payoff is non-linear in the exchange rate.

The time path of exposure over the valuation period is dependent on the time path of exchange rates and project cash flows. The domestic cash flow exposure in any given time period over the valuation period will depend on the time path of [25] :

(i) *the foreign currency cash flows*: by estimating the time path of quantities and foreign currency prices. We need to calculate the expected cash flow stream by calculating at each date: (a) the sequence of probabilities that the firm will in future be in a certain financial or operating mode. (b) the expected series of cash flows conditional on the operating and financial mode[26].

---

[23] The two most important factors affecting the price of currency options are the value of the underlying asset and the time to expiry.
[24] See Giddy (1994), p. 235.
[25] See Demacopoulos (1989), p. 104, Brealey and Kaplanis (1995), p. 779.
[26] This implies that the unconditional expected cash flows are the probability weighted means of the conditional expectations. See Brealey and Kaplanis (1995), p. 779.

(ii) *the exchange rate* (currencies of denomination of future cash flows).

Since NPV hedges suppose a static operating and financial structure, they are inappropriate for flexible firms. The relevance of ROV hedges depends on the intent of the hedge and the degree of uncertainty of the terminal ROV value.

Hedging an asymmetric exposure implies that we need to forecast the size of the positions to be hedged at maturity. This means that firms hedge anticipated cash flows that have no guarantee to materialize. The size of unhedged exposures due to errors of estimation can be important because of difficulties in forecasting[27]:

- *Competitive exposures are likely to be more difficult to forecast at long horizons* and the risk of over- or under-hedging higher. The relative importance of flexibility based operating hedging increases with quantity risk.

- *Increases in exchange rate volatility increases the real option value and reduces the efficiency of financial hedges:* a high exposure volatility increases the value of flexibility based operating hedges and affect negatively the efficiency of hedging financially.

The time frames for financial (hedging horizon) and operational hedging (time for implementation) over the valuation period are interdependent. For example, a factor that can affect the price adjustment period is the hedging policy. The horizon covered by the hedges will influence the amount of time that business units have to adjust product prices before the insurance benefits of foreign exchange hedges roll off[28].

6.1.3 Hedging Motives and Value Maximization

A. Concavity of Objective Function as Motive for Risk Management

Risk management theory gives rationales for managers to be concerned with not only expected firm value but also the distribution of firm returns around their expected value. The variability of returns matters for managers if they face a non-linear optimization function. Suppose a firm wants to maximize a non-linear objective

---

[27] See Aliber (1998), p. 327, for a discussion on this aspect.
[28] See CorporateMetrics Technical Document (1999), p. 45.

function Z, which is itself a function of expected profits, $E(P)$, and the variability of profit defined as the standard deviation of profit, σ_p [29]:

[6. 1] $Z = Z(E(P), \sigma_p)$

If the concavity of Z is due to the profit function's non-linearity, equation [6.1] can be expressed as the maximization of the expected value of profits, where the latter is itself a function of volatility:

[6. 2] $Z = E(P(\sigma_p))$

The randomness of profit around is expected value, x, is assumed to be normally distributed with mean 0 [30]. The objective of a risk management strategy m is to reduce the effect of x on E(P). The result of risk management is:

[6. 3] $E\left[\dfrac{dP}{dx} \cdot \dfrac{dx}{dm}\right] = 0$

The randomness of profit x is *associated with a vector of different uncertainties, e.g., exchange rate uncertainty,* x_i. Financial risk management is applied on each risk factor so that equation [6.3] and [6.4] hold:

[6. 4] $\text{cov}(P, x_i) = 0$

The explanation for risk aversion and the motives for hedging are based on the concavity of the objective function explained by non-linearities in the profit's function [31]:

1. *Managerial self-interest*: managers may be risk averse if they have limited ability to diversify their own personal wealth position associated with stock holdings [32].

2. *Non-linearity of taxes*: hedging could result in lower overall tax liability by stabilizing cash flows because of progressive corporate taxes (convex tax function) and the asymmetric treatment of profits and losses in the tax code [33].

---

[29] See Santomero (1995), pp. 6-7, Froot et al. (1993), pp. 1638-1639.
[30] See, e.g., Froot et al. (1993).
[31] See Santomero (1995), pp. 2-6, Froot et al. (1993) for an overview.
[32] See Stulz (1984).
[33] See Smith and Stulz (1985).

3. *Cost of financial distress*: hedging can reduce probability of default, resulting in better credit rating, lower overall financing costs.

4. *Capital market imperfections:* if firms cannot freely access capital markets, they may prefer to maintain stable cash flows to fund internally strategic options[34].

5. *Information asymmetry*: since managers know more about the firm's foreign exchange exposure, they are better qualified to determine optimal hedging.

6. *Transaction costs*: the firm is in a better position to achieve low cost hedging compared to shareholders.

According to the Modigliani-Miller Theorem, if financial markets worked perfectly, risk management activities could not increase firm market value and would not be valued by the stock market, since shareholders could costlessly manage the risks themselves through diversification of their ownership of shares in firms with different risk exposures. Because of the existence of the above market imperfections, hedging has a positive effect on firm value.

B. Variance-Minimizing and Value-Maximizing Hedging Motives

The objective of risk management can be either risk minimization/stabilization objective or value maximization/matching objectives. The academic literature has focused on volatility reduction as the primary objective of risk management.

- *Risk minimization* involves choosing a hedge ratio that minimizes the variance of cash flows by reducing the exchange rate sensitivity of cash flows. This implies that the objective of hedging is to eliminate the exposure and that firms should hedge fully. Risk minimization increases firm value but it is generally not value maximizing. For example, risk minimization is an insufficient condition for minimizing the probability of cash flows declining to a point where business disruption costs are incurred within a predetermined period of time[35].

---

[34] See Froot et al. (1993).
[35] See Copeland and Joshi (1996), p. 69, Copeland and Copeland (1999).

- *Value maximization* implies optimization of a risk-return tradeoff: to a value-maximizing firm, what matters is the possibility that exchange rate changes could cause financial distress or make it unable to pursue profitable investments options[36]. Financial hedges can increase firm value by reducing the probability of costly lower-tail outcomes and the associated expected costs of financial distress[37] and the risk of business disruption[38].

6.2 Variance-Minimizing Financial Hedges

6.2.1 Risk of Over-/Under-Hedging with Linear Financial Instruments

The relation between real price risk and quantity risk gives indications on the hedging strategy to be pursued[39]. Depending on the sign of the correlation, a firm's cash flows will exhibit either greater or lower volatility.

No Relation Real Price Risk and Quantity Risk. Real price risk and quantity risk are two separate random variables, so that the translated home currency cash flow is function of two independent random variables[40]. Quantity risk is influenced by other factors than the exchange rate and the exposure is linear and stochastic.

Quantity Risk and Real Price Risk Negatively Correlated. The negative correlation makes the exposure concave:

- *Natural hedging effect*: the quantity risk hedges some of the price risk. The negative correlation dampens fluctuations in revenues, thus producing a "natural hedge" effect. An exporter would experience increasing (declining) sales volume at the same time as its domestic currency is strengthening (weakening) in real terms. If quantity risk is perfectly negatively correlated with price risk, one could have a

---

[36] See Froot (1994), Aabo (1999), essay 1, p. 60.

[37] The expected cost of financial distress depends on the probability of financial distress and the cost of financial distress if it occurs. Financial distress reduces a company's cash flows if suppliers, employees and customers are not willing to trade with it on the same terms if distress is likely.

[38] It has been advocated that managers should only have an aversion to downside risk. Stulz (1996) for example argues that rather than putting emphasis on variance minimization, some firms may emphasize downside risk reduction of the "elimination of costly lower-tail outcomes". See also Capel (1997), pp. 93-96, Copeland and Copeland (1999), Capel (1997), Aabo (2002).

[39] See, e.g., Kerkvliet and Moffet (1991), Froot et al. (1993), Brown and Toft (2000).

[40] See CorporateMetrics Technical Document (1999), p. 40.

situation where there is price risk and quantity risk, but no cash flow risk, and hedging would be unnecessary.

- *Risk of over-hedging with linear instruments*: the optimal linear hedge ratio may be significantly low, and even zero or less[41] and there is a risk of over-hedging with static linear hedges. The risk of over-hedging is higher if quantity risk relatively higher. If the firm wants to use linear hedges, it should hedge less than its expected exposure.

- *Optimal degree of substitution between linear and non-linear instruments*: when the risk of over-hedging with linear hedges becomes a greater concern, the firm should use less linear and more nonlinear instruments[42]. Because of the negative correlation, firms should buy convexity by buying options[43], e.g., an exporter should have a long put position. High quantity volatility or low real price volatility magnifies these advantages.

Quantity Risk and Price Risk Positively Correlated. The positive correlation makes the exposure convex.

- *Amplifying effects:* a positive correlation between quantity risk and price risk exacerbates fluctuations in cash flows since output levels and real prices will move in the same direction. The resulting exposure profile is convex.

- *Linear hedge ratio higher than unity*: the optimal static linear hedge ratio surpasses unity for positive correlation and increasing cash flow uncertainty. A linear hedge can hedge some the quantity risk since quantity risk moves more in line with real price risk. An exporter that can sell more when its currency depreciates would take a larger short forward position to hedge for the quantity risk, since quantity is high when the forward price is high. The optimal non-linear hedge usually requires the firm to sell convexity by selling options[44]. High levels of quantity risk lead to more non-linear instruments in the optimal hedge[45].

---

[41] See Kerkvliet and Moffet (1991), p. 577. The optimal hedge ratio becomes negative for increasing cash flow uncertainty with negative correlation.
[42] See Gay et al. (2001).
[43] See Brown and Toft (2001).
[44] See Brown and Toft (2001).
[45] Example of interest rate in Stulz.

Exposure asymmetries exacerbate the risk of over-/under-hedging with linear instruments and provide a rationale non-linear hedges. But structuring hedges based on the correlation between price and quantity risks is not suitable for asymmetric exposures. Exposure asymmetries reflect a non-linear relation between price risk/quantity risk, while a correlation is a measure of linear dependency.

6.2.2 Portfolio of Currency Options

A non-linear/asymmetric exposure implies that the position to be hedged depends on the exchange rate at the maturity of the hedge. Typically, flexible firms that benefit from volatile exchange rates should write options, while firms that are adversely affected by exchange rate volatility should buy options. A foreign currency outflow can be hedged with a call, whereas a foreign currency inflow can be hedged with a put.

A. Portfolio of Currency Options

Options are suitable to deal with almost any kind of non-linearities. A portfolio of options can be structured with a combined payoff that approximates the cash flows in a piece-wise linear way, and hold this portfolio of options to hedge the exposure[46]. Figure 6.1 below illustrates a hypothetical exposure profile and payoff function[47].

Figure 6. 1 Piece-wise Linear Exposure Profile[48]

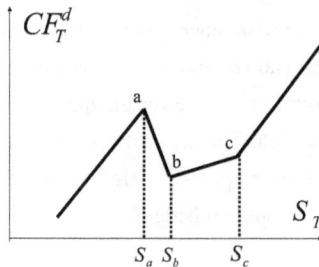

---

[46] Financial instruments whose payoff is not linear in the underlying are called contingent claims. See Stulz (2000), Ch. 11, p. 2. The same strategies can be used to hedge the payoff of an option. See Sercu and Uppal (1995), ch. 7.

[47] Example based on Stulz (2000), ch. 10. See also Sercu and Uppal (1995), pp. 504-506.

[48] Adapted from Stulz (2000), ch. 10, p. 55. Because a non-linear exposure can be fully matched with a portfolio of options, option theory can be used to describe a firm's non-linear exposure. See Stulz

Exposure is piecewise constant between the segments, and quantity risk is high around a, b, c[49]. Options are exercised at the trigger points at which exposures behave asymmetrically[50]. The slope of the exposure profile dictates the size of the option positions. Call options are used with exercise prices close to the exchange rate values a, b, c. The hedge payoffs are received at date T and are function of the exchange rate S_T, interpreted as the *nominal* price of the foreign currency in term of domestic currency[51]. CF_T^d is the *real* domestic currency cash flows. *Over the segment $\overline{ab}$: long call on foreign currency at S_a*, short call on foreign currency at S_b. The effect of the second option is to offset the payoff of the first option for exchange rates higher than S_b. *The slope is -2*: every increase in the price of the foreign currency in terms of domestic currency results in a decrease in domestic cash flows of two units of domestic currency. A portfolio of two call options on the foreign currency can hedge the segment $\overline{ab}$. A long call option position gives the right to purchase a call on two units of the domestic currency against one unit of the foreign currency with exercise price S_a. When the domestic currency price of the foreign currency equals or exceeds S_a, the option is exercised and pays off two units of domestic currency per unit of the price of the foreign currency, with payoff: $2 \cdot Max(S - S_a, 0)$. A short call option position gives the obligation to sell a call on two units of the foreign currency with exercise price S_b. This portfolio of calls pays two unit of domestic currency per increase in the domestic currency price of the foreign currency as long as the price of the underlying asset is higher than S_a and lower than S_b. The payoff of the long call position and the short call position is $2 \cdot Max(S - S_a, 0) - 2 \cdot Max(S - S_b, 0)$.

Over the segment $\overline{bc}$: short call on foreign currency at S_b, long call on foreign currency at S_c. *The slope is 0.5:* a short call option position gives the obligation to sell half a call option on the foreign currency with exercise price S_b provides this hedge. A long call option position gives the right to buy half a call option with exercise price S_c, since exposure is different for a price of the foreign currency in terms of domestic

(2000), ch. 13.
[49] The exposure profile is linear between the segments. This suggests that foreign currency cash flows are either fixed or affected by risk factors that are not related to the exchange rate.
[50] Trigger points can be assimilated to a threshold beyond which the effect is either exacerbated or reversed in sign. Holmes and Maghrebi (2002), p. 4.
[51] See Stulz (2000), ch. 10, pp. 19-22.

currency equal to or greater than S_c. The payoff of the short call position and the long call position is $-0.5 \cdot Max(S - S_b, 0) + 0.5 \cdot Max(S - S_c, 0)$.

B. Dynamic Linear Hedging Strategies

The objective of static hedging strategies with options can also be achieved with dynamic linear hedging strategies. A manager must decide whether to hedge its cash flows far into the future or on a rolling basis. A firm could hedge asymmetric exposures by structuring a non-linear hedge using a series of forward[52]. This approach consists in dividing the valuation period into several sub-periods, construct a binomial tree that matches the volatility of the exchange rate and of foreign cash flows, and hedge the exposure dynamically with a sequence of linear hedges revised every period[53]. Whenever the exchange rate or foreign cash flow changes over the hedging period, the hedge ratio is adjusted to reflect the newly acquired knowledge about the distribution of the exchange rate at maturity of the hedge. A difficulty with such as strategy is to compute the initial hedge and adjust it over time as more precise information about the exchange rate at maturity of the hedge becomes available. With a static hedge, in contrast, the factors that can affect exposure at the maturity of the hedge are evaluated at the beginning of the hedging period, and then left unchanged. The advantage of being able to adjust dynamically the hedge according to new information on the path of price risk and quantity risk can be outweighed by the possibly large transaction of implementing a dynamic strategy.

C. Exotic Currency Options[54]

If an exposure is non-linear, the use of standard options cannot entirely remove the profit uncertainty, since their payoffs are piecewise linear[55]. Exotic options can enable firms to hedge complex exposures and are more effective hedges at a lower cash cost.

---

[52] Or other linear instruments, such as swaps or indexed debts, or future contracts. See Froot et al. (1993), p. 1649.
[53] See Sercu and Uppal (1995) ch. 7, ch. 18, pp. 504-508.
[54] Exotic derivatives are all the derivatives that are not plain vanilla derivatives or cannot be created as a portfolio of plain vanilla derivatives. See Stulz (2000), ch., 1, p. 14. See Giddy (1994), p. 235. Typically cannot be replicated with forwards and a finite number of vanilla options.
[55] See Booth (1996), p. 21.

Customized exotic derivatives are typically better than vanilla contracts when correlations between prices and quantities are large in magnitude and when quantity risk is substantially greater than price risk. When the correlation between price and quantity risk is positive, exotic derivatives offer additional gains over forwards or options alone and these gains increase with greater quantity risk and less price risk[56]. Firms can benefit most from non-linear exotic payoffs when the correlation between price and quantity is negative and quantity risk is large. Two examples show the potentials of exotic options to handle complex exposure at lower costs (see sections 6.2.3 and 6.3.1.2)

6.2.3 Hedging Asymmetric Foreign Exchange Exposures: Illustrative Cases

a) Firm with Full Export Flexibility: Short Calls

A firm with full export flexibility possesses a real option to sell abroad or domestically depending on the prevailing exchange rate S_T (figure 6.2a below). Above some exchange rate level S_a, the firm starts exporting. The foreign price is assumed to be one unit of foreign currency. The firm exports n units of goods if $S_T > S_a$, or sell n units of goods domestically at a price S_a if $S_T < S_a$. The firm's income is $n[S_a + Max(S_T - S_a, 0)]$[57].

The exposure asymmetry associated with the export flexibility justifies the use of currency options. The firm can write n calls with exercise price S_a to eliminate the cash flow volatility[58]. If $S_T < S_a$, the call is not exercised, but the firm can still keep the premium collected[59]. For that reason, writing puts can be used to speculate on a rise in the exchange rate, and writing calls to speculate on an appreciation. In each case, the writer collects the premium up front and hopes that the option will expire unexercised.

A forward contract would not fully hedge a non-linear exposure since its payoff is symmetric (figure 6.2b above). Foreign cash flows from exports are offset by gains on

---

[56] See Brown and Toft (2001).
[57] See Sercu and Uppal (1995), pp. 181-182, Wong (2001), Adam-Müller and Wong (2001), p. 16.
[58] Writing options is however forbidden at some firms. From put-call parity, writing a call is equivalent to a forward sale and writing a put. See Sercu and Uppal (1995), p. 177.
[59] Put Writing options is a form of issuing risky debt. See Sercu and Uppal (1995), p. 184.

the forward hedge, but the firm would likewise gain on the forward hedge if $S_T < S_a$, making the variance-minimizing hedge less optimal than with options.

Figure 6. 2 Hedging Exposure with Full Export Flexibility: (a) Short Call, (b) Forward Sale[60]

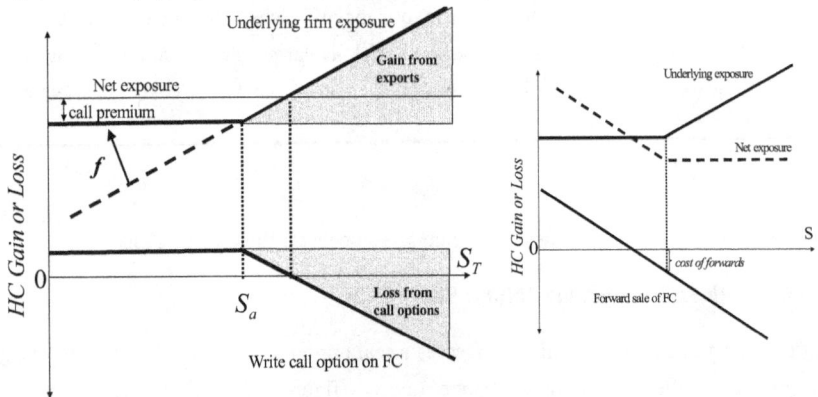

Adapted from Sercu and Uppal (1995), p. 182, Stulz (2000), ch. 10, p. 54, Adam-Müller and Wong (2001), p. 15.

b) Firm with Limited Export Flexibility: Portfolio of Forwards and Short Calls

The firm currently produces goods and plans to sell them at a future date. At this future date, the firm might sell either in its domestic market or *partially* in a foreign market, depending on the prevailing exchange rate (figure 6.3 below).

The export flexibility can be interpreted as a call on the foreign currency. Limited export flexibility implies that the firm exports a minimum level independently of the exchange rate value. Therefore, the expected profits become convex in the exchange rate with strictly positive slope everywhere. The sales allocation is assumed to be based on departures from the law of one price, which implies that the firm exercise its real call at $S_T = P_d/P_f$. The effect of flexibility is indicated by f, which represent a long put position on the domestic currency.

---

[60] The term "underlying firm exposure" refers to the before-hedge exposure.

Figure 6. 3 Hedging the Asymmetric Exposure of a Firm with Limited Export Flexibility

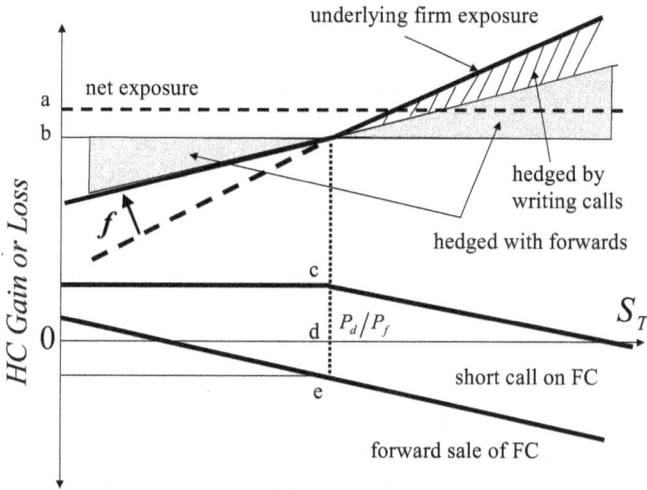

ab is the premium received from writing calls minus the costs of buying forwards. *cd* is the premium received from the short call. An increase in the exchange rate volatility would increase the call option premium. *de* is the forward costs paid. d corresponds to the level of exchange rate P_d/P_f at which the real option to increase exports is exercised. The long forward on foreign currency position hedges the exposure created by selling the minimum level in the export market against foreign currency. The call hedges the exposure created by export flexibility.

A financial hedging payoff can be designed to match the ex-post export flexibility of the firm by creating an offsetting financial position[61]. The value generated by the export flexibility can be sold in the currency call options market at a price per unit of potential exports. Writing financial calls with strike price P_d/P_f gives the firm a conditional obligation to deliver foreign exchange[62]. With full export flexibility, the firm entirely relied on fairly priced currency call options. But with limited flexibility, symmetric hedges in addition to currency options are required for $S_T < P_d/P_f$, since the minimum export level makes the slope positive even at low realizations of the exchange rate. A portfolio of futures and call options for example would make the firm's cash flows invariant to different realizations of the exchange rate[63]. The exact

---

[61] See Ware and Winter (1998), p. 301 for a structural model demonstrating this aspect.

[62] Writing call option is however forbidden at some firms. See Stulz (2000), ch. 8.

[63] Due to put-call parity, the availability of currency futures and put options yields the same result.

composition of the hedge portfolio is function of the real option value[64]. A tighter export flexibility would increase the role of futures relative to currency options.

Because cash flows are non-linear in the exchange rate, hedge ratios based on linear regressions would underestimate the exposure for $S_T > P_d/P_f$. A forward sale with size equal to the regression coefficient would not reduce completely the variance of hedged cash flow[65].

c) Firm with Production Flexibility: Portfolio of Forwards and Short Puts

A firm with a switching option to produce either domestically or abroad possesses a portfolio of American put and call. The flexibility to switch production costs from domestic to foreign location is like a long put on the foreign currency written at the money. The flexibility to switch from the foreign to the domestic location is like a long call on the foreign currency. The optimal variance-minimizing hedging strategy if the firm is currently producing domestically is to use a combination of short symmetric hedges and short put options on foreign currency, which would give the firm an implicit option premium[66]. Using forwards only would lead to a risk over-hedging, since quantity risk and price risk are positively related.

d) Firm with Strategic Real Options: Portfolio of (Exotic) Options

To illustrate, we refer to the example in section 4.2.2.2, chapter 4. A firm sells both in its domestic market and exports to a foreign market, and is subject to three sources of asymmetries:

Since the payoffs of any combination of futures, call options and put options can be replicated by any two of these three financial instruments using put-call parity, one of them is redundant. See Sercu and Uppal (1995), Adam-Müller and Wong (2001), p. 10.

[64] Contractual exposures that have been hedged through forwards will not be completely eliminated if the firm is exposed to variations in the forward exchange rate. See Sercu and Uppal (1995), pp. 482-483.

[65] See Sercu and Uppal (1995).

[66] See Hommel (2002); graphical representation in p. 18. The put-call parity relationship implies the existence of an equivalent strategy: a short put is equivalent to a forward purchase and writing a call option on foreign currency. See Sercu and Uppal (1995), p. 177.

(i)   Threat of new entrant in the *domestic* market at the exchange rate T: this can be hedged by being long call on foreign currency at T and short call on foreign currency at X.

(ii)   Export flexibility between domestic and foreign market at X: hedge by writing a call on foreign currency with exercise price X (short put on domestic currency) and long call on foreign currency at G.

(iii)   Expected foreign government intervention in exporting market at G: hedge by buying a call option on the foreign currency with exercise price G (buy a put on domestic currency).

Hedging competitive exposures must be based on the firm's currencies of determination. For example, a German manufacturer of automobiles might hedge the economic value of its share of the U.S. market by buying dollar/yen, expecting that a stronger US$/weaker yen could enhance the competitive position of the Japanese automobile industry[67].

For dealing with some types of exposure complexities, exotic options can be used. The threat of a new entrant in the domestic market could depend on an average of spot rates over past periods. *Average rate options* give the holder a payoff that depends on an average of exchange rates over some prescribed period[68]. Average rate options are advantageous when foreign/local cash flows and exchange rates are highly correlated[69]. An average rate put options on the foreign currency can be used here. If a hedging program were given a limited budget for option premiums, *barrier currency options* could be considered, since barrier features typically reduce hedge efficiency slightly but can appreciably trim up-front option premiums. A firm exposed to multiple currencies can use an option on a basket of currencies (*basket currency options*). Because the price of the option is based on the volatility of the portfolio, the basket option is generally cheaper than a collection of individual options when the currencies in the basket are imperfectly correlated[70].

---

[67] See DeRosa (1996), p. 7.
[68] See Brown (2001), p. 104, Stulz (2000), ch. 17, p. 64-65.
[69] See Giddy and Dufey (1995), p. 55.
[70] See Levich (1998), p. 442.

6.3 Value-Maximization and Strategic Management of Foreign Exchange Exposures

Competitive exposures are best managed at business unit level using structural hedges, like switching to alternative suppliers or relocating production facilities[71]. But operating hedging is costly, difficult to reverse, and takes time to be implemented. For these reasons, financial hedges are needed. The justification for financial hedging is generally viewed solely for the purpose of gaining time until operating measures are implemented or to give time for assessing the persistence of an exchange rate change[72].

However, *a value-maximizing strategy should view* operational and financial hedging as complementary rather than substitute[73]. By *combining* financial hedges and real options, a firm can achieve a higher increase in firm value. Rather than aiming at fully hedging the exposure, it can sometimes be value-maximizing to increase rather than decrease the exposure with financial hedges.

Financial and real hedging decisions should be based on overall strategic considerations. Sub-optimal real investment decisions should not be made simply because they reduce exposure to exchange rates. Foreign exchange exposure should also be managed in conjunction to other types of exposure. In contrast to financial hedges, operating hedges affects a firm's *overall* exposure profile. This means for example that operating adjustments in response to interest rate changes would affect the firm's foreign exchange exposure.

6.3.1 Strategic Real Options and the Role of Financial Flexibility Options and Derivatives

6.3.1.1 Production Possibilities Frontier, Real and Financial Hedging

Fluctuations in real exchange rates modify firms' international competitive positions, and affect their *production possibilities sets* and *production possibilities frontiers*[74].

---

[71] Other strategic changes in operations to reduce exposure include revising the marketing mix, reallocating production, choosing sourcing policies, altering the pricing strategy, adjusting the global production configuration. See, e.g., De Meza and Van Der Ploeg (1987), Dixit (1989b).
[72] This aspect is discussed in Lidbark (2003), p. 2.
[73] See, e.g., Carter et al. (2001), Hommel (2002).
[74] The production possibilites set measures the set of outputs that are feasible given the technology and the amount of inputs. The boundary of the production possibilities set is called the production possibilities frontier. See Varian (1999), p. 544.

Operational hedging increases expected cash flows and shifts the firm's production possibility frontier outwards. In contrast, *financial hedging*, at most, increases the firm's value along a production possibility frontier, e.g., by reducing expected bankruptcy costs[75]. The payoffs of financial hedges are intended to offset operating losses, but it does not affect the operating losses themselves[76].

Based on the premise that what matters to shareholders are real cash flows in domestic currency for their consumption, foreign exchange risk is function of real exchange rate/price risk and quantity risk. Ideally, one should hedge the exposure to *real* exchange rate uncertainty and structure hedge ratios on *real* amount of foreign cash flows. Managing the exposure of real cash flows should therefore ideally involve hedges that modify the operating structure of the firm. Real options give the firm the flexibility to make ex-post operating adjustments in response to exchange rate changes.

How efficient are financial and operating hedges given that economic exposure is real, long term, and uncertain.

- *Financial hedges*: financial instruments can hedge the exposure to nominal exchange rate fluctuations (*nominal* price risk), but not the exposure to unexpected changes in *nominal* foreign cash flows. Because of moral hazard, there is no instrument to hedge against nominal foreign cash flows fluctuations. Firms could manipulate the nominal prices *of their goods* or the quantities sold. Without nominal foreign cash flow risk, the optimal strategy for hedging a long position in foreign currency would be to sell the exposure forward. Exposure asymmetries imply that the nominal amount of foreign cash flow to be sold forward is function of the exchange rate level at the maturity of the hedge. For that reason, linear hedges are inappropriate.

- *Real hedges*: investing in operating flexibility can be done to set up real hedges that can hedge both quantity risk and real price risk.

---

[75] See Mello et al. (1995). The slope of the production possibilities frontier is measured by the marginal rate of transformation, which measures how much of one good the firm can get if it decides to sacrifice some of the other good. See Varian (1999), p. 545.

[76] Fairly priced foreign exchange derivatives (*NPV=0*) cannot affect the value of the company in the long run. Hedging reduces risk but does not change the mean of the cash flow distribution if the contracts are fairly priced. See Jorion (1997), p. 278.

Since the payoffs of financial hedges are based on nominal exchange rates, their efficiency to hedge economic exposure relies on the correlation between nominal and real exchange rates. There is empirical evidence that, apart from hyperinflation periods, changes in the real exchange rate are mostly a result of changes in the nominal exchange rate. The real and nominal exchange rates behavior coincide reasonably well mostly in developed countries, although the correspondence is usually weak for emerging economies[77].

6.3.1.2 Exposure Asymmetries and Cash-Flow-at-Risk (CaR) Measures of Risk[78]

A. Cash-Flow-at-Risk with Passive Management

A firm might want to know how likely it is that its cash flows will fall below some critical value over an extended period of time. The cash flow shortfall corresponding to the probability level chosen by the firm is called "Cash-Flow-at-Risk (CaR) at that probability level". "CaR at $z\%$ is a positive number such that the probability that cash flow is below its expected value by at least that number is $z\%$"[79]. This means that if we denote expected cash flow as $E(CF)$, $Prob[E(CF)\text{-}CF>CaR]=z\%$. CaR can be calculated as a translation of the standard deviation if the cash flow is normally distributed[80]. Let x be the cash flow at which the probability that a normally distributed cash flow with a mean of zero and a standard deviation of σ is less than p percent; that is, $N(x) = p\%$. Then CaR is $-x\sigma$[81]. CaR can also be estimated with simulation (see Appendix I). The normality assumption of cash flow distribution implicitly assumes:

(i)   *passive management and linear exposure*: CaR models and computer packages generally assume normal cash flows distribution and postulates that managers are passive, that they do not respond to changes in competitiveness resulting from exchange rate changes[82].

---

[77] See Sercu ad Uppal (1995), pp. 366-367.
[78] See RiskMetrics (1999), CorporateMetrics Technical Document, pp. 27-29, Stulz (2000), ch. 8.
[79] See Stulz (2000), ch. 4, p.18. For example, a CaR of $100m at the 5% level means that there is a probability of 5% that the firm's cash flow will be lower than its expected value by at least $100m.
[80] See Grinblatt and Titman (2002), pp. 777-778.
[81] For example, CaR(5% significance level) = $1.65\,\sigma$, where σ is the standard deviation of cash flow.
[82] For example, the CorporateMetrics model of the company RiskMetrics assumes that the exposures mapping stays the same for very long periods while the business environment changes. See CorporateMetrics (1999). The CaR model of NERA Consulting defines CaR to be the "probability

(ii)   normal market conditions: CaR is a risk measure that captures the combined effect of underlying volatility and exposure to financial risks. The exchange rate is assumed to be distributed normally. However, there is evidence that the distribution of currency returns is leptokurtotic[83], which necessitates stress testing for extreme events[84].

B. Cash-Flow-at-Risk and Real Options Payoffs

Figure 6. 4 Probability Distribution with Flexibility and Cash-Flow-at-Risk

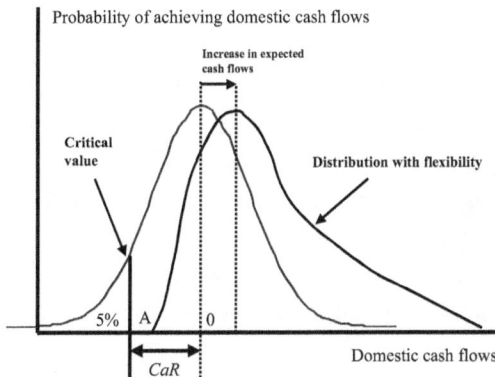

Exposure asymmetries affect firm value risk and shareholder value. Real options can affect positively shareholder value by reducing the firm's downside risk[85]. Exposure asymmetries imply that exchange rate risk, downside risk and the probability of lower-tail events cannot be inferred from a normal distribution. The effect of flexibility on *CaR* might mitigate the effect of the fat tails of the currency returns distribution. Management could then end up understating or overstating downside risk and *CaR*. In

---

distribution of a company's operating cash flows *over* some horizon in the future, *conditional on information available today*". See Stein et al. (2000), p. 1. An exception is Alesii (2003), who proposes a *CaR* model taking into account real options.

[83] See DeRosa (1996), p. 15.

[84] Stress tests are hypothetical market rates and price scenarios to reflect possible, near term changes in those rates and prices. A drawback with stress testing is that correlations between market prices are not empirically addressed as they are in CaR.

[85] See Amram and Kulatilaka (1999).

figure 6.4 below, *CaR* is the difference between the average cash flow and the fifth percentile outcome over the estimation period of the normal distribution.

The distribution curve with flexibility shows that convex asymmetric foreign exchange exposures can lead the firm to overstate the *CaR*. But *CaR* is not necessarily reduced as a result of real options. There are situations when real options take negative values and increase a firm's *CaR*. The put reduces the probability of low (negative) cash flows. This reduction in downside risk means that the *CaR* is reduced.

6.3.2 Strategic Use of Financial Hedging

Several theories have been proposed to explain why firms might prefer non-linear to linear hedges. The literature has mostly linked optimal hedging strategies to characteristics of the underlying exposures, such as (1) the correlation between hedgeable and non-hedgeable risks[86], (2) the presence of basis risk[87], (3) the existence of borrowing constraints[88], (4) the timing of production decisions[89], (5) the hedging objectives[90], (6) the financial manager has a view of volatility of rates that differ from the market's view as embodied in market option prices. An other explanation is not based on exposure characteristics but on the cost differential between internal and external funds[91].

6.3.2.1 Exposure Asymmetries and Inter-Temporal Hedging

A strategic approach to risk management can yield competitive advantage through better capital allocation[92]. "The central proposition of risk management theory is that firm value can be increased by taking financial positions that pay off when the firm's cash flow is lower than required for the firm to pursue its objectives"[93]. For asymmetric

---

[86] See, e.g., Detemple and Adler (1988), Moschini and Lapan (1995), Brown and Toft (2001).
[87] See, e.g., Wolf (1987), Moschini and Lapan (1995).
[88] See, e.g., Detemple and Adler (1988), Deep (1996).
[89] See, e.g., Moschini and Lapan (1992).
[90] Ahn et al. (1999) analyze optimal hedging strategies under assumption that firms minimize VaR.
[91] See Adam (2000).
[92] See Froot et al (1993). This is one the main reason given for the value of strategic risk management. See a survey in CFO Research Services (2002).
[93] See Stulz and Williamson (1996), p. 2.

exposures, currency options can serve such purpose by customizing hedging strategies according to the cash needed to finance foreign capital investment expenditures[94]. A currency option has both intra-temporal and inter-temporal aspects[95]:

- an *intra-temporal hedge* shifts cash flows only across states of nature: the hedge ratio of currency options is dependent on the state of nature/exchange rate.

- an *inter-temporal hedge* shifts cash flows across time: firms face an intertemporal trade-off between securing funding for current and future investments. For example, an exporter can write a call against potential foreign currency cash flows. It would "sell" the uncertain future gains for immediate cash[96], which could then be used to fund investments.

Exchange rate changes and investment opportunities can be correlated. A firm can have low profits because of an unexpectedly poor competitive position from an adverse exchange rate change and as a result low internal funds to spend on new projects. Currency options can be used to coordinate investment and financing plans and protect against the inability to fund capital spending commitments. By improving the ability to undertake valued-adding investments, currency options have an indirect effect on expected firm value[97].

Suppose a multinational corporation that has a subsidiary in a foreign country that sells in the foreign market[98]. Investment opportunities are dependent on the exchange rate. Hedging locks the ability to carry out a predetermined investment plan over the planning horizon, where that plan is based on the expected future exchange rate. S_T is the domestic currency price of the foreign currency, with the domestic currency the numeraire (figure 6.5 below).

When the domestic currency depreciates, investments abroad become less attractive due to higher input costs. Thus less foreign investment is warranted, and there is less need to hold foreign currency as a hedge against such an outcome. It is assumed that

---

[94] The economics literature on exposure usually ignores the role played by the firm's liability structure in shaping its choice of strategy. This is discussed in Mello et al. (1995).
[95] See Adam (2002), p. 9.
[96] See Froot et al. (1994), Froot (1994), Sercu and Uppal (1995), pp. 181-182.
[97] See Froot et al. (1994), Froot (1994), Chacko et al. (2000).
[98] See Froot et al (1993), pp. 1645-1646, for a similar example based on oil prices exposure.

the company does not change its capital investment expenditures for small exchange rate changes, i.e. when $S_T \in [X_p, X_c]$. Linear hedges could add value by decreasing the volatility of cash flows, but for *value maximization*, using currency options as a support for pursuing strategic objectives are more appropriate.

Because foreign investments are function of the exchange rate, we want the hedge ratio to be sensitive to the realization of the exchange rate:

- It $S_T < X_p$ at maturity: buy out-of-the-money puts on the foreign currency with exercise price X_p in addition to a linear-hedging position[99]. When S_T is low, the firm has good investment opportunities and therefore needs the additional foreign currency cash generated internally. It is necessary to hold foreign currency to guarantee a given level of foreign investment[100].

If the firm wants to hedge to avoid costly financial distress, using "deep out-of-the-money options" may be the most cost effective strategy[101], because they increase the expected value of future operating cash flows[102].

- If $S_T > X_C$ at maturity: write out-of-the-money calls on the foreign currency with exercise price X_C, since a linear-hedging position results in "too much" foreign currency cash for very large foreign currency appreciation. When S_T is high, the firm may be low on cash, but doesn't need much, since it has few attractive investment opportunities. It is optimal to hold relatively more of the domestic currency[103]. Since the firm would receive a premium at the time the option contract is settled, writing calls could be done for the purpose of coordinating investments

---

[99] Out-of-the-money options imply that immediate exercise does not generate a positive cash flow. For out-of-the-money options, the holder will not exercise immediately, and so the intrinsic value is zero. The intrinsic value is the option's value if you had to make the exercise decision right now. See Sercu and Uppal (1995), p. 167.

[100] ABB, the Swiss power and automation technology firm, for example, has consolidated market and credit exposure within its financial services division, with the goal of improving its capital usage. See CFO Research Services (2002).

[101] An option with a strike price that differs substantially form the current spot rate. See Sercu and Uppal (1995), p. 167.

[102] See Giddy (1994b) for a description of this strategy.

[103] See Froot et al. (1994), p. 1646, for an example about oil price risk. By adding out-of-the-money puts on exchange rates to its futures hedging position, the company can give itself relatively more protection against large decreases in the price of oil than against small decreases.

and financing plans. Writing a call against the potential foreign currency cash flows from exports means that the firm "sells" the uncertain future gains for immediate cash. This could be an efficient strategy if the firm needs internal fund now to finance investments[104].

The hedge ratio will depend on the expected size of the foreign investment relative to internal wealth[105].

Figure 6. 5 *Coordinating Financing and State-Dependent Investments with Options* - **Asymmetric Exposure of Foreign Investments Costs**

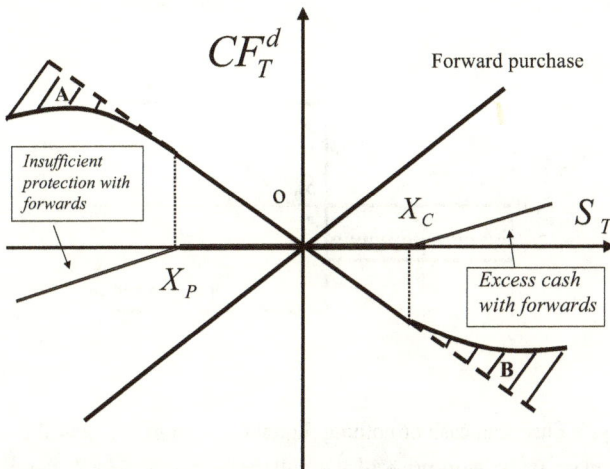

The area A represents an increase in cash outflows corresponds to an increase in foreign investment costs. Area B represents a decrease in cash outflows corresponds to a decrease in foreign capital investment expenditures.

6.3.2.2 Coordinating Financial Hedges and Strategic Real Option Exercise

A. Financing Exchange Rate Dependent Domestic Investments (Growth Options) with Digital Call Options

A cash-or-nothing digital option pays a fixed amount of cash if the underlying exceeds the exercise price. A German firm could decide to build a new plant at a certain date in

---

[104] See Froot et al. (1994), Froot (1994), Sercu and Uppal (1995), pp. 181-182.
[105] See Froot et al (1993), p. 1644.

the future only if the dollar will have appreciated to a certain level at that date. The foreign exchange exposure is thus asymmetric at that exchange rate value, S_0. The decision of the German firm to build a plant in Germany in € depends on the \$/\$ exchange rate. If $S_T > S_0$, the firm receives domestic cash flows to funds the domestic investment.

Figure 6. 6 Digital Option[106]

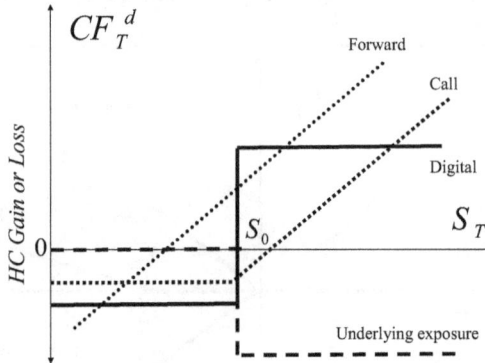

The firm buys a European cash or nothing digital call option that pays the amount need to build the plant if the euro price of the dollar exceeds S_0. At T, the payoff of the option provides the firm with the funding it requires if it is profitable to build the plant[107]. Figure 6.6 shows that a call option or a forward would not precisely hedge the exposure.

B. Preventing the Exercise of Abandonment Options

Financial hedges can provide the resources to pursue a strategy. If a poor competitive position resulting from an adverse exchange rate change is perceived to be temporary, a firm might be better off, for example, suffering short term losses in a country rather

---

[106] Adapted from Stulz (2000), ch. 17. See also Wilmott (2000), p. 35.
[107] This example is adapted from Stulz (2000), ch. 17, pp. 4-8.

than close its activities[108]. If that is the case, it has to have the resources to pursue such a strategy. It may not have these resources if it is not hedged because capital markets might be reluctant to provide funds. A reason is that it "might be difficult for capital markets participants to understand whether a strategy of financing losing operations is profitable from a long-run perspective"[109]. By preventing the exercise of this *abandonment option* in the short term, the financial hedge can increase firm value.

An implication is that financial hedges should have an economic rational based on exploiting optimally the value of its strategic real options. Suppose a multinational firm that has an unprofitable foreign operation as a result of a poor competitive position associated with an unexpected real exchange rate change. Unprofitable operations should not be kept simply because we can hedge them[110]. If the unprofitability is expected to persist in the long term, it might not be optimal to hedge them financially. The firm may be better off closing the unprofitable operation and invest in more profitable operations. The comments below made by a Wall Street analyst emphasize that argument.

"A European luxury automaker, in the late 1980s, stockpiled medium-term options and other hedging instruments to shield against the weak dollar, a move that company management considered was highly successful. However, in the long term, this may have been the wrong strategy". "The company should have been paying attention to changes in the market" says one Wall Street analyst. "Maybe they should have been moving away from luxury models, maybe building a plant in the US or maybe bringing in a new line of cars from somewhere else. But these are very low-quality earnings, and in the long run, I think the strategic planning was faulty; this kind of hedging strategy probably did more harm than good"[111].

---

[108] One reason the firm might believe that the poor competitive position is temporary is that the real exchange rates are volatile and tend to move toward their purchasing power parity level in the long run.
[109] See Stulz (2000), ch. 8, p. 47.
[110] See Stulz (2000), ch. 8, p. 49.
[111] See the Economist Intelligence Unit (1992), pp. 206-207.

6.3.3 Integrated Foreign Exchange Risk Management

6.3.3.1 Sources of Foreign Cash Flow Volatility and Effectiveness of Currency Hedges

a) Unrelated Quantity Risk and Real Price Risk: Managing Other Types of Uncertainties

If quantity risk and price risk are perfectly correlated, the home currency cash flow is function of the exchange rate only. As a result, we can eliminate all risk with currency hedging instruments because there is effectively only one source of risk, the exchange rate. As long as that random payoff is perfectly correlated with a forward price, a forward contract can be used to eliminate all risk[112].

The absence of relation between the uncertainty of the amount of foreign currency cash flows to be hedged and the exchange rate uncertainty indicates that cash flow variations are caused by other risk factors than exchange rate. In that case, it will necessarily be that hedged cash flows are risky because of the quantity risk that we cannot hedge with currency hedging instruments[113]. The effectiveness of financial hedging methods contingent on exchange rates is reduced by the presence of quantity risk[114]. If for example an exporter sells more when interest rates in the foreign country are low, the firm might benefit from hedging against interest rate increases in addition to hedging against an unexpected fall in the value of the foreign currency[115].

Hedging Foreign Currency Bids with Conditional Forwards

Viewing quantity risk as a sufficient condition for exposure to be non-linear can lead to incorrect hedging recommendations. To illustrate, we develop an example of a foreign currency bid. A firm making a bid in foreign currency faces two currency problems. First, it needs to estimate costs in multiple currencies and assume an exposure when

---

[112] See Stulz (2000), ch. 8, p.7.
[113] This residual risk is captured in a linear regression by the disturbance term. See Sercu and Uppal (1995), pp. 495-502, and the discussion in chapter 5.
[114] Quantity risk does not necessarily decrease the effectiveness of the hedge, however. "If the hedge for price risk is imperfect, it could be that quantity risk is highly negatively correlated with that part of the price risk that cannot be hedged, so that with quantity risk the hedge could become more effective". See Stulz (2000), ch. 8, for hedging foreign exchange exposures in presence of quantity risk with futures contracts.
[115] See Stulz (2000), ch. 8, p. 9.

pricing in a given currency. Second, they have to handle the exchange rate risk between bid and award date[116]. Solving the second problem can help the first, as the contractor will tend to price higher when he has exposed currency positions. It has often been argued that it is suitable to use options in dealing with the second problem. Table 6.1 gives the joint probability distribution of the exchange rate and the success of the bid that determine the future domestic currency cash flow distribution. CF_T^d, CF_T^f, S_T, are respectively the cash flows in domestic currency, foreign currency, and the exchange rate at time T. The probability of the bid success and the exchange rate risk are assumed to be independent[117]. The exposure depends on the joint probabilities of bid success and of the future exchange rate. Quantity risk is assumed to be the result of the risk related to the bid, and not of the exchange rate uncertainty.

Table 6. 1 Expected Cash Flows from Foreign Currency Bid

Distribution of exchange rate S_T (€/US\$)	*Distribution for the bid outcome*	
	Bid Accepted CF_T^f =\$200 mio., Pr = 0.5	Bid Not Accepted CF_T^f =0, Pr = 0.5
S_T=1.6, Pr =0.5	CF^d = € 320 mio., Pr = 0.25	CF^d = 0 , Pr = 0.25
S_T=1.2, Pr =0.5	CF^d = € 240 mio., Pr = 0.25	CF^d = 0 , Pr = 0.25

Probability of bid success	0.1	0.2	0.3	0.4	0.5	0.6	0.7	0.8	0.9	1.0
Expected FX exposure (mio. US\$)	20	40	60	80	100	120	140	160	180	200 = CF_T^f

The lower part of the table indicates the expected exposure values corresponding to various probabilities of bid success. When the foreign currency cash flow from the bid is highly likely, using forwards could be a reasonable solution[118].

Since $E_t(CF_T^d|S_T =1.6) = €$ 160 and $E_t(CF_T^d|S_T =1.2) = €$ 120, exposure is equal to (160-120)/(1.6-1.2) = \$ 100 mio. Figure 6.7 shows how the risk related to the bid being accepted (probability of the bid success) affect the slope but not the linear shape of the

---

[116] See Demacopoulos (1989), pp. 242-244.

[117] Since the probability to the success of the bid is assumed to be independent of the level of S_T, the probability of each state of nature is 0.5 x 0.5.

[118] Stulz (2000), ch. 13, pp. 36-41, shows that a firm that has the objective of minimizing the Cash-Flow-at-Risk of the foreign currency cash flow from the bid should use forwards if the probability of success of the bid is very high, and that when this probability is lower, it might be better not to hedge at all. The reason is that "with hedging, cash flow can be negative while absent hedging it can never be negative". Stulz (2000), Ch. 13, p. 54.

foreign exchange exposure profile. The slope is determined by the expected mean value of foreign currency cash flows from the bid.

Figure 6. 7 Foreign Exchange Exposure from Bid

(a) Foreign Currency Cash Flows	(b) Foreign Exchange Exposure Profile

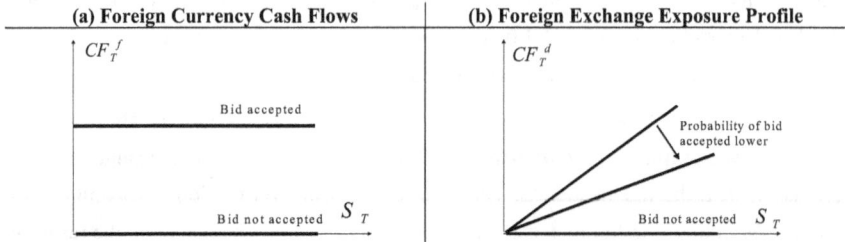

It is often argued that currency options should be used to hedge bids made in foreign currency. The argument is that options are more flexible hedging instruments than forwards or futures, since the holder cannot be forced to exercise[119]. However, if the future cash flows are uncertain and not perfectly correlated with the exchange rate, financial currency hedging is likely to be ineffective[120]. A currency option cannot efficiently hedge the cash flows from the bid. This is because the option's value is contingent on the exchange rate, while the foreign cash flow is contingent on another event, the success of the bid. The firm will exercise an in-the-money option regardless of whether the other event was favorable or unfavorable. Since the probability distribution of this other event is independent from the probability distribution of the exchange rate, currency hedges are ineffective. Quantity risk is not a sufficient condition for exposure non-linearity and for using currency options.

Ideally, the exposure to the bid risk should be hedged separately. But there is no underlying security whose price depends on the outcome of the bid[121]. A perfect hedge in this case could be achieved by a forward contract "conditional on the other source of

---

[119] For a criticism on using currency options for foreign currency bids, see Dufey and Giddy (1995), Giddy (1994), pp. 212-213.

[120] See Carter et al. (2001), p. 5.

[121] See Giddy and Dufey (1995), p. 55. Insurance contracts may be available in some cases. Insurance contracts are like derivatives; they can have a "forward-like" or an "option-like" structure. See Doherty (2000) for a discussion on how actuarial techniques can be used to improve the pricing of financial derivatives.

uncertainty"[122]. Such conditional forward contract, called "tender-to-contract forward contract", would become void if the firm loses the tender contract"[123].

b) Different Degrees of Foreign Cash Flows Uncertainty

Hedging with Hybrid Securities and Dynamic Hedging with Synthetic Options

When the exposed foreign currency cash flows are characterized by different degrees of uncertainty hybrid or synthetic hedging strategies may be needed. Suppose a German firm that expects to earn US$250,000 in export sales during 2004, and that is 95 percent confident that sales will be in the $225,000-$275,000 range[124]. The uncertainty surrounding the amount of foreign currency cash flows comes from the uncertainty of the state of the US economy. The firm's sales are assumed to be inversely correlated to the state of the US economy, as proxied by the rate of unemployment. If the US unemployment, now at 9 percent, falls to 8 percent, sales should be at the high end of the range. But if unemployment rises toward 10 percent, the sales will slump toward the $225,000 level.

Since the state of the US economy and the exchange rate are assumed to be independent, foreign exchange exposure is linear. This means that the state of the US economy is assumed to depend on factors other than the exchange rate. In figure 6.8 (a) and (b), the lower curves correspond to an unemployment rate of 10%, while the upper curves correspond to a rate of unemployment of 8%. As in the example with the foreign currency bid, exposures are function of the joint probability function of the state of the economy and the exchange rate. CF_T^d, CF_T^f, S_T, U_T, are respectively the cash flows in domestic currency, foreign currency, the exchange rate, and the unemployment rate at time T.

---

[122] See Sercu and Uppal (1995), p. 181.
[123] "Tender-to-contract options" also exist. See Sercu and Uppal (1995), p. 181.
[124] Example adapted from Levich (1998), pp. 593-594.

Figure 6. 8 Foreign Exchange Exposure with Quantity risk and Exchange Rate Risk Unrelated

        (a) Foreign Cash Flows   **(b) Foreign Exchange Exposure Profile**

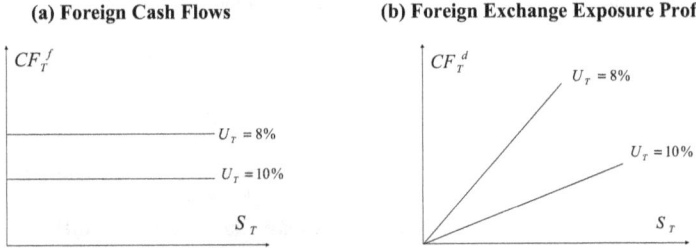

Since the exposure profile is not only linear but also random, the linearity of the exposure profile is not a sufficient condition for hedging with standard linear hedging instruments. Exposure can be highly unpredictable but linear. If the firm sells its expected US$ revenues ($250,000) forward, it will have underhedged if revenues are actually $275,000 and overhedged if revenues are only $225,000. These outcomes would leave the firm with a residual risk, from having sold forward too many or too few US$. Forwards would be suitable if the exposure is linear and certain, such as contractual exposures, or if it can be predicted with accuracy.

The foreign currency cash flows can be viewed as consisting of two components, that can be hedged according to their degree of certainty: (1) a highly predictable component: since the $225,000 amount is expected to be received with a high degree of certainty, a standard linear hedge can be used. This amount is the linear part of the firm's foreign exchange exposure to the €/$ exchange rate risk. (2) a component that is highly uncertain and that corresponds to the remaining $50'000. Because of this uncertainty, we need to find a hedge that match the probability of cash flows. We examine three hedging strategies.

(i) Hybrid Securities: Mixture of Forward and Option Contracts[125]

One strategy for dealing with cash flow uncertainty involves a hybrid security that consists of a mixture of forward and options contracts[126]. This mixed strategy requires

---

[125] Options can be employed as stand-alone contracts or embedded in financial claims such as callable bonds. This type of hedge is called "hybrid security". See Levich (1998).

[126] See Levich (1998), p. 594. Chowdhry and Howe (1999) shows that the optimal hedging of non-

selling $225,000 forward (the lower bound on the sales) and buying a put option on $50,000 (long put on US$). If sales exceed the lower bound of $225,000, the firm exercises the option for up to $50,000. And if sales are only $225,000, the firm does not exercise the put, but instead collects its terminal option value.

The first flaw of this strategy is that the firm needs a put option only if sales surpass $225,000. Similarly to the case of hedging foreign currency bids, the second flaw is that the option's value is contingent on the exchange rate, while the foreign cash flow of $50'000 is contingent on the state of the U.S. economy. If quantity risk is unrelated to price risk, a perfect hedge using currency hedges cannot be constructed. This is because the hedge contract has the same payoff in distinct states of the world, i.e. regardless of the exchange rate value.

Ideally, the firm would like to own an option to sell only the actual US$ revenue above $225,000, and no more. That would be possible if there were a hedging instrument whose payoff is function of the state of the U.S. economy or to a variable that is highly correlated to the state of the U.S. economy. If such an instrument does not exist, however, we need to find more creative solutions. However, if the transaction costs are low, the firm could find it optimal to buy a put option on $50,000.

(ii) Dynamic Hedging with Synthetic Options

An alternative approach for handling the foreign currency cash flows uncertainty is to structure a dynamic hedging with synthetic option. This dynamic strategy replicates the desired option, using the delta hedging principle[127]. The firm can create a synthetic put option for $25,000 by borrowing $25,000 and placing the proceeds (plus the fair put price) into a euro interest-bearing account[128]. As the expectation of unemployment falls, the firm can dynamically increase the size of the synthetic put option (by borrowing additional US$) toward a limit of $50,000. And as expectation of unemployment rises, we decrease the size of the synthetic put option toward a limit of zero. With this

---

linear currency exposures requires a combination of currency options and forward exchange contracts. See O'Brien (1998) for pro forma financial hedging with a combination of currency options and forward to hedge non-linear exposure. See also Shapiro (1999), p. 306, Giddy (1983), pp. 32-42.
[127] See Kulatilaka and Marcus (1994), Levich (1998), ch. 11, pp. 435-436 and p. 594.
[128] This can be thought as a put on the $50'000 with a delta of 0.50 representing the probability of reaching $50'000 in sales. See Levich (1998), p. 594.

strategy of using debt with option features, the firm always holds a position equivalent to an option on the expected amount of extra US$ sales above the $225,000 floor.

The problem with this approach is that the transaction costs of implementing the dynamic strategy could be high, perhaps higher than the cost of simply buying a put for the entire $50,000. Beside, since it is not certain (95% probability) that the foreign currency cash flows will be within the range $225'000-$275'000, both this strategy and the first strategy leave a residual exposure for the 5 percent probability that revenues will be outside the $225'000-$275'000 range.

(iii) Variance Minimizing Forward and Hedge Ratios from Regressions

If there is no hedging instrument available whose payoff is correlated to the foreign currency cash flow, a possibility is to find the currency forward position that minimizes the volatility of the hedged position, knowing that we cannot completely eliminate this volatility. This position is given by the formula: $h = Cov(C, G)/Var(G)$, where G is the forward price at maturity of the hedge, C the random cash flow, h the optimal hedge[129].

The regression approach used in chapter 5 suggests that a treasurer could smooth out stock prices with respect to exchange rate changes by undertaking a hedge dictated by the exposure coefficient[130]. For the example here, the following considerations must be taken:

- Whereas the stock price represents the net present value of all future cash flows, the treasurer may only be interested in stabilizing the cash flows in the foreseeable future. Since the market value of the firm reflects all future cash flows, a small exchange rate change could portend a large change in market value, and exposure measured using the regression approach may appear very large.

---

[129] See Stulz (2000), ch. 8, p.7, for this technique to hedge nonlinear exposures with futures and forwards. This is the hedge ratio corresponding to the regression coefficient in a linear regression of realizations of unexpected cash flow on realizations of changes in the forward price.

[130] The regression coefficient can be written as $\gamma_i = Cov(r_{it}, \Delta e_t)/Var(\Delta e_t)$, with the same notation as in chapter 5. This shows the two sources of exposure: the variance of the exchange rate and the covariance between the home currency value of the stock return and the exchange rate. This definition of exposure is a variance decomposition of a firm's returns into a component that is correlated with the exchange rate change and a component that is orthogonal to exchange rate changes.

- *Exposures coefficients are after-hedge measures*: exposure coefficients need to be adjusted for the hedging effect. These "before-hedge coefficients" can then be used to assess the suitability of existing hedging policies, and the need for, and benefits of, additional hedging[131].

- *Exposures coefficients measure marginal exchange rate effects:* firms may engage in inadequate or excessive hedging to cover their currency exposures if they fail to take into consideration the correlations between variables. Significant coefficients estimated in a series of bivariate models could be insignificant in a combined multivariate model. Conversely, insignificant coefficients estimated in a series of bivariate models may be significant in a combined multivariate. The sign of exposure coefficients could even be reversed in moving a bivariate to a multivariate model[132]. For this reason, it is important, prior to the regression analysis, to conduct a fundamental analysis to identify variables with potential economic explanatory power and that are correlated to exchange rate movements. Since the set of relevant variables may shift over time, the company should follow up the process of identification continuously[133].

In the example examined previously, we could have assumed that the state of the U.S. economy and the exchange rate were dependent rather than independent. When the price of the foreign currency is high, a recession is more likely than a boom because an expensive currency means that the foreign economy is not very competitive[134]. The difference would be that the joint probabilities of the states of nature would not be equal to the product of the exchange rate and the state of the economy probabilities. Because of the endogeneity of the state of the economy to the exchange rate, quantity risk would be indirectly affected by exchange rate changes, and the exposure would be non-linear[135].

---

[131] See Khoo (1994), p. 361, for a discussion on this aspect.
[132] See Miller (1994), p. 10.
[133] See Oxelheim (2002), p. 13.
[134] See a numerical example in Sercu and Uppal (1995), p. 500.
[135] Sercu and Uppal (1995), pp. 499-502, give a numerical example of this case, and conclude that a forward contract could hedge completely the firm's exposure resulting from the exchange rate risk. However, their example assumes only two different possible values of future exchange rates and there is residual risk.

6.3.3.2 Strategic Flexibility and Dynamic View of Natural Hedges

A. Effect of Natural Hedging on the Exposure Profile

Natural hedges are equivalent to linear financial hedges whose objective is to reduce the variance of domestic cash flows:

- *Foreign borrowings*: a firm could restructure its *long-term financing*, so as to permanently alter its financial exposure[136]. The choice of currency composition of debt can be viewed as a hedging decision since "foreign currency borrowing is equivalent to borrowing in the firm's domestic currency plus hedging via a forward contract (or swap) so that the net obligation from the two transactions is effectively denominated in the foreign currency"[137]. Borrow HC, sell forwards HC gives at maturity FC. Variance-minimizing hedges can add value but they generally will not maximize value.

- *Effect on exposure of diversification*: geographical and across products lines diversification is not a source of exposure asymmetries. Diversification refers to a firm's ex-ante operating structure. What makes exposure asymmetric are the adjustments that a firm is planning to make after the realization of unexpected exchange rate changes make[138]. Natural hedges, for example through geographical diversification, affect the linear component of a firm's exposure. Diversification is a linear real hedge, whereas forwards are linear nominal hedges.

These measures can provide protection for exposures that are relatively constant through time, such as contractual exposures, but it is less effective for competitive exposures, which are variable.

B. Dynamic Tradeoff between Strategic Flexibility and Natural Hedging

Foreign exchange exposures result from unmatched, *in a given time period*, foreign cash inflows and outflows. Natural hedges, by matching the currencies of costs and

---

[136] See Levich (1998).
[137] See Singh and Hodder (2000), p. 854.
[138] See Hommel (2002) for a hedging model of foreign exchange exposure that makes a distinction between financial hedging for a geographically diversified firm and for an operating-flexible firm.

revenues, are often viewed as an efficient way to limit foreign exchange exposure[139]. But the rationale for natural hedging is static. We need to *match the flexibility* of revenues and costs. "For instance, an exporter that sells to a foreign market and that diminished its exposure by means of a foreign currency loan. If real exchange rates change so that at some future date it is no longer profitable to sell on the foreign market, the firm ends up having foreign currency costs and no foreign currency revenues"[140].

There can be tradeoff between natural hedging and flexibility over the valuation period. Setting a natural hedge can reduce the flexibility and expected firm value. Natural hedging, by fixing a given currency basket ex-ante, reduces the firm's strategic flexibility to adjust ex-post the currency denomination of its costs and revenues after the realization of unexpected exchange rate changes. The possible tradeoff between the benefits of a natural hedge and the loss of flexibility was discussed in chapter 2/2.4.1, and in chapter 3/3.6.3. For example, invoicing prices to foreign customers in domestic currency can be viewed as a natural hedge. But by fixing ex-ante the price in domestic currency, the firm loses the exchange-rate-pass-through option associated with pricing in foreign currency.

6.3.3.3 Risk Management in a Strategic Real Options Framework

A. Linking Financial Hedging to Strategic Planning and Industry Analysis

Any financial hedging decision should be based on a detailed understanding of the firm's economic and strategic situation. The assessment of the effect of strategic real options on a firm's foreign exchange exposure is based on as industry competitive analysis and on corporate strategic planning. Figure 6.9 below shows that the process of exposure identification leading to the determination of an optimal hedge can be structured into three interrelated steps. Steps (A) and (B) assess the changes in the competitive position created by exchange rate movements and the firm's strategic responses. (A) shows that external factors affect the exposure profile and the optimal

---

[139] Natural hedges include matching revenues and costs for the same currency, e.g,. financing local operations with local currency loans, locating production in the country in which the firm sell its product, or offsetting losses in one currency with gains in another. See Fink, R., 2003, Natural Performers, CFO Magazine, June 1.

[140] See Capel (1997), p. 103.

financial hedge (III) and that strategic planning (II) is influenced by expectations about the role of the external factors. (B) indicates that financial hedging and strategic decisions are complementary; the implementation of strategic measures can be supported by financial hedges, whereas expected strategic responses to exchange rate changes influence the optimal hedge[141].

Figure 6. 9 Structuring Financial Hedges: Three Interrelated Steps

The exposure profile depends on how these three set of factors interact. Industry changes and operational adjustment expected to become active at some distinct exchange rate values create an asymmetric exposure profile, with financial hedging in turn influencing the operational adjustments. Financial hedging is assessed in accordance to these real adjustments. The firm's need for hedging is directly related to the first two set of factors. But the strategic behavior of the firm will in turn be influenced by the financial hedging strategy.

The financial risk management function of the treasury department is linked to the strategic planning of firms and the industry competitive analysis[142]. Information on the

---

[141] This means providing detailed risk information to senior planners, and requiring management to consider the risk and returns of different strategies. It also requires the risk management function to measure the threats from exchange rate changes that might affect the strategic plan. See CFO Research Services (2002).

[142] Firms can manage operating exposure by devising operating strategies that consist of combinations of different marketing initiatives, such as market selection or pricing strategy, and production initiatives, such as raw materials sourcing and production location. *Marketing strategies* such as

possibility of exercising strategic options, the exercise of which may not be correlated to changes in exchange rates but which modifies the underlying business rationale on which the financial hedge is based, is needed. The finance manager also needs to assess for which range of exchange rates and for which time horizon financial hedging is appropriate and at which points the exercise of real options take over or disqualify financial hedging. Since the relationships between all these factors are constantly shifting, hedging practices are to be constantly subject to revision.

B. Enterprise Risk Management (ERM)

Originally, risk management was implemented on an uncoordinated basis across different units of the firm. Risk management is now evolving into a firmwide exercise that addresses both short-term and long-term exposures and encompasses financial as well as operational hedges. Risk management is less frequently seen as a purely corporate finance function responsibility, and the necessity of the involvement of operating and marketing managers tends to be recognized.

Figure 6. 10 The Evolution towards Strategic Risk Management

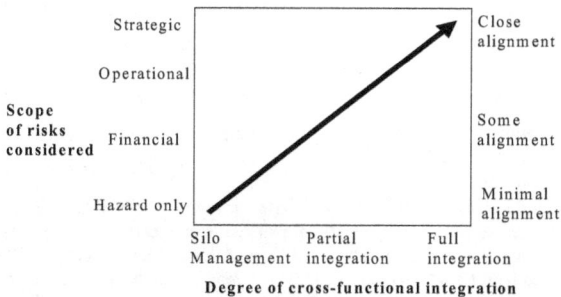

Source: CFO Research Services (2002), p. 7.

Marketing selection, Product strategy, Pricing policies, Promotional strategies. *Production strategies* such as Product sourcing, Input mix, Plant location, Raising productivity. See Shapiro (1999)

Enterprise risk management (ERM) is defined as a "method of risk management that takes an enterprise-wide approach to monitoring and managing risk in support of a company's strategic goals"[143]. With regard to currency risk management, ERM can be defined as the coordinated use of financial and operational hedges as part of an integrated risk management strategy to manage currency risk[144]. Figure 6.10 above illustrates this evolution toward greater cross-functional integration, coverage of a broader range of risks, and a more direct connection between risk and strategy. A "risk inventory" is conducted that goes through the entire organization to map out and measure all risks, then all the risks are consolidate.

The advantages of ERM resulting from the management of all risks on a consistent and integrated basis across business units, across risk categories, and across locations are multiple:

- *Recognition of the efficiency inherent in cross-hedging*: ERM includes all components that drive financial risk, accounts for interactions of risks, measures and aggregates consistently, and measures a firm's overall exposure. Foreign exchange risks are often swamped by other risks and therefore using foreign exchange derivatives is not likely to substantially reduce a company's overall cash flow volatility[145]. Contractual foreign cash flows are not fully risk-free. Foreign exchange accounts receivable can have substantial default risk. The possibility that the firm hedges forward and the debtor does not pay implies that the firm faces "reverse risk"[146].

- *Management of financial risks are in line with the firm's strategic agenda*: ERM helps division managers better understand risk management beyond their individual

---

[143] See CFO Research Services (2002), p. 2. Other terms used to describe this type of coordinated risk management are "enterprise risk management", global risk management, strategic risk management. See Miller (1992), Dowd (1999), Carter et al. (2001), p. 2, Elliot (2001), KPMG (2001), NERA/The Economist Intelligence Unit (2002), Kloman (2002). The models that have been used by corporate risk managers in the past have been adapted from those developed by banks for banks and have proven insufficient to cover all corporate risks.

[144] See Carter et al. (2001), p. 2.

[145] Copeland and Joshi (1996), p. 66, for example, pointing out specifically to a "variety of evidence that indicates that currency risk accounts for no more than 10% of cash flow volatility at most companies and often substantially less", conclude that managing FX risk is unnecessary. "Even eliminating currency risk, therefore, would be unlikely to reduce overall cash flow volatility by more than 10%." Following the import of their discussion, Shapiro (1998) concludes that "currency risk management would be most likely to be of value in the event of a catastrophic currency failure, like the Mexican peso and the East Asian currencies".

[146] See Sercu and Uppal (1995), p. 179.

departments. The objective of ERM is to reduce risk while placing the firm in a position to benefit from opportunities that arise from exchange rate changes. By embracing the strategic agenda of the firm, such as the pursuit of new markets, the capital allocation process, ERM helps structure a hedging program that generate business opportunities and create value. In turn, integrating financial risk management and corporate planning helps senior managers devise strategies that more fully account for risks. The results of the ERM risk mapping program are incorporated into their strategic plan. For example, when managers have an accurate sense of the total risk each business unit carries, they can make investment decisions based on the investment's marginal effect on risk and overall returns[147].

- *Management of foreign exchange competitive exposures can account for exposure asymmetries:* ERM can handle the factors that make foreign exchange exposures asymmetric and uncertain. Most factors of foreign currency cash flow uncertainty are likely to be firm-specific and depend on the firm's strategic behavior. With ERM, treasurers can better recognize the competitive implications of exchange rate movement for their companies, and the interrelation of this effect with other factors of competitiveness. It makes also easier for corporates to incorporate operational/production risk components into their financial risk management activities[148].

- *Coordinated use of operational and financial hedges is facilitated:* this should more effectively reduce exposure to foreign exchange risk, because it addresses the firm's exposure in a coordinated way, both in the short and in the long term.

- *Consideration of correlations between contractual and competitive exposures*: hedging contractual exposures could increase economic exposure. Suppose that the exposure of contractually fixed cash flows is naturally offset by the competitive exposure of the firm's operating cash flows. If we hedge only the contractual exposure, the firm's economic exposure could increase as a result of the financial hedge[149].

---

[147] Moreover, if a company's managers "wish to obtain higher returns from a slow-growth business, they may be more confident applying capital to higher-risk projects if their analysis reveals that the total risk level is not excessive". See CFO Research Services (2002).

[148] Din and Kouvelis (2001) discuss the effect of exposure to exchange rate risk on production plans.

[149] An example is given in Copeland and Joshi (1996), which is also discussed in Stulz (2000), ch. 8, pp. 45-46.

7. Concluding Remarks and Suggestions for Further Research

The objective of this dissertation was to provide a conceptual and analytical framework for understanding and analyzing the factors that are sources of foreign exchange exposure asymmetries. The central argument developed is that foreign exchange exposure should be asymmetric, as a result of endogenous changes in the firm's strategic behavior or exogenous changes in the competitive structure of the industry in which the firm operates, arising at distinct exchange rate values. It is shown that at some threshold exchange rate values, the nature of a firm's foreign exchange exposure may change dramatically, and that this could have important implications in terms of estimation procedures and optimal hedging policy. This proposition is supported by empirical evidence provided on German corporations. The conclusions and recommendations for further research are summarized in this chapter. Section 7.1 reviews the contributions of this study to the international corporate finance literature and the inferences which can be made from their insights. Section 7.2 suggests several research topics which might be worth pursuing.

7.1 Conclusions

Foreign exchange exposure asymmetries should be an important issue to corporate managers. The possibility that exposures could take dramatically different values for some ranges of exchange rates is of direct relevance in terms of estimation and financial hedging, and in terms of how risk management in general should be conducted. This study has shown that real options theory provides a promising conceptual framework to describe and value the foreign exchange exposure profiles of flexible firms.

In our empirical analysis, we find evidence of exposure asymmetries for the small percentage of German firms that is significantly exposed. However, there is no significant empirical evidence that some German firms are operationally capable to take advantage of fluctuations in the €/US$ exchange rate and limit the impact of detrimental movements. The result is that German firms do not seem in a position to exploit exchange rate uncertainty for the benefit of their shareholders. There is no evidence that an increase in cash flow volatility as a result of an increase in real exchange rate / price risk or quantity risk leads to an increase in equity volatility and shareholder wealth. A number of explanations for that finding have been detailed throughout our study (for a brief overview, see section 5.5.1).

Our approach emphasizes the importance in terms of risk management of analyzing foreign exchange exposures in a *dynamic multi-period valuation framework* rather than in a single-period cash flow framework as it has traditionally been done in structural models of exposure. We conclude with several general implications which have emerged from our analysis of foreign exchange exposure asymmetries.

First, it is essential for *corporate risk managers* to recognize the economic importance of the real long term competitive effects on firm value of exchange rate changes. The sole focus on the exposure of short term contractual cash flows is insufficient and overlooks the fact that foreign exchange exposure is essentially a competitive exposure that needs to be managed with strategic means. A firm might be adversely affected in the short term by unexpected exchange rate changes, but what matters ultimately for shareholders is how efficiently it copes with the effect on its competitiveness. Suppose a firm that is adversely affected by an exchange rate change. In the short term, it has a negative contractual exposure according to its foreign currency position, but in the longer term, if it pursues strategies to defend its sources of competitive advantages and economic rents more efficiently than its competitors, it could end up improving its corporate performance, i.e., its ability to generate real cash flows. Over the valuation period, the effect on firm value can be positive. Viewing foreign exchange exposure as a competitive and long term exposure implies a radically different perspective on a firm's exposure characteristics:

(a) Recognizing the *importance of the long term competitive effects* of exchange rate fluctuations rather than the short term contractual exposures should make corporate managers more aware of the *potential of investing in flexibility*. Being more flexible than competitors can improve the corporate performance of oligopolists over time. As such, the measurement and management of foreign exchange exposure needs to be linked to corporate planning.

(b) *The main determinant of a firm's exposure is not necessarily its sector of activity, but possibly the competitive structure of the industry in which it operates.* Over longer period of time, the exposure sign does not necessarily reflect a long/short position in a foreign currency. Competitive foreign exchange exposure can be viewed as being the result of a conversion effect and a competitive effect. The competitive effect can offset or even revert the sign of the exposure component resulting from the conversion effect. In presence of strategic real options and financial flexibility options, a firm's exposure can take complex forms and cannot be generalized analytically based on the sectors of activity. It is eventually a firm-specific rather than a sector- or industry-specific, as well as an empirical matter.

(c) *The measurement and management of foreign exchange exposure needs to be done in a comprehensive way with other types of risk.* Foreign exchange exposure asymmetries can be the result of other types of risk factors. For example, credit risk can create asymmetries in the foreign exchange exposure profile. The benefit of managing together different types of correlated risk is straightforward, but the practicality of such an approach is complex not only technically but organizationally since it requires the collaboration of separate corporate functions.

(d) *Exposure is to some extent a "choice variable"*[1] *that depends on managerial decisions and not solely determined by external market forces*: without knowledge of a firm's specific strategic factors, it is difficult to see why one should expect particular patterns of exposure[2]. The strategic "choice" should be based on the assessment of a trade-off between bearing foreign exchange exposures and increasing profitability through strategic measures.

(e) *We cannot generalize analytically that an increase in exchange rate volatility necessarily benefits shareholders for a flexible firm.* The value of a real option can be negative, meaning that a firm may be less valuable if it holds a real option than if it does not. For example, the effect of real options on exposure can be negative because of endogenous bounds on flexibility and strategic competition.

(f) *Dynamic perspective on profitability.* What matters is how the firm defends its sources of competitive advantages and economic rent while arbitraging forces in the goods markets are in play. For example, we argued that the flexibility of passing-through exchange rate changes into nominal prices can be interpreted as a real option for monopolistic firms. In the longer term, arbitraging forces in the

---

[1] This aspect was alluded to in Amihud (1994).
[2] Chapter 3 shows that since exposure is dependent on pricing strategy, the currency of determination of a firm's cash flow is itself to some extent a choice variable.

goods markets will erode the power of the firm to price discriminate, but what matters is how the firm manages its profitability over the valuation period during the reversion of the exchange rate to its purchasing power parity value.

(g) Exposures asymmetries have implications for foreign exchange exposure *estimation*. This finding challenges the symmetry assumption underlying the regression models used in most empirical studies. Although more data intensive, simulation analysis used for real options valuation are potentially more powerful to deal with complex asymmetries.

(h) Exposure asymmetries have implications for the elaboration of *corporate risk management policies*. There is an economic rationale for managing foreign exchange exposures with financial and strategic real options. We argue however that the *correlation between quantity risk and price risk* cannot serve as a basis for structuring hedges when the exposure is asymmetric. The use of linear statistical metrics, such as correlation coefficients would be inadequate for the assessment of hedging strategies.

Finally, our results are of interest to *newsmakers* and government decision-makers, such as *trade negotiators* and *central bankers*. For oligopolistic industries, government policies need to address strategic long term competitiveness issues rather than short term contractual effects. Whether a country's firms gains or loses from an exchange rate change depends on long term competitiveness factors[3]. Newsmakers typically draw conclusions about long term effects, based on the consideration of short term contractual effects, and overlook the long term re-distribution of industry value that follow an exchange rate change and that depends on how market participants interact strategically.

7.2 Suggestions for Further Research

We conclude with some final thoughts and suggestions for further research. A number of extensions to this study could be worth pursuing. The first observation is that the real option framework has been mostly developed for capital budgeting, but needs further development for describing and measuring risk exposures. What are needed are

---

[3] This may apply to German firms in industries such as automobiles, pharmaceuticals. Luehrman (1990), p. 226, briefly mentions these issues which are relevant for "strategic national markets".

heuristic valuation models of foreign exchange exposure. Further research could also investigate *explicitly* how exchange rate changes affect asymmetrically *firm performance*, instead of how exchange-rate movements affect stock returns[4]. That could provide better criteria to gauge the validity of the regression and market value approach.

The second observation is that in large sample research, the only practical approach is indeed to use market data in empirical tests. However, what strongly emerges from this study is that exposure is essentially firm-specific and function of a firm's strategic policies. This casts doubts on the relevance of large scale empirical studies that aim at finding general patterns at different level of analysis – firm level, industry level - based on the sectors of activity. With market data, it is generally not even possible to say if estimated exposures are actually economically too small or too large, since such approach has inherently little power to discriminate among economic models and theoretical interpretations.

A more promising research approach could be to use firm-level proprietary data, and doing empirical research based on an explicit model of firm-level behavior in order to assess whether estimated exposures are consistent and significant economically and not only statistically. Empirical studies *with strategic data* on firms would be worth pursuing. "By focusing on exchange rate and other macroeconomic exposures, previous finance research may have overlooked the most relevant economic exposures such as exposures to strategic moves by competing firms. Competitive, input supply, and product demand risks are often interrelated with movements in real exchange rates"[5] and can be important determinants of a firm's foreign exchange exposure.

---

[4] This is suggested for example by Forbes (2002).
[5] This is argued in Miller and Reuer (1998).

8. APPENDICES

APPENDIX A Economic Contractual Exposure

Comparison of Economic Contractual Exposure with Accounting Contractual Exposure[1]

Accounting Contractual Exposure

- *Time at which exposure arises: transaction date.* Accountants measure the exposure that arises from existing transactions or from financial positions that are on the books[2]. It indicates the cash flow impact of exchange rate changes on the value of the transaction that arises at the transaction date, when the transaction is entered into the books, typically when the good is shipped to or received by the buyer.

- *Exchange rate for calculation: actual exchange rates.* Accounting contractual exposure is based on actual nominal exchange rate changes. Under the accountant's definition, the transaction is originally recorded at the spot exchange rate on the transaction date and closed using the exchange rate on the settlement date. The exchange rate gain or loss is a function of the total nominal exchange rate change between these two dates.

Economic Contractual Exposure

- *Time at which exposure arises: commitment date.* From an economic perspective, contractual exposure arises the moment the firm enters a fixed nominal currency contract. That is, whenever it commits to pay or receive a specific amount of foreign currency as part of a transaction at some date in the future. Contractual exposures begins not when the transaction is entered into the books but when the agreement is reached and the terms set for the transaction to occur. This date is the "commitment date". Contractual exposure should thus also include contractual agreements not associated with booked transactions and that do not appear in the firm's balance sheet. The actual cash flow impact of exchange rate changes on the value of the transaction begins from the commitment date[3].

- *Exchange rate for calculation: expected exchange rates.* Economic contractual exposure is based upon unexpected nominal exchange rate changes[4]. This implies that, from an economic standpoint, using actual exchange rates for exposure measurement is not correct. A firm should be concerned about the amount it is expecting to receive or pay on settlement, not how much the transaction is currently worth. It is thus the present value of the expected cash flow that matters for firm value, not the value of that foreign currency cash flow at the spot rate on the transaction or commitment date. The current spot rate is irrelevant as the cash flow is occurring in the future. This measure should be based upon the firm's expectation of the exchange rate on the settlement date, and not upon the current exchange rate.

Source: adapted from Bodnar (1999).

---

[1] See Bodnar (1999).
[2] This is the measure associated with "transaction exposure" in the literature.
[3] See, e.g., Stulz (2000), ch. 8, p. 3, and Bodnar (1999), p. 1.
[4] See Bodnar (1999), p. 2.

APPENDIX B Multi-Market Monopoly Model of Foreign Exchange Exposure[5]

We can express the value of a firm, V, in terms of a stream of present and future cash flows:

[2. 1] $$V = \sum_{t=1}^{\infty} \frac{CF_t}{(1+\rho)_t}$$

where CF are the firm's cash flows, which are equal to after-tax profits less net investment, and ρ is the discount rate. If we assume that the net investment of the firm is equal to zero and that cash flows are constant from year to year[6], the expression for the firm value becomes[7]:

[2. 2] $$V = \frac{CF}{\rho} = \frac{(1-\tau)}{\rho}\pi$$

where τ is the tax rate and π is the profit before taxes. The basic measure of foreign exchange exposure is dV/dS, where S is the exchange rate expressed as the price of the foreign currency in terms of the home currency. With corporate taxes and the discount rate constant, economic exposure is proportional to the derivative of current profits with respect to the exchange rate[8]:

[2. 3] $$dV / dS = [(1-\tau)/\rho]d\pi / dS$$

It is this latter derivative, dV / dS, that will be derived explicitly below.

We assume a monopolist which practices price discrimination between markets, and which is exposed to currency risk on the revenue side[9]. It produces its inputs for production domestically and exports in k separate destination markets, indexed by i. The firm sets prices and take quantities, and solves a static profit maximization problem, where the exchange rate is the only source of uncertainty. This is a static model which does not explicitly incorporate the dynamics of exchange rates. However,

---

[5] Se Levi (1994).
[6] This is in order to "keep the model tractable so that the effect of market structure can be examined". See Bodnar et al. (2002).
[7] The after-tax profit stream is assumed to be a perpetuity. See Brealy and Myers (2000), p. 41, Levi (1994), Bodnar et al. (2002).
[8] This is a reasonable assumption "if taxes are paid to the home government which cares about profit, not where or how the profit was earned". See Levi (1994), p. 39.
[9] This part is based primarily on the model of Levi (1994), pp. 38-43. See also Marston (2001), pp. 151-153.

as long as exchange rate changes are assumed to be permanent (i.e., exchange rate follows a random walk), the results should also hold in a dynamic setting. According to [2.6], an expression for the firm value can be written as[10]:

[2. 4] $$V = \pi \left[\frac{(1-\tau)}{\rho} \right] = \left(\sum_{i=0}^{k} s_i p_i q_i - c \sum_{i=0}^{k} q_i \right) \left[\frac{(1-\tau)}{\rho} \right]$$

where V is the market value of the firm, $\sum_{i=0}^{k} s_i p_i q_i$ the total revenue, $c \sum_{i=0}^{k} q_i$ the total cost, ρ the risk-adjusted shareholder opportunity cost of capital, τ the tax rate, s_i the exchange rate in units of home currency per unit of currency i, p_i the product price in country i, q_i the quantity sold in country i, c the marginal cost of production at home, which is assumed to be constant. The exposure of the firm to the foreign currency j, $\partial V / \partial s_j$, is given by:

[2. 5] $$\frac{\partial V}{\partial s_j} = \frac{d\pi}{ds_j} \cdot \frac{(1-\tau)}{\rho} = \left[p_j q_j + s_j p_j \frac{dq_j}{dp_j} \frac{dp_j}{ds_j} + s_j q_j \frac{dp_j}{ds_j} - c \frac{dq_j}{dp_j} \frac{dp_j}{ds_j} \right] \frac{(1-\tau)}{\rho}$$

Firms and consumers regard a shift in the exchange rate as once-and-for-all change. The first-order conditions of profit maximization equates the marginal revenue from sales in each market to the common marginal cost and a destination-specific mark-up[11]:

[2. 6] $$s_j p_j + s_j q_j \frac{dp_j}{dq_j} = c$$

Alternatively, the first-order conditions can be represented by the export prices to each destination markets, which are the products of the common marginal cost and destination-specific markups:

[2. 7] $$p_j = \frac{c}{s_j \left(1 - \frac{1}{\eta_j} \right)} \qquad \forall j \qquad \text{where} \qquad \eta_j = -\frac{p_j dq_j}{q_j dp_j}$$

η_j is the elasticity of demand in the foreign market j with respect to changes in price.

---

[10] In Levi (1994), a term representing net monetary asset/liability position in currency i is added. This does not affect the main conclusions of this model. Since the value of assets and liabilities located in foreign countries ultimately gets reflected in cash flows, cash flow is all that matters to firm value. See Pringle and Connolly (1993), p.70.

[11] It is assumed that the firm's output does not affect the exchange rate.

Equation [2.11] indicates that the firm "price-to-market" by price discriminating between markets[12]. Although [2.11] represents the first-order condition for the monopolist, it could be interpreted more generally in an oligopolistic framework if we consider the elasticities to be associated with a residual demand curve that takes into account the firm's perceptions of competitors responses to changes in the firm's price. The local foreign price in country j is :

[2. 8]
$$s_j p_j = \frac{c}{\left(1 - \frac{1}{\eta_j}\right)}$$

The higher the elasticity of demand in market j, the lower the price that the firm is able to charge in that market and the lower the mark-up. From [2.11] we can see that $dp_j/ds_j = -p_j/s_j$, which implies complete exchange rate pass-through[13]. Using the pass-through expression and the definition of η_j in equation [2.11] gives:

[2. 9]
$$\frac{\partial V}{\partial s_j} = \left[p_j q_j + p_j q_j (1-\eta) + c \frac{dq_j}{dp_j} \frac{p_j}{s_j} \right] \frac{(1-\tau)}{\rho}$$

[2. 10]
$$\frac{\partial V}{\partial s_j} = \eta_j q_j \left(p_j - \frac{c}{s_j} \right) \frac{(1-\tau)}{\rho}$$

Expressed in terms of elasticity, exposure can be written as:

[2. 11]
$$\frac{\partial V}{\partial s_j} \cdot \frac{s_j}{V} = \eta_j \cdot \frac{\left[s_j q_j \left(p_j - \frac{c}{s_j} \right)(1-\tau) \right] \cdot \frac{1}{\rho}}{V}$$

If the firm is at a profit-maximizing equilibrium, equation [2.9] can be simplified by using the first-order condition for profit maximization.

---

[12] See Goldberg and Knetter (1996), Knetter (1992), for an interpretation of this expression in the context of pricing to market strategies. See also chapter 3.
[13] The most realistic case for a firm with some market power would imply partial pass-through. This possibility cannot occur in this model because marginal costs and price demand elasticities are assumed constant. In order to have partial pass-through, markups should be allowed to vary in response to exchange rate changes (see chapter 3).

[2. 12] $$\frac{\partial \pi}{\partial q_j} = \left[s_j p_j \frac{dq_j}{dp_j} \frac{dp_j}{ds_j} + s_j q_j \frac{dp_j}{ds_j} - c \frac{dq_j}{dp_j} \frac{dp_j}{ds_j} \right] = 0$$

And the expression [2.9] for exposure simplifies to:

[2. 13] $$\frac{\partial V}{\partial s_j} = (p_j q_j) \frac{(1 - \tau)}{\rho}$$

APPENDIX C Model of Exchange Rate Pass-Through and Foreign Exchange Exposure[14]

a. Foreign Consumers' Behavior

Consumers' preferences over the differentiated goods in the foreign market are represented by the CES utility function:

[3. 1] $U(q_1, q_2) = [\alpha q_1^\rho + (1-\alpha)q_2^\rho]^{1/\rho}$

where $U(.)$ represents the utility function of the consumers in the foreign market, q_1 the quantity of the exporting firm's product sold in the foreign market, q_2 the quantity of the foreign import-competing firm's product sold in the foreign market. The extent to which foreign consumers favor the exporter's goods in consumption is given by α, a preference weighting parameter, which represents the nominal expenditure share allocated to the exporter's goods. For each value of ρ, the CES function restricts the elasticity of substitution between goods to be constant for all levels of output[15].

[3. 2] $p_1 = D_1(q_1, q_2) = \dfrac{\alpha q_1^{(\rho-1)} y}{[\alpha q_1^\rho + (1-\alpha)q_2^\rho]}$

[3. 3] $p_2 = D_2(q_1, q_2) = \dfrac{(1-\alpha)q_2^{(\rho-1)} y}{[aq_1^\rho + (1-\alpha)q_2^\rho]}$

where y equals total expenditure on the two goods[16]. The own and cross-price derivatives of these demand functions are negative (i.e., $D_{ii} < 0$ and $D_{ij} < 0$), which implies that increases in outputs of either good lead to decreases in price. An expression for the market share of the exporting firm in the foreign market, defined by λ, can be obtained from [3.3]:

[3. 4] $\lambda = \dfrac{p_1 q_1}{y} = \dfrac{aq_1^\rho}{aq_1^\rho + (1-a)q_2^\rho}$

---

[14] See Bodnar, Dumas, and Marston (2002).
[15] See Dixit (2000), p. 5. ρ is related to the constant elasticity of substitution between the two goods σ by the relationship $\sigma = 1/(\rho-1)$. As ρ approaches 1, substitutability becomes perfect ($\sigma \to -\infty$). For demand functions to be positively related to the price of the other good, the two goods must be substitutes ($\rho > 0$). So $0 < \rho < 1$ and $-\infty < \sigma < -1$ are assumed. See Varian (1992), p. 112.
[16] This industry's product is assumed to be weakly separable from all other goods in the consumer's utility function. See Varian (1992), pp. 150-151.

And the share of the foreign good in its own market as $(1-\lambda)^{17}$. Using expression [3.5], the partial elasticities of demand can be expressed as functions of the industry competitive structure as defined by ρ, and the firm's market share λ.

[3. 5]
$$
\begin{bmatrix}
\dfrac{\partial q_1/\partial p_1}{q_1/p_1} & \dfrac{\partial q_1/\partial p_2}{q_1/p_2} \\[2ex]
\dfrac{\partial q_2/\partial p_1}{q_2/p_1} & \dfrac{\partial q_2/\partial p_2}{q_2/p_2}
\end{bmatrix}
= \frac{1}{1-\rho}
\begin{bmatrix}
\rho\lambda-1 & \rho(1-\lambda) \\
\rho\lambda & \rho(1-\lambda)-1
\end{bmatrix}
$$

Since λ is assumed to lie between zero and one, a rise in product substitutability ρ raises all price elasticities (in absolute value).

b. Firms' Profits

Since we define the exchange rate, S, as the price of the foreign currency in units of the exporting firm's home currency, and assume that the exporting firm produces with inputs from its home market as well as imported inputs from abroad, the profit of the exporting firm in its home currency is written as[18]:

[3. 6] $\pi_1^* = Sp_1 q_1 - (c_1^* + Sc_1)q_1$

The profit in foreign currency of the import-competing firm, which sells only in the foreign market and has costs based only in the foreign currency, is given as:

[3. 7] $\pi_2 = p_2 q_2 - c_2 q_2$

c. Industry Structure and Exchange Rate Pass-Through

Relation [3.9] represents the basic channels that transmit the effect of exchange rate changes to prices. It expresses ERPT in the form of an elasticity as follows[19]:

---

[17] If both firms sell in the foreign market, $0 < \lambda < 1$.

[18] The stars are used to denote home currency amounts. $(c_1^* + Sc_1)q_1$ is the total costs where c_1^* (c_1) is the marginal cost of the exporting firm in its home (foreign) currency.

[19] Since $d\ln p_1 /ds < 0$, this derivative is multiplied by minus 1 to ensure that the elasticity is positive. Since $\gamma < 1$, the ERPT elasticity must be greater than zero, so that $0 < \eta < 1$. However, ERPT could also be negative in practice.

[3. 8] $\eta = -\dfrac{d \ln p_1}{d \ln S} = (1 - \gamma)(1 - \rho\lambda)$

with $\gamma = Sc_1 / (c_1^* + Sc_1)$ defined as the fraction of marginal costs due to foreign currency-based inputs. The home currency markup of the exporter's is given by[20]:

[3. 9] $m_1 = \dfrac{Sp_1 - (c_1^* + Sc_1)}{Sp_1} = 1 - \rho(1 - \lambda)$

Adjustment of this home currency markup reduces the ERPT[21].

[3. 10] $\dfrac{d \ln m_1}{d \ln S} = \dfrac{(1 - \gamma)\rho^2 \lambda(1 - \lambda)}{(1 - \rho(1 - \lambda))} > 0$

An expression for the exposure γ can be derived:

[3. 11] $Exposure = \delta = \dfrac{d \ln \pi_1^*}{d \ln S} = \underbrace{1}_{\substack{CONVERSION \\ EFFECT}} + \underbrace{(1 - \gamma)\rho(1 - \lambda)}_{\substack{MARKET_t \\ SHARE \\ EFFECT}} + \underbrace{\dfrac{(1 - \gamma)\lambda\rho^2(1 - \lambda)}{[1 - \rho(1 - \lambda)]}}_{\substack{PROFIT \\ MARGIN \\ EFFECT}}$

Solution of the Model Under Quantity Competition[22]

Cost ratio $r = \dfrac{Sc_1}{c_1^* + Sc_1}$

Equilibrium market share $\lambda = \dfrac{\alpha r^\rho}{1 + \alpha r^\rho}$ where $\alpha = \alpha/(1 - \alpha)$

Exporter's price in the foreign market $p_1 = \dfrac{c_1^* + sc_1}{s\rho(1 - \lambda)}$

Exporter's quantity sold in the foreign market $q_1 = \lambda y \dfrac{s\rho(1 - \lambda)}{c_1^* + sc_1}$

---

[20] The margin is the difference between sale price and average cost, whereas the profit margin is the home-currency price in the foreign market over its costs in percentage terms.

[21] The theoretical explanations of incomplete ERPT have emphasized the role of market structure and product differentiation. Major contributions include Dornbusch (1987), Krugman (1987, 1989), Baldwin (1988), Baldwin and Krugman (1989), Dixit (1989a, 1989b), Froot and Klemperer (1989).

[22] For the solutions under price competition, see Bodnar et al. (2002), p. 205.

Foreign import-competing firm price

$$p_2 = \frac{c_2}{\rho\lambda}$$

Import-competing firm quantity sold

$$q_2 = (1-\lambda)y\frac{\rho\lambda}{c_2}$$

Exporter's profit in home currency

$$\pi_1^* = sy\lambda[Sp_1 - (c_1^* + Sc_1)]/sp_1 = sy\lambda[1 - \rho(1-\lambda)]$$

Foreign Exchange Exposure Under Price Competition

$$\delta = \frac{d\ln\pi_1^*}{d\ln S} = 1 + \frac{(1-\lambda)(1-\gamma)\rho[1-\rho(1-\lambda)]}{(1-\rho)[1-\rho^2\lambda(1-\lambda)]}$$

APPENDIX D Cournot Model of Foreign Exchange Exposure[23]

D.1 Second-order and Stability Conditions

For a maximum, the second-order condition for firm 1 is $R_1^1 + v^1 R_2^1 < 0$ and for firm 2, $R_2^2 + v^2 R_1^2 < 0$, where R_j^i is the derivative of the *ith* firm's first-order condition with respect to the output firm j. For firm 1, for instance:

$$\frac{\partial \pi_1}{\partial x_1^2} = R_1^1 = s\left[2D_1^1 + q^1 D_{11}^1 + D_2^1 v^1 + q^1 D_2^1 v^1 + q^1 D_2^1 v_1^1\right] - C_{11}^1$$

$$\frac{\partial \pi_1}{\partial x_1 \partial x_2} = R_2^1 = s\left[D_2^1 + q^1 D_{12}^1 + q^1 D_{22}^1 v^1 + q^1 D_2^1 v_2^1\right]$$

Stability conditions imply that $R_1^1 < 0$, $R_2^2 < 0$, $R = R_1^1 R_2^2 - R_2^1 R_1^2 > 0$ [24].

D.2 Foreign Exchange Exposures in the General Duopoly Model

The effect of the euro depreciation on the profits of the two firms are given by[25]:

$$\frac{d\pi_1^\epsilon}{ds} = q^1 D^1(q^1, q^2) + \{s[D^1(q^1, q^2) + q^1 D_1^1 - C_1^1]\}\frac{dq_1}{ds} + sq^1 D_2^1 \frac{dq_2}{ds}$$

$$= q^1 D^1(q^1, q^2) + \frac{sq^1 D_2^1 M(R_2^2 v^1 + R_1^2)}{R}$$

$$\frac{d\pi_2^\$}{ds} = [D^2(q^1, q^2) + q^2 D_2^2 - C_2^2]\frac{dq^2}{ds} + q^2 D_1^2 \frac{dq^1}{ds}$$

$$= \frac{-q^2 D_1^2 M(R_2^2 + v^2 R_1^2)}{R} < 0$$

---

[23] See Marston (2001). This model of exposure is based on the duopoly model of Dixit (1986), pp. 108-115.
[24] See Dixit (1986).
[25] See Dixit (1986), p. 112.

The profit of the US local firm falls. The second order conditions ensure that $R_2^2 + v^2 R_1^2 < 0$ and the stability conditions ensure that $R > 0$. If the two goods are substitutes in demand $(D_1^2 < 0)$, $d\pi_2/ds < 0$. However, the effect of the depreciation on the profits of the German exporter is indeterminate. To establish the effect on the German firm's profits, it is necessary to be more specific about the industry structure. By specifying the conjectures appropriately, we can model other industry structures in the same formal framework. These include Cournot, Bertrand, and the case with consistent conjectures. For these extensions, it is convenient to rewrite exposures as:

$$\frac{d\pi_1^\epsilon}{ds} = q^1 D^1(q^1, q^2) + \frac{sq^1 D_2^1 MR_2^2 (v^1 - r_2)}{R}$$

$$\frac{d\pi_2^\$}{ds} = \frac{q^2 D_1^2 MR_2^2 (1 - v^2 r_2)}{R}$$

with $r_2 < 0$ if $R_1^2 < 0$.

APPENDIX E Cash-Flow-at-Risk (*CaR*) Methodology[26]

Step 1: Objective function and Risk Definition	*Senior management defines the objective function, for instance cash flows over the next reporting period. Risk is then defined in terms of missing targets in the firm's business plan.*
Step 2: CaR measurement and Stress Testing	*The firm measures its CaR, an estimate of how much could be lost over a period due to financial price risk.* *(1) CaR metric specification:* specification of time horizon and confidence level. *(2) Exposure mapping:* identification of how fluctuations in exchange rates affect cash flows. This can be done in the form of (a) *equations*: that express a financial result as a function of market rates and business variables. For example, the earnings for a foreign subsidiary will be a function of both the level of exchange rates during the analysis period and the quantity of goods sold, which could itself be a function of the level of exchange rates, (b) *models*: the relationships and sensitivities that characterize quantity risk, along with the exchange rate risk, form the basis of an econometric model of risk, which measures the cash flows sensitivity, or (c) *pro forma financial statements*. *(3) Scenario generation of exchange rates:* moving from exposure to risk requires an estimate of how much the exchange rate can potentially move. ■ Identification of the distribution of exchange rate by generating the possible values of the exchange rates at each horizon, for example by Monte Carlo. ■ Exchange rate forecasting at specified time horizon. *(4) Valuation:* ■ Strategic planning could forecast future cash flows and future exchange rates. However, since one often cannot obtain a measure of the volatility of cash flow analytically because one generally does not know the distribution of cash flow even though one knows the distribution of the exchange rate changes, *CaR* cannot be computed analytically, and simulation analysis, e.g., Monte Carlo, have to be performed. ■ Calculate the expected mean, volatility, and percentile of cash flows. *(5) Risk Computation:* calculate the exchange rate risk, in absolute term and relative to target. *(6) Stress Testing:* to complement CaR, the company should stress test the impact of extreme market scenarios.
Step 3: Hedging Decision	*The CaR measure is used for implementing an informed hedging decision.*

Source: adapted from RiskMetrics (1999).

---

[26] See RiskMetrics (1999), CorporateMetrics Technical Document, pp. 27-29, Stulz (2000), ch. 8.

APPENDIX F Key Foreign Exchange Relationships

Four economic relationships are relevant to the selection of macroeconomic variables in our regression analysis in chapter 5[27]. Figure C.1 summarizes graphically the above key foreign exchange relationships.

Figure F. 1 Foreign Exchange Relationships

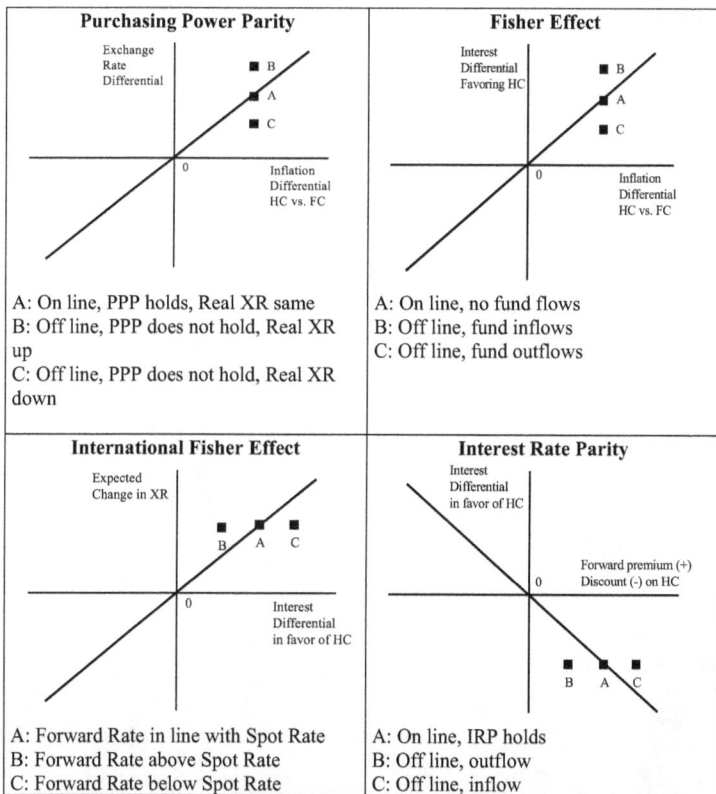

Purchasing Power Parity	Fisher Effect
Exchange Rate Differential ■ B / ■ A / ■ C 0 Inflation Differential HC vs. FC	Interest Differential Favoring HC ■ B / ■ A / ■ C 0 Inflation Differential HC vs. FC
A: On line, PPP holds, Real XR same B: Off line, PPP does not hold, Real XR up C: Off line, PPP does not hold, Real XR down	A: On line, no fund flows B: Off line, fund inflows C: Off line, fund outflows
International Fisher Effect	Interest Rate Parity
Expected Change in XR / ■ ■ B A ■ C 0 Interest Differential in favor of HC	Interest Differential in favor of HC Forward premium (+) Discount (-) on HC 0 ■ ■ ■ B A C
A: Forward Rate in line with Spot Rate B: Forward Rate above Spot Rate C: Forward Rate below Spot Rate	A: On line, IRP holds B: Off line, outflow C: Off line, inflow

Notation: HC – Home Currency, FC – Foreign Currency, XR – Exchange Rate
Source: Demacopoulos (1989), p. 274, adapted from Shapiro, A., Multinational Financial Management, Allyn and Biloon, Boston, 1986.

---

[27] Definitions from Shapiro (1999), pp. 783-797.

APPENDIX G Valuation

**Unlevered cash flows from cash
flow statement**[28]
Unlevered cash flows =

	operating cash inflow
+	investing cash inflow (which is usually negative)
+	debt interest
−	debt interest tax subsidy

**Unlevered cash flows from
EBIT**[29]
Unlevered cash flows =

	EBIT
+	Depreciation and amortization
-	Change in working capital
-	Capital expenditures
+	Sales of capital assets
-	Realized capital gains
+	Realized capital losses
-	EBIT × tax rates

**Economic Value and Equity
Value**
Value of the firm =

	present value of expected cash flows during forecast period
+	residual value
+	excess liquidity.
	Discount Free cash flow and residual value with WACC
+	value of assets that were not included in the cash-flow valuation: excess liquidity and oher non-operating assets
=	Economic value
-	value of loans, minority interests, preference stock and other non-equity financing
=	Equity value

Net Cash Flow to Shareholders
Free Cash Flow =

	Sales Revenues
-	Operating costs
=	Earnings before interest, taxes, and depreciation (EBITDA)
-	Depreciation
=	Earnings before interest and taxes (EBIT)
-	Cash taxes on EBIT
=	Net operating profit less adjusted taxes (NOPLAT)
+/-	Cash in-/outflows from (investments in) material and immaterial assets
+	Depreciation
-	Change in working capital
=	Free cash flow (FCF)

[28] See Grinblatt and Titman (2002), p. 304.
[29] See Grinblatt and Titman (2002), p. 305.

APPENDIX H   Stock Returns Data

Table H.1 DAX 30 Firms per Sector of Activity

DAX 30	DAX 100 Sector Indices
Adidas-Salomon	Retail & Consumer
Allianz	Insurance
BASF	Chemicals & Pharma
Bayer	Chemicals & Pharma
BMW (EUR1)	Automobile & Transportation
Commerzbank	Banks & Financial Services
DaimlerChrysler	Automobile & Transportation
Degussa	Chemicals & Pharma
Deutsche Bank	Banks & Financial Services
Deutsche Post	Automobile & Transportation
Deutsche Telekom	Utilities & Telecommunication
E.ON	Utilities & Telecommunication
Epcos	Software & Technology
Fres. Medical Care	Chemicals & Pharma
Henkel Vz.	Retail & Consumer
HypoVereinsbank	Banks & Financial Services
Inineon Techn.	Software & Technology
Linde	Machinery & Industrials
Lufthansa	Automobile & Transportation
MAN	Machinery & Industrials
MLP	Banks & Financial Services
Metro	Retail & Consumer
Muenchener Rueckv.	Insurance
RWE	Utilities & Telecommunication
SAP	Software & Technology
Schering	Chemicals & Pharma
Siemens	Software & Technology
ThyssenKrupp	Machinery & Industrials
TUI	Automobile & Transportation
Volkswagen	Automobile & Transportation

Sources: Börsen-Zeitung Nr. 179, 17. September 2002. Guidelines to Deutsche Börse's Equity Indices, August 2001.

Table H.2 MDAX Firms per Sector of Activity

MDAX	DAX 100 Industry Indices
Agiv Real Estate	Machinery & Industrials
Altana	Chemicals & Pharma
AMB	Insurance
AVA (50)	Retail & Consumer
AWD Holding	Banks & Financial Services
Babcock Holding	Machinery & Industrials
Beate Uhse (EUR1)	Retail & Consumer
Beiersdorf	Chemicals & Pharma
Beru	Automobile & Transportation
BHW Holding	Banks & Financial Services
Bilfinger Berger	Construction
Boss, Hugo	Retail & Consumer
Buderus	Machinery & Industrials
CargoLifter	Automobile & Transportation
Celanese	Chemicals & Pharma
Continental	Automobile & Transportation
Deutsche Boerse	Banks & Financial Services
DIS	Machinery & Industrials
Douglas Holding	Retail & Consumer
Draegerwerk Vz.	Retail & Consumer
Duerr	Machinery & Industrials
Dyckerhoff Vz.	Construction
Escada Vz.	Retail & Consumer
Fielmann (5)	Retail & Consumer
Fraport	Automobile & Transportation
Fresenius Vz.	Chemicals & Pharma
Gehe	Chemicals & Pharma
Gerry Weber Int.	Retail & Consumer
GFK	Machinery & Industrials
Gildemeister	Machinery & Industrials
Gold-Zack	Banks & Financial Services
Hannover Rueck.	Insurance
Heidelb. Druckm.	Machinery & Industrials
HeidelbergCement	Construction
Hochtief	Construction
IKB	Banks & Financial Services
Indus Hold.	Machinery & Industrials
IVG Holding	Banks & Financial Services
IWKA	Machinery & Industrials
Jenoptik	Software & Technology

Jungheinrich Vz.	Machinery & Industrials
K+S	Machinery & Industrials
Karstadt Quelle	Retail & Consumer
Koenig & Bauer	Machinery & Industrials
Kolben. Pierburg	Automobile & Transportation
Krones Vz.	Machinery & Industrials
Leoni	Software & Technology
Loewe	Software & Technology
Merck	Chemicals & Pharma
mg technologies	Machinery & Industrials
Norddt. Affinerie	Machinery & Industrials (Basic Ressources)
Phoenix	Automobile &
ProSiebenSat.1 Vz.	Retail & Consumer
Puma	Retail & Consumer
Rheinmetall Vz.	Machinery & Industrials
Rhoen-Klinikum Vz.	Chemicals & Pharma
Salzgitter	Machinery & Industrials
Schwartz Pharma	Chemicals & Pharma
SGL Carbon	Machinery & Industrials
Sixt	Automobile & Transportation
Software	Software & Technology
Stada-Arzneimittel	Chemicals & Pharma (Pharmaceutical & Healthcare)
Stinnes	Automobile & Transportation
Suedzuker	Retail & Consumer
Techem	Machinery & Industrials
Vossloh	Software & Technology
WCM Bet. Grund.	Banks & Financial Services
Wedeco W.T.	Chemicals & Pharma
Wella Vz.	Chemicals & Pharma
Zapf Creation	Retail & Consumer

Sources: Börsen-Zeitung Nr. 179, 17. September 2002. Guidelines to Deutsche Börse's Equity Indices, August 2001.

APPENDIX I DAX 100 Firms per Sector of Activity[30]

DAX 100 Sectors	Number of DAX 30	Number of MDAX Firms	Number (and %) of DAX 100 Firms
Automobile & Transportation	6	8	14
Banks & Financial Services	4	7	11
Chemicals & Pharma	5	11	16
Construction	0	4	4
Insurance	2	2	4
Machinery & Industrials	4	20	24
Retail & Consumer	3	13	16
Software & Technology	3	5	8
Utilities & Telecommunication	3	0	3

Source: Börsen-Zeitung Nr. 179, 17. September 2002.

[30] As of 17. September 2002 in the Börsen-Zeitung Nr. 179.

APPENDIX J Estimation Results – DAX Firms' Exposures to DM/US$

Table 1 Exposures to DM/US$: DAX30 Corporations – Dummy Variables Regression with market portfolio and DM/US$ as independent variables

DM or Euro appreciation relative to UD$	DM or Euro depreciation relative to UD$			
	$\gamma_i^d > 0$ (A)	$\gamma_i^d = 0$ (B)	$\gamma_i^d < 0$ (C)	Row total (4)
$\gamma_i^a > 0$	1973:1-1998:12: 0% sub-period I: 0% sub-period II: 0% sub-period III: 0% sub-period IV: 0% sub-period V: 0% (D)	1973:1-1998:12: 33.3% sub-period I: 11.1% sub-period II: 11.1% sub-period III: 16.7% sub-period IV: 16.7% sub-period V: 11.1% (E)	1973:1-1998:12: 0% sub-period I: 0% sub-period II: 0% sub-period III: 5.6% sub-period IV: 0% sub-period V: 5.6% (F)	1973:1-1998:12: 33.3% sub-period I: 11.1% sub-period II: 11.1% sub-period III: 22.3% sub-period IV: 16.7% sub-period V: 16.7% (5)
$\gamma_i^a = 0$	1973:1-1998:12: 0% sub-period I: 16.7% sub-period II: 0% sub-period III: 5.6% sub-period IV: 16.7% sub-period V: 5.6% (G)	1973:1-1998:12: 55.6% sub-period I: 72.2% sub-period II: 77.8% sub-period III: 50.1% sub-period IV: 55.6% sub-period V: 50.1% (H)	1973:1-1998:12: 0% sub-period I: 0% sub-period II: 0% sub-period III: 11.1% sub-period IV: 0% sub-period V: 11.1% (I)	1973:1-1998:12: 67.6% sub-period I: 88.9% sub-period II: 77.8% sub-period III: 66.8% sub-period IV: 72.3% sub-period V: 66.8% (6)
$\gamma_i^a < 0$	1973:1-1998:12: 0% sub-period I: 16.7% sub-period II: 0% sub-period III: 11.2% sub-period IV: 16.7% sub-period V: 5.6% (1)	1973:1-1998:12: 11.1% sub-period I: 0% sub-period II: 11.1% sub-period III: 11.1% sub-period IV: 11.1% sub-period V: 16.7% (2)	1973:1-1998:12: 0% sub-period I: 0% sub-period II: 0% sub-period III: 16.7% sub-period IV: 0% sub-period V: 16.7% (3)	
Column total	1973:1-1998:12: 0% sub-period I: 16.7% sub-period II: 0% sub-period III: 11.2% sub-period IV: 16.7% sub-period V: 5.6% (1)	1973:1-1998:12: 100% sub-period I: 83.3% sub-period II: 100% sub-period III: 77.9% sub-period IV: 83.4% sub-period V: 77.9% (2)	1973:1-1998:12: 0% sub-period I: 0% sub-period II: 0% sub-period III: 16.7% sub-period IV: 0% sub-period V: 16.7% (3)	

Table 2 Exposures to DM/US$: MDAX Corporations – Dummy Variables Regression with market portfolio and DM/US$ as independent variables

DM or Euro appreciation relative to UD$	DM or Euro depreciation relative to UD$			
	$\gamma_i^d > 0$ (A)	$\gamma_i^d = 0$ (B)	$\gamma_i^d < 0$ (C)	(4)
$\gamma_i^a > 0$	1973:1-1998:12: 0% sub-period I : 0% sub-period II : 0%: sub-period III : 0% sub-period IV :2.1% sub-period V : 0% (D)	1973:1-1998:12: 5% sub-period I : 5% sub-period II: 14.3% sub-period III : 4.3% sub-period IV : 17.0% sub-period V : 8.8% (E)	1973:1-1998:12: 0% sub-period I : 5% sub-period II: 4.8% sub-period III : 0% sub-period IV : 8.5% sub-period V : 0% (F)	1973:1-1998:12: 5.0% sub-period I : 10.0% sub-period II: 19.1% sub-period III : 4.3% sub-period IV : 31.9% sub-period V : 8.8% (5)
$\gamma_i^a = 0$	1973:1-1998:12: 5% sub-period I : 0% sub-period II: 0% sub-period III : 17.4% sub-period IV : 2.1% sub-period V : 11.8% (G)	1973:1-1998:12: 85% sub-period I : 90% sub-period II: 61.9% sub-period III : 60.9% sub-period IV : 66.0% sub-period V : 72.1% (H)	1973:1-1998:12: 0% sub-period I : 0% sub-period II: 9.5% sub-period III : 0% sub-period IV : 2.1% sub-period V : 1.5% (I)	1973:1-1998:12: 90.0% sub-period I : 90% sub-period II: 71.4% sub-period III : 78.3% sub-period IV : 70.2% sub-period V : 85.4% (6)
$\gamma_i^a < 0$	1973:1-1998:12: 0% sub-period I : 0% sub-period II: 0% sub-period III : 4.3% sub-period IV : 0% sub-period V : 1.5% (1)	1973:1-1998:12: 95.0% sub-period I : 95.0% sub-period II: 85.7% sub-period III : 73.9% sub-period IV : 85.1% sub-period V : 85.3% (2)	1973:1-1998:12: 0% sub-period I : 5.0% sub-period II: 14.3% sub-period III : 4.3% sub-period IV : 10.6% sub-period V : 1.5% (3)	1973:1-1998:12: 5.0% sub-period I : 0% sub-period II: 9.5% sub-period III : 17.3% sub-period IV : 2.1% sub-period V : 5.9%

Table 3 Exposures to DM/US$: DAX 100 Corporations – Dummy Variables Regression with market portfolio and DM/US$ as independent variables

DM or Euro appreciation relative to UD$	DM or Euro depreciation relative to UD$			
	$\gamma_i^d > 0$	$\gamma_i^d = 0$	$\gamma_i^d < 0$	
	(A)	(B)	(C)	(4)
$\gamma_i^a > 0$	1973:1-1998:12: 0% sub-period I : 0% sub-period II: 0% sub-period III : 0% sub-period IV : 1.4% sub-period V : 0% (D)	1973:1-1998:12: 18.4% sub-period I : 7.9% sub-period II: 8.2% sub-period III : 9.7% sub-period IV : 16.9% sub-period V : 9.5% (E)	1973:1-1998:12: 0% sub-period I : 2.6% sub-period II: 2.6% sub-period III : 2.5% sub-period IV : 5.6% sub-period V : 1.7% (F)	1973:1-1998:12: 18.4% sub-period I : 10.5% sub-period II: 10.8% sub-period III : 12.2% sub-period IV : 23.9% sub-period V : 11.2% (5)
$\gamma_i^a = 0$	1973:1-1998:12: 2.6% sub-period I : 7.9% sub-period II: 0% sub-period III : 12.2% sub-period IV : 7.0% sub-period V : 9.9% (G)	1973:1-1998:12: 71.1% sub-period I : 81.6% sub-period II: 69.2% sub-period III : 56.2% sub-period IV : 62.5% sub-period V : 65.5% (H)	1973:1-1998:12: 0% sub-period I : 0% sub-period II: 5.1% sub-period III : 4.9% sub-period IV : 1.4% sub-period V : 4.4% (I)	1973:1-1998:12: 73.7% sub-period I : 89.5% sub-period II: 74.3% sub-period III : 73.3% sub-period IV : 70.9% sub-period V : 79.8% (6)
$\gamma_i^a < 0$	1973:1-1998:12: 0% sub-period I : 0% sub-period II: 0% sub-period III : 4.9% sub-period IV : 0% sub-period V : 8.3% (1)	1973:1-1998:12: 7.9% sub-period I : 0% sub-period II: 10.2% sub-period III : 9.8% sub-period IV : 5.1% sub-period V : 8.1% (2)	1973:1-1998:12: 0% sub-period I : 0% sub-period II: 0% sub-period III : 2.4% sub-period IV : 0% sub-period V : 0% (3)	1973:1-1998:12: 7.9% sub-period I : 0% sub-period II: 10.2% sub-period III : 17.1% sub-period IV : 5.1% sub-period V : 16.4%
	1973:1-1998:12: 2.6% sub-period I : 7.9% sub-period II: 0% sub-period III : 17.1% sub-period IV : 8.4% sub-period V : 18.2%	1973:1-1998:12: 97.4% sub-period I : 89.5% sub-period II: 87.6% sub-period III : 75.7% sub-period IV : 84.5% sub-period V : 83.1%	1973:1-1998:12: 0% sub-period I : 2.6% sub-period II: 7.7% sub-period III : 9.8% sub-period IV : 7.0% sub-period V : 6.1%	

APPENDIX K Estimation Results – DAX Firms' Macroeconomic Exposures

Exposures ot macro risk factors – independent variables : ER1, ER2, IR1, IR2, IR3, IR4, IR5, IR6, CPI1, CPI2, CPI3 DAX 30 firms

Table 4 Exposures to macro risk factors: DAX 30 Corporations – Dummy Variables Regression as independent variables (ER1)

DM or Euro appreciation relative to US$	DM or Euro depreciation relative to UD$			
	$\gamma_i^d > 0$	$\gamma_i^d = 0$	$\gamma_i^d < 0$	
$\gamma_i^a > 0$	1985:1-1998:12: 11.8% sub-period III : 0% sub-period IV : 16.7%% sub-period V : 0% (A)	1985:1-1998:12: 82.4% sub-period III : 38.9% sub-period IV : 62.5% sub-period V : 48.3% (B)	1985:1-1998:12: 0% sub-period III : 44.4% sub-period IV : 0% sub-period V : 20.7% (C)	1985:1-1998:12: 94.4% sub-period III : 83.3% sub-period IV : 79.2% sub-period V : 69.0% (4)
$\gamma_i^a = 0$	1985:1-1998:12: 0% sub-period III : 0% sub-period IV : 8.3% sub-period V : 0% (D)	1985:1-1998:12: 5.9% sub-period III : 11.1% sub-period IV : 12.5% sub-period V : 27.6% (E)	1985:1-1998:12: 0% sub-period III : 5.6% sub-period IV : 0% sub-period V : 0% (F)	1985:1-1998:12: 5.9% sub-period III : 16.7% sub-period IV : 20.85 sub-period V : 27.6% (5)
$\gamma_i^a < 0$	1985:1-1998:12: 0% sub-period III : 0% sub-period IV : 0% sub-period V : 3.4%% (G)	1985:1-1998:12: 0% sub-period III : 0% sub-period IV : 0% sub-period V : 0% (H)	1985:1-1998:12: 0% sub-period III : 0% sub-period IV : 0% sub-period V : 20.7% (I)	1985:1-1998:12: 0% sub-period III : 0% sub-period IV : 0% sub-period V : 3.4% (6)
	1985:1-1998:12: 11.8% sub-period III : 0% sub-period IV : 25.0% sub-period V : 3.4% (1)	1985:1-1998:12: 88.3% sub-period III : 50.0% sub-period IV : 75.0% sub-period V : 75.9% (2)	1985:1-1998:12: 0% sub-period III : 0% sub-period IV : 0% sub-period V : 20.7% (3)	

Table 5 Exposures to macro risk factors: DAX 30 Corporations – Dummy Variables Regression as independent variables (ER2)

DM appreciations relative to Yen	DM depreciations relative to Yen			
	$\gamma_i^d > 0$	$\gamma_i^d = 0$	$\gamma_i^d < 0$	
$\gamma_i^a > 0$	1985:1-1998:12: 0% sub-period III : 0% sub-period IV : 0% sub-period V : 0% (A)	1985:1-1998:12: 0% sub-period III : 5.3% sub-period IV : 4.2% sub-period V : 6.9% (B)	1985:1-1998:12: 0% sub-period III : 5.3% sub-period IV : 0% sub-period V : 0% (C)	1985:1-1998:12: 0% sub-period III : 10.6% sub-period IV : 4.2% sub-period V : 6.9% (4)
$\gamma_i^a = 0$	1985:1-1998:12: 11.1% sub-period III : 36.8% sub-period IV : 8.3% sub-period V : 27.6% (D)	1985:1-1998:12: 83.3% sub-period III : 5.3% sub-period IV : 75% sub-period V : 41.4% (E)	1985:1-1998:12: 0% sub-period III : 0% sub-period IV : 8.4% sub-period V : 0% (F)	1985:1-1998:12: 94.4% sub-period III : 42.1% sub-period IV : 91.7% sub-period V : 69% (5)
$\gamma_i^a < 0$	1985:1-1998:12: 5.6% sub-period III : 47.4% sub-period IV : 0% sub-period V : 17.2% (G)	1985:1-1998:12: 0% sub-period III : 0% sub-period IV : 4.2% sub-period V : 6.9% (H)	1985:1-1998:12: 0% sub-period III : 0% sub-period IV : 8.4% sub-period V : 0% (I)	1985:1-1998:12: 5.6% sub-period III : 47.4% sub-period IV : 4.2% sub-period V : 24.1% (6)
	1985:1-1998:12: 16.7% sub-period III : 84.2% sub-period IV : 8.3% sub-period V : 44.8% (1)	1985:1-1998:12: 83.3% sub-period III : 10.6% sub-period IV : 83.4% sub-period V : 55.2% (2)	1985:1-1998:12: 0% sub-period III : 5.3% sub-period IV : 8.4% sub-period V : 0% (3)	

Table 6 Exposures to macro risk factors: DAX 30 Corporations – Dummy Variables Regression as independent variables (IR1)

Decrease in German short term interest rate	Increase in German short term interest rate		
	$\gamma_i^d > 0$ (A)	$\gamma_i^d = 0$ (B)	$\gamma_i^d < 0$ (C)
$\gamma_i^a > 0$	1985:1-1998:12: 0% sub-period III : 0% sub-period IV : 0% sub-period V : 0% (D)	1985:1-1998:12: 16.7% sub-period III : 10.5% sub-period IV : 8.3% sub-period V : 10.3% (E)	1985:1-1998:12: 16.7% sub-period III : 21.0% sub-period IV : 8.3% sub-period V : 17.2% (F)
$\gamma_i^a = 0$	1985:1-1998:12: 0% sub-period III : 5.3% sub-period IV : 4.2% sub-period V : 6.9% (G)	1985:1-1998:12: 77.8% sub-period III : 36.8% sub-period IV : 79.2% sub-period V : 51.7% (H)	1985:1-1998:12: 90.3% sub-period III : 63.2% sub-period IV : 83.4% sub-period V : 72.3% (I)
$\gamma_i^a < 0$	1985:1-1998:12: 0% sub-period III : 5.3% sub-period IV : 4.2% sub-period V : 3.4%	1985:1-1998:12: 94.5% sub-period III : 57.8% sub-period IV : 91.7% sub-period V : 65.4%	1985:1-1998:12: 0% sub-period III : 15.8% sub-period IV : 8.4% sub-period V : 10.2%

Table 7 Exposures to macro risk factors: DAX 30 Corporations – Dummy Variables Regression as independent variables (IR2)

Decrease in German long term interest rate	Increase in German long term interest rate		
	$\gamma_i^d > 0$	$\gamma_i^d = 0$	$\gamma_i^d < 0$
$\gamma_i^a > 0$	(A) 1985:1-1998:12: 0% sub-period III : 0% sub-period IV : 0% sub-period V : 0%	(B) 1985:1-1998:12: 0% sub-period III : 0% sub-period IV : 4.2% sub-period V : 3.4%	(C) 1985:1-1998:12: 0% sub-period III : 0% sub-period IV : 8.4% sub-period V : 3.4%
$\gamma_i^a = 0$	(D) 1985:1-1998:12: 22.2% sub-period III : 5.3% sub-period IV : 0% sub-period V : 10.3%	(E) 1985:1-1998:12: 22.2% sub-period III : 21.1% sub-period IV : 25% sub-period V : 24.1%	(F) 1985:1-1998:12: 72.2% sub-period III : 26.3% sub-period IV : 66.7% sub-period V : 6.9%
$\gamma_i^a < 0$	(G) 1985:1-1998:12: 0% sub-period III : 0% sub-period IV : 0% sub-period V : 0%	(H) 1985:1-1998:12: 0% sub-period III : 21.1% sub-period IV : 0% sub-period V : 41.4%	(I) 1985:1-1998:12: 5.6% sub-period III : 26.3% sub-period IV : 0% sub-period V : 13.8%
	1985:1-1998:12: 0% sub-period III : 5.3% sub-period IV : 0% sub-period V : 10.3%	1985:1-1998:12: 22.2% sub-period III : 42.2% sub-period IV : 29.2% sub-period V : 68.9%	1985:1-1998:12: 77.8% sub-period III : 52.6% sub-period IV : 70.9% sub-period V : 20.7%

Table 8 Exposures to macro risk factors: DAX 30 Corporations – Dummy Variables Regression as independent variables (IR3)

Decrease in US short term interest rate	Increase in US short term interest rate		
	$\gamma_i^d > 0$ **(A)**	$\gamma_i^d = 0$ **(B)**	$\gamma_i^d < 0$ **(C)**
$\gamma_i^a > 0$	1985:1-1998:12: 0% sub-period III : 0% sub-period IV : 0% sub-period V : 0% **(D)**	1985:1-1998:12: 16.7% sub-period III : 0% sub-period IV : 12.5% sub-period V : 6.9% **(E)**	1985:1-1998:12: 16.7% sub-period III : 0% sub-period IV : 12.5% sub-period V : 24.1% **(F)**
$\gamma_i^a = 0$	1985:1-1998:12: 0% sub-period III : 5.3% sub-period IV : 0% sub-period V : 3.4% **(G)**	1985:1-1998:12: 66.7% sub-period III : 63.2% sub-period IV : 83.3% sub-period V : 48.3% **(H)**	1985:1-1998:12: 83.4% sub-period III : 100% sub-period IV : 87.5% sub-period V : 58.6% **(I)**
$\gamma_i^a < 0$	1985:1-1998:12: 0% sub-period III : 0% sub-period IV : 0% sub-period V : 6.9%	1985:1-1998:12: 0% sub-period III : 0% sub-period IV : 0% sub-period V : 10.3%	1985:1-1998:12: 16.7% sub-period III : 0% sub-period IV : 0% sub-period V : 17.2%

Table 9 Exposures to macro risk factors: DAX 30 Corporations – Dummy Variables Regression as independent variables (IR4)

Decrease in US long term interest rate	Increase in US long term interest rate		
	$\gamma_i^d > 0$	$\gamma_i^d = 0$	$\gamma_i^d < 0$
$\gamma_i^a > 0$	(A) 1985:1-1998:12: 0% sub-period III : 0% sub-period IV : 4.2% sub-period V : 0%	(B) 1985:1-1998:12: 27.8% sub-period III : 0% sub-period IV : 8.3% sub-period V : 0%	(C) 1985:1-1998:12: 27.8% sub-period III : 0% sub-period IV : 12.5% sub-period V : 0%
$\gamma_i^a = 0$	(D) 1985:1-1998:12: 22.2% sub-period III : 26.3% sub-period IV : 0% sub-period V : 24.1%	(E) 1985:1-1998:12: 38.9% sub-period III : 73.7% sub-period IV : 75.0% sub-period V : 62.1%	(F) 1985:1-1998:12: 61.1% sub-period III : 100% sub-period IV : 79.2% sub-period V : 100%
$\gamma_i^a < 0$	(G) 1985:1-1998:12: 0% sub-period III : 0% sub-period IV : 0% sub-period V : 0%	(H) 1985:1-1998:12: 11.1% sub-period III : 0% sub-period IV : 0% sub-period V : 0%	(I) 1985:1-1998:12: 11.1% sub-period III : 0% sub-period IV : 4.2% sub-period V : 13.8%

Table 10 Exposures to macro risk factors: DAX 30 Corporations – Dummy Variables Regression as independent variables (IR5)

Decrease in Japanese short term interest rate	Increase in Japanese short term interest rate		
	$\gamma_i^a > 0$	$\gamma_i^a = 0$	$\gamma_i^a < 0$
$\gamma_i^a > 0$	(A) 1985:1-1998:12: 0% sub-period III : 0% sub-period IV : 0% sub-period V : 0%	(B) 1985:1-1998:12: 0% sub-period III : 42.1% sub-period IV : 8.3% sub-period V : 24.1%	(C) 1985:1-1998:12: 0% sub-period III : 73.3% sub-period IV : 8.3% sub-period V : 24.1%
$\gamma_i^a = 0$	(D) 1985:1-1998:12: 11.1% sub-period III : 0% sub-period IV : 0% sub-period V : 0%	(E) 1985:1-1998:12: 77.8% sub-period III : 21.1% sub-period IV : 75% sub-period V : 65.5%	(F) 1985:1-1998:12: 88.9% sub-period III : 21.1% sub-period IV : 75% sub-period V : 65.5%
$\gamma_i^a < 0$	(G) 1985:1-1998:12: 0% sub-period III : 0% sub-period IV : 4.2% sub-period V : 0%	(H) 1985:1-1998:12: 11.1% sub-period III : 5.3% sub-period IV : 12.5% sub-period V : 10.3%	(I) 1985:1-1998:12: 11.1% sub-period III : 5.3% sub-period IV : 16.7% sub-period V : 10.3%

Table 11 Exposures to macro risk factors: DAX 30 Corporations – Dummy Variables Regression as independent variables (IR6)

Decrease in Japanese long term interest rate	Increase in Japanese long term interest rate		
	$\gamma_i^d > 0$	$\gamma_i^d = 0$	$\gamma_i^d < 0$
	(A)	(B)	(C)
$\gamma_i^a > 0$	1985:1-1998:12: 0% sub-period III : 31.2% sub-period IV : 0% sub-period V : 0%	1985:1-1998:12: 5.6% sub-period III : 10.5% sub-period IV : 8.3% sub-period V : 13.8%	1985:1-1998:12: 5.6% sub-period III : 41.7% sub-period IV : 8.3% sub-period V : 13.8%
	(D)	(E)	(F)
$\gamma_i^a = 0$	1985:1-1998:12: 38.9% sub-period III : 36.8% sub-period IV : 0% sub-period V : 0%	1985:1-1998:12: 50.0% sub-period III : 5.3% sub-period IV : 91.7% sub-period V : 79.3%	1985:1-1998:12: 94.5% sub-period III : 18.6% sub-period IV : 91.7% sub-period V : 79.3%
	(G)	(H)	(I)
$\gamma_i^a < 0$	1985:1-1998:12: 0% sub-period III : 10.5% sub-period IV : 0% sub-period V : 0%	1985:1-1998:12: 0% sub-period III : 0% sub-period IV : 0% sub-period V : 6.9%	1985:1-1998:12: 0% sub-period III : 10.5% sub-period IV : 0% sub-period V : 6.9%
	1985:1-1998:12: 38.9% sub-period III : 78.5% sub-period IV : 0% sub-period V : 0%	1985:1-1998:12: 55.6% sub-period III : 15.8% sub-period IV : 100% sub-period V : 100%	1985:1-1998:12: 5.6% sub-period III : 5.3% sub-period IV : 0% sub-period V : 0%

Table 12 Exposures to macro risk factors: DAX 30 Corporations – Dummy Variables Regression as independent variables (CPI1)

US Deflation	US Inflation		
	$\gamma_i^a > 0$ (A)	$\gamma_i^a = 0$ (B)	$\gamma_i^a < 0$ (C)
$\gamma_i^a > 0$	1985:1-1998:12: 0% sub-period III : 10.5% sub-period IV : 0% sub-period V : 3.4% (D)	1985:1-1998:12: 11.1% sub-period III : 5.3% sub-period IV : 0% sub-period V : 20.7% (E)	1985:1-1998:12: 11.1% sub-period III : 15.8% sub-period IV : 0% sub-period V : 24.1%
$\gamma_i^a = 0$	1985:1-1998:12: 0% sub-period III : 36.8% sub-period IV : 41.2% sub-period V : 24.1% (G)	1985:1-1998:12: 38.9% sub-period III : 26.3% sub-period IV : 42.1% sub-period V : 37.9% (H)	1985:1-1998:12: 66.7% sub-period III : 63.1% sub-period IV : 95.8% sub-period V : 65.4%
$\gamma_i^a < 0$	1985:1-1998:12: 0% sub-period III : 52.6% sub-period IV : 41.2% sub-period V : 30.9%	1985:1-1998:12: 72.2% sub-period III : 42.1% sub-period IV : 42.1% sub-period V : 65.5%	1985:1-1998:12: 22.2% sub-period III : 21.1% sub-period IV : 4.2% sub-period V : 10.3%

Additional labeled cells shown in the table: (F) 1985:1-1998:12: 0% / sub-period III : 0% / sub-period IV : 0% / sub-period V : 0%; (I) 1985:1-1998:12: 27.8% / sub-period III : 0% / sub-period IV : 12.5% / sub-period V : 3.4%

Table 13 Exposures to macro risk factors: DAX 30 Corporations – Dummy Variables Regression as independent variables (CPI2)

Japanese Deflation	Japanese Inflation		
	$\gamma_i^a > 0$ (A)	$\gamma_i^a = 0$ (B)	$\gamma_i^a < 0$ (C)
$\gamma_i^a > 0$	1985:1-1998:12: 0%; sub-period III: 0%; sub-period IV: 0%; sub-period V: 0% (D)	1985:1-1998:12: 11.1%; sub-period III: 0%; sub-period IV: 4.2%; sub-period V: 10.3% (E)	1985:1-1998:12: 11.1%; sub-period III: 15.8%; sub-period IV: 8.9%; sub-period V: 17.2% (F)
$\gamma_i^a = 0$	1985:1-1998:12: 5.6%; sub-period III: 0%; sub-period IV: 8.3%; sub-period V: 34.5% (G)	1985:1-1998:12: 83.3%; sub-period III: 47.4%; sub-period IV: 75.0%; sub-period V: 31.0% (H)	1985:1-1998:12: 88.9%; sub-period III: 57.9%; sub-period IV: 91.6%; sub-period V: 68.9% (I)
$\gamma_i^a < 0$	1985:1-1998:12: 0%; sub-period III: 15.8%; sub-period IV: 0%; sub-period V: 3.4%	1985:1-1998:12: 0%; sub-period III: 10.5%; sub-period IV: 0%; sub-period V: 3.4%	1985:1-1998:12: 0%; sub-period III: 26.3%; sub-period IV: 0%; sub-period V: 10.2%
	1985:1-1998:12: 5.6%; sub-period III: 15.8%; sub-period IV: 8.3%; sub-period V: 37.9%	1985:1-1998:12: 94.4%; sub-period III: 57.9%; sub-period IV: 79.2%; sub-period V: 44.7%	1985:1-1998:12: 0%; sub-period III: 26.3%; sub-period IV: 13%; sub-period V: 13.7%

Table 14 Exposures to macro risk factors: DAX 30 Corporations – Dummy Variables Regression as independent variables (CPI3)

German Deflation	German Inflation $\gamma_i^a > 0$	German Inflation $\gamma_i^a = 0$	German Inflation $\gamma_i^a < 0$
$\gamma_i^a > 0$	(A) 1985:1-1998:12: 0% sub-period III : 5.3% sub-period IV : 0% sub-period V : 0%	(B) 1985:1-1998:12: 16.7% sub-period III : 5.3% sub-period IV : 8.3% sub-period V : 6.9%	(C) 1985:1-1998:12: 16.7% sub-period III : 10.6% sub-period IV : 8.3% sub-period V : 6.9%
$\gamma_i^a = 0$	(D) 1985:1-1998:12: 5.6% sub-period III : 5.3% sub-period IV : 8.3% sub-period V : 6.9%	(E) 1985:1-1998:12: 66.7% sub-period III : 26.3% sub-period IV : 62.5% sub-period V : 44.8%	(F) 1985:1-1998:12: 77.9% sub-period III : 57.9% sub-period IV : 70.8% sub-period V : 65.5%
$\gamma_i^a < 0$	(G) 1985:1-1998:12: 0% sub-period III : 0% sub-period IV : 0% sub-period V : 6.9%	(H) 1985:1-1998:12: 5.6% sub-period III : 10.5% sub-period IV : 20.8% sub-period V : 13.8%	(I) 1985:1-1998:12: 5.6% sub-period III : 21.1% sub-period IV : 0% sub-period V : 6.9%
	1985:1-1998:12: 5.6% sub-period III : 10.6% sub-period IV : 8.3% sub-period V : 13.8%	1985:1-1998:12: 89% sub-period III : 42.1% sub-period IV : 91.6% sub-period V : 65.5%	1985:1-1998:12: 5.6% sub-period III : 47.4% sub-period IV : 0% sub-period V : 20.7%

Exposures ot macro risk factors – independent variables : ER1, ER2, IR1, IR2, IR3, IR4, IR5, IR6, CPI1, CPI2, CPI3 MDAX firms

Table 15 Exposures to macro risk factors: MDAX Corporations – Dummy Variables Regression as independent variables (ER1)

DM or Euro appreciation relative to UDS	DM or Euro depreciation relative to UDS			
	$\gamma_i^d > 0$	$\gamma_i^d = 0$	$\gamma_i^d < 0$	(4)
	(A)	(B)	(C)	
$\gamma_i^a > 0$	1985:1-1998:12: 4.3% sub-period III : 0% sub-period IV : 4.1% sub-period V: 0% (D)	1985:1-1998:12: 69.6% sub-period III : 8.7% sub-period IV : 63.3% sub-period V : 30.4% (E)	1985:1-1998:12: 0% sub-period III : 13.0% sub-period IV : 2.0% sub-period V : 14.5% (F)	1985:1-1998:12: 73.9% sub-period III : 21.7% sub-period IV : 69.4% sub-period V : 44.9% (5)
$\gamma_i^a = 0$	1985:1-1998:12: 0% sub-period III : 21.7% sub-period IV : 4.1% sub-period V : 10.1% (G)	1985:1-1998:12: 21.8% sub-period III : 21.8% sub-period IV : 26.5% sub-period V : 42.0% (H)	1985:1-1998:12: 4.3% sub-period III : 21.7% sub-period IV : 0% sub-period V : 1.4% (I)	1985:1-1998:12: 26.1% sub-period III : 65.2% sub-period IV : 30.6% sub-period V : 53.5% (6)
$\gamma_i^a < 0$	1985:1-1998:12: 0% sub-period III : 4.3% sub-period IV : 0% sub-period V : 0% (l)	1985:1-1998:12: 0% sub-period III : 8.7% sub-period IV : 0% sub-period V : 0%	1985:1-1998:12: 0% sub-period III : 0% sub-period IV : 0% sub-period V : 1.4%%	1985:1-1998:12: 0% sub-period III : 13.0% sub-period IV : 0% sub-period V : 1.4%
	1985:1-1998:12: 4.3% sub-period III : 26.0% sub-period IV : 8.2% sub-period V : 10.1%	1985:1-1998:12: 91.4% sub-period III : 39.2% sub-period IV : 89.8% sub-period V : 72.4%	1985:1-1998:12: 4.3% sub-period III : 34.7% sub-period IV : 2.0% sub-period V : 17.3%	

Table 16 Exposures to macro risk factors: MDAX Corporations – Dummy Variables Regression as independent variables (ER2)

	DM depreciations relative to Yen			Total
DM appreciations relative to Yen	$\gamma_i^d > 0$	$\gamma_i^d = 0$	$\gamma_i^d < 0$	
$\gamma_i^a > 0$	1985:1-1998:12: 0% sub-period III : 0% sub-period IV : 0% sub-period V : 1.4% (A)	1985:1-1998:12: 0% sub-period III : 4.3% sub-period IV : 0% sub-period V : 1.4% (B)	1985:1-1998:12: 0% sub-period III : 0% sub-period IV : 2.0% sub-period V : 5.8% (C)	1985:1-1998:12: 0% sub-period III : 4.3% sub-period IV : 2.0% sub-period V : 8.6%
$\gamma_i^a = 0$	1985:1-1998:12: 17.4% sub-period III : 8.7% sub-period IV : 8.2% sub-period V : 15.9% (D)	1985:1-1998:12: 69.6% sub-period III : 30.4% sub-period IV : 73.5% sub-period V : 52.2% (E)	1985:1-1998:12: 0% sub-period III : 0% sub-period IV : 4.1% sub-period V : 4.3% (F)	1985:1-1998:12: 87% sub-period III : 39.1% sub-period IV : 85.8% sub-period V : 72.4%
$\gamma_i^a < 0$	1985:1-1998:12: 4.3% sub-period III : 34.8% sub-period IV : 4.1% sub-period V : 13.0% (G)	1985:1-1998:12: 8.7% sub-period III : 17.4% sub-period IV : 8.2% sub-period V : 5.8% (H)	1985:1-1998:12: 0% sub-period III : 4.3% sub-period IV : 0% sub-period V : 0% (I)	1985:1-1998:12: 13% sub-period III : 56.5% sub-period IV : 12.3% sub-period V : 18.8%
Total	1985:1-1998:12: 21.7% sub-period III : 43.5% sub-period IV : 12.3% sub-period V : 30.3%	1985:1-1998:12: 78.3% sub-period III : 52.1% sub-period IV : 81.7% sub-period V : 59.4%	1985:1-1998:12: 0% sub-period III : 4.3% sub-period IV : 6.1% sub-period V : 10.1%	

Table 17 Exposures to macro risk factors: MDAX Corporations – Dummy Variables Regression as independent variables (IR1)

Decrease in German short-term interest rates	Increase in German short-term interest rates		
	$\gamma_i^a > 0$	$\gamma_i^a = 0$	$\gamma_i^a < 0$
	(A)	(B)	(C)
$\gamma_i^a > 0$	1985:1-1998:12: 0% sub-period III : 0% sub-period IV : 0% sub-period V : 4.3%	1985:1-1998:12: 4.3% sub-period III : 4.3% sub-period IV : 8.2% sub-period V : 20.3%	1985:1-1998:12: 4.3% sub-period III : 8.6% sub-period IV : 10.2% sub-period V : 30.4%
	(D)	(E)	(F)
$\gamma_i^a = 0$	1985:1-1998:12 : 17.4% sub-period III : 4.3% sub-period IV : 2.0% sub-period V : 7.2%	1985:1-1998:12: 78.3% sub-period III : 56.5% sub-period IV : 73.5% sub-period V : 52.2%	1985:1-1998:12: 95.7% sub-period III : 86.9% sub-period IV : 85.7% sub-period V : 71%
	(G)	(H)	(I)
$\gamma_i^a < 0$	1985:1-1998:12: 17.4% sub-period III : 4.3% sub-period IV : 4.0% sub-period V : 11.5%	1985:1-1998:12: 82.6% sub-period III : 65.1% sub-period IV : 81.7% sub-period V : 72.5%	1985:1-1998:12: 0% sub-period III : 30.4% sub-period IV : 14.2% sub-period V : 17.4%

Table 18 Exposures to macro risk factors: MDAX Corporations – Dummy Variables Regression as independent variables (IR2)

Decrease in German long-term interest rates	Increase in German long-term interest rates		
	$\gamma_i^a > 0$ (A)	$\gamma_i^a = 0$ (B)	$\gamma_i^a < 0$ (C)
$\gamma_i^a > 0$	1985:1-1998:12: 0% sub-period III : 0% sub-period IV : 0% sub-period V : 4.3% (D)	1985:1-1998:12: 0% sub-period III : 4.3% sub-period IV : 6.1% sub-period V : 0% (E)	1985:1-1998:12: 0% sub-period III : 13.0% sub-period IV : 4.1% sub-period V : 1.4% (F)
$\gamma_i^a = 0$	1985:1-1998:12: 0% sub-period III : 0% sub-period IV : 2.0% sub-period V : 7.2% (G)	1985:1-1998:12: 39.1% sub-period III : 47.8% sub-period IV : 49.0% sub-period V : 36.2% (H)	1985:1-1998:12: 56.5% sub-period III : 17.4% sub-period IV : 36.7% sub-period V : 5.8% (I)
$\gamma_i^a < 0$	1985:1-1998:12: 0% sub-period III : 4.3% sub-period IV : 2.0% sub-period V : 20.2%	1985:1-1998:12: 4.3% sub-period III : 13.0% sub-period IV : 2.0% sub-period V : 27.5% 1985:1-1998:12: 43.4% sub-period III : 65.1% sub-period IV : 57.1% sub-period V : 63.7%	1985:1-1998:12: 4.3% sub-period III : 17.3% sub-period IV : 2.0% sub-period V : 44.9% 1985:1-1998:12: 95.6% sub-period III : 65.2% sub-period IV : 87.7% sub-period V : 49.2%

Table 19 Exposures to macro risk factors: MDAX Corporations – Dummy Variables Regression as independent variables (IR3)

Decrease in US short-term interest rates	Increase in US short-term interest rates		
	$\gamma_i^d > 0$ (A)	$\gamma_i^d = 0$ (B)	$\gamma_i^d < 0$ (C)
$\gamma_i^a > 0$	(D) 1985:1-1998:12: 0%; sub-period III: 0%; sub-period IV: 0%; sub-period V: 0%	(E) 1985:1-1998:12: 26.1%; sub-period III: 0%; sub-period IV: 12.2%; sub-period V: 2.9%	1985:1-1998:12: 30.4%; sub-period III: 0%; sub-period IV: 16.3%; sub-period V: 13% · (F) 1985:1-1998:12: 4.3%; sub-period III: 0%; sub-period IV: 4.1%; sub-period V: 10.1%
$\gamma_i^a = 0$	(G) 1985:1-1998:12: 0%; sub-period III: 0%; sub-period IV: 4.1%; sub-period V: 4.3%	(H) 1985:1-1998:12: 65.2%; sub-period III: 82.6%; sub-period IV: 69.4%; sub-period V: 52.2%	1985:1-1998:12: 69.5%; sub-period III: 95.6%; sub-period IV: 83.7%; sub-period V: 71% · (I) 1985:1-1998:12: 4.3%; sub-period III: 13.0%; sub-period IV: 10.2%; sub-period V: 14.5%
$\gamma_i^a < 0$	1985:1-1998:12: 0%; sub-period III: 0%; sub-period IV: 0%; sub-period V: 8.7%	1985:1-1998:12: 0%; sub-period III: 0%; sub-period IV: 0%; sub-period V: 5.8% · 1985:1-1998:12: 91.3%; sub-period III: 82.6%; sub-period IV: 81.6%; sub-period V: 60.9%	1985:1-1998:12: 0%; sub-period III: 4.3%; sub-period IV: 0%; sub-period V: 1.4% · 1985:1-1998:12: 8.6%; sub-period III: 17.3%; sub-period IV: 14.3%; sub-period V: 26%

Table 20 Exposures to macro risk factors: MDAX Corporations – Dummy Variables Regression as independent variables (IR4)

Decrease in US long-term interest rates	Increase in US long-term interest rates		
	$\gamma_i^d > 0$ (A)	$\gamma_i^d = 0$ (B)	$\gamma_i^d < 0$ (C)
$\gamma_i^a > 0$	1985:1-1998:12: 4.3% sub-period III : 0% sub-period IV : 0% sub-period V : 0% (A)	1985:1-1998:12: 39.1% sub-period III : 0% sub-period IV : 20.4% sub-period V : 0% (B)	1985:1-1998:12: 43.4% sub-period III : 0% sub-period IV : 20.4% sub-period V : 0% (C)
$\gamma_i^a = 0$	1985:1-1998:12: 0% sub-period III : 21.7% sub-period IV : 8.2% sub-period V : 37.7% (D)	1985:1-1998:12: 52.2% sub-period III : 65.2% sub-period IV : 63.3% sub-period V : 55.1% (E)	1985:1-1998:12: 52.2% sub-period III : 95.6% sub-period IV : 71.5% sub-period V : 100% (F)
$\gamma_i^a < 0$	1985:1-1998:12: 0% sub-period III : 0% sub-period IV : 0% sub-period V : 0% (G)	1985:1-1998:12: 4.3% sub-period III : 0% sub-period IV : 6.1% sub-period V : 0% (H)	1985:1-1998:12: 52.2% sub-period III : 8.7% sub-period IV : 0% sub-period V : 7.2% (I)
	1985:1-1998:12: 4.3% sub-period III : 21.7% sub-period IV : 8.2% sub-period V : 37.7%	1985:1-1998:12: 95.6% sub-period III : 65.2% sub-period IV : 89.8% sub-period V : 55.1%	1985:1-1998:12: 4.3% sub-period III : 0% sub-period IV : 10.2% sub-period V : 0%

Table 21 Exposures to macro risk factors: MDAX Corporations – Dummy Variables Regression as independent variables (IR5)

Decrease in Japanese short-term interest rates	Increase in Japanese short-term interest rates		
	$\gamma_i^d > 0$	$\gamma_i^d = 0$	$\gamma_i^d < 0$
$\gamma_i^a > 0$	1985:1-1998:12: 0% sub-period III : 13% sub-period IV : 0% sub-period V : 0% (A)	1985:1-1998:12: 0% sub-period III : 39.1% sub-period IV : 6.1% sub-period V : 17.4% (B)	1985:1-1998:12: 0% sub-period III : 52.1% sub-period IV : 6.1% sub-period V : 17.4% (C)
$\gamma_i^a = 0$	1985:1-1998:12: 4.3% sub-period III : 0% sub-period IV : 0% sub-period V : 0% (D)	1985:1-1998:12: 78.3% sub-period III : 47.8% sub-period IV : 83.7% sub-period V : 68.1% (E)	1985:1-1998:12: 86.9% sub-period III : 47.8% sub-period IV : 85.7% sub-period V : 68.1% (F)
$\gamma_i^a < 0$	1985:1-1998:12: 0% sub-period III : 0% sub-period IV : 0% sub-period V : 0% (G)	1985:1-1998:12: 13.0% sub-period III : 0% sub-period IV : 8.2% sub-period V : 14.5% (H)	1985:1-1998:12: 25.0% sub-period III : 0% sub-period IV : 8.2% sub-period V : 14.5% (I)
	1985:1-1998:12: 4.3% sub-period III : 13% sub-period IV : 0% sub-period V : 0%	1985:1-1998:12: 91.3% sub-period III : 86.9% sub-period IV : 98% sub-period V : 100%	1985:1-1998:12: 4.3% sub-period III : 0% sub-period IV : 2.0% sub-period V : 0%

Table 22 Exposures to macro risk factors: MDAX Corporations – Dummy Variables Regression as independent variables (IR6)

Increase in Japanese long-term interest rates	Increase in Japanese long-term interest rates			
	$\gamma_i^a > 0$	$\gamma_i^a = 0$	$\gamma_i^a < 0$	
	(A)	(B)	(C)	
$\gamma_i^a > 0$	1985:1-1998:12: 4.3% sub-period III : 13.0% sub-period IV : 0% sub-period V : 0%	1985:1-1998:12: 8.7% sub-period III : 4.3% sub-period IV : 14.3% sub-period V : 11.6%	1985:1-1998:12: 4.3% sub-period III : 0% sub-period IV : 0% sub-period V : 0%	1985:1-1998:12: 17.3% sub-period III : 17.3% sub-period IV : 14.3% sub-period V : 11.6%
	(D)	(E)	(F)	
$\gamma_i^a = 0$	1985:1-1998:12: 13.0% sub-period III : 20.4% sub-period IV : 0% sub-period V : 0%	1985:1-1998:12: 56.5% sub-period III : 26.1% sub-period IV : 81.6% sub-period V : 65.2%	1985:1-1998:12: 13.0% sub-period III : 0% sub-period IV : 0% sub-period V : 0%	1985:1-1998:12: 82.5% sub-period III : 46.5% sub-period IV : 81.6% sub-period V : 65.2%
	(G)	(H)	(I)	
$\gamma_i^a < 0$	1985:1-1998:12: 0% sub-period III : 4.3% sub-period IV : 0% sub-period V : 0%	1985:1-1998:12: 0% sub-period III : 8.7% sub-period IV : 4.1% sub-period V : 23.2%	1985:1-1998:12: 0% sub-period III : 0% sub-period IV : 0% sub-period V : 0%	1985:1-1998:12: 0% sub-period III : 13% sub-period IV : 4.1% sub-period V : 23.2%
	1985:1-1998:12: 17.3% sub-period III : 37.7% sub-period IV : 0% sub-period V : 0%	1985:1-1998:12: 65.2% sub-period III : 39.1% sub-period IV : 100% sub-period V : 100%	1985:1-1998:12: 17.3% sub-period III : 0% sub-period IV : 0% sub-period V : 0%	

Table 23 Exposures to macro risk factors: MDAX Corporations – Dummy Variables Regression as independent variables (CPI1)

US Deflation	US Inflation		
	$\gamma_i^d > 0$	$\gamma_i^d = 0$	$\gamma_i^d < 0$
$\gamma_i^a > 0$	1985:1-1998:12: 0% sub-period III : 0% sub-period IV : 0% sub-period V : 2.9% (A)	1985:1-1998:12: 0% sub-period III : 17.4% sub-period IV : 0% sub-period V : 15.9% (B)	1985:1-1998:12: 0% sub-period III : 21.7% sub-period IV : 0% sub-period V : 18.8% (C)
$\gamma_i^a = 0$	1985:1-1998:12: 0% sub-period III : 17.4% sub-period IV : 0% sub-period V : 11.6% (D)	1985:1-1998:12: 26.1% sub-period III : 52.2% sub-period IV : 79.6% sub-period V : 44.9% (E)	1985:1-1998:12: 43.5% sub-period III : 0% sub-period IV : 20.4% sub-period V : 4.3% (F)
$\gamma_i^a < 0$	1985:1-1998:12: 0% sub-period III : 8.7% sub-period IV : 0% sub-period V : 8.7% (G)	1985:1-1998:12: 30.4% sub-period III : 0% sub-period IV : 0% sub-period V : 8.7% (H)	1985:1-1998:12: 30.4% sub-period III : 8.7% sub-period IV : 0% sub-period V : 17.4% (I)

Table 24 Exposures to macro risk factors: MDAX Corporations – Dummy Variables Regression as independent variables (CPI2)

Japanese Deflation	Japanese Inflation		
	$\gamma_i^d > 0$	$\gamma_i^d = 0$	$\gamma_i^d < 0$
	(A)	(B)	(C)
$\gamma_i^a > 0$	1985:1-1998:12: 0% sub-period III : 0% sub-period IV : 0% sub-period V : 0% (D)	1985:1-1998:12: 0% sub-period III : 0% sub-period IV : 2.0% sub-period V : 8.7% (E)	1985:1-1998:12: 0% sub-period III : 0% sub-period IV : 2.0% sub-period V : 10.1% (F)
$\gamma_i^a = 0$	1985:1-1998:12: 0% sub-period III : 8.7% sub-period IV : 2.0% sub-period V : 7.2% (G)	1985:1-1998:12: 95.7% sub-period III : 56.5% sub-period IV : 83.7% sub-period V : 55.1% (H)	1985:1-1998:12: 95.7% sub-period III : 78.2% sub-period IV : 93.9% sub-period V : 68.1% (I)
$\gamma_i^a < 0$	1985:1-1998:12: 0% sub-period III : 4.3% sub-period IV : 0% sub-period V : 13.0% 1985:1-1998:12: 0% sub-period III : 13% sub-period IV : 2.0% sub-period V : 20.2%	1985:1-1998:12: 4.3% sub-period III : 13.0% sub-period IV : 6.1% sub-period V : 8.7% 1985:1-1998:12: 100% sub-period III : 69.5% sub-period IV : 91.8% sub-period V : 72.5%	1985:1-1998:12: 4.3% sub-period III : 21.6% sub-period IV : 6.1% sub-period V : 21.7%

Table 25 Exposures to macro risk factors: MDAX Corporations – Dummy Variables Regression as independent variables (CPI3)

German Deflation	German Inflation $\gamma_i^a > 0$	German Inflation $\gamma_i^a = 0$	German Inflation $\gamma_i^a < 0$	Total
$\gamma_i^a > 0$	(A) 1985:1-1998:12: 4.3% sub-period III : 0% sub-period IV : 2.0% sub-period V : 2.9%	(B) 1985:1-1998:12: 4.3% sub-period III : 4.3% sub-period IV : 2.0% sub-period V : 2.9%	(C) 1985:1-1998:12: 0% sub-period III : 0% sub-period IV : 0% sub-period V : 2.9%	1985:1-1998:12: 8.6% sub-period III : 4.3% sub-period IV : 4.0% sub-period V : 8.7%
$\gamma_i^a = 0$	(D) 1985:1-1998:12: 4.3% sub-period III : 0% sub-period IV : 4.1% sub-period V : 1.4%	(E) 1985:1-1998:12: 87.0% sub-period III : 60.9% sub-period IV : 81.6% sub-period V : 47.8%	(F) 1985:1-1998:12: 0% sub-period III : 13.0% sub-period IV : 6.1% sub-period V : 13.0%	1985:1-1998:12: 91.3% sub-period III : 73.9% sub-period IV : 91.8% sub-period V : 62.2%
$\gamma_i^a < 0$	(G) 1985:1-1998:12: 0% sub-period III : 4.3% sub-period IV : 2.0% sub-period V : 4.3%	(H) 1985:1-1998:12: 0% sub-period III : 17.4% sub-period IV : 0% sub-period V : 17.4%	(I) 1985:1-1998:12: 0% sub-period III : 0% sub-period IV : 0% sub-period V : 7.2%%	1985:1-1998:12: 0% sub-period III : 21.7% sub-period IV : 2.0% sub-period V : 28.9%
Total	1985:1-1998:12: 8.6% sub-period III : 4.3% sub-period IV : 8.1% sub-period V : 8.6%	1985:1-1998:12: 91.3% sub-period III : 82.6% sub-period IV : 83.6% sub-period V : 68.1%	1985:1-1998:12: 0% sub-period III : 13.0% sub-period IV : 6.1% sub-period V : 23.1%	

APPENDIX L Estimation Results – DAX Sectors' Exposures to DM/US$

Table 26 Exposures to macro risk factors: DAX Industry Sector Indexes – Dummy Variables Regression

DM appreciations relative to US$	DM depreciations relative to UD$		
	$\gamma_i^d > 0$	$\gamma_i^d = 0$	$\gamma_i^d < 0$
$\gamma_i^a > 0$	(A) 1985:1-1998:12: sub-period III : sub-period IV : sub-period V :	(B) 1985:1-1998:12: Automobile & Transportation, Banks & Financial Services, Chemicals & Pharma, Construction, Insurance, Machinery & Industrials, Retail &, Consumer, Software & Technology, Telecom & Util. sub-period III : Automobile & Transportation, Machinery & Industrials, Telecom & Util. sub-period IV : Automobile & Transportation, Banks & Financial Services, Chemicals & Pharma, Construction, Machinery & Industrials, Retail & Consumer, Software & Technology, Telecom & Util. sub-period V : Automobile & Transportation, Banks & Financial Services, Chemicals & Pharma, Insurance, Machinery & Industrials, Software & Technology, Telecom & Util.	(C) 1985:1-1998:12: sub-period III : Banks & Financial Services sub-period IV : Chemicals & Pharma Insurance sub-period V : Retail & Consumer
			1985:1- 1998:12: sub-period III : sub-period IV : sub-period V :
$\gamma_i^a = 0$	(D) 1985:1-1998:12: sub-period III : Retail & Consumer sub-period IV : sub-period V :	(E) 1985:1-1998:12: sub-period III : Telecom & Util. sub-period IV : Insurance sub-period V : Construction	(F) 1985:1-1998:12: sub-period III : sub-period IV : sub-period V :
			1985:1- 1998:12: sub-period III : sub-period IV : sub-period V :
$\gamma_i^a < 0$	(G) 1985:1-1998:12: sub-period III : Construction sub-period IV : sub-period V :	(H) 1985:1-1998:12: sub-period III : sub-period IV : sub-period V :	(I) 1985:1-1998:12: sub-period III : sub-period IV : sub-period V :
	1985:1-1998:12: sub-period III : sub-period IV : sub-period V :		1985:1- 1998:12: sub-period III : sub-period IV : sub-period V :

Table 27 Exposures to macro risk factors: DAX 100 (DAX30 / MDAX) Corporations in Sector of Activity Automobile & Transportation

DM appreciations relative to US$	DM depreciations relative to UD$ $\gamma_i^d > 0$	$\gamma_i^d = 0$	$\gamma_i^d < 0$
$\gamma_i^a > 0$	**(A)** 1985:1-1998:12: 14.3% (25%, 0%) sub-period III : 0% sub-period IV : 12.5% (25%, 0%) sub-period V : 0%	**(B)** 1985:1-1998:12: 85.7% (75%, 100%) sub-period III : 12.5% (25%, 0%) sub-period IV : 62.5% (50%, 75%) sub-period V : 61.2% (66.7%, 57.1%)	**(C)** 1985:1-1998:12: 0% sub-period III : 25% (50%, 0%) sub-period IV : 12.5% (0%, 25%) sub-period V : 7.7% (16.7%, 0%)
$\gamma_i^a = 0$	**(D)** 1985:1-1998:12: 0% sub-period III : 25% (0%, 50%) sub-period IV : 12.5% (25%, 0%) sub-period V : 0%	**(E)** 1985:1-1998:12: 0% sub-period III : 37.5% (25%, 50%) sub-period IV : 0% sub-period V : 23.1% (50%, 42.9%)	**(F)** 1985:1-1998:12: 0% sub-period III : 0% sub-period IV : 0% sub-period V : 0%
$\gamma_i^a < 0$	**(G)** 1985:1-1998:12: 0% sub-period III : 0% sub-period IV : 0% sub-period V : 0%	**(H)** 1985:1-1998:12: 0% sub-period III : 0% sub-period IV : 0% sub-period V : 0%	**(I)** 1985:1-1998:12: 0% sub-period III : 0% sub-period IV : 0% sub-period V : 7.7% (16.7%, 0%)

Table 28 Exposures to macro risk factors: DAX 100 Corporations in Sector of Activity Banks & Financial Services

DM appreciations relative to US$	DM depreciations relative to UD$		
	$\gamma_i^d > 0$	$\gamma_i^d = 0$	$\gamma_i^d < 0$
$\gamma_i^a > 0$	(A) 1985:1-1998:12: 0% sub-period III : 0% sub-period IV : 0% sub-period V : 0%	(B) 1985:1-1998:12: 50% (66.7%, 0%) sub-period III : 0% sub-period IV : 57.1% (100%, 25%) sub-period V : 20% (66.7%, 0%)	(C) 1985:1-1998:12: 12.5% (66.7%, 0%) sub-period III : 60% (75%, 0%) sub-period IV : 57.1% (100%, 25%) sub-period V : 30% (66.7%, 14.3%)
$\gamma_i^a = 0$	(D) 1985:1-1998:12: 0% sub-period III : 0% sub-period IV : 0% sub-period V : 10% (0%, 14.3%)	(E) 1985:1-1998:12: 50% (33.3%, 100%) sub-period III : 0% sub-period IV : 42.9% (0%, 75%) sub-period V : 50% (33.3%, 57.1%)	(F) 1985:1-1998:12: 50% (33.3%, 100%) sub-period III : 40% (25%, 100%) sub-period IV : 42.9% (0%, 75%) sub-period V : 60% (33.3%, 71.4%)
$\gamma_i^a < 0$	(G) 1985:1-1998:12: 0% sub-period III : 0% sub-period IV : 0% sub-period V : 0%	(H) 1985:1-1998:12: 100% (100%, 100%) sub-period III : 0% sub-period IV : 100% (100%, 100%) sub-period V : 70% (100%, 57.1%)	(I) 1985:1-1998:12: 0% sub-period III : 100% (100%, 100%) sub-period IV : 0% sub-period V : 20% (0%, 28.6%)

Table 29 Exposures to macro risk factors: DAX 100 Corporations in Sector of Activity Chemicals & Pharma

DM appreciations relative to US$	DM depreciations relative to UDS — $\gamma_i^d > 0$	$\gamma_i^d = 0$	$\gamma_i^d < 0$	(Total)
$\gamma_i^a > 0$	**(A)** 1985:1-1998:12: 12.5% (25%, 0%); sub-period III : 0%; sub-period IV : 23.1% (40%,12.5%); sub-period V : 0%	**(B)** 1985:1-1998:12: 75% (75%, 75%); sub-period III : 25% (40%, 0%); sub-period IV : 69.2% (60%, 75%); sub-period V : 43.8% (80%, 27.3%)	**(C)** 1985:1-1998:12: 0%; sub-period III : 37.5% (20%, 66.7%); sub-period IV : 0%; sub-period V : 6.3% (0%, 9.1%)	1985:1-1998:12: 87.5% (100%, 75%); sub-period III : 62.5% (60%, 66.7%); sub-period IV : 92.3% (100%, 87.5%); sub-period V : 50.1% (80%, 36.4%)
$\gamma_i^a = 0$	**(D)** 1985:1-1998:12: 0%; sub-period III : 0%; sub-period IV : 0%; sub-period V : 12.5% (0%, 18.2%)	**(E)** 1985:1-1998:12: 12.5% (0%, 25%); sub-period III : 25% (40%, 0%); sub-period IV : 7.7% (0%, 12.5%); sub-period V : 37.5% (20%, 45.5%)	**(F)** 1985:1-1998:12: 0%; sub-period III : 12.5% (0%, 33.3%); sub-period IV : 0%; sub-period V : 0%	1985:1-1998:12: 12.5% (0%, 25%); sub-period III : 37.5% (40%, 33.3%); sub-period IV : 7.7% (0%, 12.5%); sub-period V : 50% (20%, 63.7%)
$\gamma_i^a < 0$	**(G)** 1985:1-1998:12: 0%; sub-period III : 0%; sub-period IV : 0%; sub-period V : 0%	**(H)** 1985:1-1998:12: 0%; sub-period III : 0%; sub-period IV : 0%; sub-period V : 0%	**(I)** 1985:1-1998:12: 0%; sub-period III : 0%; sub-period IV : 0%; sub-period V : 0%	1985:1-1998:12: 0%; sub-period III : 0%; sub-period IV : 0%; sub-period V : 0%
(Total)	1985:1-1998:12: 12.5% (25%,0%); sub-period III : 0%; sub-period IV : 23.1% (40%, 12.5%); sub-period V : 12.5% (0%, 18.2%)	1985:1-1998:12: 87.5% (75%, 100%); sub-period III : 50% (80%, 0%); sub-period IV : 76.9% (60%, 87.5%); sub-period V : 81.2% (100%, 72.8%)		

Table 30 Exposures to macro risk factors: DAX 100 Corporations in Sector of Activity Construction

DM appreciations relative to US$	DM depreciations relative to UD$		
	$\gamma_i^d > 0$	$\gamma_i^d = 0$	$\gamma_i^d < 0$
$\gamma_i^a > 0$	1985:1-1998:12: 0% sub-period III : 0% sub-period IV : 0% sub-period V : 0% (A)	1985:1-1998:12: 75% (0%, 75%) sub-period III : 0% sub-period IV : 75% (0%, 75) sub-period V : 0% (B)	1985:1-1998:12: 12.75% (0%, 75%) sub-period III : 0% sub-period IV : 75% (0%, 75%) sub-period V : 0% (C)
$\gamma_i^a = 0$	1985:1-1998:12: 0% sub-period III : 50% (0%, 50%) sub-period IV : 0% sub-period V : 25% (0%, 25%) (D)	1985:1-1998:12: 25% (0%, 25%) sub-period III : 25% (0%, 25%) sub-period IV : 25% (0%, 25%) sub-period V : 75% (0%, 75%) (E)	1985:1-1998:12: 12.25% (0%, 25%) sub-period III : 75% (0%, 75%) sub-period IV : 25% (0%, 25%) sub-period V : 100% (0%, 100%) (F)
$\gamma_i^a < 0$	1985:1-1998:12: 0% sub-period III : 25% (0%, 25%) sub-period IV : 0% sub-period V : 0% (G)	1985:1-1998:12: 0% sub-period III : 0% sub-period IV : 0% sub-period V : 0% (H)	1985:1-1998:12: 0% sub-period III : 25% (0%, 25%) sub-period IV : 0% sub-period V : 0% (I)
	1985:1-1998:12: 0% sub-period III : 75% (0%, 75%) sub-period IV : 0% sub-period V : 25% (0%, 25%)	1985:1-1998:12: 100% (0%, 100%) sub-period III : 25% (0%, 25%) sub-period IV : 100% (0%, 100%) sub-period V : 75% (0%, 75%)	1985:1-1998:12: 0% sub-period III : 0% sub-period IV : 0% sub-period V : 0%

Table 31 Exposures to macro risk factors: DAX 100 Corporations in Sector of Activity Insurance

DM appreciations relative to U$S	DM depreciations relative to U$S		
	$\gamma_i^d > 0$	$\gamma_i^d = 0$	$\gamma_i^d < 0$
	(A)	(B)	(C)
$\gamma_i^a > 0$	1985:1-1998:12: 0% sub-period III : 0% sub-period IV : 0% sub-period V : 0%	1985:1-1998:12: 100%, (100%, 0%) sub-period III : 50% (50%, 0%) sub-period IV : 25% (25%, 0%) sub-period V : 50% (50%, 50%)	1985:1-1998:12: 100%, (100%, 0%) sub-period III : 50% (100%, 0%) sub-period IV : 25% (25%, 0%) sub-period V : 75% (100%, 50%)
	(D)	(E)	(F)
$\gamma_i^a = 0$	1985:1-1998:12: 0% sub-period III : 0% sub-period IV : 25% (0%, 25%) sub-period V : 0%	1985:1-1998:12: 0% sub-period III : 0% sub-period IV : 50% (50%, 50%) sub-period V : 25% (0%, 50%)	1985:1-1998:12: 0% sub-period III : 50% (50%, 0%) sub-period IV : 0% sub-period V : 25% (50%, 0%)
	(G)	(H)	(I)
$\gamma_i^a < 0$	1985:1-1998:12: 0% sub-period III : 0% sub-period IV : 25% (0%, 25%) sub-period V : 75% (50%, 100%)	1985:1-1998:12: 0% sub-period III : 0% sub-period IV : 0% sub-period V : 0%	1985:1-1998:12: 0% sub-period III : 0% sub-period IV : 75% (50%, 75%) sub-period V : 25% (0%, 50%)

Table 32 Exposures to macro risk factors: DAX 100 Corporations in Sector of Activity Machinery & Industrials

DM appreciations relative to US$	DM Depreciations relative to UD$		
	$\gamma_i^d > 0$ (A)	$\gamma_i^d = 0$ (B)	$\gamma_i^d < 0$ (C)
$\gamma_i^a > 0$	**(A)** 1985:1-1998:12: 10% (0%, 14.3%) sub-period III : 0% sub-period IV : 5.6% (0%, 6.7%) sub-period V : 0%	**(B)** 1985:1-1998:12: 80% (100%, 71.4%) sub-period III : 20% (33.3%, 14.3%) sub-period IV : 77.8% (100%, 73.3%) sub-period V : 34.8% (0%, 40%)	**(C)** 1985:1-1998:12: 90% (100%, 71.4%) sub-period III : 50% (100%, 28.6%) sub-period IV : 83.4% (100%, 80%) sub-period V : 60.9% (33.3%, 65%)
$\gamma_i^a = 0$	**(D)** 1985:1-1998:12: 0% sub-period III : 0% sub-period IV : 0% sub-period V : 0%	**(E)** 1985:1-1998:12: 10% (0%, 14.3%) sub-period III : 20% (0%, 28.6%) sub-period IV : 16.7% (0%, 20%) sub-period V : 34.8% (66.7%, 30%)	**(F)** 1985:1-1998:12: 0% sub-period III : 30% (0%, 42.9%) sub-period IV : 0% sub-period V : 4.3% (0%, 5%)
$\gamma_i^a < 0$	**(G)** 1985:1-1998:12: 10% (0%, 14.3%) sub-period III : 50% (0%, 71.5%) sub-period IV : 16.7% (0%, 20%) sub-period V : 39.1% (55.7%, 35%)	**(H)** 1985:1-1998:12: 90% (100%, 85.7%) sub-period III : 0% sub-period IV : 40% (33.3%, 42.9%) sub-period V : 94.5% (100%, 93.3%) sub-period V : 69.6% (66.7%, 70%)	**(I)** 1985:1-1998:12: 0% sub-period III : 30% (66.7%, 14.3%) sub-period IV : 0% sub-period V : 26.1% (33.3%, 25%)

Table 33 Exposures to macro risk factors: DAX 100 Corporations in Sector of Activity Retail & Consumer

DM appreciations relative to US$	DM depreciations relative to UDS		
	$\gamma_i^d > 0$ (A)	$\gamma_i^d = 0$ (B)	$\gamma_i^d < 0$ (C)
$\gamma_i^a > 0$	(A) 1985:1-1998:12: 0% sub-period III : 0% sub-period IV : 7.7% (33.3%, 0%) sub-period V : 0%	(B) 1985:1-1998:12: 50% (0%, 50%) sub-period III : 0% sub-period IV : 46.2% (33.3%, 50%) sub-period V : 31.3% (0%, 38.5%)	(C) 1985:1-1998:12: 50% (0%, 50%) sub-period III : 0% sub-period IV : 53.9% (66.6%, 50%) sub-period V : 75.1% (100%, 69.3%)
$\gamma_i^a = 0$	(D) 1985:1-1998:12: 0% sub-period III : 25% (0%, 25%) sub-period IV : 15.4% (33.3%, 10%) sub-period V : 12.5% (0%, 15.4%)	(E) 1985:1-1998:12: 25% (0%, 25%) sub-period III : 25% (0%, 25%) sub-period IV : 30.8% (0%, 40%) sub-period V : 12.5% (0%, 15.4%)	(F) 1985:1-1998:12: 50% (0%, 50%) sub-period III : 50% (0%, 50%) sub-period IV : 46.2% (33.3%, 50%) sub-period V : 25% (0%, 30.8%)
$\gamma_i^a < 0$	(G) 1985:1-1998:12: 0% sub-period III : 25% (0%, 25%) sub-period IV : 23.1% (66.6%, 10%) sub-period V : 12.5% (0%, 15.4%)	(H) 1985:1-1998:12: 75% (0%, 75%) sub-period III : 75% (0%, 75%) sub-period IV : 77% (33.3%, 90%) sub-period V : 43.8% (0%, 53.9%)	(I) 1985:1-1998:12: 25% (0%, 25%) sub-period III : 0% sub-period IV : 0% sub-period V : 43.8% (100%, 30.8%)

Table 34 Exposures to macro risk factors: DAX 100 Corporations in Sector of Activity Software & Technology

DM appreciations relative to US\$	DM Depreciations relative to UD\$		
	$\gamma_i^d > 0$ (A/D/G)	$\gamma_i^d = 0$ (B/E/H)	$\gamma_i^d < 0$ (C/F/I)
$\gamma_i^a > 0$	**(A)** 1985:1-1998:12: 0%; sub-period III: 0%; sub-period IV: 0%; sub-period V: 0%	**(B)** 1985:1-1998:12: 100% (100%, 0%); sub-period III: 100% (100%, 0%); sub-period IV: 75% (50%, 100%); sub-period V: 22.2% (50%, 0%)	**(C)** 1985:1-1998:12: 100% (100%, 0%); sub-period III: 100% (100%, 0%); sub-period IV: 75% (50%, 100%); sub-period V: 22.2% (50%, 0%)
$\gamma_i^a = 0$	**(D)** 1985:1-1998:12: 0%; sub-period III: 0%; sub-period IV: 0%; sub-period V: 11.1% (0%, 20%)	**(E)** 1985:1-1998:12: 0%; sub-period III: 0%; sub-period IV: 25% (50%, 0%); sub-period V: 55.6% (25%, 80%)	**(F)** 1985:1-1998:12: 0%; sub-period III: 0%; sub-period IV: 0%; sub-period V: 0%
$\gamma_i^a < 0$	**(G)** 1985:1-1998:12: 0%; sub-period III: 0%; sub-period IV: 0%; sub-period V: 22.2% (25%, 20%)	**(H)** 1985:1-1998:12: 0%; sub-period III: 0%; sub-period IV: 0%; sub-period V: 0%	**(I)** 1985:1-1998:12: 0%; sub-period III: 0%; sub-period IV: 25% (50%, 0%); sub-period V: 66.7% (25%, 100%)

Table 35 Exposures to macro risk factors: DAX 100 Corporations in Sector of Activity Telecom & Utilities

DM appreciations relative to US$	DM depreciations relative to UD$		
	$\gamma_i^d > 0$	$\gamma_i^d = 0$	$\gamma_i^d < 0$
$\gamma_i^a > 0$	**(A)** 1985:1-1998:12: 0% sub-period III : 0% sub-period IV : 0% sub-period V : 0%	**(B)** 1985:1-1998:12: 100% (100%, 0%) sub-period III : 100% (100%, 0%) sub-period IV : 50% (50%, 0%) sub-period V : 33.3% (33.3%, 0%)	**(C)** 1985:1-1998:12: 100% (100%, 0%) sub-period III : 100% (100%, 0%) sub-period IV : 50% (50%, 0%) sub-period V : 33.3% (33.3%, 0%)
$\gamma_i^a = 0$	**(D)** 1985:1-1998:12: 0% sub-period III : 0% sub-period IV : 0% sub-period V : 0%	**(E)** 1985:1-1998:12: 0% sub-period III : 0% sub-period IV : 50% (50%, 0%) sub-period V : 66.7% (66.7%, 0%)	**(F)** 1985:1-1998:12: 0% sub-period III : 0% sub-period IV : 50% (50%, 0%) sub-period V : 66.7% (66.7%, 0%)
$\gamma_i^a < 0$	**(G)** 1985:1-1998:12: 100% (100%, 0%) sub-period III : 100% (100%, 0%) sub-period IV : 100% (100%, 0%) sub-period V : 100% (100%, 0%)	**(H)** 1985:1-1998:12: 0% sub-period III : 0% sub-period IV : 0% sub-period V : 0%	**(I)** 1985:1-1998:12: 0% sub-period III : 0% sub-period IV : 0% sub-period V : 0%

References

Aabo, T., 1998, Hedging Operating Exposure Financially: The Effect of the Abandonment Option, Working Paper, The Aarhus school of Business.

Aabo, T., 1999a, Exchange Rate Exposure Management, Ph.D. Thesis, The Aarhus school of Business.

Aabo, T., 1999b, Exchange Rate Exposure Management: Bridging between Theory and Practice, in Aabo, T., 1999a, Exchange Rate Exposure Management, Ph.D. Thesis, Department of International Business, The Aarhus School of Business.

Aabo, T., 1999c, Exchange Rate Exposure Management: An Empirical Study into the Strategies of Industrial Companies, Working Paper, The Aarhus school of Business.

Aabo, T., 1999d, Exchange Rate Exposure Management: The Benchmarking Process of Industrial Companies, Working Paper, The Aarhus school of Business.

Aabo, T., 1999e, The Exchange Rate Exposure of Danish Non-Financial Companies, The Aarhus School of Business.

Aabo, T., 2001, E-Commerce and Exchange Rate Exposure Management: A Tilt towards Real Hedging, Journal of E-Business, Vol. 1, Issue 1, June.

Aabo, T., 2002a, Risk Management – Variance Minimization or Lower Tail Outcome Elimination, Working Paper, The Aarhus School of Business.

Aabo, T., 2002b, Asymmetric Exchange Rate Exposures: A Search for the Effect of Real Options, Working Paper, Department of International Business, Aarhus School of Business.

Aabo, T., 2002c, Ownership and Risk Management: Shareholder versus Stakeholder Satisfaction, Conference Proceedings for the 28th EIBA Conference, Athens, Greece, December 8-10.

Aabo, T., 2002d, Exchange Rate Exposure Management: "Speculation" in Non-Financial Companies, Paper presented at the 2nd International Conference on Banking and Finance, Greece, August 9-11.

Aabo, T., 2002e, The Interaction between Real Options and Financial Hedging: An Empirical Study of Danish Non-Financial Companies, Paper presented at the 2002 FMA European Conference, Copenhagen, June 6-8.

Aabo, T., and B.J. Simkins, 2003, Interaction between Real Options and Financial Hedging: Fact or Fiction in Managerial Decision-Making, Working Paper, Aarhus School of Business and Oklahoma State University - Stillwater - Department of Finance.

Abdel-Malek, T., 1976, Some Aspects of Exchange Risk Policies under Floating Rates, Journal of International Business.

Abuaf, N. and S. Schoess, 1988, Foreign-Exchange exposure management, Executive enterprises publications & Co. (New York, NY).

Adam-Müller, A.F.A. and K.P. Wong, 2001, Restricted Export Flexibility and Management with Options and Futures, Working Paper, Center of Finance and Econometrics, University of Konstanz.

Adam, T.R., 2000, Risk Management and the Cost of Capital, Working Paper, Department of Finance, Hong Kong University of Science & Technology.

Adam, T.R., 2002, Why Firms Use Non-Linear Hedging Strategies, Working Paper, Department of Finance, Hong Kong University of Science & Technology.

Adler, M., 1994, Exchange Rate Planning for the International Trading Firm, in Amihud, Y. and R. M. Levich (eds.), 1994, Exchange Rates and Corporate Performance, Irwin Professional Publishing, New York., ch. 8, 165-179.

Adler, M. and B. Dumas, 1980, Foreign Exchange Risk Management, in Antl, B. [Hrsg.]: Currency Risk and the Corporation, Euromoney Publications (London), 145-157.

Adler, M. and B. Dumas, 1980, The Exposure of Long-Term Foreign Currency Bonds, Journal of Financial and Quantitative Analysis 15, 973-995.

Adler, M. and B. Dumas, 1983, International Portfolio Choice and Corporate Finance: A Synthesis, The Journal of Finance, Vol. 38, No. 3, 925-984, June.

Adler, M. and B. Dumas, 1984, Exposure to Currency Risk: Definition and Measurement, Financial Management

Adolfson, M., 1999, Swedish Export Price Determination: Pricing to Market Shares?, SSE/EFI Working Paper Series in Economic and Finance No. 306

Aggarwal, R., 1981, Exchange Rates and Stock Prices: a Study of the U.S. Capital Markets under Floating Exchange Rates, Akron Business and Economic Review, 12 (4): 7-12

Agarwal, S. and S.N. Ramaswani, 1992, Choice of Market Entry Mode: Impact of Ownership, Location, and Internatlization Factors, Journal of International Business Studies 23, 1-27.

Aggarwal, R. and L. Soenen, "Managing Persistent Real Changes in Currency Values: The Role of Multinational Operating Strategies", Columbia Journal of World Business, 1989, Vol. 24, No. 3, pp. 60-67.

Aguiar, M., 2001, Devaluation, Foreign Currency Exposure and Investment: The Case of Mexico, Working Paper, Graduate School of Business, University of Chicago.

Ahkam, N.S., 1995, a Model for the Evaluation of and Response to Economic Exposure Risk by Multinational Companies, Managerial Finance, Vo. 21, No. 4, 7-22.

Ahmadi, H.Z., Sharp, P.A., and C.H. Walther, 1986, The Effectiveness of Futures and Options in Hedging Currency Risk, in Frank J. Fabozzi, ed., Advances in Futures and Options Research, Greenwich, Connecticut: JAI Press Inc.

Ahn, Boudoukh, Richardson, and Whitelaw, 1999, Optimal Risk Management Using Options, Journal of Finance 54, 359-375.

Aizenman, J., 1989, Monopolistic Competition, Relative Prices, and Output Adjustment in the Open Economy, Journal of International Money and Finance, 8, p. 5-28.

Alesii, G., 2003, Value at Risk (VaR) in Real Options Analysis, Working Paper, Università de L'Aquila.

Aliber, R. Z., 1998, A Strategy for Managing Foreign Exchange, in Wharton School, University of Chicago Graduate School of Business, London Business School, The Complete Finance Companion, Financial Times Mastering Series, 325-330.

Allayannis, G., 1995, Exchange Rate Exposure Revisited, Working Paper, Darden Graduate School of Business, University of Virginia.

Allyannis, G., 1997, The Time-Variation of the Exchange Rate Exposure: An Industry Analysis, Working Paper, Darden Graduate School of Business, University of Virginia.

Allayannis, G. and J. Ihrig, 1999, Exposure and Markups, Working Paper, Darden Graduate School of Business, University of Virginia

Allayannis, G. and A. Mozumdar, 1999, Cash Flow, Investment, and Hedging, Working Paper, Darden Graduate School of Business, University of Virginia.

Allayannis, G. and E. Ofek, 2001, Exchange Rate Exposure, Hedging, and the Use of Foreign Currency Derivatives, Journal of International Money and Finance, 20, 273-296.

Allayannis, G. and J.P. Weston, 1999, The Use of Foreign Currency Derivatives and Firm Market Value, Working Paper, Darden Graduate School of Business, University of Virginia

Allayannis, G. and J.P. Weston, 1999, The Use of Foreign Currency Derivatives and Industry Structure, Darden School of Business Working Paper, University of Virginia

Allen, L. and C. Pantzalis, 1996, Valuation of the Operating Flexibility of Multinational Corporations, Journal of International Business Studies, 27(4): 633-653

Amihud, Y., 1994, Evidence on Exchange Rates and Valuation of Equity Shares, in Amihud, Y. and R. M. Levich (eds.), Exchange Rates and Corporate Performance, Irwin Professional Publishing, New York.

Amihud, Y. and R. M. Levich (eds.), 1994, Exchange Rates and Corporate Performance, Irwin Professional Publishing, New York.

Amram, M. and N. Kulatilaka, 1999, Real Options: Managing Strategic Investments in an Uncertain World, Boston: Harvard Business School Press.

Amram, M. and N. Kulatilaka, 2000, Strategy and Shareholder Value Creation: The Real Options Frontier, Journal of Corporate Finance, Vol. 13, No. 2, 8-21.

Andren, N., 2000, Macroecomic Exposure of European Firms, Working Paper, Department of Business Administration, Lund University.

Andren, N., 2000, Do Country and Industry Explain Macroeconomic Exposure?, Working Paper, Department of Business Administration, Lund University.

Andren, N., 2001, Is Macroeconomic Exposure Asymmetric, Working Paper, Department of Business Administration, Lund University.

Andren, N., 2001, International Finance FEK 562, Department of Business Administration, Lund University.

Andren, N. and L. Oxelheim, 2001, Exchange-Rate and Interest-Rate Driven Competitive Advantages in the EMU, Working Paper Series No 2001/8, Institute of Economic Research, Lund University

Ang, A. and G. Bekaert, 2001, Stock Return Predictability: Is it There?, NBER Working Paper Series, April.

Appeltofft, J., Petrykowski, M. and M. Svensson, 2000, Corporate Macroeconomic Exposure Management: Domtar Inc. and Westvaco Corporation, FEK 562 International Finance, Spring, Institution of Business Administration, Lunds University.

Archinard, G. and B. Guerrien, 1988, Analyse Mathématique pour Economistes, 3e édition, Economica. Paris.

Arden, R., Cook, S., Holly, S. and P. Turner, 1998, The Asymmetric Effects of Monetary Policy: Some Results from a Macroeconomic Model, Working Paper, Department of Applied Economics, University of Cambridge.

Aspesi, C., and Vardhan, D., 1999, Brilliant Strategy, but Can You Execute? The McKinsey Quarterly No.1, pp. 88-99.

Auckenthaler, C. und J. Gabathuler, 1999, Gedanken zum Konzept eines Total Enterprise Wide Risk Management (TERM), KPMG Consulting

Avenarius, C., 1996, Management von Waehrungsrisiken, in Eller, R., Handbuch Derivater Instrumente: Produkte, Strategien und Risikomanagement, Schaeffer-Poeschel Verlag Stuttgart.

Axel F.A. and Muller, A., 1997, Export and Hedging Decisions under Exchange Rate Risk: A Note, European Economic Review 41, pp. 1421-1426.

Baba, N. and K. Fukao, 2000, Currency Risk Exposure of Japanese Firms with Overseas Production Bases: Theory and Evidence, Discussion Paper No. 2000-E-1, Institute for Monetary and Economic Studies, Bank of Japan.

Bailey, W. and K. Bhaopichitr, 2002, How Important Was Silver? Some Evidence on Exchange Rate Fluctuations and Stock Returns in Colonial-Era Asia, Working Paper, Johnson Graduate School of Management, Cornell University.

Baldwin, R., 1988, Hysterisis in Import Prices: The Beachhead Effect, The American Economic Review, Vol. 78 No. 4, Sept., pp. 773-785.

Barber, B.M., Click, R.W. and M.N. Darrough, 1999, The Impact of Shocks to Exchange Rates and Oil Prices on U.S. Sales of American and Japanese Automakers, Japan and the World Economy 11(1), p. 57-93.

Baron, D.P., 1976, Fluctuating Exchange Rates and the Pricing of Exports, Economic Inquiry, Sept., 14, 425-438.

Bartov, E. and G.M. Bodnar, 1994, Firm Valuation, Earnings Expectations and the Exchange Rate Exposure Effect, Journal of Finance 49, p. 1755-85.

Bartov, E. and G.M. Bodnar, 1995, Foreign Currency Translation Reporting and the Exchange Rate Exposure Effect, Journal of International Financial Management and Accounting, Vol. 6, No. 2, p. 93-114.

Bartov, E., Bodnar, G.M. and A. Kaul, 1996, Exchange Rate Variability and The Riskiness of US Multinational Firms: Evidence From The Breakdown of The Bretton Woods System, Journal of Financial Economics 42, p. 105-132

Bartram, S.M., 1999, Corporate Risk Management - Eine empirische Analyse der finanzwirtschaftlichen exposures deutscher Industrie- und Handelsunternehmen, Uhlenbruch Verlag

Bartram, S.M., 2000, Corporate Risk Management as a Lever for Shareholder Value Creation, in Financial Markets, Institutions & Instruments - New York University Salomon Center, V. 9, N. 5, December, Blackwell Publishers, Cambridge, MA.

Bartram, S.M., 2001, The Interest Rate Exposure of Nonfinancial Corporations, Working Paper, Graduate School of Management, Lancaster University. (Also in European Finance Review, Vol. 6 (1), 2002, 101-125).

Bartram, S.M., 2002, Linear and Nonlinear Foreign Exchange Rate Exposures of German Nonfinancial Corporations, Working Paper, Graduate School of Management, Lancaster University. (Journal of International Money and Finance, forthcoming 2002)

Bartram, S.M., Karolyi, G.A. and S. Kleimeier, 2002, The Impact of the Euro on Foreign Exchange Rate Risk Exposures, Working Paper, Limburg Institute of Financial Economics, Maastricht University.

Batten, J., R. Mellor and V. Wan, 1993, Foreign Exchange Risk Management Practices and Products Used by Australian Firms, Journal of International Business Studies, p. 557-573.

Baum, C.F., Caglayan, M. and J.T. Barkoulas, 2000, Exchange Rate Uncertainty and Firm Profitability, Working Paper, Department of Economics, Boston College.

Beder, T.S., 1995, VAR: Seductive but Dangerous, Financial Analysts Journal, Sep-Oct.

Beike, R., 1995, Devisenmanagement, S+W Steuer- und Wirtschaftsverlag (Hamburg)

Bekaert, G. and C. Harvey, 1995, Time-Varying World Market Integration, Journal of Finance, 50, 403-443.

Bekaert, G. and R.J. Hodrick, 1992, Characterizing Predictable Components in Equity Foreign Exchange Rates of Returns, Journal of Finance 47, p. 467-509.

Belk, P.A. and M. Glaum, 1990, The Management of Foreign Exchange Risk in UK Multinationals: an Empirical Investigation, Accounting and Business Research, Vol. 21, No. 81, p. 3-13.

Belk, P. and M. Glaum, 1993, The UK's Entry into the ERM: some Views of Group Treasures in UK and German Multinational Corporations, European Business and Economic Development, 2(3): p. 9-17.

Bellalah, M., 2000, Les Entreprises Exportatrices Face a l'Euro, Working Paper Universite de Paris-Dauphine.

Benet, B. A. and C.F. Luft, 1995, Hedge Performance of SPX Index Options and S&P 500 Futures, Journal of Futures Markets, September, p. 691-717.

Bergbom, L., 1998, Exchange Rate Variability Inside and Outside the EMU, Working Paper, Uppsala University.

Bergman, U.M. and J. Hansson, 2000, Real Exchange Rates and Switching Regimes, Working Paper, Department of Economics, Lund University.

Bergin, P. R. and R. C. Feenstra, 2001, Pricing-to-Market, Staggered Contracts, and Real Exchange Rate Persistence, Journal of International Economics 54, p. 333-359.

Berkowitz, J., 1998, Evaluating the Forecasts of Risk Models, Working Paper, Federal Reserve Board.

Berkowitz, J., 1997, Long-Horizon Exchange Rate Predictability, Working Paper, International Monetary Fund

Bernard, A.B. and J.B. Jensen, 1997a, Understanding the US Export Boom, Working Paper, MIT Industrial Performance Center 97-006WP, March.

Bernard, A.B. and J. B. Jensen, 1997b, Why Some Firms Export: Experience, Entry Costs, Spillowers, and Subsidies, Yale Mimeo.

Bernard, A.B. and J. Wagner, 1998, Export Entry and Exit by German Firms, Working Paper, MIT Industrial Performance Center 98-002WP, April.

Bessembinder, H., 1992, Exchange Rate Exposure and the Hedging of Currency Risk, in Recent Developments in International Banking and Finance, Vol. VI.

Best, A., 1999, Hedging Asian Currency Risk, The Chase Guide to Corporate Treasury in Asia.

Betts, C. and M.B. Devereux, 1998, Exchange Rate Dynamics in a Model of Pricing-To-Market, Department of Economics, University of Southern California, Los Angeles.

Bilson, J.F.O., 1994, Managing Economic Exposure to Foreign Exchange Risk: a Case Study of American Airlines, in Amihud, Y. and R. M. Levich (eds.), Exchange Rates and Corporate Performance, Irwin (New York University), p. 221-246

Bird, J., 2001, Currency Fluctuations, Earnings Announcements, and Market Capitalization, Bank of America Journal of Risk Analysis.

Bishop, M., 1996, A Survey of Corporate Risk Management, The Economist, February 10, Special Section, p. 3-22.

Bishop, P. and D. Dixon, 1992, Foreign Exchange Handbook: Managing Risk and Opportunity in Global Currency Markets, McGraw-Hill, Inc.

Black, F. and M. Scholes, 1973, The Pricing of Options and Corporate Liabilities, Journal of Political Economy, May-June, 637-659.

Black, A., 2002, International Financial Management, R. Buckland & South-Western College Publishing.

Black, A., Fraser, P., and N. Groenewold, 2000, US Stock Prices and Macroeconomic Fundamentals, Working Paper, Department of Accountancy and Finance, University of Aberdeen.

Bodart, V. and P. Reding, 2001, Do Foreign Exchange Markets Matter for Industry Stock Returns? An Empirical Investigation, Working Paper, Catholic University of Louvain.

Bodie, Z., Kane, A. and A.J. Marcus, 1993, Investments, Second Edition, Irwin.

Bodnar, G. M., 1998, Exchange Rate Exposure and Market Value, in Wharton School, University of Chicago Graduate School of Business, London Business School, The Complete Finance Companion, Financial Times Mastering Series

Bodnar, G. M., 1999, Corporate Exposure to Exchange Rates, International Finance – FNCE 719 WEMBA, Spring.

Bodnar, G. M., Dumas, B. and R. C. Marston, 2002, Pass-through and Exposure, The Journal of Finance, Vol. 58, No. 1, Feb., 199-231.

Bodnar, G. M. and G. Gebhardt, 1998, Derivatives Usage in Risk Management by U.S. and German Non-Financial Firms: A Comparative Study, Working Paper, Wharton School, University of Pennsylvania.

Bodnar, G. M. and W.M. Gentry, 1993, Exchange Rate Exposures and Industry Characteristics: Evidence from Canada, Japan and the USA, Journal of International Money and Finance 12, p. 29-45

Bodnar, G.M., Marston, R.C. and G. Hayt, 1998, 1998 Survey of Financial Risk Management by U.S. Non-Financial Firms, George Weiss Center for International Financial Research, Wharton School, University of Pennsylvania and CIBC World Markets, July, p. 1-21.

Bodnar, G.M., Hayt, G.S. and R.C. Marston, 1996, 1995 Wharton Survey of Derivatives Usage by US Non-Financial Firms, Financial Management, Vol. 25, No.4, p.113-133.

Bodnar, G.M. and R.C. Marston, 2000, A Simple Model of Foreign Exchange Exposure, Working Paper, Wharton School, University of Pennsylvania.

Bodnar, G. M., Tang, C. and J. Weintrop, 1998, Both Sides of Corporate Diversification: The Value Impacts of Geographic and Industrial Diversification, Working Paper, Wharton School, University of Pennsylvania.

Bodnar, G. M. and M. H. F. Wong, 1999, Estimating Exchange Rate Exposures: Some "Weighty" Issues, Working Paper, Haas School of Business, University of California at Berkeley, also NBER Working Paper 7497, January 2000

Bodurtha, J.N., 1993, Integrating Interest Rate and Currency Risk Management, School of Business Georgetown University.

Bookstaber, R., 1997, Global Risk Management: Are We Missing the Point, The Journal of Portfolio Management, Spring.

Bollerslev, T., 1986, Generelized Autoregressive Conditional Heteroscedasticity, Journal of Econometrics, 31, pp. 307-327.

Bollerslev, T. and J.M. Wooldridge, Quasi-Maximum Likelihood Estimation and Inference in Dynamic Models with Time Varying Covariances, Econometric Reviews, 1992, Vol. 11, p. 143–172.

Booth, L., 1996, On the Nature of Foreign Exchange Exposure, Journal of Multinational Financial Management, Vol. 6, Issue 1, January, p. 1-24.

Booth, L., 1998, What Drives Shareholder Value?, Working Paper, Rotman School of Management, University of Toronto.

Booth, L. D. and W. Rotenberg, 1990, Assessing Foreign Exchange Rate Exposure: Theory and Application Using Canadian Firms, Journal of International Financial Management and Accounting, Vol. 2 (1), p. 1-22.

Borenstein, S. and A. Shepard, 1993, Dynamic Pricing in Retail Gasoline Markets, NBER Working Paper No. 4489, National Bureau of Economic Research, October.

Boudoukh, J. and M. Richardson, 1993, Stock Returns and Inflation: a Long-Run Perspective, American Economic Review, Vol. 83, No. 5, 1346-1355.

Boudoukh, J. and M. Richardson, 1993, The statistics of Long-Horizon Regressions Revisited, Mathematical Finance 4, p. 103-119.

Boyer, M., Gravel, E. and P. Lasserre, 2004, Real Options and Strategic Competition: A Survey, Working Paper, University of Montreal, May.

Bradley, K., 1996, Economic Currency Exposure and Its Determinants: A Survey of British Companies, Working Paper 96.12, Center for Financial Markets Research, Management School, The University of Edinburgh.

Bradley, K. and Moles, P., 1998, The Nature and Determinants of the Economic Currency Exposure of Non-Financial UK Firms, Working Paper 98.8, Center for Financial Markets Research, Management School, The University of Edinburgh.

Bradley, K. and Moles, P., 2001, The Effects of Exchange Rate Movements on Non-Financial UK Firms, International Business Review 10, p. 51-69.

Brandenburger, A. and B. Nalebuff, 1996, Co-opetition, New York: Currency Doubleday.

Brander, J.A. and B.J. Spencer, 1985, Export Subsidies and International Market Share Rivalry, Journal of International Economics 18, 83-100.

Branson, W. H. and R. C. Marston, 1989, Price and Output Adjustment in Japanese Manufacturing, Working Paper No. 2878, National Bureau of Economic Research, March.

Brealey, R.A. and E.C. Kaplanis, 1995, Discrete Exchange Rate Hedging Strategies, Journal of Banking and Finance 19, pp. 765-784.

Brealy, R. A. and S. C. Myers, 2000, Principles of Corporate Finance, 6th Edition, Irwin McGraw-Hill

Bresnahan, T. F., 1987, Competition and Collusion in the American Automobile Industry: the 1955 Price War, The Journal of Industrial Economics, XXXV, p. 457-482.

Brockwell, P. J. and R. A. Davis, 1996, Time Series: Theory and Methods, Second Edition, Springer Series in Statistics.

Broll, U., 1999, Export as an Option, International Economic Journal, Spring, 19-26.

Broll, U. and S. Hansen, 2004, Labour Demand and Exchange Rate Volatility, Discussion Paper 28 - June, Center for Globalization and Europeanization of the Economy, Georg-August-Universität Göttingen.

Broll, U., Welzel, P. and K. P. Wong, 1999, Strategic Hedging, Working Paper, Department of Economics, Saarland University.

Brooks, R. and L. Catao, 2000, The New Economy and Global Stock Returns, IMF Working Paper 216, Dec.

Brooks, R. and M.D. Negro, 2002, The Rise in Comovement Across National Stock Markets: Market Integration or Global Bubble?, IMF Working Paper 147, Sept.

Brown, G.W., 2001, Managing Foreign Exchange Risk with Derivatives, Journal of Financial Economics 60, 401-448.

Brown, G.W., 2001, Seeking Security in a Volatile World, in Mastering Risk, Vol. 1: Concepts, Financial Times/Prentice Hall.

Brown, G.W. and Z. Khokher, 2000, Corporate Hedging with a View, Working Paper, Kenan-Flager Business School, The University of North Carolina at Chapel Hill.

Brown, G.W. and K.B. Toft, 2001, How Firms Should Hedge, Working Paper, Kenan-Flager Business School, The University of North Carolina at Chapel Hill.

Bulow, J., Geanakoplos, J. and P. Klemperer, 1985, Multimarket Oligopoly: Strategic Substitutes and Complements, Journal of Political Economy, June, p. 488-511.

Burgess, S. and M. M. Knetter, 1996, An International Comparison of Employment Adjustment to Exchange Rate Fluctuations, Working Paper No. 5861 (December), National Bureau of Economic Research, December.

Burgman, T.A., 1996, An Empirical Examination of Multinational Corporate Capital Structure, Journal of International Business Studies, Third Quarter.

Butler, K.C., 2000, Multinational Finance, South-Western College Publishing.

Campa, J. and L.S. Goldberg, 1995, Investment in Manufacturing, Exchange Rates and External Exposure, Journal of International Economics 38, p. 297-320.

Campa, J. and L.S. Goldberg, 1995, Investment, Pass-through and Exchange Rates: A Cross-Country Comparison, NBER Working Paper no 5139.

Campa, J. and L.S. Goldberg, 1997, The Evolving External Orientatio of Manufacturing Industries: Evidence from Four Countries, NBER Working Paper No. 5919.

Campa, J. and L.S. Goldberg, 1998, Employment Versus Wage Adjustment and the U.S. Dollar, Working Paper, Stern School of Business, New York University.

Campa, J. and L.S. Goldberg, 1998, Investment, Pass-through and Exchange Rates, Working Paper, Stern School of Business, New York University.

Campa, Jose and L. S. Goldberg, 2001, Exchange Rate Pass-Through into Import Prices: A Macro or Micro Phenomenon?, Working Paper, IESE Business School and N.B.E.R.

Campbell, J.Y., 1987, Stock Returns and the Term Structure, Journal of Financial Economics, Vol. 18 (2), 373-399.

Campbell, J.Y., 1993, Why Long-Horizons? A Study of Power Against Persistent Alternatives, Working Paper, Princeton University.

Capel. J., 1997, A Real Options Approach to Economic Exposure Management, Journal of International Financial Management & Accounting, Vol. 8, No. 2, p. 87-113.

Carter, D.A., Pantzalis, C. and B.J. Simkins, 2001, Firmwide Risk Management of Foreign Exchange Exposure by U.S. Multinational Corporations, Working Paper, Oklahoma State University.

Carter, D.A., Pantzalis, C. and B.J. Simkins, 2003, Asymmetric Exposure to Foreign-Exchange Risk: Financial and Real Option Hedges Implemented by U.S. Multinational Corporations, Working Paper, College of Business Administration, Oklahoma State University.

Ceglowski, J., 1989, Dollar Depreciation and U.S. Industry Performance, Journal of International Money and Finance, 8: p. 233-251.

CFO Research Services, 2002, Strategic Risk Management: New Disciplines, New Opportunities, CFO Publishing Corp.

Chamberlain, S., Howe, J. S. and Popper,H., 1997, The Exchange Rate Exposure of U.S. and Japanese Banking Institutions, Journal of Banking and Finance, 21(6), p. 871-892.

Chang, B.-K. and H. E. Lapan, 2001, Price Commitment vs. Flexibility: The Role of Exchange Rate Uncertainty and Its Implications for Exchange Rate Pass-Through, Working Paper, Department of Economics, Iowa State University.

Chen, N.F., Roll, R. and S.A. Ross, 1986, Economic Forces and the Stock Market, Journal of Business 59, 383-403.

Cheung, Y. W., M. Chinn, and E. Fujii, 1999, Market Structure and the Persistence of Sectoral Real Exchange Rates, Working Paper, Department of Economics, University of California, Santa Cruz.

Cheung, Y.W. and F. Westermann, 2000, Equity Price Dynamics Before and After the Introduction of the Euro: A Note, Working Paper, Department of Economics, University of California, Santa Cruz.

Chiao, C. and K. Hung, 2000, Exchange-Rate Exposure of Taiwanese Exporting Firms, Review of Pacific Basin Financial Markets and Policies, Vol. 3, No. 2, p. 201-233.

Chinn, M.D. and R.A. Meese, Banking on Currency Forecasts: How Predictable is Change in Money?, Journal of International Economics, 1995, No. 38, pp. 161-178.

Choi, J.J., 1986, A Model of Firm Valuation with Exchange Rate Exposure, Journal of International Business Studies, Summer, 153-160.

Choi, J.J., 1988, Diversification, Exchange Risk, and Corporate International Investment, Journal of International Business Studies, Spring.

Choi, J.J., 1996, Derivative Exposure and the Interest Rate and Exchange Rate Risks of U.S. Banks, Working Paper, The Wharton School, University of Pennsylvania.

Choi, J.J. and E. Elyasiani, 1997, Derivative Exposure and the Interest Rate and Exchange Rate Risk of U.S. Banks, Journal of Financial Services Research, Vil. 12 (2-3), 267-286.

Choi, J.J. and Y.-C. Kim, 2000, The Asian Exposure of U.S. Firms: Risk Management and Operating Strategies, Working Paper, Department of Finance, Fox School of Business and Management, Temple University.

Choi, J.J. and A.M. Prasad, 1995, Exchange Risk Sensitivity and Its Determinants: A Firm and Industry Analysis of U.S. Multinationals, Financial Management, 24(3): p. 77-88.

Choi, J.J., Hiraki, T. and N. Takezawa, 1998, Is Foreign Exchange Risk Priced in the Japanese Stock Market, Journal of Financial and Quantitative Analysis, Sept., Vol. 33, No. 3, 361-382.

Choudhri, E.U. and D.S. Hakura, 2001, Exchange Rate Pass-Trough to Domestic Prices: Does the Inflationary Environment Matter?, IMF Working Paper, WP/01/194.

Chow, E.H. and H.-L. Chen, 1998, The Determinants of Foreign Exchange Rate Exposure: Evidence on Japanese Firms, Pacific-Basin Finance Journal, Vol. 6 (1/2), p. 153-174.

Chow, E., Lee, W. and M. Solt, 1997, The Exchange Rate Risk Exposure of Asset returns, Journal of Business 70, p. 105-123.

Chow, E.H., Wayne, Y.L. and M.E. Solt, 1997, The Economic Exposure of U.S. Multinational Firms, The Journal of Financial Research, Summer, Vol. 20, No. 2, p. 191-210.

Chowdhry, B., 1995, Corporate Hedging of Exchange Risk When Foreign Currency Cash Flow Is Uncertain, Management Science, Vol. 41, No. 6, June, 1083-1090.

Chowdhry, B. and J.T.B. Howe, 1996, Corporate Risk Management for Multinational Corporations: Financial and Operational Hedging Policies, UCLA Working Paper.

Chowdhry, B. and J.T.B. Howe, 1999, Corporate Risk Management for Multinational Corporations: Financial and Operational Hedging Policies, European Finance Review 2, p. 229-246.

Clark, T., Kotabe, M. and D. Rajaratnam, 1999, Exchange Rate Pass- Through and International Pricing Strategy: A Conceptual Framework and Research Propositions, Journal of International Business Studies, 30, 2.

Clarke, R. and S. W. Davies, 1982, Market Structure and Price Cost Margins, Economics, Vol. 49, 277-287.

Clifton, E.V., 1985, Real Exchange Rates, Import Penatration, and Protectionism in Industrial Countries, IMF Staff Papers, Vol. 32, No. 3 (Sept.), 513-536.

Clifton, E.V., 1998, The Decline of Traditional Sectors in Israel: The Role of the Exchange Rate and the Minimum Wage, IMF Working Paper, WP/98/167.

Cohen, M.A. and A. Huchzermeier, 1998, Global Supply Chain Management: A Survey of Research and Applications, in: Tayur, S., Magazine, M. and R. Ganeshan (Eds.), Quantitative Models for Supply Chain Management, Kluwer Academic Press, Ch. 21.

Cohen and Huchzermeier, 1999, Global Supply Chain Network Management under Price/Exchange Rate Risk and Demand Uncertainty, Working Paper.

Colquitt, L.L. Hoyt R.E. and E.B. Lee, 1999, Integrated Risk Management and the Role of the Risk Manager, Risk Management and Insurance Review, Vol.2, No.3, 43-61.

Connolly, R.A., Ozoguz, A. and D.J. Ravenscraft, 2000, Foreign Market Cash Flow Exposure: A Multi-Country, Firm-Level Study, Working Paper, Kenan-Flager Business School.

Copeland, T., 2001 (a), The Right Stuff: Cutting Edge Applications in Corporate Finance / European Financial Management Association, Monitor Company Group, L.P.

Copeland, T., 2001 (b), Value-Based Management, White Paper, Monitor Group.

Copeland, T.and V. Antikarov, 2001, Real Options - A Practitioner's Guide, Texere, New York.

Copeland, T. and M. Copeland, 1999, Managing FX Risk - A Value Maximizing Approach, Financial Management, Vol. 28, No. 3, Autumn, 68-75.

Copeland, T. and Y. Joshi, 1996, Why Derivatives Don't Reduce Currency Risk, The McKinsey Quarterly, Number 1, pp. 66-79

Copeland, T. Koller, T. and J. Murrin, 1994, Valuation: Measuring and Managing the Value of Companies, 2nd ed., New York, NY, John Wiley & Sons.

Copeland, T. and J. F. Weston, 1992, Financial Theory and Corporate Policy, 3rd edition, Addison Wesley

Copeland, T. and Keenan, P., 1998, How Much is Flexibility Worth?, The McKinsey Quarterly, Number 2, pp. 38-49

Copeland, T. and Keenan, P., 1998, Making Real Options Real, The McKinsey Quarterly, Number 3, pp. 128-141.

Coppe, B., Graham, M. and T. M. Koller, 1996, Are you Taking the Wrong FX Risk?, The McKinsey Quaterly, Number 1, pp. 80-89

Cornell, B. and A.C. Shapiro, 1983, Managing Foreign Exchange Risks, Midland Corporate Financial Journal, Vol. 1, No. 3, 16-31.

Cormier, D., Magngnan, M. and D. Zeghal, 1999, Earnings, Cash Flows and Value-Added as Performance Metrics: an International Comparison, Cahier de Recherche du CETAI, HEC-Montreal, Feb.

Cosset, J. C. and B. D. de la Rianderie, 1985, Political Risk and Foreign Exchange Rates: An Efficient-Markets Approach, Journal of International Business Studies, Fall.

Cote, A., 1994, Exchange Rate Volatility and Trade: a Survey, Banque du Canada, Document de Travail 94-5.

Cottrell, T.J. and G. A. Sick, 2001, First Mover (Dis)advantage and Real Options, Journal of Applied Corporate Finance 14(2): 41-51.

Coughlin, C. and P.S. Pollard, 2000, Exchange Rate Pass-Through in U.S. Manufacturing: Exchange Rate Index Choice and Asymmetry Issues, Working Paper 2000-022A, Federal Reserve Bank of St. Louis.

Courtney, H., Kirkland, J. and P. Viguerie, 1997, Strategy Under Uncertainty, Harvard Business Review, Nov.-Dec., 67-79.

Coval, J., 1998, Financial Management in the International Corporation: Assessing the Risk of Foreign Exchange Exposure, Lecture Notes, Michigan Business School, March 30.

Cox, J.C., Ross, S.A. and M. Rubinstein, 1979, Option Pricing: A Simplified Approach, Journal of Financial Economics, 7, pp. 229-263.

Cox, M., 1986, A New Alternative Trade-Weighted Dollar Exchange Rate Index, Federal Reserve Bank of Dallas Economic Review 67.

Culp, C.L. and M.H. Miller, 1995, Mettalgesellschaft and the Economics of Synthetic Storage, Journal of Applied Corporate Finance 7, 62-76.

Culp, C.L. and M.H. Miller, 1995, Hedging in the Theory of Corporate Finance: A Reply to Our Critics, Journal of Applied Corporate Finance 8, Spring, p. 122.

Culp, C.L. and Merton M. Miller and Andrea M.P. Neves, "Value At Risk: Uses and Abuses", Journal of Applied Corporate Finance, 1998, Vol. 10, No. 4, pp. 26-38.

Cumby, R. E., 1994, Coments on Dornbusch, Levi, and Amihud, in Amihud, Y. and R. M. Levich (eds.), Exchange Rates and Corporate Performance, New York University

Cumming, C.M. and B.J. Hirtle, 2001, The Chalenges of Risk Management in Diversified Financial Companies, Federal Reserve Bank of New York Economic Policy Review, March.

Cummins, J.D., Phillips, R.D., and S.D. Smith, 1997, Derivatives and Corporate Risk Management: Participation and Volume Decisions in the Insurance Industry, Working Paper, Federal Reserve Bank of Atlanta, November.

Dahl. F.M., 1996, Revision im Waehrungsmanagement, in Eller, R. (Hrsg.), Handbuch Derivater Instrumente: Produkte, Strategien und Risikomanagement, Schaeffer-Poeschel Verlag Stuttgart.

Dahlquist, M. and G. Robertsson, 2001, Exchange Rate Exposure, Risk Premia, and Firm Characteristics, Working Paper, Fuqua School of Business, Duke University.

Damodaran, A., 2003-a, Value and Risk: Beyond Betas, Working Paper, Stern School of Business, New York University (NYU).

Damodaran, A., 2003-b, Measuring Company Risk Exposure to Country Risk, Working Paper, Stern School of Business, New York University (NYU).

Damodaran, A., 2004-a, Value Creation and Enhancement: Back to the Future, Working Paper, Stern School of Business, New York University (NYU).

Damodaran, A., 2004-b, Estimating Risk Free Rates, Working Paper, Stern School of Business, New York University (NYU).

Darvas, Z., 2001, Exchange Rate Pass-Through and Real Exchange Rate in EU Candidate Countries, Discussion Paper 10/01, Economic Research Center of the Deutsche Bundesbank.

d'Aspremont, C., Dos Santos Ferreira, R. and L.-A. Gerard-Varet, 1996, On the Dixit-Stiglitz Model of Monopolistic Competition, The American Economic Review, Vol. 86, Issue 3, June, 623-629.

Davis, J. L. and A. S. Desai, 1998, Stock Returns, Beta and Firm Size: The Case of Bull, Bear, and Flat Markets, Working Paper, Department of Finance, Kansas State University.

Dechow, P.M., 1994, Accounting Earnings and Cash Flows as Measures of Firm Performance: the Role of Accounting Accruals, Journal of Accounting and Economics 18, 3-42.

Deep, A., 1996, Optimal Dynamic Hedging Using Futures under a Borrowing Constraint, Yale University, Working Paper.

De Fiore, F., 1998, The Transmission of Monetary Policy in Israel, IMF Working Paper 98/114, Washington: International Monetary Fund.

De Jong, A., Ligterink, J. and V. Macrae, 2002, A Firm-Specific Analysis of the Exchange-Rate Exposure of Dutch Firms, Working Paper ERS-2002-109-F&Ajuh, Erasmus Research Institute of Management (ERIM).

De Meza and Van Der Ploeg, 1987, Production Flexibility as a Motive for Multinatioality, The Journal of Industrial Economics 35, no. 3, 343-351.

Demirag, I.S., 1988, Assessing Foreign Subsidiary Performance: The Currency Choice of U.K. MNCs, Journal of International Business Studies, Summer.

Demacopoulos, A.C., 1989, Foreign Exchange Exposure in International Construction, Ph.D. Dissertation, MIT, June.

DeRosa, D.F., 1996, Managing Foreign Exchange Risk, Advanced Strategies for Global Investors, Corporations and Financial Institutions, Irwin.

De Santis, G. and B. Gérard, 1998, How Big is the Premium for Currency Risk?, Journal of Financial Economics 49, 373-412.

De Santis, G., Gérard, B., and P. Hillion, 1999, The Relevance of Currency Risk in the EMU.

Deschamps, P., 1988, Cours de Mathématiques pour Economistes, Dunod, Paris.

Detemple, J.B., and M. Adler, 1988, Hedging with Futures and Options, Studies in Banking and Finance 5, 181-197.

Deutsche Boerse, 2001, Guidelines to Deutsche Boerse's Equity Indices, Version 4.2, August.

Deutsche Bundesbank, 1996, Monatsbericht der Deutschen Bundesbank, Vol. 48 (11), Deutschen Bundesbank, May, Frankfurt am Main.

Deutsche Bundesbank, 1997, Zur Entwicklung der Kapitalverflechtung der Unternhemen mit dem Ausland von Ende 1993 bis Ende 1995, Monatsberichte der Deutschen Bundesbank, May, Frankfurt am Main.

Dewenter, K.L., Higgins, R.C. and T.T. Simin, 2001, Estimating the Exchange Rate Exposure of US Multinational Firms: Evidence from an Event Study Methodology, in Frenkel, M., Hommel, U. and M. Rudolf (eds), Risk Management – Challenge and Opportunity, Springer Verlag, Berlin.

Di Iorio, A. and R. Faff, 2000, An analysis of Asymmetry in Foreign Currency Exposure of the Australian Equities Market, Journal of Multinational Financial Management, 10(2), p. 133-159.

Di Iorio, A. and R. Faff, 2001, Foreign Exchange Exposure and Pricing in the Australian Equitites Market: A Fama and French Framework, Working Paper, School of Economics ad Finance, RMIT University.

Diebold, F. X., 1999, Financial Risk Management in a Volatile Global Environment, The Wharton School, University of Pennsylvania.

Dimson, E. and Marsh, P., 1988, Svenska Neuhaus, Cases in Corporate Finance, London Business School, John Wiley & Sons.

Din, Q. and P. Kouvelis, 2001, On the Interaction of Production and Financial Hedging Decisions in Global Markets, Working Paper, Olin School of Business, Washington University in St. Louis.

Dixit, A.K., 1986, Comparative Statics for Oligopoly, International Economic Review, Vol. 27, No. 1, February, 107-122.

Dixit, A.K., 1989a, Entry and Exit Decisions under Uncertainty, Journal of Political Economy, Vol. 97, No. 3, p. 620-638.

Dixit, A.K., 1989b, Hysterisis, Import Penetration, and Exchange Rate Pass-Through, The Quarterly Journal of Economics, Vol. CIV, Issue 2, May, p. 205-228.

Dixit, A.K., 2000, Some Reflections on Theories and Applications of Monopolistic Competition, Working Paper, Department of Economics, Princeton University.

Dixit, A.K., and J. E. Stiglitz, 1977, Monopolistic Competition and Optimum Product Diversity, The American Economic Review, Vol. 67, Issue 3, June, 297-308.

Dixit, A.K., and J. E. Stiglitz, 1993, Monopolistic Competition and Optimum Product Diversity: Reply, The American Economic Review, Vol. 83, No. 1, March, 302-304.

Dixit, A.K., and R.S. Pindyck, 1994, Investment under Uncertainty, Princeton University Press.

Dixit, A.K., and R.S. Pindyck, The Options Approach to Capital Investment, Harvard Business Review, May-June 1995, p. 105-115.

Doan, T. A., 1995, RATS User's Manual, Version 4, Estima, Evanston, IL.

Doherty, N.A., 2000, Integrated Risk Management, Techniques and Strategies for Managing Corporate Risk, McGraw-Hill, Inc.

Doidge, C., Griffin, J., and R. Williamson, 2000, An International Comparison of Exchange Rate Exposure, Working Paper, Fisher College of Business, Ohio State University.

Doidge, C., Griffin, J., and R. Williamson, 2002, Does Exchange Rate Exposure Matter?, Working Paper, Fisher College of Business, Ohio State University.

Dolde, W., 1993, The Trajectory of Corporate Financial Risk Management, Journal of Applied Corporate Finance, Vol. 6, Fall, No. 3, p. 33-41.

Dolde, W., 1993, Use of Foreign Exchange and Interest Rate Risk Management in Large Firms, University of Connecticut, School of Business Administration, Working Paper, p. 93-142.

Domian, D.L. and J.E. Gilster, 1996, Expected Inflation, Interest Rates, and Stock Returns, Financial Review 31, 809-830.

Dominguez, K.M., 1998, The Dollar Exposure of Japanese Companies, Discussion Paper No. 414, Research Seminar in International Economics, Ford School of Public Policy, University of Michigan.

Dominguez, K.M. and L.L. Tesar, 2001, A Re-Examination of Exchange Rate Exposure, Working Paper 8128, National Bureau of Economic Research, February.

Dominguez, K.M. and L.L. Tesar, 2001, Exchange Rate Exposure, Mimeo, Gerald R. Ford School of Public Policy, University of Michigan.

Dominguez, K.M. and L.L. Tesar, 2001, Trade and Exposure, Working Paper, Ford School of Public Policy, University of Michigan.

Domowitz, I., Hubbard, G., and B. Petersen, 1986, Business Cycles and the Relationship between Concentration and Price-Cost Margins, Rand Journal of Economics, 17, Spring, p. 1-17.

Donaldson, G. and J. W. Lorsch, 1993, Decision Making at the Top, Basic Books, 1983. The Economist Intelligence Unit, Strategic Financial Risk Management, Research Report.

Donnelly, R. and E. Sheehy, 1996, The Share Price Reaction of U.K. Exporters to Exchange Rate Movements: An Empirical Study, Journal of International Business Studies, 27(1): p. 157-165

Dornbusch, R., 1987, Exchange Rates and Prices, The American Economic Review, Vol.77, p. 93-106.

Doukas, J., Hall, P.H. and L.H.P. Lang, 1998, Exchange Rate Exposure, Stock Returns and the Pricing of Currency Risk in Japan, Working Paper, Old Dominion University.

Doukas, J., Hall, P.H. and L.H.P. Lang, 1999, The Pricing of Currency Risk in Japan, Journal of Banking and Finance 23(1), 1-20.

Doukas, J., Hall, P.H. and L.H.P. Lang, 2001, Exchange Rate Exposure at the Firm and Industry Level, Working Paper, Old Dominion University.

Dufey, G., 1972, Corporate Finance and Exchange Rate Variations, Financial Management, 1(2): p. 51-57.

Dufey, G. and I.H. Giddy, 1978, International Financial Planning, California Management Review, Vol. 21 (1), p. 69-81.

Dufey, G. and I.H. Giddy, 1997, Management of Foreign Exchange Risk, in: Choi, F.D.S. [Hrsg.]: International Accounting and Finance Handbook, 2. Aufl., John Wiley & Sons Inc. (New York, NY), Kapitel 31, p. 31.1-31.30.

Dufey, G. and U. Hommel, 1996, Currency Exposure Management in Multinational Companies: Centralized Coordination as an Alternative to Centralization, in Engelhard, J. [Hrsg.], Strategische Fuehrung internationaler Unternehmen, Wiesbaden, S. p. 199-220.

Dufey, G. and S.L. Srinivasulu, 1983, The Case for Corporate Management of Foreign Exchange Risk, Financial Management, Winter, Vol. 12, p. 54-62.

Dukas, S. P., Fatemi, A.M. and A. Tavakkol, 1996, Foreign Exchange Exposure and the Pricing of Exchange Rate Risk, Global Finance Journal, Vol. 7, No. 2, p. 169-189.

Dumas, B., 1978, The Theory of the Trading Firm Revisited, Journal of Finance 33, p. 1019-1029.

Dumas, B., 1994, Short- and Long- Term Hedging for the Corporation, CEPR Discussion Paper No. 1083.

Dumas, B. and B. Solnik, 1995, The World Price of Foreign Exchange Risk, Journal of Finance, June, Vo. 50, No. 2, p. 445-479.

Eaker, M.R., 1981, The Numeraire Problem and Foreign Exchange Risk, The Journal of Finance, Vol. 36, No. 2, May, 419-426.

Eiteman, D.K., Stonehill, A.I. and M.H. Moffett, 2000, Multinational Business Finance, Ninth Edition, Addison-Wesley Publishing Company.

Eller, R., 1996, Handbuch Derivater Instrumente: Produkte, Strategien und Risikomanagement, Schaeffer-Poeschel Verlag Stuttgart.

Elliot, M.W., 2001, The Emerging Field of Enterprise Risk, View Point, The Marsh & McLennan Companies Journal, Vol. XXX, Number 2, p. 33-39.

Elton, E.J. and M.J. Gruber, 1995, Modern Portfolio Theory and Investment Analysis, Fifth Edition, John Wiley & Sons, Inc.

Emmons, W.R. and F.A. Schmid, 2000, The Asian Crisis and the Exposure of Large U.S. Firms, Federal Reserve Bank of St. Louis Review, January/February.

Enders, W., 1995, Applied Econometric Time Series, John Wiley & Sons, Inc.

Enders, W. and S. Dibooglu, 2001, Long-run Purchasing Power Parity with Asymmetric Adjustment, Working Paper No. 01-02-04, Economics, Finance and Legal Studies, University of Alabama, forthcoming in Southern Economic Journal.

Engel, C. and J. D. Hamilton, 1990, Long Swings in the Dollar: Are They in the Data and Do the Markets Know It?, American Economic Review 80, p. 689-713.

Engle, R. F., Autoregressive Conditional Heteroskedasticity with Estimates of the Variance of United Kingdom Inflation, Econometrica, July 1982, Vol. 50, No. 4, p. 987–1007.

Espinosa, R. and K. Ramlochan, 2000, Economic Exposures: An Overview, Bank of America, 6 Nov, GT NEWS.

Essaides, N., 1999, Rewriting FX Policy? Read this First, International Treasurer, June 7.

Entorf, H., 2000, Der deutsche Aktienmarkt, der Dollar und der Außenhandel: Eine ökonometrische Analyse, Zeitschrift für Betriebswirtschaft (ZfB) 70, Mai, S. 515-539.

Entorf, H. and M. Kabbalakes, 1998, Der Dollar und der deutsche Aktienmarkt: Eine Analyse des Zusammenhangs auf Branchenebene, ifo-Studien 44, S. 199-204.

Entorf, H. and G. Jamin, 2002, Dance with the Dollar: Exchange Rate Exposure on the German Stock Market, Working Paper, Department of Economics, Darmstadt University of Technology.

Erdal, B., 2001, Investment Decisions Under Real Exchange Rate Uncertainty, The Central Bank of the Republic of Turkey - Central Bank Review 1, 25-47.

Eun, C., Kolodny, R. and B. Resnick, 1991, US-Based International Mutual Funds: A Performance Evaluation, Journal of Portfolio Management, 17.

Everett, R. M., A. M. George and A. Blumberg, Appraising Currency Strengths and Weaknesses: An Operational Model For Calculating Parity Exchange Rates, Journal of International Business Studies.

Faff, R. and D. Hillier, 2000, The Determinants of Stock Price Exposure in Mining and Extractive Industries: An Analysis of the Oil Industry, Working Paper, Royal Melbourne Institute of Technology.

Falk, M. and R. Falk, 1998, Pricing to Market of German Exporters: Evidence from Panel Data, Discussion Paper No. 98-28, Zentrum fuer Europaeische Wirtschaftsforschung (ZEW), Mannheim.

Fama, E., 1990, Asset Returns, Expected Returns and Real Activity, The Journal of Finance, Vol. 45, No. 4, Sept., 1089-1108.

Fama, E. and K.K. French, 1988, Dividend Yields and Expected Returns, Journal of Financial Economics 22, p. 3-25.

Fama, E. and K.K. French, 1989, Business Conditions and Expected Returns on Stocks and Bonds, Journal of Financial Economics, Vol. 25 (1), 23-49.

Fatemi and M. Glaum, 2000, Risk Management Practices of German Firms, Managerial Finance.

Feenstra, R.C., J.E. Gagnon, and M.M. Knetter, 1996, Market Share and Exchange Rate Pass-through in World Automobile Trade, Journal of International Economics, 40, p. 187-207.

Feenstra, R.C., 1987, Symmetric Pass-Though of Tariffs and Exchange Rates Under Imperfect Competition: An Empirical Test, Journal of International Economics, 27, August, p. 25-45.

Finnerty, J., 1988, Financial Engineering in Corporate Finance: An Overview, Financial Management 17, p. 14-33

Flood, E. Jr. and D.R. Lessard, 1986, On the Measurement of Operating Exposure to Exchange Rates: a Conceptual Approach, Financial Management, Spring, Vol.15, 25-37.

Forbes, K. J., 2002, How Do Large Depreciations Affect Firm Performance?, Working Paper 9095, NBER Working Paper Series.

Frachot, A., 2001, Theorie et Pratique des Instruments Financiers, Ecole Polytechnique, Paris.

Frankel, A.B. and D.E. Palmer, 1996, The Management of Financial Risks at German Non Financial Firms: The Case of Metallgesellschaft, International Finance Discussion Paper No. 560

Frenkel, M. and P. McCracken, 2001, Economic Risks of EMU, in Frenkel, M., Hommel, U., and M. Rudolf (eds) , Risk Management - Challenge and Opportunity, Springer Verlag, Berlin.

Friberg, R., 1996, On the Role of Pricing Exports in a Third Currency, Stockholm School of Economics.

Friberg, R., 1998, Prices, Profits and Exchange Rate Uncertainty: The Case of Bertrand Competition in Differentiated Goods, Updated Version of Working Paper 196, Stockholm School of Economics.

Friberg, R., 1998, In Which Currency Should Exporters Set Their Prices?, Journal of International Economics 45, p. 59-76.

Friberg, R. and S. Nydahl, 1997, Openness and the Exchange Rate Exposure of National Stock Markets – A Note, Working Paper Series in Economics and Finance N0. 195, Stockholm School of Economics.

Friberg, R. and A. Vredin, 1996, Exchange Rate Uncertainty and The Microeconomic Benefits of EMU, Working Paper No.127, Stockholm School of Economics.

Froot, K.A., 1993, Currency Hedging Over Long Horizons, NBER Working Paper No. 4355, May.

Froot, K.A., 1994, Comments on Exchange Rates and Corporate Strategic Management, in Amihud, Y. and R. M. Levich (eds.), Exchange Rates and Corporate Performance, Irwin, New York University, p. 253-255.

Froot, K.A. and P. Klemperer, 1989, Exchange Rate Pass-Through When Market Share Matters, American Economic Review, September, p. 637-654.

Froot, K.A. and K. Rogoff, 1995, Perspectives on PPP and Long-Run Real Exchange Rates, Handbook of International Economics, Vol. III, Edited by G. Grossman and K. Rogoff.

Froot, K., Scharfstein, D. and J. Stein, 1993, Risk Management: Coordinating Corporate Investment and Financing Policies, Journal of Finance 48, p. 1629-1658.

Froot, K., Scharfstein, D. and J. Stein, 1994, A Framework for Risk Management, Harward Business Review, November

Froot, K. and J. Stein, 1991, Exchange Rate and Foreign Direct Investment: an Imperfect Capital Markets Approach, Quarterly Journal of Economics, p. 1191-1217.

Froot, K. and J. Stein, 1997, Risk Management, Capital Budgeting, and Capital Structure Policy for Financial Institutions: An Integrated Approach, Journal of Financial Economics, 47:55-82.

Fudenberg, D. and J. Tirole, 1992, Game Theory, The MIT Press, Cambridge, Massachusetts.

Gagnon, J. and M. Knetter, 1994, Markup Adjustment and Exchange Rate Fluctuations: Evidence from Panel Data on Automobiles, Journal of International Money and Finance.

Galbraith, J.W. and G. Tkacz, 2000, Testing for Asymmetry in the Link between the Yield Spread and Output in the G-7 Countries, Journal of International Money and Finance, October, 657-672.

Gao, T., 2000, Exchange Rate Movements and the Profitability of U.S. Multinationals, Journal of International Money and Finance 19, p. 117-134.

Garcia, R. and H. Schaller, 1995, Are the Effects of Monetary Policy Asymmetric?, Scientific Series, No. 95s-6, CIRANO, Centre Interuniversitaire de Recherche en Analyse des Organisations, Montreal.

Garner, C.K. and A.C. Shapiro, 1984, A Practical Method of Assessing Foreign Exchange Risk, Midland Corporate Finance Journal, Fall, 6-17.

Gasmi, F., Laffont J.-J., and Q. Vuong, 1992, Econometric Analysis of Collusive Behavior in a Soft-drink Market, Journal of Economics and Management Strategy, 1, 277-31.

Gay, G.D., Nam J. and M. Turac, 2001, How Firms Manage Risk: The Optimal Mix of Linear and Non-linear Derivatives, Working Paper, Georgia State University.

Gebhardt, G. and O. Russ, 1998, Einsatz von derivaten im Risikomanagement bei deutschen Industrie-, Hnadels- und Dienstleistungsunternehmen, Working Paper, Frankfurt.

Geczy, C., Minton, B.A., and C. Schrand, 1997, Why Firms Use Currency Derivatives, The Journal of Finance 52, October, 1323-1355.

Geczy, C., Minton, B.A., and C. Schrand, 2000, Choices Among Alternative Risk Management Strategies: Evidence From the Natural Gas Industry, The Wharton School, University of Pennsylvania.

Gendreau, B. C., 1994, Comments on Exchange Rates, the Macroeconomic Environment, and the Firm, in Amihud, Y. and R. M. Levich (eds.), Exchange Rates and Corporate Performance, Irwin Professional Publishing, New York.

Gernon, H., 1983, The Effect of Translation on Multinational Corporations' Internal Performance Evaluation, Journal of International Business Studies, Spring/Summer.

Ghymers, C., 1981, Taux de Change Tendenciels et Specialisation, Revue d'Economie Politique 91e annee, No. 1, p. 25-55.

Gibson, R., Zimmermann, 1994, The Benefits and Risks of Derivative Instruments: An Economic Perspective, Institute of Banking and Financial Management, HEC Lausanne.

Giddy, I.H, 1977, A note on the Macroeconomic Assumptions of International Financial Management, Journal of Financial and Quantitative Analysis, 12(November): p. 601-605.

Giddy, I.H, 1983, The Foreign Exchange Option as a Hedging Tool, Midland Corporate Finance Journal, Fall, pp. 32-42.

Giddy, I.H., 1994a, Global Financial Markets, D.C.Heath and Company, Houghton Mifflin, Illinois.

Giddy, I.H., 1994b, Exchange Rate Volatility, Hedging, and the Cost of Capital, in Amihud, Y. and R. M. Levich (eds.), 1994, Exchange Rates and Corporate Performance, Irwin Professional Publishing, New York., p. 37-48.

Giddy, I.H. and G. Dufey, 1992, The Management of Foreign Exchange Risk, in The Handbook of International Accounting and Finance, F.D.S. Choi, ed., John Wiley and Sons.

Giddy, I.H. and G. Dufey, 1995, Uses and Abuses of Currency Options, Journal of Applied Corporate Finance, Vol. 8, Number 3, Fall, 49-57.

Giliberto, M., 1985, Interest Rate Sensitivity in the Common Stocks of Financial Intermediaries: A Methodological Note, Journal of Financial and Quantitative Analysis, 20, 123-126.

Gil-Pareja, S., 2000, Exchange Rates and European Countries' Export Prices: An Empirical Test for Asymmetries in Pricing to Market Behavior, Weltwirtschaftliches Archiv 136(1), 1-23.

Giovannini, A., 1988, Exchange Rates and Traded Goods Prices, Journal of International Economics 24, p. 45-68.

Glaum, M., 1990, Strategic Management of Exchange Rate Risks, Long Range Planning, August, Vol. 23, No. 4, p. 65-72.

Glaum, M., 1998, Foreign Exchange Risk Management in German Non-Financial Corporations: An Empirical Analysis, Working Paper, Justus-Liebig University Giessen, Germany.

Glaum, M., 2000, Industriestudie: Finanzwirtschaftliches Risikomanagement deutscher Industrie- und Handelsunternehmen, Price Waterhouse Coopers, Fachverlag Moderne Wirtschaft

Glaum, M., 2000, Foreign Exchange Risk Management in German Non-Financial Corporations: An Empirical Analysis, in Frenkel, M., Hommel, U. and M. Rudolf (Hrsg.): Risk Management - Challenge and Opportunity, Springer Verlag, Berlin, 373-393.

Glaum, M., 2002, The Determinants of Selective Exchange-Risk Management – Evidence from German Non-Financial Corporations, Journal of Applied Corporate Finance, Vol. 14, Nr. 4, S. 108 – 121

Glaum, M., Brunner M., and H. Himmel, 2000, The DAX and the Dollar: The Economic Exchange Rate Exposure of German Corporations, Journal of International Business Studies, 31, 4, p. 715-724.

Glaum, M. and A. Roth, 1993, Wechselkursrisiko-Management in deutschen internationalen Unternehmen, Zeitschrift fur Betriebswirtschaftslehre, Vol. 63(11), p.1181-1206.

Göppl, H., Lüdecke, T., Schlag, C. and H. Schütz, 1995, The German Equity Market: Risk, Return, and Liquidity, Diskussionspapier Nr. 183, Institut für Entscheidungstheorie und Unternehmensforschung, Universität Karlsruhe.

Goetzman, W. and P. Jorion, 1993, Testing the Predictive Power of Dividend Yields, Journal of Finance 48, p. 663-679.

Goldberg, L. and J. Tracy, 1999, Exchange Rates and Local Labor Markets, NBER Working Paper 6985.

Goldberg, P. K., 1995, Product Differentiation and Oligopoly in International Markets: The Case of the U.S. Automobile Industry, Econometrica 63(4), 891-951.

Goldberg, P. K., and M. M. Knetter, 1996, Goods Prices and Exchange Rates: What Have We Learned?, NBER Working Paper 5862.

Goldberg, S.R., Godwin, J.H., Kim, M.S., Trischler, C.A., 1994, On the Determinants of Corporate Hedging with Financial Derivatives, Purdue University.

Goeppl, H. and H. Schuetz, 1995, Die Konzeption eines Deutschen Aktienindex fuer Forschungszwecke (DAFOX), Diskussionspapier Nr. 162, Institut fuer Entscheidungstheorie und Unternehmensforschung, Universitaet Karlsruhe (TH).

Gottfries, N., 1991, Customer Markets, Credit Market Imperfections and Real Price Rigidity, Economica 58, 317-323.

Gottfries, N., 1994, Market Shares, Financial Constraints, and Pricing Behavior in the Export Industry, Seminar Paper No. 586, December, Institute for International Economic Studies, Stockholm.

Grable, J., Lytton, R.H., 1999, Financial Risk Tolerance Revisited: The Development of a Risk Assessment Instrument, Financial Services Review 8.

Graham, J. R. and D. A. Rogers, 2000, Does Corporate Hedging Increase Firm Value? An Empirical Analysis, Working Paper, Fuqua School of Business, Duke University.

Granger, C.W.J., Huang B.-N. and C.-W. Yang, 2000, A Bivariate Causality between Stock Prices and Exchange Rates: Evidence from the Recent Asian Flu, The Quarterly Review of Economics and Finance, 40(3), p. 337-354.

Greene, W. H., 2000, Econometric Analysis, Fourth Edition, Prentice-Hall International, Inc..

Grenadier, S. R., 2002, Option Exercise Games : An Application to the Equilibrium Investment Strategies of Firms, Review of Financial Studies 15(3) : 691-721.

Griffin, J.M. and Karolyi G.A., 1998, Another Look at the Role of the Industrial Structure of Markets for International Diversification Strategies, Journal of Financial Economics 50, p. 351-373.

Griffin, J.M. and R. M. Stulz, 2001, International Competition and Exchange Rate Shocks: a Cross-Country Industry Analysis of Stock Returns, The Review of Financial Studies.

Grinblatt, M. and S. Titman, 2002, Financial Markets and Corporate Strategy, Irwin/McGraw-Hill, Inc.

Grossman P.Z., 2000, Determinants of Share Price Movements in Emerging Equity Markets: some Evidence from America's past, The Quarterly Review of Economics and Finance 40, p. 355-374.

Guay, W. R., 1999, The Impact of Derivatives on Firm risk: An Empirical Examination of New Derivatie Users, Journal of Accounting and Economics 26, p.319-351.

Guo, J.T. and R.C Wu, 1998, Financial Liberalization and the Foreign Exchange Exposure Effect: A Nonparametric Analysis of Taiwan, Multinational Finance Journal, vol. 2, no. 1.

Hagelin, N. and B. Pramborg, 2001, Hedging Foreign Exchange Exposure: Risk Reduction from Transaction and Translation Hedging, Working Paper, Department of Corporate Finance, School of Business, Stockholm University.

Hagelin, N. and B. Pramborg, 2002, Foreign Exchange Exposure, Risk Management, and Quarterly Earnings Announcements, Working Paper, Department of Corporate Finance, School of Business, Stockholm University.

Hahn, F. H., 1962, The Stability of the Cournot Oligopoly Solution, Review of Economic Studies, p. 329-331.

Hakkarainen. A., Kasanen. E., Puttonen. V., 1994, Exchange Rate and Interest Rate Risk Management in Major Finnish Firms. Helsinki School of Economics and Business Administration, Helsinki.

Hakkarainen. A., Kasanen. E., Puttonen. V., 1997, Interest Rate Risk Management in Major Finnish Firms, European Financial Management, Vol. 3 (3), 255-268.

Hall, S., Walsh, M. and A. Yates, 1997, How Do UK Companies Set Prices?, Bank of England.

Hallerbach, W. and B. Menkveld, 1999, Value at Risk as a Diagnostic tool for Corporates: The Airline Industry, Working Paper, Tinbergen Institute, Erasmus University Rotterdam.

Hamilton, J. D., 1994, Time Series Analysis, Princeton University Press

Hanneman, J. F., 2000, Exchange Exposure Measurement, Global Tresury News, March

Hansen, L.P., 1982, Large Sample Properties of Generalized Method of Moments Estimation, Econometrica 50, p. 1029-1054.

Hansen, L.P. and R.J. Hodrick, 1980, Forward Rates as Predictors of Future Sport Rates: an Econometric Analysis, Journal of Political Economy 88, p. 829-853.

Harvey, A. C., 1994, Time Series Models, second edition, MIT Press.

Harvey, C., 1991, The World Price of Covariance Risk, Journal of Finance, 46, 111-157.

Harvey, C., 1991, Interest Based Forecasts of German Economic Growth, Weltwirtchaftliches Archiv, Vol. 127, 701-718.

Harris, T.S. Melumad, N.D. and T. Shibano, 1996, An Argument Against Hedging By Matching the Currencies of Costs and Revenues, Bank of America – Journal of Applied Corporate Finance, Fall, 90-97.

Hau, H., 1999, Comment on "Corporate Risk Management for Multinational Corporations: Financial and Operational Hedging Policies" European Finance Review 2: p. 247-249.

Hassan, I., Francis, B. and C. Pantzalis, 2000, Operational Hedges and Coping with Foreign Exchange Exposure: the Case of U.S. MNCs during the Asian Financial Crisis of 1997, Working Paper, New York University.

Haugen, R.A., Stroyny, A.L. and D.W. Wichern, 1978, Rate Regulation, Capital Structure, and the Sharing of Interest Rate Risk in the Electricity Utility Industry, Journal of Finance, Vol. 33 (3), 707-721.

Hayashi, F., 2000, Econometrics, Princeton University Press.

Hayt and Song, 1995, Handle with Sensitivity, Risk, 8(9), 94-99.

He, J., L. Ng and X. Wu, 1996, Foreign Exchange Exposure, Risk and the Japan Market: Old Issues and New Insights, Working Paper, Dept. of Economics and Finance, City U. of Hong Kong.

He, J. and L. Ng, 1998, Foreign Exchange Exposure, Risk, and the Japanese Stock Market, Journal of Finance 53, p. 733-753.

He, J. and L. K. Ng, 1998, The Foreign Exchange Exposure of Japanese Multinational Corporations, Journal of Finance, April, Vol. 53, No. 2. p. 733-753.

Heckerman, D., 1972, The Exchange Risks of Foreign Operations, Journal of Business 45, no. 1, Jan., p. 42-48.

Heiliger, H.G., 2000. How Has the Euro Changed Financial Risk Management for Corporates, Global Treasury News, 18 May.

Hekman, C.R., 1981, Foreign Exchange Risk: Relevance and Management, Managerial and Decision Economics, Vol. 2, No. 4.

Hekman, C.R.,1983, Foreign Exchange Exposure: Accounting Measures and Economic Reality, Journal of Cash Management, Feb/Mar, Vol. 3, No. 1.

Hekman, C.R., 1985, A Financial Model of Foreign Exchange Exposure, Journal of International Business Studies, Summer, 16, 83-99.

Hekman, C.R., 1988, The Real Effects for foreign Exchange Rate Changes on a Competitive, Profit-Maximizing Firm, unpublished manuscript, Peter F. Drucker Graduate Management Center, The Claremont Graduate School.

Hekman, C.R., 1989, Measuring the Impact of Exposure, in: Management of Currency Risk, Boris Antl, Euromoney Publications, Chapter 6.

Hentschel, L., Kothari, S.P., 1999, Are Corporations Reducing or Taking Risks with Derivatives?, Simson School, University of Rochester, Sloan School, Massachusetts Institute of Technology.

Higgins, C. Robert, 1980, Discussion: The Exposure of Long-Term Foreign Currency Bonds, Joural of Financial and Quantitative Analysis, Vol. 15, Nov, p. 995-996.

Hin, L.K. and C.K. Thim, 2001, Corporate Finance Lessons from the Impact of the Asian Financial Crisis on Different Economic Sectors in Malaysia, Research Paper Series, Division of Business and Management, The University of Nottingham in Malaysia.

Hodder, J., 1982, Exposure to Exchange Rate Movements, Journal of International Economics 13, 375-386.

Hodrick, R.J., 1981, International Asset Pricing with Time-Varying Risk Premia, Journal of International Economics, November, 573-587.

Holmes, M.J. and N. Maghrebi, 2002, Non-linearities, Regime Switching and the Relationship between Asian Equity and Foreign Exchange Markets, Working Paper, Department of Economcis, Loughborough University.

Hommel, U., 2001, Sachgerechte Bewertung von Wachstumsunternehmen mit dem Realoptionsansatz, European Business School, Finance Group Working Paper No. 01-02, June.

Hommel, U., 2002, Financial versus Operative Hedging of Currency Risk, Working Paper, European Business School Finance Group, Oestrich-Winkel, No. 02-01

Hommel, U. und G. Pritsch, 1998, Derivative Finanzierungsinstrumente - Notwendigkeit des unternehmerischen Risikomanagement aus Shareholder-Value-Sicht, in Handbuch Corporate Finance, Deutscher Wirtschaftsdienst, Maerz

Hommel, U. and G. Pritsch, 1998, Bausteine des Risikomanagement-Prozesses, Handbuch Corporate Finance (Achleitner/Thoma), Deutscher Wirtschaftsdienst, Köln.

Hommel, U. and G. Pritsch, 1998, Notwendigkeit des unternehmerischen Risikomanagement aus Shareholder-Value-Sicht, Handbuch Corporate Finance (Achleitner/Thoma), Deutscher Wirtschaftsdienst, Köln.

Hommel, U. und G. Pritsch, 1999, Investitionsbewertugn und Unternehmensfuehrung mit dem Realoptionsansatz, Handbuch Corporate Finance, Ergaenzungslieferung 4, Deutscher Wirtschaftsdienst, 1-68.

Hu, H. T. C., 1996, Behind the Corporate Hedge: Information and The Limits of „Shareholder Wealth Maximization", Bank of America Journal of Applied Corporate Finance, Vol. 9 (3), Fall, 39-51.

Huang, R.D. and W.A. Kracaw, 1984, Stock Market Returns and Real Activity : A Note, The Journal of Finance, Vol. 39, No.1, March, 267-273.

Huang, R.D. and H.R. Stoll, 2001, Exchange Rates and Firms' Liquidity: evidence from ADRs, Journal of International Money and Finance 20, 297-325.

Huchzermeier, A., 2001, Bewertung von Realoptionen in globalen Produktions- und Logistiknetzwerken, in: Hommel, U., Scholich, M. and R. Vollrath, Realoptionen in der Unternehmenspraxis: Wert schaffen durch Flexibilität, Springer.

Huisman, K.J.M., 2001, Technology Investment: A Game Theoretic Real Options Approach, Kluwer Academic Publishers, 272 pp.

Huisman, K.J.M. and P.M. Kort, 1999, Effects of Strategic Interactions on the Option Value of Waiting, VentER Disccusion Paper 9992, Tilburg University, The Netherlands.

Hung, J., 1992, Assessing the Exchange Rate's Impact on U.S. Manufacturing Profits, Quarterly Review, Federal Reserve Bank of NY, Winter.

Hughes, B., 1998, Currency Risk Management - No Longer an Option, European Journal of Purchasing & Supply Management 4, p. 195-197.

Hyun-Han Shin, Luc Soenen, 1999, Exposure to Currency Risk by US Multinational Corporations, Journal of Multinational Financial Management 9: p. 195 - 207.

Ibrahimi, F., L. Oxelheim and C. Wihlborg, 1995, International Stock Markets and Fluctuations in Exchange Rates and Other Macroeconomic Variables, in R. Aggarwal and David C. Schirm, editors, Global Portfolio Diversification: Risk Management, Market Microstructure, and Implementation Issues, Boston.

Ihrig, J., 2001, Exchange-Rate Exposure of Multinationals: Focusing on Exchange-Rate Issues, International Finance Discussion Papers Number 709, Board of Governors of the Federal Reserve System, Aug.

Jacque, L.L., 1981, Management of Foreign Exchange Risk: A Review Article, Journal of International Business Studies, Spring/Summer: p. 81-101.

Jacquillat, B. and B. Solnik, 1978, Multinationals are Poor Tools for Diversification, Financial Analyst Journal, Winter, 8-12.

Jensen, M.C., Self-Interest, Altruism, Incentives, and Agency Theory, Journal of Applied Corporate Finance, Summer 1994, p. 40-45.

Jensen, M.C., 2001, Value Maximization Stakeholder Theory, and The Corporate Objective Function, Bank of America Journal of Applied Corporate Finance, Vol. 14, Number 3, Fall, 8-21.

Jensen, M.C. and W.H. Meckling, Theory of the Firm: Managerial Behavior, Agency Costs and Ownership Structure, Journal of Financial Economics, October 1976, p. 305-360.

Jesswein, K.R., Kwok, C.C.Y., Folks, Jr. W.R., 1995, Corporate Use of Innovative Foreign Exchange Risk Management Products, The Columbia Journal of World Business.

Jesswein, K.R., Kwok, C.C.Y., Folks, Jr. W.R., 1995b, What New Currency Risk Products are Companies Using, and Why?, Journal of Applied Corporate Finance, Vol. 8, Number 3, Fall, 103-114.

Johansson, A. and L. Rolseth, 1998, The Effects of Firm-Specific Variables and Consensus Forecasts Data on the Pricing of Large Swedish Firm's Stocks, Working Paper, Department of Economics, University of Gothenburg.

Johnston, K. and E. Scott, 2000, Garch Models and the Stochastic Progress Underlying Exchange Rate Price Changes, Journal of Financial and Strategic Decisions Vol. 13, No. 2.

Jorion, P., 1990, Exchange Rate Exposure of US Multinationals, Journal of Business, Vol.63(3), 331-345

Jorion, P., 1991, The Pricing of Exchange Rate Risk in the Stock Market, Journal of Financial and Quantitative Analysis, Vol.26(3), p. 3631-376.

Jorion, P., 1994, Currencies and Long-Term Interest Rates, in Amihud, Y. and R. M. Levich (eds.), Exchange Rates and Corporate Performance, New York University, Ch. 6, pp. 97-117.

Jorion, P., 1996, Risk2: Measuring the Risk in the Value at Risk, Financial Analysts Journal, Nov-Dec

Jorion, P., 1997, Value at Risk: The New Benchmark for Controlling Market Risk, McGraw-Hill

Jorion, P., and S.J. Khoury, 1996, Financial Risk Management: Domestic and International Dimensions, Oxford: Basil Blackwell

Jumah, A. and R.M. Kunst, 2001, The Effects of Exchange-Rate Exposures on Equity Assets Markets, Economic Series 94, Institute for Advanced Studies (IHS), Vienna, Jan.

Juselius, K. and R. MacDonald, 2000, International Parity Relationships Between Germany and the united States: A Joint Modelling Approach, Working Paper, University of Copenhagen.

Kanas, A., 1995, Hedging Exchange Rate Economic Exposure: Real Options or Currency Option?, University of Stirling, Department of Accountancy and Finance working paper 95/06.

Kanas, A., 1995, Is Economic Exposure Asymetric between Depreciations and Appreciations? Testing Using Cointegration Analysis, Discussion Paper No. 95/07 Department of Accountancy & Finance, University of Stirling.

Kandil, M., 2000, The Asymmetric Effects of Exchange Rate Fluctuations: Theory and Evidence from Developing Countries, IMF Working Paper 00/184, Nov.

Kaplan S.N. and R. Leftwich, 1998, Value at Risk and Hedging: Pitfalls for the Unwary, in Wharton School, University of Chicago Graduate School of Business, London Business School, 1998, The Complete Finance Companion, Financial Times Mastering Series

Kaplan S.N. and R. S. Ruback, 1994, The Valuation of Cash Flow Forecasts: An Empirical Analysis, NBER Working Paper Series No. 4724.

Kaplan S.N. and R. S. Ruback, 1996, The Market Pricing of Cash Flow Forecasts: Discounted Cash Flow vs. The Method of "Comparables", Bank of America Journal of Applied Corporate Finance, Vol. 8 (4), Winter, 45-60.

Kedia, S. and A. Mozumdar, 1999, Is Foreign Currency Denominated Debt a Hedging Instrument?, Working Paper, Graduate School of Business Administration, Harvard University.

Kadiyali, V., 1997, Exchange Rate Pass-Through for Strategic Pricing and Advertising: An Empirical Analysis of the U.S. Photographic film Industry, Journal of International Economics 43(3/4), 437-461.

Kaplanis, E. and S.M. Schaefer, 1991, Exchange Risk and International Diversification in Bond and Equity Portfolios, Journal of Economics and Business 43, pp. 287-307.

Kendall, J.D., 1989, Role of Exchange-Rate Volatility in US Import price Pass-Through Relationships, Ph.D. Dissertation, University of California, Davis.

Kerkvliet, J. and M.H. Moffett, 1991, The Hedging of an Uncertain Future Foreign Currency Cash Flow, Journal of Financial and Quantitative Analysis, Vol. 26, No. 4, December, 565-578.

Khoo, A., 1994, Estimation of Foreign Exchange Exposure: An Application to Mining Companies in Australia, Journal of International Money and Finance, Vol.13(3), p. 342-363.

Khoury, S.J. and K.H. Chan, 1988, Hedging Foreign Exchange Risk: Selecting the Optimal Tool, Midland Corporate Finance Journal 5 (4), p. 40-52.

Kilian, L., 1997, Exchange Rates and Monetary Fundamentals: What Do We Learn From Long-Horizon Regressions?, University of Michigan.

Kim, J., Malz, A.M. and J. Mina, 1999, LongRun Technical Document, RiskMetrics Group

Klitgaard, T., 1996, Coping with the Rising Yen: Japan's Recent Export Experience, Current Issues in Economics and Finance, Federal Reserve Bank of New York, Vol. 2, Number 1, January.

Klitgaard, T., 1999, Exchange Rates and Profit Margins: The Case of Japanese Exporters, FRBNY Economic Policy Review, April.

Kloman, H.F., 2002, Integrated Risk Management: Current Views of Risk Management, GARP paper

Knetter, M.M., 1989, Price Discrimination by U.S. and German Exporters, American Economic Review, 79, March, p. 198-210.

Knetter, M.M., 1993, International Comparisons of Pricing-to-Market Behavior, American Economic Review, 83, June, p. 473-486.

Knetter, M., 1994a, Exchange Rates and Corporate Pricing Strategies, in Y. Amihud and R. Levich, Eds: Exchange Rates and Corporate Performance, Business One Irwin, Ill.

Knetter, M., 1994b, Is Export Price Adjustment Asymmetric?: Evaluating the Market Share and Marketing Bottlenecks Hypothesis, Journal of International Money and Finance, 13, 55-70.

Knetter, M., 1995, Pricing to Market in Response to Unobservable and Observable shocks, International Economic Journal, Volume 9, Number 2, Summer.

Knetter, M., 1997, Why are Retail Prices in Japan so High: Evidence from German Export Prices, International Journal of Industrial Organizations, 15, 5, pp. 549-572.

Kogut, B., 1983, Foreign Direct Investment as a Sequential Process, in: Kindelberger, C.P. and D. Audretsch (eds.), The Multinational Corporations in the 1980s, MIT Press, Cambridge, M.A, 38-56.

Kogut, B. and N. Kulatilaka, 1994, Operating Flexibility, Global Manufacturing, and the Option Value of a Multinational Network, Management Science, 40: p. 123-139.

Kogut, B. and N. Kulatilaka, 1999, Capabilities as Real Options, Working Paper, Wharton School, University of Pennsylvania, March 14.

Koutmos, G. and A.D. Martin, 1999, Asymmetric Exchange Rate Exposure: Theory and Evidence, Working Paper, School of Business, Fairfield University.

KPMG, 1995, Financial Instruments: Einsatzmoeglichkeiten, Risikomanagement und Risikocontrolling, Rechnungslegung, Besteuerung.

KPMG, 1996, Solving the Mystery of Swaps.

KPMG, 2000, International Accounting Standards: Financial Instruments Accounting, Sept.

KPMG, 2001, Financial Risk Management.

KPMG LLP, 2001, Understanding Enterprise Risk Management: an Emerging Model for Building Shareholder Value.

Krahnen, J.P., 1998, Where Do We Stand in the Theory of Finance?, A Selective Overview with Reference to Erich Gutenberg, Working Paper, Center for Financial Studies, Frankfurt.

Kreinin, M., Stephen, M. and E. J. Sheehy, 1987, Differential Response of U.S. Import Prices and Quantities to Exchange Rate Adjustments, Weltwirtchaftliches Archiv 123(3), 449-462.

Krishnamoorthy, A., 2001, Industrial Structure and the Exchange-Rate Exposure of Industry Portfolio Returns, Global Finance Journal 12, 285-297.

Krugman, P., 1986, Pricing to Market When the Exchange Rate Changes, NBER Working Paper No. 1926, May.

Krugman, P., 1995, The Age of Diminished Expectations: U.S. Economic Policy in the 1990s, Revised and Updated Edition, The MIT Press.

Krugman, P. and R.E. Baldwin, 1987, The Pesistence of the U.S. Trade Deficit, Brookings Papers on Economic Activity 1987:1, 1-55.

Krugman, P. and M. Miller, 1993, Why Have a Target Zone, Carnegie Rochester Conference Series on Public Policy 38, 279-314.

Krugman, P. and M. Obstfeld, 1991, International Economics, New York, HarperCollins.

Krugman, P, 1987, Pricing to Market When the Exchange Rate Changes, in S.W. Arndt and J.D. Richardson, editors, Real-Financial Linkages among Open Economies, Cambridge: MIT Press, p. 49-70.

Krugman, P., 1989, Exchange Rate Instability, Cambridge, MA: The MIT Press.

Kulatilaka, N. and A. Marcus, 1994, Hedging Foreign Project Risk, Journal of International Financial Management and Accounting, 5, no. 2, June, p. 142-56.

Kulatilaka, N. and E.C. Perotti, 1999, Time-to-Market Capability as a Stackelberg Growth Option, Working Paper, School of Management, Boston University.

Kumakura, M., 2001, Exchange Rates and Dynamics of Traded Goods Prices: Does Exchange Rate Uncertainty Matter?, Working Paper Faculty of Economics and Politics, University of Cambridge.

Kuno, P.M., Huisman, K.J.M., Pawlina, G., and J.J. Thijssen, 2003, Strategic Investment under Uncertainty: Merging Real Options with Game Theory, Working Paper No. 2003-06, Center for Economic Research, Tilburg University.

Kupiec, P., 1995, Techniques for Verifying the Accuracy of Risk Measurement Models, Journal of Derivatives 2, December, p. 73-84.

Lackman, C.L., 1996, Exchange Risk: A Capital Asset Pricing Model Framework, Journal of Financial and Strategic Decisions, Vol. 9, Number 1, Spring.

Lamont, O., 1997, Earnings and Expected Returns, University of Chicago.

Lardaro, L., 1993, Applied Econometrics, HarperCollins College Publishers.

Lee, A.Y., 1999, CorporateMetrics - The Benchmark for Corporate Risk Management, RiskMetrics Group.

Lee, W. Y. and M. E. Solt, 2000, Economic Exposure and Hysteresis: Evidence from German, Japanese, and US Stock Returns, Working Paper, Sam M. Walton College of Business Administration, University of Arkansas.

Leslie, K. J., and Michaels, M.P., 1997, The Real Power of Real Options, The McKinsey Quarterly No.3, p.97-108.

Lessard, D.R., 1976, The Determinants of Common Stock Returns Volatility: An International Comparision : Discussion, The Journal of Finance, Vol. 31, No. 2, May, 751-752.

Lessard, D.R., 1979, International Financial Management : Theory and Application, Warren Gorham and Lamont, Boston, MA.

Lessard, D.R., 1988, Finance and Global Competition: Exploiting Financial Scope and Coping with Volatile Exchange Rates, in Stern, J.M. and D.H. Chew (Hrsg.): New Developments in International Finance, Oxford, p. 3-26.

Lessard, D. and J.B. Lightstone, 1986, Volatile Exchange Rates Can Put Operations at Risk, Harvard Business Review, Vl. 64 (4), p. 107-114.

Lessard, D. and J.B. Lightstone, Operating Exposure, in Management of Currency Risk, Boris Antl (ed.), 1989, Euromoney Publications, London, p. 29-40.

Levi, M.D.., 1994, Exchange Rates and Valuation of Firms, in Amihud, Y. and R. M. Levich (eds.), Exchange Rates and Corporate Performance, Irwin Professional Publishing, New York., Chapter 3, p. 37-48.

Levi, M. D, 1996, International Finance, 3.rd edition., McGraw-Hill, New York, NY

Levi, M.D. and P. Sercu, 1991, Erronous and Valid Reasons for Hedging Foreign Exchange Exposure, Journal of Multinational Financial Management, p. 25-37.

Levich, R. M., 1998, International Financial Markets: Prices and Policies, McGraw-Hill, version prior to publication.

Lewent, J.C. and A.J. Kearney, 1990, Identifying, Measuring, and Hedging Currency Risk at Merck, Continental Bank, Journal of Applied Corporate Finance, Vol.2(4), p. 19-28.

Lewis, K.K., 1994, Puzzles in International Financial Markets, National Bureau of Economic Research, No. 4951.

Lewis, K.K., 1995, Puzzles in International Financial Markets, Handbook of International Economcis, Vol. III, Edited by G. Grossman and K. Rogoff.

Lidbark, J., 2003, Exposure Identification and Hedging: Does Time Horizon Matter?, Bank of America Global Corporate and Investment Bank, Global Treasury News, 25 Nov.

Lidbark, J. and A. Middleton, 2002, Back-testing FX Hedging Strategies from a EUR Perspective, Journal of Risk Analysis, Monograph #175, Summer.

Liebel, H., 1996, A Currency Risk Management Strategy, Treasury Management International, September.

Linares, J.C., 1999, Methoden, Instrumente und Strategien des Waehrungsrisiko-Managements in international taetigen Unternehmen, Dissertation, Universitaet St.Gallen, Schweiz

Linck, J., 1998, Foreign Currency Changes and Corporate Cash Flow, Working Paper, University of Rochester.

Lipsey, R.G., 1969, An Introduction to Positive Economics, 2nd Edition, Weidenfeld and Nicolson.

Loderer, C. and K. Pichler, 2000, Firms, Do you Know your Currency Risk Exposure? Survey Results, Working Paper, Institut fuer Finanzmanagement, Universitaet Bern.

Logue, D.E., 1981, The Effects of International Operations on the Market Value of the Firm: Theory and Evidence: Discussion, The Journal of Finance, V 36, No. 2, May, 439-440.

Logue, D.E., 1995, When Theory Fails: Globalization as a Response to the (Hostile) Market for Foreign Exchange, Bank of America Journal of Applied Corportate Finance, V. 8 (3), p. 39-48.

Loudon, G.F., 1993a, Foreign Exchange Exposure and the Pricing of Currency Risk in Equity Returns: Some Australian Evidence, Pacific-Basin Finance Journal, 1(4), p. 335-354.

Loudon, G.F., 1993b, The Foreign Exchange Operating Exposure of Australian Stocks, Accounting and Finance, Vol.33(1) p. 19-32.

Lucas, R., 1982, Interest Rates and Currency Prices in a Two-Country World, Journal of Monetary Economics, November.

Lucke, D., 1998, The Degree of Dependence of German Exports on the Real External Value of the D-Mark, Economic Bulletin 3/1998, DIW Berlin and Gower Publishing.

Luehrman, T.A., 1990, The Exchange Rate Exposure of a Global Competitor, Journal of International Business Studies, Vol.21 (2), 225-242.

Luehrman, T.A., 1991, Exchange Rate Changes and The Distribution of Industry Value, Journal of International Business Studies, 22 (4), 619-649.

MacMinn, R.D., 1998, On Corporate Risk Management and Insurance, Working Paper

Mahul, O., 2002, Hedging Price Risk in the Presence of Crop Yield and Revenue Insurance, Working Paper, INRA, Department of Economics, Rennes, France.

Malindretos, J. and D. Tsanacas, 1995, Hedging Preferences and Foreign Exchange Exposure Management, Multinational Business review, Fall, Vol. 3, No.2, p. 56-66.

Maloney, P.J., 1990, Managing Currency Exposure: the Case of Western Mining, Journal of Applied Corporate Finance, Vol. 3, No. 2, p. 29-34.

Mann, C.L., 1989, The Effects of Exchange Rate Trends and Volatility on Export prices: Industry Examples from Japan, Germany, and the United States, Weltwirtschaftliches Archiv, 125, p. 588-618

Mark, N.C., 1995, Exchange Rates and Fundamentals: Evidence on Long-Horizon Predictability and Overshooting, American Economic review 85, March, no.1, p. 201-18.

Marshall, A.P., 2000, Foreign Exchange Risk Management in UK, USA and Asia Pacific multinational companies, Journal of Multinational Financial Management 10, 2000, p. 185-211.

Marston, R.C., 1996, The Effects of Industrial Structure on Economic Exposure, Working Paper, University of Pennsylvania., alos NBER Working Paper 551823

Marston, R.C., 2001, The Effects of Industrial Structure on Economic Exposure, Journal of International Money and Finance, 20, 149-164.

Marston, R., Hayt, G.S. and G.M. Bodnar, 1998, Derivatives as a Way of Reducing Risk, in Wharton School, University of Chicago Graduate School of Business, London Business School, The Complete Finance Companion, Financial Times Mastering Series

Marston, R.C., 1990, Pricing to Market in Japanese Manufacturing, Journal of International Economics, 29, November, p. 217-236.

Martin, A. D., 2000, Exchange Rate Exposure of the Key Financial Institutions in the Foreign Exchange Market, International Review of Economics and Finance, 9(3), p. 267-286.

Martines-Solano, P., 1998, Foreign Exchange Exposure on the Spanish Stock Market: Sources of Risk and Hedging, Working Paper, Department of Accounting and Finance, Lancaster University.

Mathieson, G. and P. Moles, 1998, Company Value and Economic Currency Risk: An Empirical Study of UK-Listed Importers and Exporters, Working Paper 98.10, Center for Financial Markets Research, Management School, The University of Edinburgh.

Mayrhofer, H.H., 1992, Methodenorientiertes Waehrungsrisikomanagement, Verlag Paul Haupt (Bern), zugl. Diss. Hoschule St. Gallen.

McCloskey and Ziliak, 1996, The Standard Error of Regressions, Journal of Economic Literature, March.

McCloskey and Ziliak, 2004, Size Matters: the Standard Error of Regressions in the American Economic Review, Journal of Socio-Economics, forthcoming.

Meese, R., 1990, Currency Fluctuations in the Post-Bretton Woods era, Journal of Economic Persepectives, 4(1): p. 117-134

Mellios, C. et J.-L. Viviani, 2001, Exposition au Risque de Change et Couverture par les Entreprises Francaises a l'Aide des Produits Derives, de la Bruslerie H. (coordonne par), Finance d'Entreprise: Recherches du CREFIB, Economica, Paris.

Mello, A.S., Parsons, J.E., and A.J. Triantis, 1995, An Integrated Model of Multinational Flexibility and Financial Hedging, Journal of International Economics 39, p. 27-51.

Menon, J., 1995, Exchange Rate Pass-though, Journal of Economic Surveys, 9, p. 197-231

Menon, J., 1999, Flexible Exchange Rates and Traded Goods Prices: A Theory of the Short-Run, General Paper No. G-108, Centre of Policy Studies, Monash University.

Merton, R.C., 1974, On the Pricing of Corporate Debt: the Risk Structure of Interest Rates, Journal of Finance 29, 449-470.

Mian, S.L., 1996, Evidence on Corporate Hedging Policy, The Journal of Finance and Quantitative Analysis, September.

Miller, M., 1986, Financial Innovations: The Last Twenty Years and the Next, Journal of Financial and Quantitative Analysis 21, p. 459-471.

Miller, K.D., 1992, A Framework for Integrated Risk Management in International Business, Journal of International Business Studies, Second Quarter.

Miller, K.D., 1998, Economic Exposure and Integrated Risk Management, Strategic Management Journal, Vo. 19, p. 497-514.

Miller, K.D. and J.J. Reuer, 1998, Firm Strategy and Economic Exposure to Foreign Exchange Rate Movements, Journal of International Business Studies, 29(3): p. 493-514.

Miller, K.D. and J. J. Reuer, 1995, Asymmetric Corporate Exposures to Foreign Exchange Rate Changes, Working Paper 95-004, Krannert Graduate school of Management, Center for International Business Education and Research (CIBER), Purdue University.

Milley, F., 2000, How Corporations Can Manage FX Risk Outside of the Financial Markets, Global Treasury News, 13 Apr.

Minton, B.A. and C. Schrand, 1998, The Impact of Cash Flow Volatility on Discretionary Investment and the Costs of Debt and Equity, Working Paper, The Wharton School, University of Pennsylvania.

Miyamoto, A., 2003, The 2003 Risk Management Survey, Bank of America Global Corporate and Investment Bank.

Moffet. M.H., 1999, Lufthansa, Case Study, Thunderbird, The American Graduate School of International Management.

Moffet, M.H., 1999, British Columbia Hydro, Thunderbird, The American Graduate school of International Management.

Moffett, M. H. and J. K. Karlsen, 1994, Managing Foreign Exchange Rate Economic Exposure, Journal of International Financial Management and Accounting. Vol.5(2), p. 157-175.

Moguillansky G., 2001, Non Financial Corporate Risk Management and Foreign Exchange Rate Volatility in Latin America, second draft.

Moore, S., 2003, Commodity Price Management – Can You Afford the Risk?, Global Treasury News, 16 December, originally pulished in InterAct, The Quaterly Journal of the Irish Association of Corporate Treasurers.

Moschini, G. and H. Lapan, 1992, Hedging Price Risk with Options and Futures for the Competitive Firm with Production Flexibility, International Economic Review 33, 607-618.

Moschini, G., and H. Lapan, 1995, The Hedging Role of Options and Futures under Joint Price, Basis, and Production Risk, International Economic Review 36, 1025-1049.

Muralidhar, A.S., 1992, Volatility, Flexibility and the Multinational Enterprise, Ph.D. dissertation, Sloan School of Management, MIT, May.

Myers, S.C., 1977, Determinants of Corporate Borrowing, Journal of Financial Economics, 5, 6-13.

Myers, S.C. and N. S. Majluf, 1984, Corporate Financing and Investment Decisions When Firms Have Information That Investors Do Not Have, Journal of Financial Economics, Vol. 13, p. 187-221.

Nance, D.R., Smith C.W. Jr. and C.W. Smithson, 1993, On the Determinants of Corporate Hedging, Journal of Finance 48, p. 391-405.

Newey, W.K. and K.D. West, 1987, A Simple, Positive Semi-Definite, Heteroskedasticity and Autocorrelation Consitent Covariance Matrix, Econometrica, V. 55, No. 3 (May), p. 703-708.

Nickerson, D. and R.J. Sullivan, 2004, Financial Innovation, Strategic Real Options and Endogenous Competition: Theory and an Application to Internet Banking, Working Paper, Department of Economics, Colorado State University.

Nilsson, K., 1999, Alternative Measures of the Swedish Real Effective Exchange Rate, Working Paper No. 68, Dec., National Institute of Economic Research.

Nydahl, S., 1999, Exchange Rate Exposure, Foreign Involvement and Currency Hedging of Firms - Some Swedish Evidence, Working Paper, Uppsala University.

O'Brien, T.J., 1997, Accounting Versus Economic Exposure to Currency Risk, Journal of Financial Statement Analysis, summer, p. 21-29.

O'Brien, T.J., 1998, International Production Location and "Pro Forma" Financial Hedging of Exchange Rate Risk, Journal of Applied Corporate Finance, Fall, pp. 100-108.

O'Brien, T.J., 1998, Corporate FX Exposure, A Review, Working Paper, University of Connecticut.

Obstfeld, M. and K. Rogoff, 2000, The Six Major Puzzles in International Macroeconomics: Is There a Common Cause?, NBER Macroeconomics Annual.

Ochynsky, W., 2003, To Hedge or Not to hedge?, Global Treasury News, 7 October.

Oertmann, P., Rendu, C., and H. Zimmermann, 2000, Interest Rate Risk of European Financial Corporations, European Financial Management, Vol. 6 (4), 459-478.

Ohno, K., 1989, Export Pricing Behavior of Manufacturing: A U.S.-Japan Comparison, International Monetary Fund Staff Papers, 36, September, p. 550-579.

Oi, W.Y., 1961, The Desirability of Price Instability under Perfect Competition, Econometrica, vol. 29, p. 58-64.

Oi, W.Y., 1962, Labor as a Quasi-fixed Factor, Journal of Political Economy 70, December: 538-55.

Oliveira Martins, J., 1993, Market Structure, International Trade and Relative Wages, OECD Economics Department Working Papers No. 134.

Oliveira Martins, J., Scarpetta, S. and D. Pilat, 1996, Mark-Up Ratios in Manufacturing Industries: Estimates for 14 OECD Countries, OECD Economics Department Working Papers No. 162.

Oxelheim, L., 2003, The Impact of Macroeconomic Variables on Corporate Performance – What Shareholders Ought to Know, Financial Analyst Journal.

Oxelheim, L. and C.G. Wihlborg, 1987, Macroeconomic Uncertainty: Interantional Risks and Opportunties for the Corporation, New York: John Wiley.

Oxelheim, L. and C.G. Wihlborg, 2002, Recognizing Macroeconomic Fluctuations in Value Based Management, Working Paper No. 574, IUI, The Research Institute of Industrial Economics.

Oxelheim, L. and C.G. Wihlborg, 1991, Corporate Strategies in a Turbulent World Economy, Management International Review, Vol.31(4), p. 293-315.

Oxelheim, L.and C.G. Wihlborg, 1995, Measuring Macroeconomic Exposure: The Case of Volvo Cars, European Financial Management, Vol.1(3), p. 241-263.

Oxelheim, L. and C.G, Wihlborg, 1998, Managing in the Turbulent World Economy - Corporate Performance and Risk Exposure, New York: John Wiley & Sons.

Oxelheim, L. and C.G. Wihlborg, C.G, 2000, Recognizing Macroeconomic Fluctuations in Value Based Management, Working Paper, Institute of Economic Research, School of Economics and Management, Lund University.

Palia, D. and J. Thomas, 1997, Exchange Rate Exposure and Firm Valuation: New Evidence for Market Efficiency, Working Paper, Graduate School of Business, Columbia University.

Pan, M.-S., R. C.-W. Fok and Y.A. Liu, 2001, Dynamic Linkages Between Exchange Rates and Stock Prices: Evidence from Pacific Rim Countries, Working Paper, Department of Finance, Decision Sciences, and Information Systems, Shippensburg University.

Pantzalis, C., Simkins, B.J., Laux, P., 1999, Operational Hedges and the Foreign Exchange Exposure of US Multinational Corporations, Working Paper, University of South Florida.

Parsley, D. C. and H. Popper, Exchange Rate Pegs and Foreign Exchange Exposure in East Asia, Vanderbilt University - Owen Graduate School of Management and Santa Clara University - Department of Economics

Patro. D.K., Wald, J.K. and Y. Wu, 2000, The Impact of Macroeconomic and Financial Variables on Market Risk: Evidence from International Equity Returns, Working Paper, Department of Finance and Economics, Faculty of Management, Rutgers University.

Peltzman, S., 2000, Prices Rise Faster than they Fall, Journal of Political Economy 108(3), 466-502.

Perry, M.J., 1998, Financial Management in the International Corporation: Economic Exposure, Michigan Business School, March 16.

Petersen, M. A. and S. R. Thiagarajan, 1998, Risk Measurement and Hedging: With and Without Derivatives, Working Paper, J.L. Kellog Graduate School of Management, Northwestern University.

Phelphs, E.S. and S. G. Winter, 1970, Optimal Price Policy under Atomistic Competition, in Phelphs, E.S. (ed.): Microecnomic Foundations of Employment and Inflation Theory, Norton New York.

Phylaktis, K. and F. Ravazzolo, 2000, Stock Prices and Exchange Rate Dynamics, Working Paper, City University Business School.

Pinches, G. E., "Myopia, 1982, Capital Budgeting and Decision Making", Financial Management, Vol. 11, No. 3, p. 6-19.

Pindyck, R.S., 1991, Irreversibility, Uncertainty and Investment, Journal of Economic Literature 26 (3), September, 1110-1148..

Poncet, P., 2001, Theorie de la Courverture: Application aux Risque de Taux de Change et d'Interet d'une Entreprise Multinationale, de la Bruslerie H. (coordonne par), Finance d'Entreprise: Recherches du CREFIB, Economica, Paris.

Poniachek, H.A., 1989, International Corporate Finance, Unwin Hyman ltd.

Porter, M.E., 1980, Competitive Strategy, The Free Press, New York.

Porter, M.E., 1998, Clusters and the New Economics of Competition, Harvard Business Review, November-December, 77-90.

PriceWaterhouseCoopers, 2000, International Accounting Standards: Financial Instruments, Understanding IAS 39.

Priestley, R. and B.A. Odegaard, 2001, Exchange Rate Regimes and Exchange Rate Exposures, Department of Financial Economics, Norwegian School of Management BI.

Priestley, R. and B.A. Odegaard, 2002, New Evidence on Exchange Rate Exposure, Working Paper, Department of Financial Economics, Norwegian School of Management BI.

Priestley, R. and B.A. Odegaard, 2002, Linear and Nonlinear Exchange Rate Exposure and the Price of Exchange Rate Risk, Working Paper, Department of Financial Economics, Norwegian School of Management BI.

Pringle, J.J., 1991, Managing Foreign Exchange Exposure, Continental Bank of America, Journal of Applied Corporate Finance, Vol.3(4), p. 73-82.

Pringle, J., 1995, A Look at Indirect Foreign Currency Exposure, Journal of Applied Corporate Finance 8, p. 75-81.

Pringle, J.J. and R.A. Connolly, 1993, The Nature and Causes of Foreign Currency Exposure, Journal of Applied Corporate Finance 6 (3), p. 61-72.

Price Waterhouse, 1997, Risk Management for Financial Institutions - Advances in Measurement and Control, RISK publications.

Pritamani, M., Shome, D.K. and V. Singal, 2001, Exchange Rates and Stock Prices: Are they Related?, Working Paper, Department of Accounting and Finance, School of Business Administration, Oakland University.

Radebaugh, L.H., Accounting for Price-Level and Exchange-Rate Cases for U.S. International Firms: An Empirical Study

Raeburn, R., Bennett, D., and N. Morgan, 1994, Organising and Controlling your Treasury, Financial Times / Pitman Publishing Series.

Ragnitz, J., 1994, Zinsstruktur and Witschaftswachstum, Kredit und Kapital, Vol. 27 (1), 11-29.

Ramasamy, B., 2000, Foreign Exchange Rate Exposure During a Financial Crisis: the Case of Malaysian Multinationals, Research Paper Series, Division of Business and Management, The University of Nottingham in Malaysia.

Ramasamy, B. and M. Yeung, 2001, The Causality Between Stock Returns and Exchange Rates: Revisited, Research Paper Series, Division of Business and Management, The University of Nottingham in Malaysia.

Ramlochan, K., 2001, Managing Economic Exposures from a Top-Down Perspective, Bank of America Journal of Risk Analysis, Sept.

Rangan, S., 1998, Do Multinationals Operate Flexibly? Theory and Evidence, Journal of International Business Studies 29 (2), 217-237.

Rappaport, A., 1986, Creating Shareholder Value, New York: Free Press.

Reeb, D.M., Kwok, C.C.Y and H.Y. Baek, 1998, Systematic Risk of the Multinational Corporation, Journal of International Business Studies, 29, 2 (Second Quarter), p. 263-279.

Rees, W. and S. Unni, 1999, Exchange Rate Exposure Amongst European Firms: Evidence from France, Germany, and the UK, Working Paper 99/8, Department of Accounting & Finance, University of Glasgow.

Rhee, S. G., R. P. Chang and P. E. Koveos, 1985, The Currency of Denomination Decision for Debt Financing, Journal of International Business Studies, Fall.

Rodriguez, R. M., 1981, Corporate Exchange Risk Management: Theme and Abberations, The Journal of Finance, Vol. 36, No. 2, May, 427-439.

Rolseth, L., 1998, Adjusting Stock Market Values to Exchange Rate Exposure: The Case of ASTRA, SCA and STORA, Working Papers in Economics no. 6, Department of Economics, Goeteborg University.

Ronner, A. and M. Blok, 2001, Hedging Foreign Currency Exposure: Consequences of FAS 133, Journal of Applied Finance.

Ross, M. P., 1997, Corporate Hedging: What, Why and How?, Working Paper, Haas School of Business, University of California, Berkeley.

Ruland, R. G. and T. S. Doupnik, 1988, Foreign Currency Translation and The Behavior of Exchange Rates, Journal of International Business Studies, Fall.

Salop, S., 1979, Monopolistic Competition with Outside Goods, Bell Journal of economics, p. 141-156.

Samuelson, P., 1965, Proof That Properly Anticipated Prices Fluctuate Randomly, Industrial Management Review, 41-49.

Santomero, A.M., 1995, Financial Risk Management: The Whys and Hows, in Financial Markets, Institutions & Instruments - New York University Salomon Center, V. 4, N. 5, December, Blackwell Publishers, Cambridge, MA.

Sarno, L., 2001, Towards a New Paradigm in Open Economy Modeling: Where Do We Stand?, Federal Reserve Bank of St. Louis, May/June.

Sauer, A., 1991, Die Bereinigung von Aktienkursen: Ein kurzer Überblick über Konzept und praktische Umsetzung, Version 1.0, Institut für Entscheidungstheorie und Unternehmensforschung, Universität Karlsruhe.

Schnabel, J.A./Laurier, W., 1994, Real Exposure to Foreign Currency Risk, Managerial Finance. Vol.20(8), p. 69-77.

Schrand, C., Unal, H., Hedging and Coordinated Risk Management: Evidence from Thrift Conversions, University of Pennsylvania.

Schwert, W., 1990, Stock Returns and Real Activity: A Century of Evidence, The Journal of Finance, Vol. 45, No. 4, Sept. 1237-1257.

Scognamiglio, D., 1995, Motive des Waehrungsrisiko-Managements, Working Paper, Institut fuer Finanzmanagement, Universitaet Bern.

Sender, G.L., 1994, Option Analyis at Merck, Harvard Business Review, January-February, 92

Sercu, P. and R. Uppal, 1995, International Financial Markets and the Firm, South-Western College Publishing, Cincinnati.

Shaked, I., 1986, Are Multinational Corporations Safer?, Journal of International Business Studies, Vol. 17 (1), p. 83-106.

Shapiro, A. C., 1974, Exchange Rate Changes, Inflation and the Value of the Multinational Corporation, Journal of Finance 30(2), p. 485-502.

Shapiro, A.C., 1999, Multinational Financial Management, 6th Edition, Prentice Hall International, Inc.

Shapiro, A.C. and S. Titman, 1985, An Integrated Approach to Corporate Risk Management, Midland Corporate Finance Journal 3 (2), p. 41-56.

Shi, L., 2003, Real Options Approach for Evaluation of Managerial Flexibility, Department of Industrial Engineering , University of Wisconsin-Madison , March 27.

Shin, H.H. and L. Soenen, 1999, Exposure to Currency Risk by US Multinational Corporations, Journal of Multinational Financial Management 9, p. 195-207.

Shin, H.H., and R. Stulz, 2000, Shareholder Wealth and Firm Risk, Working Paper, Ohio State University.

Shirvani, H. and B. Wilbratte, 2000, Does Consumption Respond More Strongly to Stock Market Declines than to Increases?, International Economic Journal, Vol. 14, Number 3, Autumn, 41-49.

Sick, G., 1995, Real Options, ch.21, 631.691, in: Jarrow et al., 1995, Vol. 9, First Edition, Inform, Handbook in Operations Research and Management Sciences.

Siegel, J.J., 1998, Stocks for the Long Run, second edition, McGraw-Hill.

Simkins, B.J and P. Laux, 1997, Derivatives Use and the Exchange Rate Risk of Large US Corporations, Working Paper, Oklahoma State University, Weatherhead School of Management, Case Western Reserve University.

Singh, K. and J.E. Hodder, 2000, Multinational Capital Structure and Financial Flexibility, Journal of International Money and Finance 19, pp. 853-884.

Sjaastad, L.A., 1998, Why PPP Real Exchange Rates Mislead, Journal of Applied Economics, Vol. 1, No. 1, Nov., p. 179-207.

Slade, M.E., 1986, Conjectures, Firm Characteristics, and Market Structure, International Journal of Industrial Organization, 4, p. 347-369.

Slade, M.E., 1995, Empirical Games: the Oligopoly Case, Canadian Journal of Economics, XXVIII, p. 368-402.

Sloan, R. G., 1996, Using Earnings and Free Cash Flow to Evaluate Corporate Performance, Bank of America Journal of Applied Corporate Finance, Vol. 9, Number 1, Spring, 70-78.

Smith, C.E., 1999, Exchange Rate Variation, Commodity Price Variation and the Implications for International Trade, Journal of International Money and Finance, 18, p. 471-491.

Smith, C.W., Jr., 1995, Corporate Risk Management: Theory and Practice, Journal of Derivatives, p. 21-30.

Smith, C.W., Jr. and R. Stulz, 1985, The Determinants of Firms' Hedging Policies, Journal of Financial and Quantitative Analysis 20, pp. 391-405.

Smithson, C.W., Smith, C.W. and W.D. Sykes, 1995, Managing Financial Risk: A Guide to Derivative Products, Financial Engineering, and Value Maximization, Chicago et. Al.: Irwin

So, J. C., 1986, The Behavior of Foreign Exchange Rates - Comment, Journal of International Business Studies, Fall, p. 165-180.

Soenen, L.A. and J. Madura, 1991, Foreign Exchange Management - a Strategic Approach, Long Range Planning, 29, p. 119-124

Solnik, B., 1974, An Equilibrium Model of the International Capital Market, Journal of Economic Theory, August, 500-524.

Solnik, B., 1984, Stock Prices and Monetary Variables: The International Evidence, Financial Analysts Journal, Vol. 40 (2), 69-73.

Solnik, B., 1996, International Investments, Third Edition, Addison-Wesley Publishing Company, Inc.

Soros, G., 1994, The Alchemy of Finance, John Wiley & Sons, Inc.

Spanos, A., 1986, Statistical Foundations of Econometric Modelling, Cambridge University Press.

Sparla, T., 2001, Strategic Real Options - with the German Electric Power Market in View, Ph.D. Thesis, Dortmund University.

Spindler, C., 1996, Waehrungsmanagement in internationalen Unternehmen, in Eller, R. (Hrsg.), Handbuch Deriverater Instrumente: Produkte, Strategien und Risikomanagement, Schaeffer-Poeschel Verlag Stuttgart.

Srinivasulu, S.L., 1981, Strategic Response to Foreign Exchange Risks, Columbia Journal of World Business, Spring, 16(1), p. 13-23.

Statistisches Bundesamt, 1996, Statistisches Jahrbuch 1996, Metzler-Poeschel Verlag, Stuttgart.

Stein, J.C., Usher, S.E., LaGattuta, D. and J. Youngen, 2000, A Comparable Approach to Measuring Cashflow-at-Risk for Non-Financial Firms, Working Paper #39, NERA Consulting Economists.

Stulz, R., 1981, A Model of International Asset Pricing, Journal of Financial Economics, December, 383-406.

Stulz, R., 1984, Optimal Hedging Policies, Journal of Financial and Quantitative Analysis 19.

Stulz, R., 1996, Rethinking Risk Management, Bank of America Journal of Applied Corporate Finance 9(3), Fall, p. 8-24.

Stulz, R., 2002, Derivatives, Risk Management, and Financial Engineering, Southwestern College Publishing, Cincinnati, forthcoming.

Stulz, R. and R. Williamson, 1996, Identifying and Quantifying Exposures, Working Paper, Ohio State University.

Stutzmann Y. and V. Popov, 2003, How is Foreign Exchange Risk Managed? An Empirical Study Applied to two Swiss Companies, master theses Nr. 0314, Department of Banking and Finance, HEC Lausanne, University of Lausanne.

Subramanyam, K.R. and M. Venkatachalam, 2001, Earnings, Cash Flows and Ex post Intrinsic Value of Equity, Working Paper, Graduate School of Business, Standford University.

Sundaram, A.K. and S. Black, 1992, The Environment and Internal Organization of Multinational Enterprises, Academy of Management Journal, 17, p. 729-757.

Sundaram, A.K. and V. Mishra, 1990, Currency Movements and Corporate Pricing Strategy, in K.S. Khoury, Recent Developments in International Banking (p. 203-241), Amsterdam, Netherlands: Elsevier Science.

Swanson, P.E. and S.C. Caples, 1987, Hedging Foreign Exchange Risk Using Forward Foreign Exchange Markets: An Extension, Journal of International Business Studies, spring, 75-82.

Tai, C.-S., 2004, Asymmetric Currency Exposure of US Bank Stock Returns, Unpublished Paper, Department of Economics and Finance, College of Business Administration, Texas A&M University-Kingsville.

Taylor, M.P., 1995, The Economics of Exchange Rates, Journal of Economic Literature, Vol. 33, p. 13-47.

Taylor, M.P. and D.A. Peel, 2000, Nonlinear Adjustment, Long-Run Equilibrium and Exchange Rate Fundamentals, Journal of International Money and Finance, February, 33-53.

The Association of Corporate Treasurers, 2000, Advanced Risk Management and Evaluation.

The Economist, 2001, American Manufacturers and the Dollar: A Bunch of Cry-Babies?, August 18th, p. 49-50.

The Economist, 2004, Economic focus: Signifying Nothing?, Jan. 31st – Feb. 6th, p. 71.

The Economist Intelligence Unit, 1992, Building the Next-Generation Global Treasury.

The Economist Intelligence Unit, 1993, Strategic Financial Risk Management, Research Report.

The Economist Intelligence Unit, 2001, Country Finance: Germany.

The Economist Intelligence Unit, 2001, Country Finance: United States.

The Economist Intelligence Unit and MMC Enterprise Risk, 2001, Enterprise Risk Management: Implementing New Solutions.

Tirole, J., 1990, The Theory of Industrial Organization, The MIT Press, Cambridge, Massachusetts.

TMAC, 1999, Hedging Volume Risk, The Canadian Treasurer, 14 Nov.

Trema Management Consulting, 2001, Corporate Risk Disclosure Survey 2001.

Trigeorgis, L., 1993, Real Options and Interactions with Financial Flexibility, Financial Management, Autumn, Vol. 22, No. 3, p. 202-224.

Trigeorgis, L., 1996, Real Options: Managerial Flexibility and Strategy in Resource Allocation, MIT Press, Cambridge, Massachusetts, First Edition.

Trigeorgis, L., 2002, Real Options and Investment Under Uncertainty: What do we Know?, Working Papers No. 22, May – Research Series, National Bank of Belgium.

Tufano, P., 1996, Who Manages Risk? An Empirical Analysis of Risk Management Practices in the Gold Mining Industry, Journal of Finance 53, p. 1015-1052

Tufano, P., 1998, Agency Costs of Corporate Risk Management, Financial Management 27, Spring 98, p. 67-77.

Tufano, P., How Financial Engineering Can Advance Corporate Strategy, Harvard Business Review, January-February 1996, p. 136-146.

Tzokas, N., Hart, S., Argouslidis, P. And M. Saren, 2000, Industrial Export Pricing Practices in the United Kingdom, Industrial Marketing Management 29, 191-204.

Van den Broek, M., 2000, Currency Blues, Global Treasury News, 3 June

Van Roden, J., 1995, Bank of America Roundtable on Corporate Risk Management, Journal of Applied Corporate Finance, Fall, Vol. 8, No. 3.

Varian, H. R., 1992, Microeconomic Analysis, Third Edition, W. W. Norton & Company, Inc., New York.

Varian, H.R., 1999, Intermediate Microeconomics: a Modern Approach, Fifth Edition, W. W. Norton & Company, Inc., New York.

Verbeek, M., 2000, A Guide to Modern Econometrics, John Wiley & Sons, Ltd, West Sussex, England.

Vontobel, E., 1996, Waehrungsrisiken - eine empirische Studie, Working Paper, Institut fuer Finanzmanagement, Universitaet Bern.

von Ungern-Sternberg, T., and C.C. von Weizsacker, 1990, Strategic Foreign Exchange Management, Journal of Industrial Economics, Vol. 38, June, p. 381-395.

Vuolteenaho, T., 2002, What Drives Firm-Level Stock Returns?, The Journal of Finance, Vol. LVII, No. 1, Feb., 233-264.

Wallace, J. B., 1998, Benchmarking in Foreign Exchange, Treasury Management International, Sept., p. 39-42.

Wallace, J.B., 1999, The Group of 31 Report: Core Principles for Managing Multinational FX Risk, Greenwich Treasury Advisors LLC.

Wallace, J.B., 1999, How to Manage Multinational FX Risk, The Treasurer, Sept.

Walleck, A., Steven, J., D. O'Halloran and C.A. Leader, Benchmarking World-Class Performance, The McKinsey Quarterly, 1991, Number 1, p. 3-24

Walsh, E.J., 1994, Operating Income, Exchange Rate Changes, and the Value of the Firm: An Empirical Analysis, Journal of Accounting, Auditing & Finance, Vol.9(4), p. 703-724.

Ware, R. and R. Winter, 1988, Forwards Markets, Currency Options and the Hedging of Foreign Exchange Risk, Journal of International Economics, Vol. 25 (3/4), p. 291302.

Wharton School, University of Chicago Graduate School of Business, London Business School, 1998, The Complete Finance Companion, Financial Times Mastering Series

Whitaker, M.B., 1994, Strategic Management of Foreign Exchange Exposure in an International Firm, in Amihud, Y. and R. M. Levich (eds.), Exchange Rates and Corporate Performance, Irwin Professional Publishing, New York.

Wihlborg, C., 1980, Economics of Exposure Management of Foreign Subsidiaries of Multinational Corporations, Journal of International Business Studies, Winter.

Wihlborg, C., 1980, Currency Exposure: Taxonomy and Theory, in R.M. Levich and C. Wihlborg, editors, Exchange Risk and Exposure: Current Developments in International Financial Management, Lexington (Mass.).

Williamson, R.G., 2001, Exchange Rate Exposure and Competition: Evidence from the Automotive Industry, Journal of Financial economics 59, p. 441-475.

Wolf, 1987, Optimal Hedging with Futures Options, Journal of Economics and Business 39, 141-158.

Wolfson, A. and J. Emanuelsson, 1997, Commodities – The Risk of Substance, Corporate Finance Risk Management & Derivatives Yearbook 197, 25-28.

Wong, K.P., 2001, Currency Hedging for Export-Flexible Firms, International Economic Journal, Vol. 15, Number 1, Spring.

Woolridge, J. R., 1995, Do Stock Prices Reflect Fundamental Values?, Bank of America Journal of Applied Corporate Finance, Vol. 8 (1), Spring, 64-69.

Wu, Y., 2000, Stock Prices and Exchange Rates in a VEC Model – The Case of Singapore in the 1990s, Journal of Economics and Finance, Vol. 24, Fall, 260-274.

Xiaokai, Y. and B.J. Heijdra, 1993, Monopolistic Competition and Optimum Product Diversity: Comment, The American Economic Review, Vol. 83, No. 1, March.

Yang, J., 1997, Exchange Rate Pass-Through in U.S. Manufacturing Industries, Review of Economics and Statistics 79(1), 95-104.

Zugel and T. Copeland, 1998, Responding to the Stock Price Challenge: The Monitor Company Value Audit, Monitor Group.

Wihlborg, C., 1980, Currency Exposure: Taxonomy and Theory, in R.M. Levich and C. Wihlborg, editors, Exchange Risk and Exposure: Current Developments in International Financial Management, Lexington (Mass.).

Williamson, R.G., 2001, Exchange Rate Exposure and Competition: Evidence from the Automotive Industry, Journal of Financial economics 59, p. 441-475.

Wolf, 1987, Optimal Hedging with Futures Options, Journal of Economics and Business 39, 141-158.

Wolfson, A. and J. Emanuelsson, 1997, Commodities – The Risk of Substance, Corporate Finance Risk Management & Derivatives Yearbook 197, 25-28.

Wong, K.P., 2001, Currency Hedging for Export-Flexible Firms, International Economic Journal, Vol. 15, Number 1, Spring.

Woolridge, J. R., 1995, Do Stock Prices Reflect Fundamental Values?, Bank of America Journal of Applied Corporate Finance, Vol. 8 (1), Spring, 64-69.

Wu, Y., 2000, Stock Prices and Exchange Rates in a VEC Model – The Case of Singapore in the 1990s, Journal of Economics and Finance, Vol. 24, Fall, 260-274.

Xiaokai, Y. and B.J. Heijdra, 1993, Monopolistic Competition and Optimum Product Diversity: Comment, The American Economic Review, Vol. 83, No. 1, March.

Yang, J., 1997, Exchange Rate Pass-Through in U.S. Manufacturing Industries, Review of Economics and Statistics 79(1), 95-104.

Zugel and T. Copeland, 1998, Responding to the Stock Price Challenge: The Monitor Company Value Audit, Monitor Group.

www.ingramcontent.com/pod-product-compliance
Lightning Source LLC
Chambersburg PA
CBHW020909210326
41598CB00018B/1819